When States Come Out

In the last two decades, the LGBT movement has gained a momentum that is arguably unprecedented in speed and suddenness when compared to other human rights movements. This book investigates the recent history of this transnational movement in Europe, focusing on the diffusion of the norms it champions and the overarching question of why, despite similar international pressures, the trajectories of socio-legal recognition for LGBT minorities are so different across states. The book makes the case that a politics of visibility has engendered interactions between movements and states that empower marginalized people – mobilizing actors to demand change, influencing the spread of new legal standards, and weaving new ideas into the fabrics of societies. It documents how this process of "coming out" empowers marginalized social groups by moving them to the center of political debate and public recognition, and making it possible for them to obtain rights to which they have due claim.

Phillip M. Ayoub is Assistant Professor of Politics at Drexel University. Ayoub's doctoral dissertation received the biennial 2013–2014 award for the best dissertation from the European Union Studies Association, as well as the 2014 Kenneth Sherrill Award for the best dissertation in the field of sexuality and politics, and the 2014 award for the best dissertation in the field of human rights from sections of the American Political Science Association. He is also the recipient of Cornell University's 2011 Kahin Prize and co-recipient of the 2014 Esman Prize for distinguished scholarship. His articles have appeared in the *European Journal of International Relations*, *Mobilization*, the *European Political Science Review*, the *Journal of Human Rights*, and *Perspectives on Europe*.

Advance Praise for *When States Come Out*

"This innovative book breaks new ground in the study of human rights, international relations, social movements, and identity politics. Phillip Ayoub provides a deep and rigorous multi-method analysis of a critical issue at the frontiers of the struggle for human dignity."

Alison Brysk, Mellichamp Professor of Global Governance,
University of California, Santa Barbara

"A revolution has swept across the countries of Europe, transforming LGBT persons from criminal degenerates into upstanding and even celebrated members of society. But the revolution has not changed all countries equally. Some have moved quickly to grant LGBT citizens the same rights and protections accorded to their fellows. Other countries have showed greater reluctance, and even now fall short of equal incorporation. Accounting for the overall trends and especially the enduring variations are Phillip Ayoub's central tasks, and he fulfills them brilliantly in this masterful and incisive book."

David John Frank, Professor of Sociology and Courtesy Professor
of Education and Political Science at the University of California, Irvine

"*When States Come Out* is a masterful analysis of the domestic and transnational currents of Europe's LGBT politics. Based on a rich trove of new qualitative and quantitative data, Ayoub's compelling argument shows how and why the politics of visibility is at the center of the human rights and dignity movement."

Peter J. Katzenstein, Walter S. Carpenter, Jr. Professor of
International Studies, Cornell University

"This brilliant study provides a compelling answer to the question of what drives policy success of LGBT movements in particular and of social movements, more generally. Phillip Ayoub anchors his empirically rich, meticulously researched, and theoretically sophisticated argument in the idea that norm visibility is the key to policy success. This book is a must-read for scholars and activists interested in how marginalized groups gain agency and generate political change."

Sabine Lang, Associate Professor, Jackson School of International
Studies, University of Washington, and author of *NGOs,
Civil Society, and the Public Sphere* (Cambridge, 2012)

"Why, like their counterparts in the United States, have some European Union states advanced LGBT rights much more rapidly than others in recent years? In *When States Come Out*, Phillip Ayoub marries a sophisticated theoretical framework to a wealth of empirical data to advance a compelling argument about the importance of transnational norms and the domestic politics of visibility to shaping real progress on the rights of sexual minorities. This is an important contribution not only to the literature on LGBT politics, but also to that on comparative social movements and the politics of social change more broadly."

Robert Singh, Professor of Politics, Birkbeck College, University of London

"*When States Come Out* sheds new light on longstanding questions about the conditions under which weak, marginalized, and stigmatized groups are able to bring about political and social change. Focusing on the inconsistent diffusion of rights and recognition for lesbian, gay, bisexual, and transgender people across European Union states, Phillip Ayoub draws on a wealth of evidence to demonstrate the important role of individual and collective visibility in provoking both recognition of but also resistance to justice and equality for LGBT people. His analyses lead to important and often surprising insights about the sources and consequences of both movement victories and setbacks, offering reasons for optimism at the same time as they deliver sobering reminders about continued persecution and barriers to justice."

Dara Z. Strolovitch, Associate Professor, Department
of Politics, Princeton University

"There are many well-trained scholars of social movements; many others who are experts on European transnational politics; and still others who specialize on the LGBT movement. But there is no one who has encompassed all three more elegantly than Phillip Ayoub has done in this richly documented, carefully researched, and intellectually inspiring book. More than a consummate exercise in comparative research, and more than an in-depth inquiry into the LGBT movement in both parts of Europe, it is also a profoundly enlightening inquiry into the factors that produce cultural openness to diversity and those that inhibit it."

Sidney Tarrow, Emeritus Maxwell M. Upson Professor of Government at
Cornell University, and author of *Power in Movement* (Cambridge, 2011)
and *The Language of Contention* (Cambridge, 2013)

Cambridge Studies in Contentious Politics

Editors

Mark Beissinger   *Princeton University*
Jack A. Goldstone   *George Mason University*
Michael Hanagan   *Vassar College*
Doug McAdam   *Stanford University and Center for Advanced Study in the Behavioral Sciences*
Sarah Soule   *Stanford University*
Suzanne Staggenborg   *University of Pittsburgh*
Sidney Tarrow   *Cornell University*
Charles Tilly (d. 2008)   *Columbia University*
Elisabeth J. Wood   *Yale University*
Deborah Yashar   *Princeton University*

Ronald Aminzade, *Race, Nation, and Citizenship in Post-Colonial Africa: The Case of Tanzania*

Ronald Aminzade et al., *Silence and Voice in the Study of Contentious Politics*

Javier Auyero, *Routine Politics and Violence in Argentina: The Gray Zone of State Power*

Phillip M. Ayoub, *When States Come Out: Europe's Sexual Minorities and the Politics of Visibility*

W. Lance Bennett and Alexandra Segerberg, *The Logic of Connective Action: Digital Media and the Personalization of Contentious Politics*

Amrita Basu, *Violent Conjunctures in Democratic India*

Clifford Bob, *The Marketing of Rebellion: Insurgents, Media, and International Activism*

Charles Brockett, *Political Movements and Violence in Central America*

Valerie Bunce and Sharon Wolchik, *Defeating Authoritarian Leaders in Postcommunist Countries*

Lars-Erik Cederman, Kristian Skrede Gleditsch, and Halvard Buhaug, *Inequality, Grievances, and Civil War*

Christian Davenport, *How Social Movements Die: Repression and Demobilization of the Republic of New Africa*

Christian Davenport, *Media Bias, Perspective, and State Repression*

Gerald F. Davis, Doug McAdam, W. Richard Scott, and Mayer N. Zald, *Social Movements and Organization Theory*

Donatella della Porta, *Clandestine Political Violence*

Mario Diani, *The Cement of Civil Society: Studying Networks in Localities*

Todd A. Eisenstadt, *Politics, Identity, and Mexico's Indigenous Rights Movements*

Daniel Q. Gillion, *The Political Power of Protest: Minority Activism and Shifts in Public Policy*

(continued after Index)

When States Come Out

Europe's Sexual Minorities and the Politics of Visibility

PHILLIP M. AYOUB

CAMBRIDGE
UNIVERSITY PRESS

CAMBRIDGE
UNIVERSITY PRESS

32 Avenue of the Americas, New York, NY 10013

Cambridge University Press is part of the University of Cambridge.

It furthers the University's mission by disseminating knowledge in the pursuit of education, learning, and research at the highest international levels of excellence.

www.cambridge.org
Information on this title: www.cambridge.org/9781107115590

© Phillip M. Ayoub 2016

First published 2016

Printed in the United States of America by Sheridan Books, Inc.

A catalog record for this publication is available from the British Library

Library of Congress Cataloging-in-Publication data
Names: Ayoub, Phillip, 1983– author.
Title: When states come out : Europe's sexual minorities and the politics of visibility / Phillip M. Ayoub.
Description: Cambridge, United Kingdom: Cambridge University Press, 2016. |
Series: Cambridge studies in contentious politics |
Includes bibliographical references and index.
Identifiers: LCCN 2016008235| ISBN 9781107115590 (hardback) |
ISBN 9781107535893 (paperback)
Subjects: LCSH: Gay rights – Europe. | Gay liberation movement – Europe. |
Sexual minorities – Political activity – Europe. | Identity politics – Europe. |
BISAC: POLITICAL SCIENCE / Government / General.
Classification: LCC HQ76.8.E85 A96 2016 | DDC 323.3/264094–dc23
LC record available at http://lccn.loc.gov/2016008235

ISBN 978-1-107-11559-0 Hardback
ISBN 978-1-107-53589-3 Paperback

For my parents,
Reinhild and Anwar Ayoub

Contents

List of figures		*page* x
List of tables		xii
Preface and acknowledgments		xiii
List of abbreviations		xix
1	Introduction	1
2	The politics of visibility and LGBT rights in Europe	21
3	Transnational movement: Opportunities, actors, and mechanisms	53
4	Complying with new norms: LGBT rights legislation	87
5	Internalizing new norms: Attitudes toward sexual minorities	127
6	Poland and Slovenia's responses to international norms	158
7	Visibility in movement and transnational politics	199
Methodological appendix		225
References		247
Index		271

Figures

1.1 Variation in attitudes toward homosexuality
across EU states   *page* 9
1.2 Variation in LGBT rights legislation across EU states   10
2.1 (In)direct and mediated channels of norm diffusion and
compliance outcomes   37
2.2 Processes of internalization   43
2.3 Internalization outcomes based on conditions of threat and
channels of visibility   43
2.4 Variation in attitudes toward homosexuality between new
and old EU states   50
2.5 Variation in objections toward homosexual neighbors
between new and old EU states   50
3.1 Influence of European institutions on state compliance   57
3.2 Influence of European institutions on societal internalization   58
3.3 Number of LGBT social spaces (restaurants, cafes, bars,
and clubs) in Berlin and Warsaw, 1990–2004   68
3.4 Number of LGBT organizations (political, religious, and
health groups) in Berlin and Warsaw, 1990–2004   68
3.5 "Solidarność Gejów," Berlin, 2009   74
3.6 "Catholics We Love You," Warsaw, 2010   78
3.7 European frames in Warsaw, 2006   78
4.1 Mapping the introduction of LGBT rights legislation in
EU states, 1980–2010   89
4.2 Expected change in the predicted probability of passing
LGBT legislation when norm brokers exist in new EU states   110
4.3 International dynamics of "passing" same-sex marriage   122
5.1 Mapping attitudes toward homosexuality in EU states,
1990–2010   129

5.2 Correlation between aggregate attitudes and combined
      channels in new EU states   144
5.3 Religiosity and perceived threat   150
5.4 National pride and perceived threat   150
5.5 Effect of pro-LGBT legislation on societal attitudes   154
6.1 The "defend the nation" frame   176
6.2 NOP symbols   185
6.3 Type of norm reception process described by respondents (%) 191

Every effort has been made to contact the relevant copyright-holders for the images reproduced in this book. In the event of any error, the publisher will be pleased to make corrections in any reprints or future editions.

Tables

3.1 Political opportunity structures, mobilizing structures,
     transnational actors, and mechanisms   *page* 64
4.1 European LGBT organizations' reliance on external
     funding sources   93
4.2 Predicting pro-LGBT legislation in Europe, 1970–2010   107
4.3 EU-12 determinants of year passing anti-discrimination,
     criminal law, and partnership legislation, 1970–2010   114
4.4 EU-15 determinants of year passing anti-discrimination,
     criminal law, partnership, and parenting legislation,
     1970–2010   116
5.1 Predicting tolerance toward homosexuality in the EU   142
5.2 Predicting tolerance toward homosexuality in new
     and old EU states   147
5.3 Predicting the effect of pro-LGBT legislation on
     tolerance toward homosexuality   152
6.1 Transnational social channels and norm brokers   167
6.2 Legal framework for LGBT people in Poland and Slovenia 168
6.3 Church authority and national vulnerability in
     Poland and Slovenia   175
6.4 Slovenian mobilization in the public sphere, 2000–2009 183
A.1 Dependent and independent variables summarized
     (Chapter 4)   233
A.2 Descriptive statistics and correlations (Chapter 4)   236
A.3 Dependent and independent variables summarized
     (Chapter 5)   237
A.4 Descriptive statistics and correlations (Chapter 5)   239

Preface and acknowledgments

Like many students of social movements, I first became interested in the
LGBT rights movement through personal experience. This project dates
back to 2004–2006, when I was completing a master's degree in Berlin
at a time when many Berliners were organizing to participate in marches
for LGBT equality in various Polish cities. It was in Berlin that I came
across a flier concerning a march in Warsaw, which sparked a long curi-
osity about the transnational nature of LGBT politics and the questions
it raises. The political behavior that seemed obvious to many of the participants challenged fundamentals of what I had learned of politics in
the classroom: what was rational about marching for rights in a foreign
context, where such rights would not benefit you directly? Why did such
activism meet forceful resistance in some cases and not in others? The
uneven diffusion of legal rights and societal recognition across states –
the goals of the movement – also puzzled me.

During the decade I spent thinking about the issues related to this
book, I would be amazed most of all by the striking changes that
occurred around the globe. Under the right conditions, it seemed,
LGBT people could be their own emancipators (in some sense of that
word), in that their visibility could be the path toward rights. Moreover,
these politics of visibility were transnational in nature, as so many varied states – including ones that many observers thought of as highly
unlikely – adopted new LGBT rights norms into the framework of the
state. The contentious politics of visibility thus became the subject of
this endeavor, and this book is about the political power of coming out
for individuals, groups, and states. It is a story of how local activists can
channel transnational support to affect domestic politics, a story about

how a norm can become salient, and about how people can come out under broader conditions of visibility.

For all the words in this book, I could easily devote as many to thanking the various people who have made it possible. It is only fitting that I begin by thanking the many unnamed activists who offered me their time and insight as interviewees. So many of the LGBT activists who shared their stories for this book taught me the truth of the statement articulated so elegantly by author-activist bell hooks: "All the great movements for social justice in our society have promoted a love ethic" (2001, 98). To love and to be loved has driven the mobilization of the many people who comprise a truly great social movement of our times. It has been a privilege to learn from people who led and lead the struggle; their work and stories will inspire me for years to come.

My greatest intellectual debts go to the members of my doctoral committee who, throughout my six years of graduate studies at Cornell University, provided valued mentorship and invested long hours to guide this book project. In meeting their high demands, I received far more guidance than is typical or expected. Peter Katzenstein was an exceptional mentor. He replied to emails within minutes (whether at 7 a.m. or 11 p.m.), put Goethe on my reading list, and struck that fine balance between vigorously demanding excellence and voicing sincere encouragement and praise. His skill as an advisor is already legendary, but I would argue that the legend is an understatement, as his work ethic and his commitment to his students – both in their professional development and in their personal lives – are truly remarkable. They have left an undeniable mark both on this book and the role I have come to fill as a scholar.

To Sid Tarrow I owe an incredible debt of gratitude, not least for influencing this book's focus on contentious politics. Early on, he told me quite directly that I was "writing about movements" and left me little room to explain how this might not be the case. Judging by the series home this book has found for itself, he was, of course, correct. The breadth and richness of his insights – often going back to the French Revolution – and the plethora of time he has invested in my work have made the outcome much better. Matt Evangelista was enthusiastic about the subject of this book from the start, and the combination of intellectual and moral support that he provided was of great importance to me as I conducted my research. LGBT politics is only now beginning to capture the attention of political scientists (still far too little attention, but more than when I stumbled into his office in 2007), but Matt encouraged the project from the start. Concerned that my courses were not covering much of the work specifically related to gender and LGBT politics, Matt and I went over such readings together, discussing each piece as I wrote the earliest drafts of the prospectus. In response to my later drafts, he always asked the difficult questions while simultaneously showing excitement for my work. I doubt that this book's topic would have developed without Matt's early enthusiasm, and I know that the outcome would have been weaker without his input.

Sarah Soule offered brilliant comments on my various projects, while simultaneously helping me to navigate the pragmatic elements of the profession. Her understanding of sociology and politics is astonishing, and she helped me hone in on the feasible dimensions of this project and execute them. Even when I was in Europe conducting research, I could schedule phone meetings with her to vet the first iteration of my ideas in brainstorming sessions. I have an extraordinary amount of respect for Sarah's scholarship, kindness, and humility, all of which shine through in the better parts of this completed work. Finally, Chris Anderson has graciously supported my fascination with European politics; like Sarah, he also imparted a great deal of knowledge concerning methodology. Together, these five individuals have guided the stronger parts of this work.

At Cornell University, I benefited from the dedication and advice offered to me by Tom Pepinsky, Peter Enns, Jessica Weeks, Chris Way, Jonathan Kirshner, Alex Kuo, and Syd van Morgen. Historian Holly Case, who has read every word of this book, has always encouraged and improved my work. Her East European Circle gave me an interdisciplinary platform to present and vet ideas. Jay Barry at the Cornell Statistical Consulting Unit was willing to talk through my models from afar. It is impossible to list all the graduate student friends who inspired my intellectual trajectory, so I will focus on a few: Deondra Rose, Chris Zepeda-Millán, Jaimie Bleck, Idrissa Sidibe, Julie Ajinkya, Ben Brake, Igor Logvinenko, Don Leonard, Pablo Yanguas, Desmond Jagmohan, Janice Gallagher, Tariq Thachil, Pinar Kemerli, Simon Gilhooley, Sinja Graf, Robert Braun, Sophia Wallace, Martha Wilfahrt, Jen Hadden, Lucia Seybert, Jennifer Erickson, and Noelle Brigden. Of my accomplishments in graduate school, these friendships have been the most valuable; they have shaped how I understand politics and society (especially concerning marginalized peoples), and they have taught me that the best scholars are those who also leave the library to experience the world around them.

I revised much of this book during the three years after I left Cornell University. Under the warmth of the Tuscan sun, I found so much clarity during my Max Weber postdoctoral fellowship at the European University Institute in Florence. I benefited greatly from energizing conversations with my friends and colleagues, including Donatella della Porta, Ludivine Broch-Hinks, Franziska Exeler, Eirini Karamouzi, Akis Psygkas, Mary Anne Madeira, Valerie McGuire, Philip Balsiger, Pablo Kalmanowitz, Zoe Lefkofridi, Alyson Price, and Laurie Anderson. At my current home at Drexel University, my generous colleagues have offered me the most enthusiastic and stimulating environment. Special thanks is owed to Zoltán Búzás, Amelia Hoover-Green, Erin Graham, George Chiccariello-Maher, Rose Corrigan, Melissa Mansfield, and Scott Barclay for helping me to cross the finish line.

Many scholars from other campuses have commented on and encouraged me in this project, notably David Paternotte, Agnès Chetaille, Beth Kier, John McCarthy, Jeff Checkel, Anna Grzymała-Busse, Verta Taylor, Markus Thiel, Kelly Kollman, Isa Engeli, Samantha Majic, Jocelyn Viterna, Shawn Schulenberg, Lisa Dellmuth, David Frank, and Jasna Magic. Alison Brysk and Dara Strolovitch made large commitments of time to prepare outstanding and invaluable comments, as well as travel to Philadelphia for the book workshops hosted by Drexel University. They deserve special thanks. For influencing my early academic trajectory, I thank Sabine Lang and Christine Ingebritsen at the University of Washington, and John Stephens and Christiane Lemke at the University of North Carolina at Chapel Hill.

I am so grateful for the efforts of Lew Bateman, my editor at Cambridge University Press, for putting his weight behind this project and shepherding it through review and production. The anonymous readers for the press were incisive and brilliant in their comments, which played a tremendous role in guiding the revisions. Kathleen Kearns' meticulous eyes did an exceptional job to help me edit this work. Olaf Hajek, the renowned and talented artist, offered to create the cover because he was committed to the story being told. I thank him for his generous gift. I thank Cambridge University Press, Sage, and Routledge for permission to use portions of my earlier work (Ayoub 2013, 2014, 2015a), in parts of Chapters 3, 4, and 6, respectively. This research was generously supported by an Alexander von Humboldt Chancellor Fellowship, a Fulbright Schuman Fellowship for the European Union, a Michelle Sicca Research Fellowship (Cornell), a Luigi Einaudi Fellowship (Cornell), and three Foreign Language and Area Studies (FLAS) Fellowships for Polish.

Between 2009 and 2012, I spent twenty-five months in Europe to conduct research for this book. During that time, I incurred many debts to the people and institutions that warmly welcomed me. For their intellectual feedback and for hosting me as a guest researcher, I thank Michael Zürn, Ruud Koopmans, Martin Binder, and Matthias Ecker-Ehrhardt at the Wissenschafts Zentrum Berlin; Ingo Peters and Thomas Risse at Free University Berlin's Center on Transnational Relations; David Paternotte at the Université Libre de Bruxelles; and Martin Nagelschmidt at Humboldt University's Berlin Graduate School of Social Sciences. I thank Lena Renz for her able research assistance in transcribing interviews and helping to compile and clean my legislation data set, as well as Jakob Tesch for coding work on the attitudinal data set, and Christine Hammell and Ryan Spavlik for help in formatting the manuscript.

I also benefited from valued friendship during my many stints in the field. I want to thank Blanca Biosca, Olga Brzezinska, and Brigid O'Shea for standing by me whenever the process felt difficult. They are the ones who put up with me as I tuned out of conversation to scribble a new idea into my notepad, and who graciously accepted that I would always travel with my laptop. Remo Kaufmann, Volker Hagen, Olly Hopwood, the M18 crew (Robert Radu, Alex Rahn, Christoph Schippel, and Björn Weiss), Mikael Ronsmans, Tomasz Koko, Olaf Szymanski, Greg Czarnecki, Hanna Schmidt Hollaender, Jordan Long, Laurent Fierens Gevaert, and Bruno Selun made me feel at home in Germany, Poland, and Belgium. I thank the Alexander von Humboldt group from China, Russia, and the United States, especially Emily Yates, Emilie Mathieu, Sarah Kelly, Özge Guzelsu, Jack Gieseking, and Johanna Schuster-Craig, for the enriching experiences we shared as we trekked all over Germany (from coal mines to the Chancellery).

Thanks also go to my oldest friends, Nate Fronk, Matt Simo, Krista Johnson, Rachel Streeter, Caitlyn Clauson, and Graham Van der Zanden, who have stayed in my life and have fervently pretended to be interested in my work (as well as read it) for more than ten years. Nate has read almost every chapter and deserves special thanks for his unwavering support. My grandmother's sisters – Edith Gier, Gaby Gier, Anneliese Dörr, Waldraud Königsberger, and Ria Mäder – who live(d) along the Franco-German border and experienced war and the rebuilding of Europe, taught me the fundamentals about the European project. I attribute my scholarly interest in Europe to them and to my siblings, Miriam and Darren Ayoub.

Finally, this book is for my father and mother. Though my father believed in me beyond any realistic measure of my capabilities, his motivation and encouragement are responsible for all the better things I have achieved in life. This book is one of them, and I thank him for it. He passed away shortly before I defended the dissertation version in 2013, in what was (and continues to be) a very painful and difficult reality to accept: to say goodbye to a wonderful man who left us far too soon. Before he passed, I was able to show him a draft of the dissertation's dedication page to him. In his typical style, he rejected any credit, saying, "It should be for your mother," rightly for the wonderful inspiration and model of excellence she has been in my life. After some debate I was able to appease him by promising him my mother would get due credit next time. And that was how he pushed me higher again. It was the pivotal nudge to write this book, which is for both of them.

Abbreviations

ACT UP	AIDS Coalition to Unleash Power
CCOO	Comisiones Obreras [The Workers' Commissions]
CDU	Christlich Demokratische Union Deutschlands [Christian Democratic Union of Germany]
CEE	Central and Eastern Europe(an)
COC	Cultuur en Ontspanningscentrum [Center for Culture and Leisure]
CoE	Council of Europe
CSU	Christlich-Soziale Union [Christian Social Union of Bavaria]
ECJ	European Court of Justice
ECtHR	European Court of Human Rights
EU	European Union
EVS	European Values Study
FRA	European Agency for Fundamental Rights
GDR	German Democratic Republic (East Germany)
IGLYO	International Lesbian, Gay, Bisexual, Transgender, Queer Youth and Student Organization
ILGA	International Lesbian, Gay, Bisexual, Trans and Intersex Association
ILGA-Europe	International Lesbian, Gay, Bisexual, Trans and Intersex Association Europe
KPH	Kampania Przeciw Homofobii [Campaign against Homophobia]
KUL	Institute of Family Life and Culture, Slovenia
LGBT	lesbian, gay, bisexual, and trans
LPR	Liga Polskich Rodzin [League of Polish Families]

LSVD	Lesben-und Schwulenverband in Deutschland [Lesbian and Gay Federation Germany]
MEP	Member of the European Parliament
NGO	nongovernmental organization
NOP	Narodowe Odrodzenie Polski [National Rebirth of Poland]
NUTS	Nomenclature of Units for Territorial Statistics
ONR	Obóz Narodowo-Radykalny [National Radical Camp]
OSCE	Organization for Security and Co-operation in Europe
PiS	Prawo i Sprawiedliwość [Polish Law and Justice Party]
RFSL	Riksförbundet för homosexuellas, bisexuellas och transpersoners rättigheter [Swedish Federation for Lesbian, Gay, Bisexual, and Transgender Rights]
SDS	Slovenska Demokratska Stranka [Slovenian Democratic Party]
SLD	Sojusz Lewicy Demokratycznej [Polish Democratic Left Alliance]
SRP	Samoobrona Rzeczpospolitej Polskiej [Self-Defense of the Polish Republic]
TFP	The American Society for the Defense of Tradition, Family, and Property
TGEU	Transgender Europe
WWII	Second World War

I

Introduction

On the gray late spring day of June 19, 2010, Judith Butler, the renowned philosopher and public intellectual, took to the stage at the Brandenburg Gate to address Berlin's Christopher Street Day parade. The annual event celebrates the visibility of lesbian, gay, bisexual, and trans (LGBT)[1] identities, and that year it had again attracted almost a million guests from across the continent. A bird's-eye view of the colorful throng of people on the tree-lined street that connects the Brandenburg Gate and the Victory Column – the Prussian military monument that Berlin's gay community symbolically claimed as their own – clearly suggested that the organizers had achieved their goal of generating visibility. While some participants simply came to celebrate (though by making their identities visible, their presence was still political [V. Taylor, Rupp, and Gamson 2004]), others purposefully enhanced the colorful nature of the event by carrying signs and banners that articulated political grievances. Many of these statements championed or targeted the governments of foreign states.

---

[1] Scholarship on lesbian, gay, bisexual, trans, queer, intersex, and asexual (LGBTQIA) people defines its subjects in diverse ways. For simplicity, I use the umbrella terms *LGBT* and *sexual minority* to encompass people marginalized because of sexual orientations and/or gender identities that are deviant from heteronormative frameworks. My organizational data refer to LGBT people, and my policy and attitudinal data are often limited to LG people. While most academic scholarship uses the term *transgender*, I use *trans* because many of the groups I interviewed prefer it (or *trans**) as more inclusive. International norms of appropriate behavior concerning trans people have been less well established than those concerning lesbian and gay people (Balzer and Hutta 2014), especially in the period covered by this project's quantitative analyses. The study did not include data to extensively explore anti-institutional queer movements or the situations of people with questioning, intersex, or asexual identities.

reflecting political action that reached far beyond the city and the state. Butler stood before a crowd peppered with diverse national symbols – in recent years they have included a Swedish flag, a banner with the words *Solidarność Gejów* ("gay solidarity" in Polish), an image of Russian President Vladimir Putin's face painted in drag, and floats foreign embassies and expatriate communities had commissioned.

The scene illustrates the transnational dynamics of a movement that has spilled over the borders of nation states, a dimension of visibility that is central to this book. Visibility for LGBT people often has its roots in transnational sources. Indeed, the Berlin parade's name, Christopher Street Day, refers to the street in New York City where police raided the Stonewall Bar in 1969, subsequently spawning the gay liberation movement that moved LGBT people out of the closet and into the streets. With the parade's audience spread across both halves of a once-divided city where the Berlin Wall stood, the location itself represented both persistence and change in the role transnational movements play in an integrating Europe. Berlin was the avant-garde city that housed the world's first research center on homosexuality in 1897 but then stood aside in fearful silence as the capital of a state that brutally persecuted gay identity during the Third Reich. Today it symbolizes the unification of Europe, with Butler standing only meters away from where Ronald Reagan delivered his "Tear down this wall!" speech in 1987, and where countless East and West Berliners celebrated when the Berlin Wall did fall in 1989. Beyond the symbolic resonance of the location, the transnational makeup of the guests in Butler's audience reflects the new dimensions of space, both local and transnational, for minority rights movements.

Butler, an American, was invited to receive the prestigious *Zivilcouragepreis* (Civil Courage Award), which local Christopher Street Day organizers give to recognize persons and organizations that combat discrimination against, and prosecution of minorities. Yet, unbeknownst to the organizers and onlookers, Butler would use the stage to reject the award. She had come to shed light on the invisibility of specific LGBT groups, which remained hidden among the spectacular masses before her, by publically distancing herself from what she called the "racist complicity" in the divisions between the increasingly commercialized parade and local immigrant LGBT organizations. What was clearly an event of great visibility also reflected, in Butler's view, the invisibility of LGBT immigrants and people of color. While highlighting invisibility, Butler's performance simultaneously demonstrated the discursive political power of making the invisible visible. With her words, she shed light on the groups who are often left out of the discourses on LGBT recognition, recognizing that, in some states, these broader discourses have reshaped the lived experiences of only *some* marginalized groups that fall under the broad umbrella of LGBT categories.

Invisibility is not only a challenge for specific subgroups within LGBT communities, but also a broader issue across states and societies, among which the levels of recognition for sexual minorities vary tremendously. While Berliners in the hundreds of thousands could celebrate LGBT identities, four weeks later an even more transnational Pride event, the EuroPride in neighboring Poland, attracted a record 15,000 marchers. "Visitors from abroad said they'd come specifically because they'd heard the situation for gays in Poland was bad. 'I wouldn't go on a gay pride march in Brussels,' said [an attendee] from Belgium" (Cragg 2010). The contested nature of the Polish event also distinguished it from Berlin's Christopher Street Day parade. In Warsaw, the 15,000 marchers were accompanied by a 2,000-strong Polish police force necessary to fend off eight counterdemonstrations. Scenes such as this are common in contexts where LGBT issues are just beginning to enter the popular and political discourse. During the first parade in Podgorica, Montenegro, in 2013, 2,000 police officers protected 150 marchers from 1,500 counterdemonstrators (*Economist* 2014). At parades like the one in Berlin in 2010, there were no recorded protesters. The only additional demonstrations involved were other LGBT groups who organized their own parade to critique the commercialized nature of the main Christopher Street Day parade. Across Europe, the topography of LGBT recognition and (in)visibility in the public sphere is strikingly varied.

The politics of visibility and transnational movements

The subject of this book is how minority and marginal groups come to assert their rights in a transnational process that makes the invisible visible and, ultimately, transform the politics of states. Butler's speech at Christopher Street Day – a performance that embodies the themes of (in)visibility, movement, and transnationalism – is part of that transnational process on behalf of invisible LGBT communities. By providing a theoretical lens through which to view it, I hope to make this process clearer. Butler's presence at a local German event symbolizes a politics that cuts across borders, connecting people for mobilization in a movement and struggle that is so central to contemporary politics. Regardless of Butler's intentions, or individual reactions to her political position, her performance made it clear that a movement composed of diverse transnational ideas and actors places a high value on the power of visibility, within contentious politics, to diffuse new ideas into sociopolitical discourses.

This book thus explains how the politics of visibility affects relations among states and the political power of marginalized people within them. I show that the key to understanding processes of social change lies in a closer examination of the ways in which – and the degree to which – marginalized groups make governments and societies see and interact with their ideas. It is this process of "coming out" that leads to the sociopolitical recognition of rights that alters the situation for such groups. The attainment of rights by Swedish women, for example, originated in their demand for nationally subsidized childcare – active labor market participation facilitated their political emancipation. German women achieved less (and much later), as structural incentives to remain in the home kept them relatively invisible to the larger political culture (Huber and Stephens 2001, 125–6; Torstendahl 1999). Similarly, in 2006, the organizers of unprecedented episodes of immigrant collective action in the United States borrowed the term *coming out* to describe their mobilization. Fear of deportation had silenced undocumented immigrants for decades, but visibility gave them a voice as they began to engage political elites (Zepeda-Millán 2011). In a remarkable act of defiance, the Mothers of the Disappeared destabilized the predominant narrative of the Argentine military – who denied both that they had systematically disappeared "undesirable" segments of the population and, subsequently, that the disappeared had ever existed – by occupying the public sphere to declare, "Where are they?" (Brysk 2013, 63–5). The *Madres* made their children's identities visible, attaining widespread international recognition and destabilizing the bedrock narrative of the Argentine state. In the 1990s, Queer Nation activists in the United States, frustrated with violent homophobia and political impotence in dealing with the AIDS crisis, used a related slogan to make visible their presence in society: "We're here. We're queer. Get used to it." By contrast, invisibility has rendered marginalized groups weak in their efforts to demand change. Poor people's social movements in the United States, for example, were eventually silenced in the wake of widespread incarceration (Piven and Cloward 1977). To be sure, history is rife with examples of "weak" groups influencing states, but only under conditions of visibility.

Visibility has engendered the interactions between movements and states that empower people, mobilizing actors to demand change, influencing the spread of new legal standards, and weaving new norms into the fabrics of societies. For many marginalized groups, such visibility has its roots in both domestic and transnational sources. Consequently, I theorize two modes of the practice of coming out (as an identity marker and as a presence in the public sphere), demonstrating in Chapter 2 how opportunities for making norms visible through interaction can unfold at multiple levels. Coming out has heretofore been considered an individual experience, but Alexander Wendt's (1999) formative argument – that states have malleable identities of their own – suggests that they too can come out by recognizing certain groups as part of their rights frameworks. Take, for example, the Swedish Peace and Arbitration Society's creative campaign to mark the country's territorial waters. In response both to broader Swedish opposition to Russian antigay propaganda laws and to reports of rogue Russian submarines in Swedish waters, the society transmitted from the territorial boundaries Morse code that proclaimed, "Sweden, gay since 1944" (A. Taylor 2015). The act illustrates that LGBT politics can merge with state identities, whether real or imagined, and play a role in contemporary world politics.

The politics of LGBT visibility encompasses a group that many observers have referred to as "an invisible minority," but whose newfound presence and influence in many different nation states is a development that offers fresh opportunities for the study of sociopolitical change and the diffusion of norms.[2] Indeed, it is quite remarkable that Catholic Ireland would adopt same-sex marriage by popular vote, or that the small island of Malta would become a trailblazer on trans recognition. The fact that, for example, so many states have approved same-sex unions "is not a mere coincidence," as Kelly Kollman (2013, 3) has argued. It calls on us to take seriously the international dimension of these trends. While I analyze LGBT rights to develop the politics of visibility framework, the framework has powerful implications for other movements pertinent to political science and sociology, such as those I have mentioned. I use the LGBT case to explore how actors are mobilized across borders and explain why the outcome of their mobilization varies across national contexts.

Why, despite similar international pressures from European institutions, has the social and legal recognition of sexual minorities changed to such

---

[2] For example, Hillary Clinton referred to LGBT people as "an invisible minority" in her Human Rights Day speech delivered on December 6, 2011, at the United Nations in Geneva. Text: www.huffingtonpost.com/2011/12/06/hillary-clinton-gay-rights-speech-geneva_n_1132392.html

differing degrees and at such different rates across European states? My answer is simple but consequential: I argue that differing degrees of visibility have produced different outcomes for sociopolitical change across states. Building on theories of international relations and contentious politics that deal with international norm diffusion, this book focuses on variation in the changed legal status and societal perceptions of sexual minorities. Put most broadly, it explains changing ideas of the state and society in world politics, using the case of norms governing LGBT rights. In doing so, it deals with the existential conflict between various actors and the tension between two sets of norms: ideas that are new and international, and ideas that are rooted in the heteronormative nation and local tradition. The two sets of ideas usually do not coexist harmoniously. That said, I do not view domestic politics as passive, or reactionary to "progressive" international norms, nor do I suggest a false dichotomy between enlightened civil society and norm-violating governments (see Seybert 2012). Norm politics are never a one-way street, and many of the most forward-thinking proponents of LGBT rights are domestic actors within target states who champion the issue, often seeking out transnational ties to further their cause. Norm evolution does not stop once it reaches the international realm; echoing Lucia Seybert (2012), I argue that it continues through interaction with domestic spheres. Consequently, this book focuses on interactions between actors – both proponents and opponents of LGBT rights – at both domestic and transnational levels. "From the clash of identities and social systems we learn how worlds change," as Alison Brysk (2000, 1) notes. The LGBT rights revolution provides an ideal platform from which to study such interactions.

How LGBT rights vary across Europe

My research question focuses specifically on Europe, the only region of the world with internationally binding protections based on sexual orientation, a region that is a leader on LGBT rights but nonetheless exhibits great variety in the degree to which its states adopt international norms governing LGBT rights. The fall of the Berlin Wall and subsequent European integration gave former Communist Bloc states unprecedented exposure to norms and institutions developed in response to the early politicization of sexual identity in several Western European states. The rapidly increased social and political interaction between new European Union (EU) member states in Central and Eastern Europe (CEE) with older member states provides an ideal methodological framework for international norm diffusion theory, which stipulates that state and non-state actors spread ideas from areas where those ideas are more accepted to areas where they are not. I use the terms *first mover/leading* and *new adopter* to distinguish states that politicized LGBT issues relatively early from those where the issue has become politicized more recently.[3] An *international norm* defines appropriate behavior for a specific set of actors (Katzenstein 1996, 5), standards that governments or nongovernmental organizations (NGOs) wish to export (Finnemore and Sikkink 1998, 891) or that receiving actors feel they ought to adopt or emulate. By *diffusion*, I refer to the spread of an innovation to a state or society, when the decision to adopt the innovation is influenced by some other state or society (Graham, Shipan, and Volden 2013, 676). In this case, diffusion is related partly to the processes by which people work to effect social and political change (that is, change in society, institutions, or the law), for instance building alliances, exerting pressure, and spreading and adapting knowledge across national borders (Roggeband 2010, 19). Diffusion can also include indirect interactions in which purposiveness is not necessary, such as the transmission of new ideas via the media.

In Europe, a number of transnational actors – the EU institutions, the European Court of Human Rights (ECtHR), and a transnational network of activists – have fostered change by propagating an international norm of LGBT rights and introducing, or at least amplifying, the issue in the domestic discourses of various European states (Kollman 2013). A recent example from Romania exhibits these trends. In 2010, the ACCEPT Association, a transnationally linked Romanian LGBT organization, brought a case against George Becali in the European Court of Justice (ECJ). Becali, a Romanian politician and owner of a soccer club, had made public statements opposing the transfer and employment in his club of a

---

[3] Proponents of LGBT rights refer to the former as leading or first movers because they are generally endowed with more LGBT movement actors, more comprehensive LGBT rights, and more favorable attitudes. I distinguish leading/first movers from new adopters merely as a heuristic device to acknowledge differing levels of LGBT norm development across states. The distinction is not meant to conceal the intolerance and injustice that LGBT people still experience in states labeled as leading – for instance, the Netherlands holds a top spot in the leading category, yet 40 percent of Dutch respondents expressed discomfort at seeing two men kiss in public, as opposed to only 13 percent who objected to a man and a woman doing the same (Keuzenkamp and Ross 2010, 355–6). Nor is this distinction intended to deem new-adopter states of lesser worth or to "other" them as a new type of abnormality to "Western" scripts (Binnie and Klesse 2013; Kulpa and Mizielińska 2011; Stychin 1998). Finally, the labels don't correspond with old and new EU member states. While older EU states are more likely to be leading states (see Figure 2.4 and Figure 2.5), there are exceptions, notably Italy and Greece.

soccer player rumored to be gay. The court's ruling in favor of ACCEPT placed Romania's implementation of the EU's anti-discrimination directive under scrutiny and has already had far-reaching implications. It put LGBT rights on the agenda of the Romanian National Council for Combating Discrimination and encouraged proposed amendments to the country's anti-discrimination act. Becali's prominence has also spurred a societal discourse, with LGBT advocates hammering home a central message: "Homophobia has no place in sports, has no place in employment, and has no place in a *European* state" (Berbec-Rostas 2013, emphasis added).

The norm that LGBT people are entitled to fundamental human rights, and deserving of state recognition and protection, is clearly articulated in both the rhetoric and the legal framework of the institutions of the EU and the Council of Europe (CoE). Examples include: Article 13 of the Amsterdam Treaty, Article 49 of the Lisbon Treaty, the 2000 Employment Anti-Discrimination Directive, the EU Charter of Fundamental Rights, the 1993 Copenhagen Criteria, various European Parliament resolutions (e.g. *European Parliament Resolution on Homophobia in Europe 2005/2666* and *2007/2543*), ECtHR decisions (e.g. *Bączkowski and others v. Poland*, 1543/06), and ECJ decisions (e.g. C-13/94, *P. v. S. and Cornwall County Council*) (see Ayoub and Paternotte 2014; Mos 2014; Slootmaeckers and Touquet in press). Despite strikingly similar exposure to European norms and regulations, however, newly admitted member states differ greatly in both societal attitudes and in the introduction of legal protections for sexual minorities, challenging the direct top-down power of norms (Finnemore 1996). Figure 1.1 shows the mean country value, on a scale of 1 to 10, for attitudes toward homosexuality across three periods (1990–1993, 1999–2001, and 2008–2010) in EU member states. The top graph includes the new EU-12 member states (2004 and 2007 waves) and the bottom, the original EU-15 member states.[4] Figure 1.2 illustrates the variation in the adoption of pro-LGBT legislation across EU-27 member states.[5] All states meet the

---

4 I use *EU-12* to refer to the twelve *new* states that came after the EU-15 (within the EU-27 enlargement). These should not be confused with the original EU-12 of the late 1980s and early 1990s.

5 The combined legislation score includes the following provisions: anti-discrimination in employment, goods and services, and constitutional recognition; recognition of hate crimes based on sexual orientation as an aggravating circumstance and/or prohibition of incitement to hatred based on sexual orientation; recognition of same-sex partnership for cohabitation, registered partnership, and marriage; recognition of same-sex couples' parenting rights for joint adoption and second parent adoption; and sexual

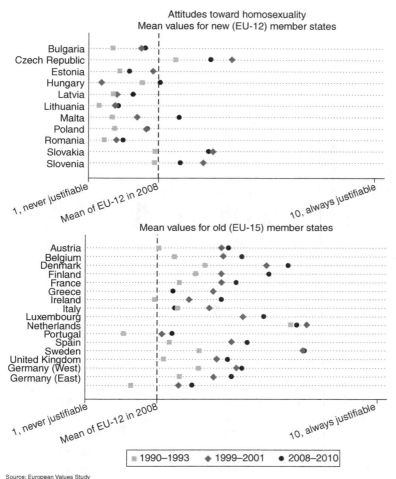

FIGURE 1.1. Variation in attitudes toward homosexuality across EU states.

sexual minority protections the EU requires of its members (decriminalization of same-sex acts; the same age of consent for both opposite-sex and same-sex acts; no discrimination in employment; and, more recently, asylum on the basis of sexual orientation), but some states provide additional protections, for example, parenting and partnership rights.

offense provisions that specify an equal age of consent for same-sex and opposite-sex activity (cf. Table A.1, Appendix).

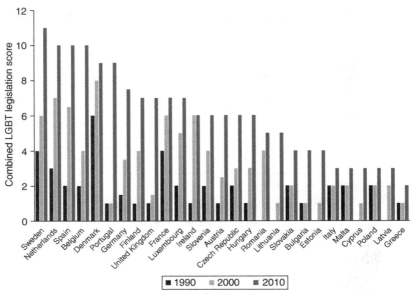

FIGURE 1.2. Variation in LGBT rights legislation across EU states.

Why countries grant or withhold LGBT rights

Most, though not all, EU states and societies find nonheterosexualities more acceptable today than they did in 1989, but the LGBT norm has permeated different domestic contexts at different rates. For example, some traditionally Catholic countries blaze new trails on LGBT rights, while some modern, wealthy democracies remain laggards. Existing theories for successful diffusion cannot adequately explain this discrepancy, though such theories – differences in international pressures, the fit between domestic and international norms, modernization, low implementation costs – are useful for a baseline understanding of how and why norms change in a multitude of states. From this baseline, my evidence suggests that the degree to which international norms resonate in a given state – and become internalized within it – depends on specific transnational channels and on domestic interest groups that make political issues visible. I show that the extent of a state's openness to international organizations and information flows (the exchange of ideas and images with other countries) has demonstrable effects on diffusion because it allows new ideas to enter the domestic discourse. These social and political channels prime a context for diffusion by making the issue visible. Furthermore, the degree to which domestic actors are embedded in transnational advocacy networks illuminates the issue and shapes the speed and direction of diffusion. These transnational actors mediate between international and domestic norms both to frame the message so it fits locally and to quell the perceptions of threat that some states assign to LGBT norms.

Yet states do not react to the external environment in the same way. A second component of my argument is that the degree of religious nationalism in the domestic sphere moderates the way international norms are received and internalized. The book reflects on the politics of the link between national identity and religion to argue that different perceptions of threat in distinct national contexts can influence responses to LGBT norms. I propose not that religion bars the advancement of LGBT movements, but that politicizing the historical antecedents of the popular idea of the nation can make religion a force for countermobilization. In sum, differing perceptions of threat define how distinct domestic realms receive international norms, and threat perception increases where religion is historically embedded in the popular conception of the nation. Whether resistance is effectual, however, is a separate question. Where sexual minorities become visible, contestation is common, if not expected, but rarely leads to the demise of the movement or sustained backlash in the public sphere (see also Bishin *et al.* 2015 on backlash). The evidence suggests that in high-threat contexts, resistance to the LGBT movement can be self-defeating, in that it can galvanize the movement and enhance both the visibility and the salience of the LGBT rights norm (O'Dwyer 2012; Ayoub 2014).

My findings suggest that norm visibility is necessary for diffusion – both to governments and publics – in world politics, since elites and publics within states do not always see or care about issues that first develop elsewhere. By *norm visibility,* I refer to the relative ability of publics and governments to see and interact with the ideas and images that define standards of appropriate behavior. By defining new standards of acceptability, these international sources of normative change introduce "new ways of understanding oneself" (Altman 1999, 563). This is true both for LGBT people and for societies at large. Norm visibility is critical for mobilizing the people who spread new standards and attitudes, for influencing the timing and likelihood of legal changes, and for determining the pathway to, and level of, internalization in society.

A unique aspect of the LGBT rights norm is that it is inherently contentious in most societies, to the point that it is often portrayed as violating the moral foundation on which nationhood is structured (Stychin 1998). Even after the issue was initially politicized, first-mover states required decades to introduce legislation, such as protection against discrimination, akin to the legal protection won by other groups represented in the rights revolution.[6] This calls into question why new EU member states have so quickly begun to digest this contentious LGBT norm – politicized only recently – at home and respond to it within their legal and social structures. The visibility explanation presented here assumes that these states want to identify as part of "Europe." Europe perceives itself on the macro level as adherent to the rights revolution that has transformed world politics – and it perceives LGBT rights as among these newly won rights. Adopting the LGBT rights norm, then, is part of what it means to be a member of contemporary Europe. This conceptualization draws from scholars who argue that states adopt standards to remain or become legitimate (J. W. Meyer *et al.* 1997); however, I emphasize agency by arguing that deliberation, which comes with visibility, is a key mechanism for diffusion and change. For this process to happen, states must see that with which they are meant to conform. Efforts by new EU member states to identify with this community have driven the social movements that have made the norm visible. I will argue that the norm must be made visible in the domestic context before societies can deliberate on it and internalize it. The felt intensity of a norm varies across cases, depending on its visibility.

Alternative explanations

The spread of norms concerning the rights of sexual minorities complicates existing explanations about diffusion and social change, both arguments about international norms and those about domestic sociolegal

---

[6] LGBT rights are part of the broader rights revolution. Both the 2006 Yogyakarta Principles on the Application of International Human Rights Law in Relation to Sexual Orientation and Gender Identity and UN resolutions have established LGBT rights firmly within the discourses of the rights revolution. This marks a change from the 1960s and 1970s, when it was common for other movements to exclude LGBT people from this discourse (Skrentny 2002). This exclusion was partly related to discomfort at including LGBT people and fear that societies were not yet "ready" for homosexual and trans issues; these movements tended to sideline LGBT rights (Bernstein 2002, 546), though there were notable exceptions – for example, Huey Newton's pioneering 1970 article on the intersection of race, gender, and sexuality (Newton 1970).

changes. The diversity of the states that today promote LGBT rights mud-
dles previous theories about the domestic factors that affect recognition
of these rights: religious-cultural context (Finke and Adamczyk 2008),
economic wealth and modernity (Inglehart and Norris 2003), societal
openness toward homosexuality (Badgett 2009), the development of the
welfare state (Wilson 2013), the organizing capacity of domestic social
movements (Adam, Duyvendak, and Krouwel 1998), the strength of democracy (Encarnación 2014), and the pluralization of sexual practice and
meaning (including revolutionized gender hierarchies, and the separation
of sex and reproduction) (Weeks 2007).[7] Many of these arguments grew
out of the experiences charted in first-mover states, such as the Protestant
Nordic countries and the Netherlands, but became complicated in the
new century. For example, at the time of writing this book more than
twenty European states have adopted some form of same-sex union at
the federal level, and few of them resemble the first movers in terms of
the domestic factors listed above.

The idea that international norms diffuse successfully when they
match domestic beliefs and understandings (Checkel 2001; Cortell and
Davis 1996; Finnemore 1996; Keck and Sikkink 1998, 204) also does
not hold among new adopters. Despite the contentious nature of LGBT
rights, surprising "misfits," such as more religious and less democratic
states, have embraced them. Three of Europe's most religious states –
Catholic Spain, Portugal and, most recently, Ireland – have seen some of
the most rapid social and legal change concerning these rights (Casanova
2009, 209). The small island of Malta, where 95 percent of the population self-identifies as Roman Catholic and more than half the population
attends church services regularly (Harwood 2015), became a trailblazer on trans recognition. Furthermore, though Estonia and the Czech
Republic are equally secular, Estonia is more intolerant than the Czech
Republic, and attitudes among former East Germans are more unfavora-
ble to LGBT people than in less secular western Germany. Other misfits include post-socialist countries such as Poland which, though it has
democratized and complied with many costly EU regulations (Petrova
2012), has struggled to adopt basic measures to protect the rights of
LGBT minorities. Within and outside Europe, the increasingly diverse set
of states that adopt LGBT rights norms challenges us to think beyond the
factors that explained changes in first-mover states.

---

[7] David Paternotte (2015) eloquently summarizes several of these explanations.

I also find that universal "low-cost" norms elicit powerful reactions from states and societies. Scholars have argued that states should always take low-cost moral action (Kaufman and Pape 1999), especially when it helps facilitate access to the bundle of economic benefits that come with EU membership (Schimmelfennig 2007; Vachudova 2005). However, attempting to apply purely rational logic to state behavior around LGBT rights raises as many questions as answers. States can enhance their international reputations by recognizing and protecting sexual minorities, without direct monetary costs to themselves or to individuals. Yet some moral norms low in monetary cost are difficult to transmit. Equally puzzling are cases where state authorities stake their domestic reputations on recognizing and protecting sexual minorities despite the presumed political costs (see Putnam 1988 on two-level games in world politics). Then too, states such as Germany have opposed expanding EU anti-discrimination directives for LGBT people even though they would face no implementation cost because their domestic standards exceed EU requirements. Even when states commit to international human rights treaties simply to avoid criticism, I argue, these acts produce tangible outcomes, a stance in line with Beth Simmons' (2009) challenge to the idea that human rights norms are hollow and costless. The uneven rate of diffusion across states is also puzzling, given that previous scholarship shows human rights norms are the most successfully and uniformly adopted norms in the EU accession process (Checkel 1997, 480) when accession states have similar material incentives. The fact that the same norm meets forceful resistance in some cases and not in others cannot be understood without thinking more carefully about varied state identities.

Furthermore, theories resting on a hard-law understanding of conditionality explain the diffusion of LGBT rights only insofar as they help to make the norm visible and legitimize it. Conditionality can also provoke unwanted responses and prompt anti-LGBT organizers to argue that the issue is being externally imposed. Thus, conditionality affects the diffusion of norms, but not in the way commonly theorized. Not only do the "soft" socialization mechanisms behind a visibility approach have a more positive effect on both compliance and internalization, as I show in Chapters 4 and 5, but hard-law conditionality may work indirectly, leading to backlash before the visibility that that backlash generates can fuel the salience of the norm (Chapter 6). In contrast to arguments based on conditionality, localization, and norm fit, I argue that contestation can lead to visibility.

The diffusion of LGBT norms also challenges the widely held assumption that modernization correlates with the adoption of post-material values, such as accepting homosexuality (Inglehart 1997; Inglehart and Norris 2003). While the first states to expand LGBT rights were often the wealthy states that modernization theorists expect to change (e.g. the Nordic states), many new adopters do not exhibit similar economic wealth (Chapter 4). The level of per capita gross domestic product (GDP) is not a robust or reliable predictor of change, because poorer states often adopt the norm before wealthier ones. Studies that combine data from dissimilar world regions in one model overemphasize the importance of economic wealth for social change (Inglehart and Norris 2003). Several of the field's dominant explanations lose traction when we study a region bound by strong supranational institutional structures.

Contrary to expectations, LGBT actors have mobilized where domestic political opportunities are most closed, which prompts us to consider multilevel and transnational opportunities for mobilization. The high risk of LGBT mobilization may still prevent mobilization in "culturally closed" contexts (Blumenfeld and Raymond 1988), but activists have responded to roadblocks at home by looking elsewhere. For example, when state and local governments in Poland banned LGBT activists from public assembly in multiple cities, Polish activism continued because of opportunities beyond the country's borders. The social movement field's traditional political process approach, rooted as it is in the nation state, would predict otherwise. In fact, mobilization often intensified *before* states granted LGBT actors access to political participation, these actors acquired influential domestic allies, the state's elite split, or the state's resolve to repress mobilization declined (Kriesi 2004; McAdam 1999). The mobilization of LGBT minorities shows that the multilevel structure of the European polity can shift the opportunities described by this approach to new levels, including those outside the nation state (Sikkink 2005).

Another competing explanation is that the post-communist legacy has affected LGBT rights in many of the new EU member states. This line of scholarship proposes that the material and ideational bankruptcy of civil society in CEE, and the impact of the past on new institutions (Jowitt 1992), have restricted the development of LGBT rights there. Indeed, the Soviet reordering of relations at the legal, political, and social levels did influence state and societal behavior around sexuality, which was repressed and stigmatized in the Eastern Bloc, and aspects of that legacy do manifest themselves in the contemporary politics of the region. That said, I take a more nuanced stance on the Soviet legacy (see Beissinger and Kotkin 2014). Post-communist states have gone their separate ways on a multitude of political and cultural variables (Darden and Grzymała-Busse 2006; Easter 1997). Indeed, one of the central puzzles in this book is that states emerged from communism to follow different paths on LGBT rights and attitudes toward LGBT people – variations that the post-communist legacy thesis cannot explain on its own. That the legacy of communism does not have a uniform grip on the relationship between the state and social perceptions of sexuality becomes quickly apparent with a cursory look at the sociopolitical data surrounding the issue. Notably, even the three Baltic states, once part of the Soviet Union, look different from each other, as do the states that once made up Yugoslavia and Czechoslovakia.

This book offers a new explanation not only for variation between old and new EU member states but also for variation within these groupings. Chapter 6, in particular, examines how the historical antecedents of the idea of the nation can prompt countermobilization fueled by religious nationalism, which is one factor that explains the differences among CEE countries. In doing so, it builds on what other scholars of LGBT politics have noted, that a deterministic post-Soviet thesis artificially homogenizes CEE countries (Kulpa and Mizielińska 2011). Sexual minorities had different histories in these countries before and after the Berlin Wall fell. The chapter also explains both the persistence and the decay of the post-Soviet legacy, something the thesis overlooks, by thinking through new experiences and factors that now play an active role in the region. Namely, as Beissinger and Kotkin (2014, 5–6) state:

While the social ramifications that flowed from the upheaval of communist collapse have been studied in great detail, the role of the outside world has often remained a blank spot or has been reduced to a focus on democracy promotion efforts. Relatively few scholars, for instance, have examined how postcommunist societies have been shaped (or not shaped) by ... global cultural currents, or the role of possible models for emulation.

The outside world, I argue, matters a great deal for the politics of sexuality in Europe, and its influence varies according to how connected states are to it (via sociopolitical channels of visibility that transnational activist networks help to facilitate).

Finally, taking seriously the variation in compliance and internationalization across states also extends arguments of the World Polity

School, which posits that a global civil society, comprised of organized and rule-like models, constitutes the capabilities and interrelationships of societal actors (J. W. Meyer *et al.* 1997). According to this school of thought, a global society advances not functional needs or actor interests, but rather general universal truths, which leads to a global isomorphism in institutions and norms (Soysal 1994). While this explanation can describe some changes surrounding sexuality – for example, reforms in incest law, bestiality law, and adultery law have often occurred without visible advocacy (cf. Frank, Camp, and Boutcher 2010) – the basic postulate requires refinement if it is to explain the diffusion of the more expansive LGBT rights norm. The postulate portrays global culture as secular and rational (J. W. Meyer *et al.* 1997, 154), slighting the tensions that derive from domestic norms when they are incompatible with international LGBT norms, as well as the substantial differences I identify between processes of compliance and internalization. Instead of expecting states and societies to respond to the external environment in the same way, I emphasize the contentiousness of global change by privileging agency, specifying the relational mechanisms, and charting the transnational channels and domestic differences inherent in processes of norm diffusion. *Too much*

Considering how change occurs

I support the visibility argument by explaining differences in social attitudes and state laws concerning sexual minorities across European states (Figure 1.1 and Figure 1.2). Is change due to heightened exposure to individuals and groups in states that have previously adopted the norm? Under what domestic preconditions (of the recipient state) do international norms of sexual minority rights successfully spread, and to what degree will they be opposed? Who are the agents of change and how are they mobilized? Finally, what are the transnational pathways of diffusion? The outcomes I explore – my dependent variables – tap into two dimensions of international norm diffusion: change in the behavior of the state and change in the behavior of individuals within society. I analyze legal compliance and societal internalization as related but separate processes. (By *internalization*, I refer to a process by which certain behaviors come to feel inappropriate for one's identity as one's group develops new collective expectations [Abdelal *et al.* 2006, 697].) Distinguishing between these processes is essential, given that legal protections do not necessarily correlate highly with decreasing levels of social stigmatization. Furthermore, the commonly used dependent variable – the socialization of state elites (e.g. Checkel 1997) – does not capture an attitudinal shift (or lack thereof) in most of society.

In this book, I look at both indices of norm diffusion – legal compliance and societal internalization – because norms are ultimately about changes in behavior. As Peter Katzenstein and Tim Byrnes (2006, 683) note, "The behavioral dimension is shaped by the regulative and constitutive effects of rules that operate at the individual level through internalization and habituation and at the collective level through various sanctioning mechanisms." Since norms are difficult to observe directly, I look to two behavioral measures to analyze consequences of changed norms. To measure change at the state level, I collected and analyzed data on the number of LGBT rights laws adopted by states. These include protective and equality laws that go beyond decriminalization. To capture change at the individual level, I looked to survey data on social attitudes toward sexual minorities.

As the methodological description suggests, while my evidence and arguments have normative implications, my primary goal is not to evaluate the normative substance of LGBT rights norms. Many excellent studies in international relations and queer theory rightly question the normative content of the demands made by mainstream LGBT rights activists (R. Conrad 2014) and critique the power dynamics and western essentialism inherent in some forms of transnational activism (Amar 2013; Picq and Thiel 2015; Rahman 2014). While I am sympathetic to such arguments and call attention to them at various points in the text, a critical normative engagement of transnational LGBT activism falls outside the scope of this book. Instead, I observe that LGBT norms, regardless of the quality of their content, have spread to multiple domestic contexts, and I attempt to explain when and how that happens.

Throughout this book, I argue that a politics of visibility explains how and when "weak" groups bring about change in social and political systems, that the struggle for rights occurs through pathways of visibility, and that such visibility increasingly has transnational sources. While social institutions and actors can transform the lived experience of marginalized peoples, we know too little about why such groups have wielded power in some states and lacked power in others. A visibility framework provides answers.

Plan of the book

In highlighting the importance of visibility for change in world politics, the following chapters explore why the trajectories of sociolegal recognition for marginalized groups are remarkably dissimilar across states. Chapter 2 presents the intricacies of my theory about the causes of this variation and of change itself; it explores why and how visibility influences sociolegal change concerning sexual minorities. In it, I conceptualize a framework for how visibility influences the processes of both state compliance and societal internalization, and I reflect on the transnational channels of visibility, their interaction with domestic politics, and the resistances they can provoke. I close the chapter by summarizing my methods of inquiry.

Chapter 3 introduces the various actors and mechanisms at play in the transnational movement for LGBT rights. It explores how transnationalization influences the mobilization of marginalized people, focusing on the mobilization of norm entrepreneurs and on how they navigate transnational and domestic spheres to create a local resonance for LGBT rights norms. I call these agents *norm entrepreneurs* because they purposefully detach their causes from the confines of one nation, seek to influence popular and political support in more than one state, and contribute to the functioning of like-minded organizations in other countries (Acharya 2004, 248; Nadelmann 1990).[8] Specifically, the chapter addresses the question of how marginalized actors are mobilized across borders and illustrates the visibility mechanisms that these actors employ in their attempts to influence state and society. I use the cases of Germany and Poland, within the framework of European institutions, to trace cross-border connections between norm entrepreneur and target state.

Chapters 4 and 5 present cross-national empirical findings on the central research question: why has the social and legal recognition of minorities changed to such differing degrees and at such different rates across states? Chapter 4 explores the varied adoption of pro-LGBT legislation in Europe. It analyzes an original LGBT legislation data set and employs event history and ordered logit modeling techniques to explain the timing, rate, and adoption of various LGBT rights laws in EU states across forty years. Chapter 5 considers the varied attitudinal shifts toward LGBT people in Europe. It uses multilevel random intercept models to

---

[8] The term *norm entrepreneur* is related to the term *policy/issue entrepreneur* used in research on interest groups (Baumgartner and Jones 2009), but shifts the focus to the transnational level.

explain the state's contextual influence over individual attitudes toward homosexuality across three points in time, as well as the differences in societal attitudes across states.

In Chapter 6, the second qualitative component of the book, I use the case studies of Poland and Slovenia to compare differences in domestic norm reception and sociolegal outcomes, asking why the visibility of norms governing LGBT rights provoked resistance in one case and not in the other. I analyze how resistance is rooted in the relationship between religion and nationalism, explore how these factors interact with transnational channels of visibility, and explain the conditions under which visibility can improve the sociolegal situation for LGBT minorities.

Finally, in Chapter 7, I discuss my findings and summarize the role of visibility in movement and transnational politics. The chapter outlines those elements of my argument that are limited to Europe, as well as those that are generalizable to issues of global change on minority rights. It discusses the implications of my findings for theory and practice in world politics, as well as the project's importance in light of current events, both within Europe and beyond.

2

The politics of visibility and LGBT rights in Europe

Come out, stand up and let that world know. That would do more to end prejudice overnight than anybody would imagine. I urge them to do that, urge them to come out. Only that way will we start to achieve our rights.
– Harvey Milk, 1977

In the 1980s, activists of the AIDS Coalition to Unleash Power (ACT UP) in New York coined the slogan "Silence = Death," an expression that came to define much of the LGBT movement in that decade. In the spirit of Harvey Milk, who rejected what he called a "conspiracy of silence," the activists were responding to the Reagan administration's silence on the HIV/AIDS epidemic that had brought the gay community to its knees. ACT UP adopted a logo that featured, above the words "Silence = Death," a pink triangle symbolizing the patch that gay concentration camp prisoners were forced to wear during the Second World War (WWII). That historical context also evoked the theme of silence and death: in the 1940s, the silence of a nation and the silence of a social group resulted in death in the camps of Dachau, just as it did in the hospital beds of Chelsea in the 1980s. Equating silence with death is therefore neither new nor unique to a particular context. Indeed, nearly a century earlier in 1896, a German gay advocate (using the pseudonym Ludwig Frey) wrote that *"Stillschweigen ist der Tod"* (staying silent is death) (Beachy 2014, 107). At various points during the twentieth century, members of a marginalized group who sometimes had the ability to disguise their sexual orientation and gender identity were compelled to come out, to act up, and to make themselves visible.

Extending the logic of the "Silence = Death" campaign, I argue that visibility explains the transnational diffusion of LGBT rights in Europe. The premise that visibility leads to change is not new among European rights activists, many of whom share Harvey Milk's theory that gay and lesbian people should publicly declare their orientation if they wish to see society accept them (Herek 2004, 14). That said, they also caution that coming out – especially on an individual basis – is a privilege that can be more or less difficult depending on context (a point I return to at the end of this chapter). Visibility functions by facilitating the interactions that empower groups at the political periphery. It helps LGBT people find each other in contexts where their identities are invisible – increasing the potential for their mobilization – and it brings states and societies into contact with new norms. Increasingly, this process is both domestic and transnational, as external sources of visibility influence the spread of new legal and societal standards into the framework for the nation state. I thus define the core concept of *norm visibility* as the relative ability of governments and publics to see and interact with new ideas and images that define the standards of appropriate behavior within their international societies.

In this chapter I develop a theoretical framework around norm visibility that specifies the conditions under which states comply with, and societies begin to internalize, norms of tolerance toward sexual minorities. Norm visibility engenders this broader diffusion of images and ideas that empower the political margins. It moves the margin – in this case LGBT people – to the center of political debate and public recognition, making it possible for them to claim the rights that are their due. Coming out is thus a social and political process – one that brings states, publics, and marginalized groups together – for making the invisible visible and cashing in on the human rights and dignity movements that have marked European and world politics after WWII.

Such a conception of visibility goes beyond strategic movement choices. For Ashley Currier (2012), whose pioneering work integrated the concept into theories of contentious politics, visibility is primarily a social movement strategy that activists can choose to implement (or not) in their work (see also Zivi 2012). While this is true of LGBT activists in Europe, who also view visibility as a goal, my definition of norm visibility involves a more diffuse transnational process. Visibility can be the source of the identities that lead to mobilization in the first place, provide the political inspiration for both movement actors and state authorities, and be the involuntary transmission of ideas and images via information flows that cross borders. Social interaction is at the core of all of these aspects of visibility that bring disparate actors and states into dialogue transnationally via brokerage, deliberation, and processes of learning.

In the remainder of this chapter, I elaborate on the mechanisms and processes through which norm visibility functions in the transmission of the movement and its ideas across borders. First, I break down the functioning of norm visibility into two related subcomponents: inter-personal visibility and public visibility. Through social relationships, *interpersonal visibility* brings individuals into interaction with people identifying as LGBT. These interactions can be both among people who come to identify as LGBT (in-group) and between LGBT people and their broader social networks. Put most simply, it is about members of the group seeing each other and being seen by segments of their other communities. *Public visibility* is the collective coming out of a group to engage and be seen by society and state. Both interpersonal and pub-lic visibilities have political consequences for the diffusion of norms. Second, I discuss the channels of visibility (transnational political, social, and movement channels) that connect states and societies to the norms of the international communities in which they are embedded. I describe how these channels can lead to compliance with LGBT norms by states.

Finally, I turn to contestation and internalization in the domestic realm. Contestation heightens the norm's salience and subsequently leads to further interaction with the norm, via well-connected actors in the movement and, in some cases, their opposition. Channels of visibility and contestation have effects on state compliance and societal international-ization. I close by discussing the scopes and caveats of the theory in terms of the valence of visibility and then briefly introduce the methods for analysis that drive the subsequent chapters.

The politics of visibility

Seeing each other

Visibility facilitates the construction of politically salient identity markers and can inspire marginalized people to create the networks of trust and solidarity that lead to mobilization. A large part of LGBT identity devel-ops later in life in interaction with other LGBT people and their allies, and such identities that distinguish the group from heteronormative cul-ture have been used as a strategy to mobilize people (Bernstein 2002). It is this aspect of visibility, which I call interpersonal visibility, that provides the foundation for such interactions to take root and for collective action to materialize. The visibility of LGBT norms brings to light the shared experiences of many gender and sexual minorities, both among the activists and among the constituents they represent. Gloria Steinem (2014), an American activist in the women's movement, described this process vividly when she recollected her own mobilization and politicization:

I don't think I understood the need for a movement until I went to cover an abortion hearing. I had had an abortion when I first graduated from college and I'd never told anyone. And I listened to women testify about all that they had to go through: the injury, the danger, the infection, [and] the sexual humiliation to get an illegal abortion. I began to understand that my experience was not just mine ... And that meant that only if you got together with other women was it going to be affected in any way.

The idea that "the personal is political" – that is, social and systemic instead of isolated and individual (Crenshaw 1991) – mobilized the second and third wave of feminists once they came to see themselves as part of a collective and discover who "they" were (Whittier 2010). Similarly, many LGBT people experienced a fusion of the personal and the political as relatable sexualities became visible. The pioneering homosexual activist Karl Heinrich Ulrichs described a related experience of discovery when he left Göttingen – where "as far as he could see, there was no one else like him" – for Berlin in the 1840s (Beachy 2014, 9). It was there that he would meet other men with same-sex desires, whom he would describe (using the term *urning*) in writings that inspired the world's first homosexual rights movement just one generation later.

Most of the contemporary activists I interviewed mentioned the centrality of (in)visibility to their work, because in many European contexts LGBT people find it difficult to show themselves openly. Being visible is thus a privilege (Bernstein and Reimann 2001, 10), and the visibility of LGBT life varies greatly by context. Fearing rejection from family, friends, and employers, LGBT people often conceal their sexuality and gender identity, rendering part of themselves invisible. Thus, many LGBT identities have been built in safe spaces – such as cafes, bars, and private homes – that remain secluded from society and state. While these spaces have been transformational by fostering an awareness of collective grievances and social solidarity, they lack the public dimension that scholars have found to be important for a group's democratic participation (Evans and Boyte 1992).

Private or designated safe spaces remain invisible to society at large almost by definition, as they exist to shield the identity of LGBT people from out-group members. While invisibility can provide security, it stifles domestic movements for change because there are few actors to mobilize in public and too few openly LGBT people for the nation to perceive the issue as local. In many European states, activists interviewed described difficulty in recruiting potential activists at the turn of the century because of fears and discomfort associated with coming out to friends and family members (interviews no. 8, 9, 129, 131, 139, and 140). Many possible LGBT activists had to keep low public profiles because they did not want their families to see them in the media. In Slovakia, a campaign, simply called "Come Out," was started specifically to address the centrality of this issue for political mobilization: "People did not come out in Slovakia; we needed them to see role models" (interview no. 118). Similarly, activists in Malta emphasized that Maltese LGBT people found it difficult to see their situation as collectively shared before the issue became visible: "Discrimination is very systemic and insidious, making it hard to get people to *see* that their rights are being infringed. Visibility politicizes gay people themselves" (interview no. 112, emphasis added). These obstacles are acute in countries where the discourse on LGBT rights is new.

While coming out strategies (Chabot and Duyvendak 2002, 726) are effectual movement repertoires, they are arduous to realize in such contexts. The activists' testimonies echo what Brett Stockdill (2003, 17) argued years ago, that "the transformation of collective consciousness is a crucial aspect of social movement development: people in marginalized groups must be able to see their situation as shared before they can collectively challenge both cultural and institutional symbols" (see also McAdam 2013 on cognitive liberation, and Weeks 2015 on collective consciousness).[1] The visibility of LGBT life, even when examples come from external contexts, can aid LGBT people in seeing their situation as shared and can inspire them to become politically active (interviews no. 5, 12, 16, 118, and 138).

Transnational visibility also helps establish networks of solidarity among LGBT people across borders (Altman 1996). Like many of her colleagues in the European LGBT movement, a Swedish-born activist with Latvian roots describes her involvement and political activism this way: "I was deeply bothered that LGBT people were invisible in Latvia" (interview no. 138). Like her, many LGBT people were appalled by the

---

[1] Jeffrey Weeks (2015, 47) writes that "by coming out, people could begin to show the world that they existed, but as important it would show other lesbians and gay men that they were not alone, that through coming out all could come together, and construct new narratives about who and what they were."

first LGBT Pride parade in Riga, in 2005, which was a "huge, violent disaster, with counterprotesters outnumbering protesters ten to one" (interview no. 138). In the winter of 2006, along with fifteen other activists, she established an organization called Mozaika, which lobbied the Open Society Foundations for funding to organize campaigns of sociolegal recognition, including subsequent Pride parades in the Baltic states. The Mozaika activists are examples of *rooted cosmopolitans*, individuals and groups who carry out their activities by maintaining ties within transnational networks and to other countries, while remaining deeply connected to their societies of origin (della Porta and Tarrow 2005, 237). But the arrows run both ways. Interpersonal visibility is also important for mobilization in states that lead on LGBT rights. When the Swedish Federation for Lesbian, Gay, Bisexual, and Transgender Rights (RFSL) organizes to send LGBT youth to the Riga Pride, they wish not only to make the issue more visible in Latvia but also to motivate apathetic youth at home in Sweden by showing them that anti-LGBT prejudices are "a serious problem" (interview no. 138).

In sum, visibility can trigger clandestine groups to rise up and tap into their latent movement potential. Verta Taylor (1989) has called such groups "movements in abeyance" because they have the potential to mobilize under the right conditions, when new opportunities arise. In what follows, I suggest that these opportunities are often transnational in contemporary European politics. First, though, I elaborate on the political potential of moving a once private issue into the public sphere. Through this transitional dimension, norm visibility affects in-group dynamics by making members visible to each other across multiple domestic contexts. I argue that the fact that LGBT groups in some of the most unexpected places have found the ability to assert themselves and to formulate demands of their societies and states supports norm visibility's transformative transnational effect.

Being seen by state and society

On June 27, 1969, officers from Manhattan's Sixth Precinct raided the Stonewall Inn, an LGBT bar on Christopher Street in New York City. Unlike those previously subject to such routine raids, patrons of the bar fought back, capturing the community's attention and giving rise to a long-repressed subculture that had established covert networks in abeyance. Events like Stonewall and the gay rights demonstrations at Independence Hall in Philadelphia each July 4 from 1965 to 1969 greatly amplified the public nature of gay activism and the public visibility of sexual minorities.[2] The Gay Liberation Front that emerged as a result was paramount in redefining the experience of coming out as a repertoire for sociopolitical change – both in the United States and in Europe. What was once an isolating and atomized individual experience shifted to the public sphere (D'Emilio 1998). The European and American leadership of the postwar Homophile Movement of the 1950s and 1960s had, to a much lesser degree, engaged the issue publically, but they rarely advised their constituents to do so. On both continents, post-Stonewall gay liberation politics went much further. Its understanding of coming out, according to John D'Emilio, was the:

> open avowal of one's sexual identity, whether at work, at school, at home, or before television cameras, [that] symbolized the shedding of the self-hatred that gay men and women internalized … [The act] quintessentially expressed the fusion of the personal and political that the radicalism of the late 1960s exalted. Coming out also posed as the key strategy for building a movement. Its impact on an individual was often cathartic. The exhilaration and anger that surfaced when men and women stepped through the fear of discovery propelled them into political activity. Moreover, when lesbians and homosexuals came out, they crossed a critical dividing line. They relinquished their invisibility, made themselves vulnerable to attack, and acquired an investment in the success of the movement in a way that mere adherence to a political line could never accomplish. Visible lesbians and gay men also served as magnets that drew others to them. Furthermore, once out of the closet, they could not easily fade back in. Coming out provided gay liberation with an army of permanent enlistees. (1998, 235–6)

By the beginning of the 1980s, the public visibility of gay liberation had done wonders for the movement, both fueling organizational capacity and increasing the numbers of mobilized participants. "In a relatively short time, gay liberation achieved the goal that had eluded homophile leaders for two decades – the active involvement of large numbers of homosexuals and lesbians in their own emancipation effort" (D'Emilio 1998, 238). Modern LGBT movements may not retain the radical politics of gay liberation, but they have kept at their core the profoundly political act of coming out, which makes visibility an end and a means for changing the personal and collective experience of gay and lesbian people. Pride marches and parades are at the center of this collective coming out process, occupying the public space in resistance to heteronormativity. Still today, European LGBT activists refer to Pride as "more political, more

---

[2] It is important to emphasize that change was already afoot before Stonewall, even if the riots in New York are remembered as the most symbolic representation of that change (Weeks 2015).

aggressive, more visible than other cultural events" (interview no. 119; see also Carlson-Rainer 2015). Others elaborated that "[G]ay pride is powerful because it leads to visibility. 'LGBT' becomes a key topic after Pride, as discourse and media attention begin to happen" (panel no. 205).

Simultaneously with Stonewall and the formation of the Gay Liberation Front in the United States, other radical groups were created in contexts as diverse as Australia, Belgium, Britain, Canada, France, Germany, and the Netherlands (Jackson 2015, 41; Rimmerman 2014). In Paris, the Front Homosexuel d'Action Révolutionnaire staged a public demonstration in 1971, just a year after the premier gay pride march down the streets of Greenwich Village in Manhattan. In West Germany, gay action groups emerged following Rosa von Praunheim's 1971 film, *Nicht der Homosexuelle ist Pervers, sondern die Situation in der er lebt* (Not the Homosexual is Perverse, But the Society in which He Lives). In 1972, they staged the first "gay demo" in provincial Munster (Griffiths 2015).[3] Building on a long history of homophile activism in Europe, gay liberation supported a simple but powerful idea: that sexuality itself must be visible – a matter of public, not just private, concern – before it can serve as a basis for mobilization.

Indeed, the public visibility of LGBT norms is built on the foundation of a ripe history of activism in Europe, beginning when Magnus Hirschfeld founded the Weltliga für Sexualreform (World League for Sexual Reform) in Germany in 1928.[4] While persecution and repression during the Third Reich destroyed such LGBT organizing (except in neutral Switzerland) and the little visibility that had been attained, a new wave of activism, called the "homophile movement," would flourish after 1945.[5] The homophile movement existed amidst a challenging period of Cold War politics, including active antigay policing and surveillance. Nonetheless, it developed and maintained the movement's characteristically transnational

---

[3] In later decades, organizational models of activism in response to the AIDS epidemic – mainly those of the Gay Men's Health Crisis and ACT UP – similarly spread around the world from their center in the United States (Broqua 2015).

[4] While visibility has changed over the decades, and took new meaning after Stonewall, other forms of coming out existed in pre-WWII metropolitan areas such as New York, Amsterdam and Berlin. Then, coming out referred to an initiation into the gay world, though there remained a pattern of wearing a double-mask in society at large. George Chauncey's (1994, 7) description of the formal presentation of gay men at drag balls in New York City is one of the best examples of coming out in the pre-WWII years.

[5] WWII gave many homosexual military men mobility, furthering interpersonal visibility by offering an escape from life rooted in family structures (Chauncey 1994).

features, connecting activists in the Netherlands, Belgium, France, Germany, Scandinavia, and the United Kingdom (Rupp 2011).[6] As noted earlier in this chapter, this more clandestine and private – though not timid – activism would become increasingly public in the late 1960s and 1970s. Formal transnational networking ties thus started in the 1940s and multiplied in the 1970s. The early objectives were both to advance the human rights agenda and to serve as networks of solidarity in times of difficulty.

In 1978, following gay liberation activism, the International Lesbian, Gay, Bisexual, Trans, and Intersex Association (ILGA), called the International Gay Association until 1986, was founded in Coventry, United Kingdom (Paternotte 2012). ILGA's founders were oriented toward European frameworks from the start, recognizing that they could provide a fruitful venue for their activism and a possible pressure point through which to influence reluctant states to address gay rights. In many cases, domestic movements for LGBT rights were impotent, even while a handful of other European states were paving the way forward in some domains of lesbian and gay rights. This imbalance caused great frustration among gay and lesbian activists in Europe, many of whom saw their situation as shared. In response, these movement actors envisioned a role for the EU on LGBT rights before the EU itself had a social mandate, as David Paternotte and I have argued (Ayoub and Paternotte 2014). The view among these multinational activists that supranational institutions could serve as a venue for minority rights politicking has proven to be both farsighted and revolutionary for LGBT rights politics in the European polity.

As I elaborate in Chapter 3, the transnational movement has targeted European institutions (the EU, the CoE, the Organization for Security and Co-operation in Europe) ever since. This tactic has further enhanced the public visibility of LGBT rights and multiplied the presence of LGBT rights groups across the continent. In 2010 ILGA-Europe – funded predominantly by the European Commission and the largest and richest of ILGA-International's six regional organizations – counted 291 member organizations. The idea, or imagination, of contemporary Europe as LGBT-friendly is itself an evolutionary process, built on the interaction between these movements and supranational institutions. This

---

[6] The Netherlands replaced Germany as a central node in the 1950s, due largely to the active role played by a Dutch organization, inconspicuously named the Cultuur en Ontspanningscentrum (COC, Center for Culture and Leisure), as well as to the annual meetings organized by the International Committee for Sexual Equality (ICSE).

relationship – between LGBT rights and the idea of Europe – has become increasingly pronounced and further cemented as activists in new-adopter states take the EU flag with them to protest for LGBT rights, framing their struggle in terms of European democratic values and human rights (Ayoub and Paternotte 2014). In turn, European institutions play a central role in this process by legitimating the norm and signaling to states and societies how to behave "appropriately." In this sense, the EU has come to play an important institutional role in furthering the publicness of the norm's visibility. The movement and its complex relationship with political institutions explains much about where visibility originates and how institutions have come to adopt it.

While visibility took root in many European states, the politics that surround the idea were far from uniform across the European continent, especially on the eastern half of the Iron Curtain. This continental divide at least partly reflects the fact that some European states defined the issue earlier than others through developments that produced visibility, such as the 1960–70s sexual revolution, including gay liberation, and the politicization of the HIV/AIDS crisis in the 1980s (Chetaille 2011, 122–3; Owczarzak 2009); with *politicization* referring to "making previously apolitical matters political" (de Wilde and Zürn 2012, 139–40). While fears about coming out exist in every EU member state, several interviewees argued that it is more difficult to come out in a context like Poland's, where surveys carried out in 2000 found that only 10 percent of Poles claimed to have ever encountered a gay person (interview no. 9). Similarly, an Estonian activist explains:

> In Estonia our goals are to generate visibility. The problem is that we [LGBT people] have no role models, no open politicians, and not even the Social Democrats have a clear stance on the issue. This is why we have to find the new sources for visibility. Visibility leads to debate, and even if that debate is at first hateful, it gets us over the hump. Through it we learn how to talk about sexuality as a society. (interview no. 105)

In societies where LGBT people are mostly invisible, it is also not costly for state and societal authorities to target LGBT people for their own political gain, because such actors can assume that none of their constituents are LGBT. Public visibility reveals such falsity, because it sheds light on local LGBT people. Transnational channels of visibility also signal that substantial change is indeed possible and mobilize new potential activists. The European context of social sanctions changes standards of conduct and connects LGBT actors across states with differing degrees of LGBT visibility. While the extent of change depends on both international and domestic normative structures, in states that have recently begun learning about the norm, widespread public visibility depends especially on transnational interactions.

How visibility brings about change

To theorize that the visibility of international norms can lead to social and legal change, I draw from evidence in social psychology suggesting that engagement can lead to a reduction in prejudice among individuals. This research makes clear that conditions of invisibility, such as those I described in preaccession Estonia and Poland, are not conducive to change. According to one activist in Warsaw, "The problem in Poland at the time of EU accession was that no one was coming out – everyone stayed in their closets. In terms of socialization, there is a strong correlation between knowing a gay person and being agreeable toward gay rights" (interview no. 9). Indeed, studies have repeatedly found that respondents who know at least one person in their in-group with friendship ties to an out-group member report decreased levels of prejudice toward that out-group (Wright *et al.* 1997). Gordon Allport's (1954) seminal contact hypothesis rested on this same idea: interactions among different groups could change intergroup relations by leading to positive perceptions of the other. In addition, a long tradition of research finds support for the negative relationship between contact and prejudice (Pettigrew and Tropp 2006). The finding is especially true under conditions of cooperation, common goals, and institutional support, some of which the "idea of Europe" provides. While these studies usually measure change at the individual level, there is also evidence for the understudied effect of contact on societal change (Dixon, Durrheim, and Tredoux 2005). Several studies have found that a positive interaction, whether direct or imagined, is more likely to reduce prejudice than a neutral one (Stathi and Crisp 2008).[7] Yet, psychologists note that anxiety – or perceived threat – is likely to lessen after contact, as adopters "come to realize they have

---

[7] Recent experiments show that even imagined interactions, if they are positive, can significantly reduce negative feelings toward unfamiliar out-groups (Crisp and Turner 2009; Mazziotta, Mummendey, and Wright 2011). These findings hold for studies of interactions between heterosexual and homosexual groups, with heterosexual participants displaying more positive attitudes and fewer stereotypes about gay people after imagining an interaction (Turner, Crisp, and Lambert 2007). Imagined contact is entirely cognitive, referring only to an image or story of interaction.

nothing to fear from such interactions" (Crisp and Turner 2009, 235).[8]
Learning through interaction is a central mechanism for change because
it reduces the level of threat associated with the out-group.

Through social and political channels across borders, transnational
movements play a role in socialization by linking the LGBT norm to
membership in modern Europe, by setting rules of compliance, and by
dispensing ideas and images about LGBT people that make them visible.
As a Lithuanian respondent emphasized, "Litigation at home is long
and cumbersome, but discourse is changing. A discourse exists and it is
growing. Young Lithuanians might not have known there was a community out there, but now they hear about [same-sex] marriage because of
what's going on in Brussels" (interview no. 144). A Portuguese respondent described a related transnational process of legitimization, "Discourse
itself leads to change. If politicians – be they in Brussels or at home –
support it rhetorically, it influences what becomes acceptable" (interview
no. 100). The European polity is effectual in this regard, in that it shifts
the dynamics of movement out of the nation state, which historically
has a long history of silencing LGBT people (Weeks 2000). Providing a
new platform for visibility can engage publics and governments at home,
when the channels of visibility exist.

   While psychological research supports the general theory that visibility, through interaction, produces change, psychological studies are confined to laboratories, devoid of politics, and removed from the relational
ties between actors across states. My argument moves beyond cognitive
mechanisms and takes into account the fact that similar interventions,
such as the ones described in psychological experiments, mean different
things in various contexts. The support of institutions, law, or custom can
have a strong effect on individual shifts in prejudice – and they make it
possible for activists to engage a politics of visibility at home (a point that
I elaborate on later in this chapter).[9]

---

[8] Richard Crisp and Rhiannon Turner (2009, 234) point out that a "positive tone is also
important to guard against a possible negative tone, which might emerge if the participants are left to their own devices." The authors go on to note that participants are left to
their own devices under conditions of segregation, or arguably under conditions of invisibility. Anxiety about interaction, in which an in-group associates threat with the "other,"
"can arise when there has been minimal previous contact" (Crisp and Turner 2009, 235).

[9] As Crisp and Turner (2009, 232) suggest in their call for future research, "Contact can
only work where the opportunity for contact exists." Thus, as Pettigrew also argues,
"institutional and societal norms structure the form and effects of contact situations"
and "societal norms of discrimination [can] poison intergroup contact." Referring to a

Acknowledging that these norms are contested requires us to rethink the traditional set of mechanisms that drive diffusion processes. Constructivist scholars highlight the mechanisms of argument and persuasion to explain political and social outcomes. The mechanism of argument has to do with the ongoing discourse between norm entrepreneurs and followers, which fosters shared understandings. The mechanism of persuasion has to do with the expectation to conform to international, universalistic, liberal values – interactions with international society socialize states to alter policies and practices (Finnemore and Sikkink 1998).[10] I argue that the effectiveness of these cognitive mechanisms of appropriateness is limited when transnationally embedded domestic LGBT organizations do not exist to make the issue visible and clearly interpret it. Deliberative mechanisms of diffusion are complicated when the moral hierarchy between contending norms is difficult for states and societies to establish. I deal with these shortcomings by bridging cognitive mechanisms (framing, learning, and deliberation) with relational ones (norm brokerage and sociopolitical channels of visibility), and by theorizing cases of norm rejection and contending norms.

The European polity furthers norm visibility by connecting states through channels of social information and political rules, as well as by connecting LGBT actors across states to help broker and interpret the norm. Put simply, transnational and international channels of visibility provide for interaction among social actors that leads to a change of ideas.[11] Through mechanisms of learning and deliberation,

---

study during apartheid in South Africa, he notes that "even there, modest improvements emerged in white attitudes toward their neighbors of color. Yet the larger social context constrained these effects. Alternatively, when a society embraces intergroup harmony, equal-status contact between groups is no longer subversive. Normative support makes attainment of other optimal conditions far easier" (1998, 79).

[10] Socialization is "a process of inducting actors into the norms and rules of a given community"; it implies "that an agent switches from a logic of consequences to a logic of appropriateness" (Checkel 2005, 804). One type of socialization is role playing, whereby actors learn what is appropriate and behave accordingly. A second type involves actors adopting the interests and identity of the community – in such a case *taken-for-grantedness* replaces instrumental calculation.

[11] I use the customary definitions for transnational and international: I think of *transnational* relations as involving the cross-border activities of nonstate actors. Nonstate actors can include, for example, activists, NGOs, religious actors, multinational corporations, and terrorism rebels. *International* relations involve the activities between states or between states and international institutions. While most of the channels I refer to are transnational, they were often facilitated by processes of political internationalization (e.g. increased mobility via the EU's Schengen Treaty) and continue to be supported

these ideational changes can influence the ways the legal and social structures of the state adopt the norm. Other mechanisms of European institutional influence, such as pressures of competition and political sanction via hard law, also play a role, but the following analyses will demonstrate that these mechanisms are more limited in their ability to produce change. The mechanisms most central to this argument are social, and they include:

- *Norm brokerage:* the process by which actors endowed with local knowledge mediate between often-divergent new international norms and domestic norms. Norm brokers aid diffusion by framing the international elements of the norm – in a domestically familiar discourse – so that they resonate with the domestic traditions of the society. They also connect disparate actors across contexts to politicize and draw external attention to the domestic situations of LGBT people.[12]
- *Framing:* the process of "presenting and packaging ideas" to fashion meanings for a given audience (Khagram, Riker, and Sikkink 2002, 10; see also Snow and Benford 1992).
- *Deliberation:* the communicative and thought processes by which groups (subnational, national, and transnational) weigh and debate conflicting norms after new norms become visible (cf. Risse 2000).
- *Learning:* the process by which individuals and communities reassess their fundamental beliefs, values, and ways of doing things through interacting with new ideas and norms. Learning can refer to the transfer of knowledge between international organizations, governments, societies, and individuals, and it includes both simple learning, which leads to instrumental change, and complex learning, which leads to change in beliefs.[13]

These mechanisms of socialization can have a transformative effect on prevailing societal behaviors and state institutions by making international norms visible. They come together to prime the contexts for

by international channels between state and international institutions. For simplicity, I occasionally use the terms *transnational channels* or *channels* to refer collectively to transnational and international channels. I do this especially when I contrast the *international/transnational* with the *domestic*.

[12] The first part of my definition of brokerage is a slight variation of Sidney Tarrow's (2005b) emphasis on the brokers who connect actors in different contexts.

[13] My broad definition of learning draws upon a vast literature on processes of learning, both individual and collective (Deutsch 1963; Haas 1991), and both complex and simple (Checkel 2005; Zito 2009).

diffusion by signaling to society and state that they (as publics and governments) must react to the norm. For the LGBT norm to resonate in various states, it helps for the issue to be clearly associated with Europe and be visible within the domestic contexts of the state. In this dimension, new member states vary in important ways. While European directives set a minimal hard-law standard,[14] I find the diffusion of the issue beyond these basic measures relies largely on both the extent to which transnational channels make the issue visible and on the effectiveness of transnational actors who identify the issue as one of singular importance to membership in modern Europe.

Norm brokers help the state and individuals in society give meaning to the issue – which constitutes a new idea in many of the domestic spheres analyzed – by framing the LGBT norm as a European value of human rights. Not only do they help states and societies, more broadly, to interpret international information, they also help to frame that information in ways that resonate in local contexts (Hafner-Burton 2013, 5). In my conceptualization, brokers connect domestic LGBT organizations to a transnational network of actors and to European institutions. Ryan Thoreson (2014) also speaks of the important role of brokers in transnational LGBT activism, taking us a long way in understanding the intricacies of how LGBT activism is negotiated and campaigned for across borders. My related concept of *norm brokers* is slightly different, in that I place emphasis on the translation of the international to the local and vice versa. I am thus focused on both domestic organizations that are transnationally embedded – that is, doing the groundwork in their own local contexts – and on the actors within external organizations like ILGA-Europe. Thus, brokers are not only the umbrella organizations that connect disparate actors, they are also domestic LGBT groups and rooted cosmopolitans who frame and graft international scripts to make them fit specific domestic contexts.

The premise of a visibility argument is that, for states and societies to understand how to "behave appropriately," they must see the norm and receive cues about how to interpret it. Societies must come to understand – often through the brokerage and deliberation spurred by contestation – how the universal elements of the norm connect to their

---

[14] The EU's directives on anti-discrimination reflect the late emergence of LGBT issues in the international rights revolution. Sexual orientation, along with disability, is protected in only one category (employment), compared to four for race (employment, social protection, social advantages, and access to goods and services) and two for gender (employment and access to goods and services).

own, local understandings of self. In the next two sections, I posit that norm visibility is a transnational process.

Channels of visibility

Drawing from the contentious politics literature, I argue that the nature of the channels between the originator and the receiver of a social norm influences diffusion (Givan, Roberts, and Soule 2010).[15] Channels can be relational (*direct*) or non-relational (*indirect*), in that they are direct and personal, indirect and impersonal, or brokered by institutions or organizations (Tarrow 2005b). Within direct channels, ideas diffuse most rapidly to new European states with domestic LGBT rights activists who are in close and frequent contact with their counterparts in leading European states. Relational ties to transnational organizations provide domestic LGBT groups with credibility, funding, and expertise, legitimizing domestic political and social campaigns to make the issue visible in their respective domestic contexts. More resource-rich transnational LGBT organizations can set the agenda around certain functional goals and help certain issues to get transnational traction (Carpenter 2011, 72). The actors most effective at engendering change in this case are domestic LGBT rights organizations that can command transnational resources from first-mover states. Transnational organizations provide resources that domestic actors are then able to use to enhance visibility by organizing demonstrations, engaging the press, lobbying government, and demanding outside intervention when necessary. In turn, transnational activism leads to deliberation and social learning in the target state.

State compliance

Figure 2.1 illustrates three important types of channels for state compliance. The presence of local LGBT actors who are embedded in transnational networks makes the norm visible by sending signals to state and society. As the right side of Figure 2.1 shows, visibility is higher in contexts with transnationally embedded actors – norm brokers – who send strong and clear signals with their presence and information on how to approach

---

[15] Sarah Soule (2004a) isolates four attributes required for diffusion: a *transmitter*, an *adopter*, an *innovation*, and a *channel* that passes the innovation from transmitter to adopter. In my case, the *transmitters* are transnational LGBT organizations in leading European states, the *adopters* are societies and states, the *innovation* is the LGBT rights norm, and the *channels* are networks of activists and channels of social transnationalization and political internationalization.

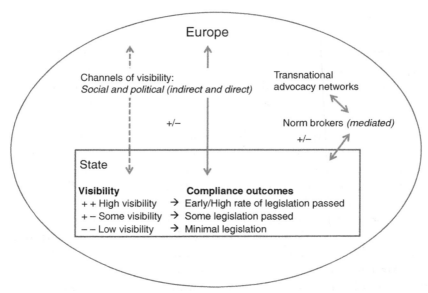

FIGURE 2.1. (In)direct and mediated channels of norm diffusion and compliance outcomes.
Note: + (channel exists), – (channel does not exist).

the issue. Political authorities respond to grievances most in cases where movements can send strong signals, in terms of their presence and strength in numbers (Gillion 2013; Lohmann 1993). Social movement actors can help state authorities interpret messages. I find that especially when they are embedded in transnational networks, European LGBT groups disperse guidelines and rules of best practice that converge to send clear and strong signals.[16] In addition, transnationally linked LGBT rights groups mediate diffusion when they act as brokers connecting disparate activists and grafting international ideas to domestic ones, which accelerates the diffusion of information and frames the message appropriately – especially when confronted with domestic resistance. They often guide this

[16] Conor O'Dwyer and Katrina Schwartz's (2010) excellent work correctly privileges the influence of the socialization mechanisms of Europeanization in the realm of LGBT rights in their case studies of Poland and Latvia. However, they are somewhat indifferent to the importance of transnational advocacy networks in this process. Their brief mention of the ILGA-Europe refers to the organization as a small NGO in Brussels, sidestepping its importance as an instigator of social change. As Chapter 3 demonstrates in detail, it is also the work of a wide network of norm entrepreneurs that helps establish the mechanisms of social change that O'Dwyer and Schwartz find to be important.

process of transnationalization by "appeal[ing] to the values consistent with the self-concept of [local] individuals and supported by their important reference groups" (Herek 2004, 13). This mediation is a necessary step, because when a society – especially one in which LGBT people are invisible – is left to its own devices to interpret new contentious ideas, its reactions will tend to be more negative (Pettigrew 1998, 79).

Also shown in Figure 2.1, the visibility of the LGBT rights norm also diffuses through political and social channels (both relational and non-relational) between first-mover and new-adopter states. First, the extent of relational ties between the state and international organizations – what I refer to as *political channels* – furthers norm visibility. These relational ties include state membership in international organizations, the signing of bi- and multilateral treaties, the number of host embassies and high commissions, and involvement in United Nations (UN) peace missions (Dreher, Gaston, and Martens 2008). Second, drawing on Sarah Soule (2004a) and David Strang and John Meyer (1993), I also identify in Figure 2.1 two mechanisms of indirect diffusion that lead to norm visibility, which I call *social channels*: (1) a sense of shared political identification between adopter and transmitter; and (2) the presence of social information flows that broadcast the issues of the transmitter to potential adopters. These international and transnational channels prime the contexts by providing legitimacy and scripts for interpretation of the issue, both of which are critical for the norm brokers trying to make their case. They help bring states and societies into contact with LGBT people.

Norm brokers are better able to mobilize and to credibly diffuse their arguments in an environment where the visibility of the issue has been fostered by these channels. It is under these conditions of visibility that actors can harness ideas and adapt them to manufacture resonance in their domestic contexts, even when the ideas did not previously have local appeal. A visibility argument thus dovetails with the research of social problems theorists, who emphasize that issue salience leads to public and social action (Hilgartner and Bosk 1988). The visibility of a problem – or the construction of LGBT rights as a problem – explains much about the timing of state actions to combat homophobia, despite the persistent marginalization of sexual minorities previously.

In sum, direct and indirect channels of visibility prime the domestic contexts by introducing images and ideas about the LGBT norm to the state. If domestic LGBT organizations become transnationally linked to organizations in leading states, they fuel domestic norm visibility, in large part through engaging state and societal institutions (e.g. by lobbying the state, staging demonstrations, and attracting media attention). They act as brokers between the movement and the state, framing and interpreting the norm to make it fit locally. Varying degrees of visibility lead to diverse outcomes in regard to state recognition of the norm.

Contestation: perceiving threat, internalizing new norms

What we know about mediated, direct, and indirect channels of norm diffusion offers plausible concepts and mechanisms for understanding the spread of new ideas from one state to another, but the contentious element of the LGBT rights norm requires us to pay special attention to resistance in the domestic realm.[17] My theoretical framework also deals with cases of diffusion that fuel an active social opposition, such as the mobilization of resistance movements that challenge and externalize the positions endorsed by proponents of LGBT rights. The argument thus requires expanding the pool of usual actors and rethinking what part of the domestic context matters for diffusing contentious norms. In particular, studies often conceptualize transnational actors as "good" norm entrepreneurs and overlook contention in the domestic sphere.[18] At the

---

[17] Robert Benford and David Snow (1999) suggest four agential relationships: (1) *reciprocation*: cases of diffusion in which both the transmitter and the adopter favor the item being diffused; (2) *adaptation*: cases with an active/copying adopter and a passive transmitter; (3) *accommodation*: cases of diffusion in which the transmitter promotes the diffusion of a foreign practice by tailoring it to the needs of a passive adopter; and (4) *simple contagion*: cases in which neither party wants to diffuse the innovation. Often the adopter is welcoming or passive. Above, I am also describing as adopters larger social entities who are in fact resistant to the innovation. I am thus also interested in a relationship not suggested by Benford and Snow: active transmitter, resistant adopter.

[18] International relations theories of diffusion are largely silent about such countermovements as an element of domestic and transnational opportunity structures, which explains why international norms that elicit active resistance have received so little scholarly attention. As one critic put it, much of the research "overestimate[s] diffusion to the domestic level and underestimate[s] possible domestic conflict between norms" (Landolt 2004, 585). Those scholars who are sensitive to the misfit between the international and domestic often study socially noncontentious issues (Acharya 2004). However, it is commonly difficult to make LGBT rights norms congruent with local beliefs (Manalansan 1995), which is why framing the issue as one of European standards becomes an attractive tool at the disposal of transnational activists. Finally, scholars of transnationalism typically addressed the "common good" (Risse-Kappen 1995), which says little about the many transnational issues that deal with minority rights. This omission is critical, because minorities, arguably more than others, have incentives to look beyond their states to join forces with those who share a common identity.

national level, the actors relevant to diffusion go far beyond state elites to include societal actors and countermovements. In the case of LGBT rights, pro- and anti-LGBT groups are mutually constitutive because they exist partly on their own initiative and partly as a response to opposing actors (Fetner 2008). They compete to define the nation according to their perceptions of what is appropriate and legitimate in their particular society.

This second element of my theoretical framework thus takes into consideration the domestic political and social contexts in which actors operate and how these contexts affect the diffusion and reception of ideas. For example, how might the Catholic Polish context mediate the influence of a well-networked LGBT organization and active sociopolitical channels that affirm LGBT rights? Not all societies will find the imported norm equally threatening, depending on the perception and legitimacy of social institutions within the domestic context. As such, we must not view states as undifferentiated rational actors. Instead, their varied state and national identities emerge "from their interaction with different social environments, both domestic and international" (Katzenstein 1995, 92).

While states increasingly do nod to the LGBT norm by complying with some level of legislation, the process of internalization is more complex.[19] The domestic context in which individuals are socialized mediates the ability of societies to internalize international norms. Different societies associate different levels of threat with the LGBT norm, and threat perception facilitates the interaction between domestic and international norms. I define *threat* as the anticipation of danger to a set of values that defines a group, and *perception* as the process of apprehending by means of the senses.[20] It is important to note that these definitions assume that threat can have a symbolic value at the collective level, in that threat is socially constructed through discourse among political authorities and publics (C. O. Meyer 2009). Drawing on Carl Schmitt's (1996) 1932 thesis, Peter Katzenstein (2003, 736) argues that:

conceptions of identity, of self versus other, are always part of threat perceptions. The norms and identities that trigger different threat perceptions are not merely

---

[19] Internalization must also take into account a distinction between state and national identities. Whereas state identities "are primarily external; they describe the actions of governments in a society of states," national identities "are primarily internal; they describe the processes by which mass publics acquire, modify, and forget their collective identities" (Katzenstein 1997, 20).

[20] This international relations definition can be related to the social movement literature's definition of threat, where it "denotes the probability that existing benefits will be taken away or new harms inflicted if challenging groups fail to act collectively" (Almeida 2003).

derivative of material capabilities … The threat perceptions of groups and states are embedded instead in systems of meaning that affect what is and what is not defined as a threat.

My sociological interpretation of perceived threat stipulates that social understandings within the domestic realm define the way state actors respond to international pressures (Andrews 1975, 524–35). Thus, similarly strong channels of LGBT visibility will have differing effects depending on the level of threat that societies attribute to the norm. I find that the degree to which the LGBT norm is perceived as a threat is at its highest in domestic contexts in which religion is deeply embedded in the national identity.[21] Where this religious-nationalist relationship exists, contending actors can better cast external LGBT rights norms as threatening.

The strength and legitimacy of competing (heteronormative versus LGBT rights) norms in distinct domestic environments explain the variation in the internalization trajectories of LGBT norms. Due to the religious and national basis of much LGBT rights denial, anti-LGBT rights mobilization is politically effective when narratives of nation hinge on religious identity, because sexual politics then become indirectly linked with nationalism. Take, for example, the cultural paradigm that Russian President Putin advocates, which directly juxtaposes "traditional" values of nation and religion with "alien" norms of homosexuality – a trope he and other Russian leaders have used to justify political maneuvers ranging from a domestic "gay propaganda" ban to opposing intensified Ukraine–EU relations (Riabov and Riabova 2014). In this sense, societies and social groups define their domestic identity and use this identity to evaluate and determine which outside norms are acceptable to internalize (Rousseau 2006, 211). Societies thus assign different levels of threat to the norm import, depending on how domestic social institutions perceive it. The EU's standards of appropriate behavior on LGBT rights norms are perceived as outside imposition to some societies and welcome modernity to others. As the example above illustrates, I do not argue simply that historically religious states will oppose the norm; Russian leaders link

---

[21] This concept builds on the notion that "the normative and organizational arrangements which form the 'state,' structure society, and link the two in the polity" influences the availability of channels for transnational actors to enter the political realm, and the ability of these actors to form winning coalitions that change policy (Risse-Kappen 1995, 6; see also Evangelista 1999). However, for processes of internalization, the emphasis here is on normative structures that facilitate legitimacy, as opposed to state structure, conceived of as central versus fragmented governance models.

religious values and national identity even though Russia has not been a religious state in recent history. In many cases, religious institutions lose their clout to hinder the societal internationalization of LGBT norms: "In recent Estonian politics, [for example,] religious groups tried to get their message across but they were simply not legitimate" (interview no. 105). Instead, I find that traditionalist religious scripts are only legitimate – and subsequently effective – if they are tied to the popular nation.

Religious institutions – when they have mobilized to challenge EU pressures on behalf of LGBT rights – have varying degrees of social legitimacy in different states, and cannot always frame the "external" LGBT norms as threatening to the national identity of the state. Whereas in some Catholic cases, for example, the church has political authority and has been successful in fueling resistance and framing a message of threat to resonate with popular beliefs (e.g. Poland, Lithuania, and, until the turn of the century, Ireland), in other plausible cases it has not (e.g. the Czech Republic, Slovenia, and Spain). In the latter cases, LGBT groups, using their European frames, found earlier success. To explain this difference, I demonstrate that the church's political and moral authority depends on its history as a political actor in the domestic realm. In Poland, the Catholic Church, as a champion of the Solidarity movement, created a role for itself as an autonomous, progressive, moral entrepreneur with deep ties to the popular nation. In contrast, the Slovenians linked the Catholic Church to Nazi German occupation, the Czechs and Slovaks linked it to state socialism in Czechoslovakia, and the Spaniards linked it to Franco's regime in Spain. Strong resistance is less likely in states where the church fell on the "wrong" side of democratic transition and lost its political authority as a constitutive part of national identity.

Societal internalization

In sum, state and societal responses to European norms concerning LGBT rights developed differently, depending on levels of the LGBT norm's visibility and on the different domestic perceptions of threat associated with the norm. Figure 2.2 (process) and Figure 2.3 (outcomes) predict a set of internalization outcomes depending on norm visibility and the level of threat perception. Since norm visibility is a function of both transnational and domestic factors, one can anticipate an initial backlash in many new-adopter states, as they are cases where the issue is made more visible from the periphery.

A *Type I process* results in minimal change. Few channels of visibility in states with low perceived threat will have little deliberation and minimal

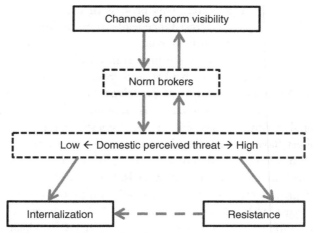

FIGURE 2.2. Processes of internalization.

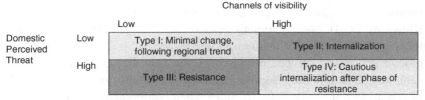

FIGURE 2.3. Internalization outcomes based on conditions of threat and channels of visibility.

change. A *Type II process* results in internalization and societal attitudes improve. In this case, the LGBT norm generates deliberation once visible. Norm brokers illuminate historical narrations of LGBT people in their respective countries, leading to learning. International ideas of democratic responsibility/human rights resonate and states steadily conform to the standards of a community to which they belong. A *Type III process* results in resistance and societal attitudes worsen. Here we can expect the intensification of anti-LGBT politics by some religious and nationalist sectors of society that can take advantage of LGBT invisibility by targeting the group for political gain. Since few channels of visibility exist, a discourse of threat goes unchecked. Finally, a *Type IV process* results in cautious internalization after a period of resistance and social attitudes eventually improve. In this case, norm brokers call attention to resistance, and transnational and international attention heightens, fueling active deliberation in the target state. This process of contestation suggests a strategic relationship, where resistance leads to more visibility – and ultimately learning – if norm brokers exist.

In sum, Figure 2.3 reasserts the importance of strong transnationally connected domestic actors to broker and frame the message according to context. Whereas high levels of perceived threat foster active resistance, in the long run that resistance is only effective if the presence of transnational channels of visibility in the domestic realm is weak. Where norm brokers have existed, they have channeled international EU attention, which has led to the deployment of additional outside pressures on states for breaching appropriate standards. Ironically, the mobilization of anti-LGBT groups creates a type of visibility on its own, which in many cases has proved to work against their cause.[22] Activists repeatedly noted that, in a context such as Europe's, they preferred backlash to silence because the former made LGBT people visible and their rights politically salient (cf. spiral model, Risse, Ropp, and Sikkink 2013). Indeed, a recurrent theme of the study was that resistance opens doors for internalization. In cases as varied as Ukraine (outside of the EU) and the United Kingdom, LGBT organizations reported that "the [LGBT] issue became more visible because of the homophobic rhetoric of politicians," "the religious right would campaign and speak out heavily against it whilst the general public generally became in favor," and "improved attitudes followed an initial backlash in attitudes when conservative parties, antigay movements, and clergy started to organize" (surveys no. 19, 28, and 94). There is thus an interactive relationship between political opportunity and threat (Almeida 2003). Political opportunities can lead to enduring social movement organizations and networks that, when in place, can further fuel the movement if they are faced with threat. However, backlash on its own is not a sufficient condition. Norm brokers need to be present and well networked to draw international attention and reshape the local interpretation of the norm. If the backlash meets LGBT norms without domestic actors to guide the discourse, the deliberation that emerges may fail to localize the issue in an effective way. Chapter 6 presents and discusses the findings of my organizational survey, showing that the large majority of respondents described such Type II or Type IV outcomes.

---

[22] As I address in Chapter 6, the church no longer monopolizes anti-LGBT rhetoric during phases of resistance. Instead, the populist far right also adopts an anti-LGBT politics as a central issue to oppose outside influences (e.g. Jobbik in Hungary, or the League of Polish Families in Poland).

I expect that transnational channels, which connect states to each other and to their international community, make norms visible (both in terms of interpersonal and public visibility). This leads to heightened mobilization of movement actors, who frame the norm for a local audience and help to guide deliberation in the domestic sphere. In many cases, states will start complying with the norm by adopting it into their legislative frameworks at this stage. Depending on the level of perceived threat domestically, norm visibility can produce social learning in low-threat contexts. It can provoke contestation in high-threat contexts, especially as state actors start to pass laws that anti-LGBT groups begin to mobilize against. Such resistance leads to heightened public visibility and deliberation. I also expect additional mobilization by norm brokers who channel international attention and support to their cause. In these high-threat contexts, cautious societal learning and internationalization should follow on an extended time horizon. These expectations apply to states embedded in international communities that extend the LGBT norm legitimacy, such as the EU states analyzed here.

Scopes and caveats: the valence of visibility

While my research gives credence to the optimism that proponents of LGBT rights express for change (even in hard cases, like Poland [Chapter 3]), it remains attuned to the struggles they describe in many facets of their work. Just as feminist scholarship has critiqued linear progress narratives, sequential and teleological theory is limited at explaining change related to human rights (Risse, Ropp, and Sikkink 2013). While the interactive model presented above suggests an analytic sequence, its focus remains on mechanisms of change, which do not depend on a rigid empirical sequence. Instead, I hope that the model describes a framework for the processes involving the introduction of norms, both in terms of transnational channels and domestic structures. While broad visibility is indeed new and different in its attractiveness during the period that I analyze, history reminds us that previous advances for LGBT people have been followed by repression. The *valence of visibility* is thus particularly important; its intrinsic attractiveness or averseness – and, possibly, its helpfulness or harmfulness – is contextual.

Germany is a key example of the visibility of homosexuality making social and political gains that were followed with forceful repression. Wilhelmine Berlin (1871–1918) had a laissez-faire stance toward gay social spaces, such as bars and clubs, and Magnus Hirschfeld freely led a pathbreaking research initiative on homosexuality, the Wissenschaftlich-humanitäre-Komitee (Scientific Humanitarian Committee), starting in 1897. Weimar Berlin (1919–33) was even more of a home to vibrant gay visibility, in the form of political and research organizations and within the arts (especially in literature, film, and music), as Alex Ross (2015, 76) describes:

During the golden years of the Weimar Republic ... gays and lesbians achieved an almost dizzying degree of visibility in popular culture. They could see themselves onscreen in films like "Mädchen in Uniform" [Girls in Uniform] and "Different from the Others" – a tale of a gay violinist driven to suicide, with Hirschfeld featured in the supporting role of a wise sexologist. Disdainful representations of gay life were not only lamented but also protested.

Such visibility had remarkable social and political impacts. According to historian Robert Beachy, Germany was at the cusp of a mass movement, and the Reichstag was poised to decriminalize homosexuality in 1929, just as the tremor of the stock market crash threw a final vote out of orbit (2014, 220–40). The rise of Hitler in 1933 extinguished what remained of that visibility and, subsequently, that potential, as narrated so beautifully in Christopher Isherwood's aptly titled novel, *Goodbye to Berlin*. Despite the relative tolerance that visibility had engendered, with a changed institutional environment Germany would in 1935 revise Paragraph 175 of its Criminal Code to more broadly criminalize homosexuality, leading to the internment and deaths of thousands of gay men during the Third Reich. In those times, invisibility became a survival strategy for marginalized people.

Thus, variation in threat perceptions is an important moderating component of this argument. As the example from Germany illustrates, my argument has conditions of institutional and regional scope, in that the marginalized population must have claims to legitimacy from the international community in which the state is embedded. This condition for positive valence is embedded in the concept of norm visibility. While I see great potential for the presence of such norms outside the state, if no norm exists at any level relevant to the state, the valence of visibility may not be attractive. When the Third Reich began, no norms legitimizing LGBT people had yet won standing among political institutions.

At any given time, norm visibility and threat perception play a role in the valence that visibility has for marginalized groups. The valence of visibility also makes certain aspects of the theory work uniquely in the set of EU states I analyze here, which are embedded in a polity that has bestowed a considerable degree of legitimacy on LGBT rights claims. If a wider authoritative context offers such legitimacy, then visibility is paramount to achieving change in the sociopolitical fabric of the state, even if the process begins with resistance. If a wider authoritative context offers illegitimacy, then both visibility and invisibility become rotating strategies for LGBT activists and their survival. Visibility is deeply dependent on time and place, as Ashley Currier (2012) has argued. For example, the introduction of an LGBT norm has fueled resistance in many African countries, a region in which actors have struggled to frame the norm successfully in the local context. There, many forms of internationalization are seen as "un-African" because they hark of colonial – that is, *external* – imposition (Currier 2012). The "un-African" frame is operative; even if it is ironic, given that British colonialism criminalized homosexuality in much of Africa in the first place, and conservative networks of American evangelicals have played no small part in fomenting and inflating the threat associated with LGBT rights (Bob 2012). By contrast, in Europe transnational actors have an important frame at their disposal: "We are all European." There, Europeanization can at least sometimes be seen as self-reflection and internal learning, not external imposition. Indeed, Estonians are both Estonians and Europeans, just as Swedes are both Swedes and Europeans.

Consequently, the valence of visibility, and ultimately the direction that norm compliance and internalization take, is influenced greatly by the international community in which the state is embedded. For LGBT rights, these international communities vary. With *norm polarization*, a term I borrow from Jonathan Symons and Dennis Altman (2015), different spheres of influence impact LGBT rights and result in starkly different perceptions of the legitimacy of those rights. While Europe (broadly conceived) has become a champion of LGBT rights in the imaginations of many states, Russia has become a vocal opponent of them, using the issue to champion a moral conservatism that purposefully distinguishes Russia from "Europe" and "the West." The Ukraine crisis that began in 2013 illustrates the situation of a state caught between the EU and Russia, where Russian authorities framed the Maidan protesters as "gay" and westward alignment as an abandonment of Ukraine's moral and traditional values. This imaginary "European" or "Western" plot to spread gay rights has led Russian popular commentary to use the term *Gayropa* when referring to Europe – a concept "bound up with a traditional, perceived opposition between Russia and Europe" (Riabov and Riabova 2014). The trope works for some in contemporary Russian geopolitics.

As Alexei Pushkov, the Chairman of the Russian Duma's Foreign Affairs Committee, explained to Ukrainians, turning toward a demasculinized Gayropa would mean "an expansion of the sphere of the so-called gay culture, which has now turned into the official policy of the EU" (Ayoub and Paternotte 2014, 1). In sum, the international communities to which states belong facilitate the valence of visibility, and visibility's effectiveness depends on how easily movements can destabilize the "external" tinge of frames used by the opposition.

Indeed, norm brokers are always aware of the valence of visibility in the ways they frame their cause. This explains why many of my interviewees in new-adopter states approach *transgressive visibility* – visibility that challenges culture head on – cautiously (see also the concept of defiant visibility in Bruce in press). When issues are new, norm brokers are not organizing marches that display naked torsos on floats – scenes we would expect at the Berlin or Madrid pride parades.

Globally, the power of visibility is contingent on time and place, and local movements must determine that time and place for themselves. The same is surely also true for visibility politics on an individual level. While the group process of coming out has the potential to change cultural politics and better lives, that is not to say that all individuals must come out to be "model" LGBT people. Indeed, the often-challenging act of coming out also involves a great deal of privilege that is not equally available to all people. LGBT people are well aware of the risks that can accompany coming out, such as a threat to their safety and losing the support of their social networks, which vary according to context, social situation, and intersectional identities of the individual at hand. In sum, an individual's coming out can be a political matter, but it is always a personal one, one that LGBT people must navigate individually. While this book is about the power inherent in visibility, we might still hope that this very challenging step of coming out – especially on an individual basis – will itself be increasingly less necessary for individuals one day.

For states, my theory proposes that visibility can have a great deal of potential when times are ripe (in terms of the valence some international environments can provide visibility), even if the domestic discourse is not ready. Indeed, visibility can be especially important within states that suppress LGBT rights, if those states are embedded in international communities that champion an LGBT norm. In contemporary times, the international level has offered a venue for legitimization outside of the state, one that can affect this calculation in favor of visibility. The European activists in this story have the good fortune of readily available political opportunities at the international level, opportunities that the vision of their predecessors in the movement enabled in the first place (Ayoub and Paternotte 2014). These specifications should clarify the theoretical scope of the project, as well as the methodological decisions made to investigate the problem at hand.

Research design and methods

Case selection

I addressed the study's overarching research questions by collecting data on (1) the EU-27 and (2) the case studies of Germany, Poland, and Slovenia. Europe offers the ideal laboratory for testing and refining my theory because of the EU norm to protect sexual minorities and the presence of states on both ends of the "gay friendliness" spectrum. Furthermore, the EU is a very likely case for diffusion (Checkel 1997). The fact that it provides the mechanisms that regularly function to constrain states to conform to international norms makes the varied adoption of LGBT rights all the more fruitful for analysis.

The book uses quantitative methods to test correlations between predictors in all EU member states, and qualitative methods to trace channels of diffusion from Germany and the EU to Poland and Slovenia. Within the first large-*n* set of states, I also analyzed the 2004 and 2007 waves of EU member states (the EU-12) separately, because after 1989 these states experienced greater exposure to advanced norms on homosexuality (originating in Western Europe, the United States, etc.) and all were successful in gaining membership in the EU. Here the EU-12 refers to the new members of the EU, including the ten ex-Communist Bloc countries, plus Cyprus and Malta. As demonstrated by Figure 2.4 and Figure 2.5, on average, these states score markedly lower on rates of acceptance of sexual minorities compared to the pre-2004 EU member states (the EU-15). The new EU-12 emerged from transition having had little discourse on the LGBT rights issue prior to beginning the EU accession process, which subjected them to the only internationally recognized legal protections for sexual minorities in the world (Swiebel 2009). Even in the most secular of these states, discussion of homosexuality was rarely public prior to the fall of the Berlin Wall (McCajor Hall 2009). The year 1989 was thus a turning point for Europe, the reintegration of the continent, and the proliferation of new international channels. The time frame of the study,

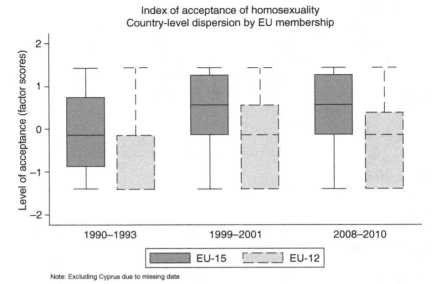

FIGURE 2.4. Variation in attitudes toward homosexuality between new and old
EU states.

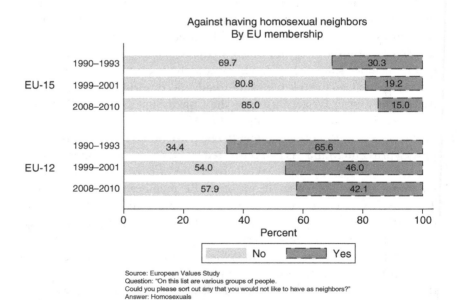

FIGURE 2.5. Variation in objections toward homosexual neighbors between new
and old EU states.

beginning with gay liberation in the early 1970s and tracking differences through post-Cold War Europe to the present, is thus methodologically useful for understanding diffusion processes and explains why I put the needle on the record when I do.

The second set of states, for qualitative analysis, represents ideal cases for understanding the mechanisms by which ideas are diffused. I compared Poland and Slovenia on their different rates of change along both indicators of the dependent variable: social attitudes and laws toward sexual minorities (see Figures 1.1 and 1.2). The different outcomes in these two historically Catholic countries merit analysis (Chapter 6). Germany represents a "norm entrepreneur" case for analysis (the norm also originates elsewhere, a fact I explore in the large-*n* analysis of channels to recipient states). In particular, the cases of Germany and Poland illustrate how ideas moved from a first-mover to new-adopter state, a process in which actors based in Germany became involved in Poland. Many analogous examples exist, making the involvement of groups within and across German borders a valuable case for the study of the transnationalization of LGBT rights activism.

Finally, the LGBT norm lends itself to cross-national analysis because it applies to a minority that exists – in various forms – in all societies. The data also show a bimodal trend in attitudes, a trend apparent in other data on homosexuality (T. W. Smith 2011) (survey respondents usually position themselves at the ends of a scale by answering that homosexuality is either "always" or "never" acceptable), suggesting that individuals in society rarely take a middle position on the issue. In other words, people either embrace or reject equal rights for sexual minorities. Thus, there is little contention about the specific content of the norm, a situation that is an important precondition for norm implementation (Dimitrova and Rhinard 2005). LGBT rights are a case of a contentious norm at an early phase of development and a symbol of sociocultural modernity (Carrillo 2007) from which we can generate theory to explain other contentious norms – for example, those concerning gender and immigrant rights politics.

Research methods

I developed an eclectic multimethod research design to discern the processes by which LGBT rights norms diffuse. Using both quantitative and qualitative methods, I considered the transnational actors and transnational channels that carry international LGBT rights norms, as well as the domestic structures that welcome or reject those norms. Data gathering included more than two years of on-site fieldwork, semistructured interviews, participant observation, and archival research, as well as an organizational survey of transnationally linked LGBT organizations. My qualitative research focused on my case studies (Germany, Poland, Slovenia, and the European institutions), although I also interviewed numerous actors from other European states. My data collection resulted in three data sets for analysis. The Appendix provides a more detailed description of my research methods.

3

Transnational movement: Opportunities, actors, and mechanisms

When the late Polish president and former then-mayor of Warsaw, Lech Kaczyński, banned marches for LGBT equality in 2004 and 2005, LGBT organizations began organizing to hold the event illegally and generating press by contacting international authorities and media outlets. What was unique about the Parada Równości (Equality March) of June 11, 2005, compared to similar gay pride events in major cities where LGBT visibility had become common, was that a transnational group of activists organized the event from both Poland and neighboring Germany. Many of these activists were expatriate Poles who used resources made available to them in Berlin. Prominent European politicians were among the roughly 5,000 illegal marchers who took to the streets of Warsaw that day to demand the right of assembly for sexual minorities in Poland, and more than one-third of the marchers came from foreign contexts (interview no. 125). According to Tomasz Bączkowski, the activist who organized the march:

It was organized in Berlin because I lived there ... I had a lot of experiences in Germany, I knew how to do this – or how one should do it – and I thought, in these times ... it shouldn't be a problem organizing from the outside. Naturally, through the personal contacts with [German parliamentarian] Claudia Roth and others, it was much easier for me to organize it from [Germany] than for Polish activists in Poland, where the environment in general is very hostile. In retrospect, these international political pressures were much more important than if I would have just done this in Poland. (interview no. 124)

The illegal march provided the political opportunity to link the social situation of Polish sexual minorities to Poland's recent accession to the EU through the frames of democratic values and human rights. Many activists remember it as one of the most important public assemblies for the rights of LGBT Poles and as a turning point for Polish LGBT activism.[1] A member of Lambda Warsaw described the situation in Poland in terms that echo what representatives of other LGBT organizations across many new-adopter states expressed in my interviews with them:

> Polish homosexuals live hidden and in fear. Our organization, however, wants our presence recognized in society, that we are here, we are sending a signal to gays and lesbians: you are visible and get used to it. It is the end of silence, the end of hiding in the closet. (Kubica 2009, 136–7)

Polish LGBT activism – one experience within a larger campaign for LGBT rights in Europe – illustrates the increasing influence that transnational sources have on the visibility of LGBT people, as well as the effect that Europeanization has on the political mobilization of norm entrepreneurs and their tactics. This chapter reflects on transnational LGBT activism in Europe, emphasizing the role Europe plays in facilitating the mobilization of these actors. It also illustrates the mechanisms that these actors engage in their attempt to impact both society and state. These socialization mechanisms include norm brokerage, framing, learning, and deliberation.

To what extent do processes of Europeanization facilitate the political mobilization and influence the strategies of LGBT norm entrepreneurs in the EU? This chapter emphasizes that European integration alters political opportunities for mobilization. As a result, transnational European networks of LGBT activists form, and they employ mechanisms of socialization to push for the social and legal visibility of LGBT people in various member states.

The EU's multilevel system offers a host of political opportunities for advocacy groups to mobilize around social issues, opportunities that are more complex than conventionally thought. I argue that the Europeanization of LGBT activism is facilitated by a vertical (top-down and bottom-up) interaction between domestic states and Brussels; it also functions horizontally by facilitating networks of actors across member states. I demonstrate these interactions by focusing on the discrepancies in opportunities for LGBT mobilization in two member states, one open to norm entrepreneurs and thus facilitating mobilization, the other a closed target state. Interaction occurs in a type of activism similar to

---

[1] The Kultura dla Tolerancji events in 2004 and 2005 also generated considerable attention. The Warsaw march was also banned in 2004, and activists responded by organizing an illegal rally.

what Doug Imig and Sidney Tarrow call "cooperative transnationalism" (2001, 17); the actors are transnational and the foreign target of contention is domestic.[2] Furthermore, I contend that vertical and horizontal opportunities for mobilization bring together different types of actors who rely on mechanisms of socialization and frame their demands in a European discourse.

This chapter's argument proceeds in three steps. First, I argue that the Europeanization of LGBT rights begins primarily as a vertical process in which the EU imposes formal rules on member states and builds the capacities of civil society organizations to lobby domestic institutions. Second, I make a case for looking at the Europeanization of LGBT mobilization horizontally. I argue that Europeanization facilitates transnational activism around LGBT issues through the free movement of peoples and through transnational advocacy networks, granting actors from the new-adopter states access to important mobilizing structures in other member states. Third, in arguing that much LGBT activism is mobilized among member states, I show that mechanisms of socialization through EU-level frames and elites almost always accompany such mobilization. My focus on the member states of Germany and Poland makes explicit the connections between a leading and a new-adopter state, with Polish and German norm entrepreneurs using resources available to them in Germany to mobilize in Poland.

Europeanization and opportunities for transnational activism

The Europeanization of a norm

European institutions have actively championed the norm of protecting sexual minorities both rhetorically, through various resolutions and reports, and directly, through various court rulings, anti-discrimination directives, and EU accession requirements. Following the 1981 case of *Dudgeon v. the United Kingdom*, in which the ECtHR ruled that same-sex intercourse be decriminalized in Northern Ireland, the CoE became an instrumental player in LGBT rights (Johnson 2012; van der Vleuten 2014). Its ECtHR would rule on issues as diverse as LGBT freedom of

---

[2] By contrast, collective transnationalism (cf. Imig and Tarrow 2001) is rare for LGBT rights groups. ILGA-Europe is the only direct pressure point on the EU Commission and it functions almost exclusively through legal challenges (see also Marks and McAdam 1996, on targets of activism in Europe).

assembly, expression, and association; age of consent; partnership benefits and family life; military access; and gender reassignment. In groundbreaking legislation in 2015, the ECtHR ruled in *Oliari and others v. Italy* that Italy must recognize same-sex couples legally. The European Community, later the EU, joined the struggle for LGBT rights with its 1984 Squarcialupi Report. Its European Parliament would go on to become the LGBT movement's central partner within the EU institutions, adopting numerous resolutions in defense of LGBT people, including the pivotal 1994 Roth Report. In 1997, the EU adopted the Treaty of Amsterdam, which resulted three years later in a directive banning discrimination on the ground of sexual orientation in employment (Beger 2004; Mos 2014; Waaldijk and Bonini-Baraldi 2006). The ECJ as well as the European Agency for Fundamental Rights (FRA) (established in 2007), have also created new venues for LGBT activists to make claims. For example, a historic 2013 ruling by the ECJ granted asylum to LGBT people seeking refuge in the EU.

While the EU provides a sound methodological scope for the analysis, my conception of how Europeanization drives transnationalization encompasses more than the EU. The relationship between Europe and LGBT rights is a fluid one, and while the EU has been more vocal on the issue in recent years, other institutions (e.g. the CoE and the Organization for Security and Co-operation in Europe [OSCE]) have been actively involved. Furthermore, noninstitutional and informal transnational interactions date back to the early twentieth century, when shared regional geography and efficient transportation networks allowed LGBT people to sustain collaborative networks that spanned the continent. David Paternotte and I (Ayoub and Paternotte 2014) have argued that earlier movement activists (primarily in the 1970s) saw a visionary role for European institutions long before the European Community had a social mandate. European institutions have moved at the request of the movement. While the EU position on the rights of sexual minorities is a conglomeration of member states' positions, with some states far ahead of the Union, it has acted as a semiautonomous leading actor in pressuring its other member states – the ones that fall behind – to adopt the LGBT rights norm. Both proponents and opponents of European integration agree that norms governing LGBT rights have become part of the symbolic set of values that define the idea of contemporary Europe (Ayoub and Paternotte 2014, 1–4).

While European institutions directly contribute to a minimum level of policy change across all member states (i.e. decriminalization of adult

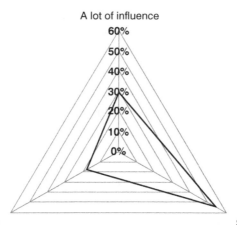

A lot of influence

Not much influence   Some influence

FIGURE 3.1. Influence of European institutions on state compliance.
Organizational responses to the question: In your opinion, how much influence do
European-level institutions – that is, institutions like the European Commission,
the European Parliament, the European Court of Justice, or the European Court
of Human Rights – have on your country's politics and policies related to the
rights of LGBT people?[3]
Source: Author's Transnational LGBT Organizations Survey (see Appendix), *n* = 186.

same-sex relations, anti-discrimination in employment, and asylum), most
other changes come about indirectly through the facilitation of transnational
advocacy networks. While an expert survey of European LGBT organizations shows the direct effect of European institutions is substantial, it also
leaves much to be explained, especially in terms of change in social attitudes.
Figure 3.1 illustrates a strong direct link between European institutions and
domestic LGBT politics and policy, with representatives from 82 percent
of the responding LGBT organizations reporting "some" (53 percent) or
"a lot" (29 percent) of influence. Figure 3.2 demonstrates that the direct
nature of this link is less pronounced when the outcome concerns domestic attitudes toward LGBT people, with only 46 percent reporting "some"
(39 percent) or "a lot" (7 percent) of influence. Indeed, 57 percent of the
respondents said that the European institutions do not have much direct
influence over the hearts and minds of ordinary Europeans.

Europeanization[4] as a process is not always directly tied to formal
institutional politics between elites in the member states and European

[3] This question is adapted from one formulated by Conor O'Dwyer (2010, 236–7) and
used in his survey of Polish activists and politicians.
[4] Scholars broadly define Europeanization as "processes of (a) construction, (b) diffusion,
and (c) institutionalization of formal and informal rules, procedures, policy paradigms,

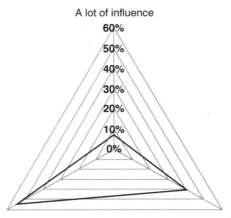

A lot of influence

Not much influence   Some influence

FIGURE 3.2. Influence of European institutions on societal internalization. Organizational responses to the question: In your opinion, how much influence do European-level institutions – that is, institutions like the European Commission, the European Parliament, the European Court of Justice, or the European Court of Human Rights – have on what people in your country think about the rights of LGBT people?
Source: Author's Transnational LGBT Organizations Survey (see Appendix), *n* = 184.

institutions, or to top-down EU processes such as persuasion or sanctions. A series of other indirect processes also affect change. While a logic of consequences tied to the EU institutions prevails before accession, after accession a logic of appropriateness quickly assumes a primary role. As the secretary of the European Parliament's Intergroup on LGBTI Rights explained, "The EU is more effective when we have a carrot to dangle. There is no EU army, all we have is dialogue" (interview no. 126). For example, in April 2015, the Parliament adopted nonbinding resolutions on Albania and Bosnia-Herzegovina that respectively called for same-sex partnership rights (paragraph 22, European Parliament 2015a) and the inclusion of sexual orientation and gender identity in hate crime law (paragraphs 25 and 28, European Parliament 2015b). The EU does require states to make changes to accompany accession, but it becomes cautious about "embarrassing its own members" once they are in (interviews no. 15 and 138), bringing into question the successful implementation

styles, 'ways of doing things' and shared beliefs and norms, which are first defined and consolidated in the EU policy process and then incorporated in the logic of domestic discourse, political structures and public policies" (Radaelli 2004, 3).

and promotion of new LGBT policies (O'Dwyer 2010; Kristoffersson, van Roozendaal and Poghosyan in press). Instead, the brunt of the effort to induct "actors into the norms and rules of a given community ... [so] that an agent switches from a logic of consequences to a logic of appropriateness" (Checkel 2005, 804) is left to a transnational network of activists, suggesting a fascinating relationship between European intergovernmental organizations and international nongovernmental organizations. As an LGBT activist clarified, "Most EU institutions don't feel comfortable shaming their member states, so they instead look to organizations, for example in the Netherlands, to do it for them" (panel no. 205).

Transnational LGBT advocacy networks play a central role in Europeanization, because direct EU competences in sanctioning states for infringing upon the rights of LGBT peoples remain limited.[5] An LGBT advocacy network composed of transnationally linked civil society groups, international human rights NGOs, and sympathetic political elites at the national and supranational levels has exacerbated the political opportunities for mobilization tremendously. ILGA-Europe now connects more than 300 domestic and local organizations across the EU and CoE member states. It both lobbies European institutions to improve the legal standing of LGBT people in the states and contributes to capacity building in its member organizations by dispersing know-how and mediating ties between national LGBT groups. Following the Treaty of Amsterdam, Brussels-based ILGA-Europe became an official partner of the European Commission, from which it has since received its core funding (Paternotte 2012). Similarly, the European Parliament's Intergroup on LGBTI Rights grew out of the cooperation between ILGA-Europe and sympathetic members of the European Parliament (MEPs), providing an elite EU response to LGBT issues around Europe. According to MEP Ulrike Lunacek, co-president of the Intergroup:

Governments have to learn how to talk about the issue, even if they don't like [the issue itself] ... Our job in the European Parliament and the Intergroup is to promote visibility of the issue, and to ask governments that don't want to move ahead some tough questions. And I assure you, that we do." (panel no. 215)

In 2011, the Intergroup included 115 parliamentarians representing 20 EU member states (interview no. 126). That number grew to 150 parliamentarians by 2015 (despite the historic gains by far-right MEPs in the

---

[5] Celeste Montoya (2008, 360) has charted a similar process in the European woman's movement.

2014 parliamentary elections), making the Intergroup on LGBTI Rights the largest of the parliament's twenty-eight intergroups. In 2016, the Parliament voted to actively promote fundamental EU values—including the protection of LGBI people—through intercultural dialogue and education. These networks share resources and pool information to develop tactics for promoting the visibility of LGBT people in Europe.

Such networks of advocates and political elites come together via new political opportunities provided by the EU's multilevel framework, which increasingly facilitates a space for horizontal interaction. By horizontal, I mean the conduits and actors mobilized across member states, using European frames. For example, while ILGA-Europe actively lobbies the EU on some LGBT rights (but less on domestic partnership, which is outside the EU's direct purview), several indirect influences affect horizontal and transnational activism on the partnership issue. At the annual ILGA-Europe conferences, activists have several panels on tactics and strategies for advancing partnership claims (panel no. 212). For LGBT actors, who have long relied on safe spaces to express their identity, such horizontal interaction is an important precondition for their mobilization, because the EU does not directly offer such public spaces. The concept of political opportunities provides a useful theoretical lens through which to think about horizontal and vertical processes of Europeanization.

Varied political opportunities in leading and new-adopter states
Political opportunity structures were traditionally defined as the circumstances surrounding a political system, in particular the availability of alliances and the strength of opponents in a given context. Most opportunities, however, are not structural, but rather subject to attribution and situational, in that they need to be both perceived by and visible to potential actors (McAdam, Tarrow, and Tilly 2001, 43).[6] The fact that political opportunities must be made visible to facilitate mobilization is clearly relevant to this book's argument. Likewise, the process of Europeanization modifies our conceptual understanding of political opportunity structures, as social movement actors in one state increasingly have ties to those in another, and actors in one state can target another's government.

---

[6] As Sebastiaan Princen and Bart Kerremans (2008, 1132) synthesize, "the actual effects of political opportunities on social movements depend on (1) the identification of those opportunities, (2) the existence of collective identities and frames that are favorable to specific forms of political activity, and (3) organizational resources and capabilities that allow social movements to take advantage of those opportunities."

Consequently, multilevel frameworks come to have an effect on movement mobilization and tactics at local, national, and supranational levels (della Porta and Caiani 2007).[7] The relationship between the EU and LGBT activists is generally harmonious, with activists seeing Brussels as an ally in a struggle against sometimes-hostile domestic governments. Indeed, the European Commission generously funds ILGA-Europe with the primary purpose of lobbying EU institutions. Europeanized opportunity structures become interesting for LGBT mobilization because they have an effect on the types of transnational and domestic actors mobilized at various levels and on the strategies these actors implement in various member states.

LGBT advocacy groups operate in an interactive environment that depends on the openness of political opportunity structures at domestic and international levels. If we think of this openness in terms of the social and legal acceptance of LGBT people, where there is still considerable variance, we can adapt Kathryn Sikkink's (2005) understanding of openness as receptiveness to NGO activity. For instance, when the domestic level is closed and interacting with an open international opportunity structure, she expects "boomerang" or "spiral model" patterns, wherein domestic actors sidestep their governments to pressure from above (Risse, Ropp, and Sikkink 2013). She notes that activists in an open domestic context can aid those in a closed one, forming what she calls an insider–outsider coalition. Poland, Germany, and the EU are all open to advocacy groups, yet present discrepancies in visibility for LGBT people. Because LGBT people are often invisible and must fear both social and political costs associated with mobilization, we must reconceptualize open and closed opportunity structures for LGBT people across Europe.

How LGBT mobilization occurs: Germany and Poland
Horizontal and vertical Europeanization have differing effects on LGBT mobilization, but they come together to make it effective. The former provides access to social spaces and organizational resources in open member states that mobilize LGBT publics (both elite and ordinary citizens) from one member state to another. Horizontal opportunities are particularly useful for noninstitutionalized mobilization in a target state's

---

[7] This type of contention – and the mechanisms of brokerage and diffusion that this book highlights – is closely related to the social movement concept of "scale shift," the "process through which contention at one level is transposed to a higher (or a lower) one" (Tarrow and McAdam 2005). See also Andrew Yeo (2011).

public sphere. Vertical opportunities provide the legitimacy and institutional clout to mobilize European political elites and socialize authorities in the target state, as well as the frames and socialization mechanisms that activists use to make their message effective there.

For the purposes of this analysis, I conceive of the political opportunities for LGBT mobilization around the time of Polish accession (2004) as closed in Poland and open both in Germany and at the macro EU level. Poland had little discourse on the LGBT issue prior to beginning the EU accession process, during which the state was subjected to new EU standards on LGBT rights. In contrast, the 1960s' student and sexual revolution and the 1980s' HIV/AIDS epidemic politicized LGBT issues earlier throughout the Federal Republic of Germany. If both domestic and international levels are open (as they were in Germany), activists will "privilege domestic political change, but will keep international activism as a complementary and compensatory option" (Sikkink 2005, 165).

I used three measures – based on Ronald Holzhacker (2012) – to compare legal standing and societal and elite opinion in Germany and Poland. To measure legality at the state level, I collected data on protective and equality LGBT laws adopted in all twenty-seven EU states by 2005. I then scored the states on measures of LGBT legal standing, such as the status of recognized partnerships, anti-discrimination protections, and adoption rights (see Table A.1 in the Appendix). Scoring ranges between 2 and 12 points, and Poland (2 points) scores comparatively low, Germany (7.5) comparatively high, in the top third, for 2005.[8] To compare the societal situation, I use available survey data on social attitudes toward sexual minorities (*European Values Study 1981–2008* 2011).[9] The percentage of Poles who approve of homosexuality (by selecting 6–10 on a scale of 1 to 10) was 15.63 percent in 2008, compared to 51.03 percent of Germans surveyed that same year.

For elite opinion, I rely on interviews with politicians and national LGBT experts in Poland and Germany and at the EU institutions. Here again I recognize discrepancies in elite opinion between Germany and Poland. In Germany, all five federal political parties have LGBT committees that represent LGBT constituencies. While some members of these parties clearly hold homo- or transphobic views, a taboo exists against

---

[8] By 2005, Poland had introduced anti-discrimination employment measures and equal sexual offenses provisions; Germany had introduced the same, plus registered partnership, second-parent adoption, and anti-discrimination in goods and services.

[9] The 2008 survey wave (fourth) was selected because it is the wave closest to the 2005 Equality March.

expressing them. In Poland the situation is changing, but all interviewees explicitly cite openly hostile rhetoric among political parties in 2005 (see also Bączkowski 2008). Political elites in Poland went so far as to propose a bill to remove homosexual schoolteachers from schools because of their supposed threat to children – this type of public discourse no longer has credibility among political elites in Germany.

Since the EU, as an international organization, has different competences than nation states, the same measures do not apply. That said, there is evidence that the EU is the most progressive organization of nation states on LGBT issues, and more progressive than the UN (Swiebel 2009). As in Germany, a taboo against elite homophobic rhetoric exists in the EU – this was particularly evident in 2004, when the prospects of a favored candidate for commission president were scuppered after he expressed religious views that conflicted with the acceptance of homosexuality. The EU institutions have a clear mandate to promote LGBT rights in member states and abroad. Table 3.1 provides a sketch of what will follow.

Mobilizing through the structures of gay life

The abundant LGBT social spaces and organizational resources in neighboring Germany were critical variables for bringing together the main actors, defining their common identity, and empowering them with the necessary resources for transnational activism in Poland. By *LGBT social spaces*, I refer to the centers for gay life that make the community visible and serve as safe spaces where LGBT people can meet and express their identity. These spaces facilitate ties "by demonstrating the co-presence of others, thus showing people that issues they thought taboo can be discussed, and strengthening collective identity by providing tangible evidence of the existence of a group" (Polletta 1999, 25).[10] Social spaces, which for LGBT people have traditionally existed in the private sphere or taken the form of cafes, bars, and clubs, can foster collective consciousness by making the issue visible to potential movement actors. They thus

---

[10] Drawing on James Scott (1990, 118), Chris Zepeda-Millán (2016, 277) notes the importance of social spaces, created by marginalized groups, for the emergence of political action on their behalf: "According to Scott, 'the practices and discourses of resistance' cultivated by the oppressed cannot exist 'without tacit or acknowledged coordination and communication within the subordinate group.' For this to occur, 'the subordinate group must carve out for itself social spaces insulated from control and surveillance from above'" (see also Chauncey 1994, 5). In the EU, insulated social spaces for activists can exist in foreign member states.

TABLE 3.1. *Political opportunity structures, mobilizing structures, transnational actors, and mechanisms*

	Poland	Germany	EU
I. Political opportunity structures			
Legal standing of LGBT people in 2005 (0–12)	Low (2)	High (7.5)	N/A
Societal opinion approving of homosexuality in 2008	Low (15.63%)	High (51.03%)	N/A
Elite opinion toward LGBT equality in 2005	Opposed/Split *Closed (new target state)*	Supportive *Open (leading horizontal norm entrepreneur)*	Supportive *Open (leading vertical norm entrepreneur)*
II. Mobilizing structures			
Social spaces (Average # 1990–2005)	Low (5.5)	High (117.5)	N/A
LGBT organizational resources (Average # 1990–2005)	Low (4.9)	High (48.5) Resources for protest in the public sphere	High (EU-linked umbrella organizations) Resources for institutionalized lobbying of government
III. Types of external transnational actors		*Horizontal*	*Vertical*
Mobilization of Polish expatriates/rooted cosmopolitans		+	–
Mobilization of foreign political elites		+	+
Mobilization of foreign publics		+	–
IV. Mechanisms			
Norm brokerage†	+	–/+	–
Legitimate frames for deliberation in target state	+	–	+
Legitimate frames for learning in target state	+	–	+

Note: †Norm brokers connect the often-contrasting international norms and domestic norms, and aid diffusion by framing norms – in a domestically familiar discourse – so they fit better locally. In this case study, they are transnationally connected local actors in Poland, and specifically the Polish rooted cosmopolitans in Germany.

promote interpersonal visibility. Organizational capacity refers to the presence of LGBT organizations that endow LGBT communities with resources and capabilities, including financial capital, know-how, legitimacy, and access to existing networks (Princen and Kerremans 2008, 1131–2). Organizational capacity also exists at the European level (e.g. ILGA-Europe), but it serves a different function, because these umbrella organizations are more likely to pursue formal lobbying than domestic organizations, who are often devoted to public sphere work (Lang 2013). Social spaces and organizational capacity in open EU member states provided the mobilizing structures that engendered a process not available in Poland.

The difficult social situation for LGBT Poles made headlines in Europe, as activists and media highlighted the paradox that Poland's successfully democratizing state and society was struggling to recognize sexual minorities. Despite some institutional changes associated with accession, like passing the anti-discrimination in employment directive, Poland showed itself resistant to many protective policy measures, societal attitudes toward sexual minorities remained largely negative, and cases of state-sponsored discrimination abounded (Bączkowski 2008). Several city governments violated the right to freedom of assembly for LGBT marches, even though the march has a long history within the tactical repertoire for expressing political grievances in Poland. Alongside more formal advocacy work, LGBT activists stressed the importance of mobilization in the public sphere as an important type of Europeanization, because LGBT activism is geared toward both society and state.

While other EU member states (both old and new) also experienced troubles with recognizing sexual minorities, a homophobic government, coupled with an emerging civil society and several engaged LGBT organizations, made Catholic Poland a prototype for improving the situation of sexual minorities in the EU (Chetaille 2011; European Parliament 2006). Polish LGBT activists made progress in the three years leading up to Poland's accession to the EU by implementing innovative campaigns and founding a new national LGBT organization, Kampania Przeciw Homofobii (KPH, Campaign against Homophobia). According to the former president of KPH, the debate on homosexuality entered the public realm most visibly just before EU accession (interview no. 8). In 2003, the Niech Nas Zobaczą (Let Them See Us) campaign – during which twenty-seven billboards, funded substantially by the Swedish, Danish, and Dutch embassies, showed same-sex couples holding hands – fueled national debate on the issue. The euphoria associated with EU membership was not long lived, however, as hostile political and social opposition began forming in response (interviews no. 9 and 140). In large part, allies from abroad aided local Polish activism by organizing demonstrations and placing demands on the Polish state from foreign contexts during this time.

The topography of LGBT recognition – both socially and legally – is complex, with stark variation between and within states, and between rural and urban areas. In Europe, Europeanization processes indirectly facilitate access to centers of gay life through the free movement of people, goods, and services, making established gay communities, such as those in Berlin, more accessible to non-nationals. This creates dense nodes of gay social spaces and activist kinships in specific national contexts and urban areas that outpace their surroundings – for example, Amsterdam, London, and Berlin became known as "gay capitals" at various points in the 1970s, 1980s, and 1990s. European integration accelerates access to such spaces, where openly LGBT populations and their social spaces are more present. This is especially true for post-socialist countries, where social spaces and organizational resources are comparatively less developed. Thus, the political opportunities for transnational LGBT mobilization lie not only in Brussels, but also in the EU member states' centers of gay life.

Gay life in Berlin and Warsaw, 1990–2005

In Germany, openly LGBT people have a long history as part of the state's fabric (including both persecution and tolerance), which has resulted in long-term LGBT organizations and a presence in some parts of the public space in cities such as Berlin, Cologne, and Hamburg.

Berlin, in particular, provided a host of opportunities for mobilization, absent in Poland, that were also different from those available at the EU level.[11] Berlin's large Polish expatriate community, its geographic proximity to the Polish border, and its status as an LGBT-friendly European city with

---

[11] While I focus on Berlin and Warsaw here, similar connections exist between other cities in Germany and Poland. For example, the mayor of Nuremberg addressed the importance of LGBT rights as part of cooperation on a visit to Cracow – one of Nuremberg's sister cities (interview no. 103). Activists from Cologne – another center of gay life with a large Polish community – were also engaged in Poland. Alongside Warsaw, targets included Cracow, Poznan, and other cities with banned marches. Similarly, the work of Jon Binnie and Christian Klesse (2013) shows that Polish migration flows in other European countries have aided the development of activist networks.

dozens of LGBT social spaces and organizations provided fertile ground for transnational activism to take root there, beginning in the late 1990s. First, a long history of immigration by Polish workers to Germany has left a visible mark on German demography. Berlin's second-largest immigrant group is Polish, numbering nearly 41,000 registered Polish citizens (Amt fuer Statistik Berlin-Brandenburg 2011). The population of Berliners of Polish descent is estimated to be 130,000, counting both undocumented Polish immigrants and those who were born and raised in Poland but have since taken German citizenship. Berlin is particularly appealing to Polish sexual minorities, who seek it out as a destination to reside in and travel to because of the comparatively high level of LGBT tolerance within the city (interviews no. 5 and 113). A Polish presence – for example, through flags, pamphlets, and information booths – is renowned and visible at all of Berlin's major LGBT events, including the annual Christopher Street Day parade and the Gay-Lesbian Street Fair. Second, geographic proximity became a critical factor for visibility after the dissolution of the Iron Curtain, since Berlin is just over sixty kilometers from the Polish border, and train connections such as the Berlin–Warszawa Express make travel between the two capitals quick and affordable – the 5.5-hour journey to Warsaw cost less than 40 euros in 2005.

Then too, Berlin has a long history as a center of gay life, as I mentioned in Chapter 2. The institutions Magnus Hirschfeld founded were the earliest precursors to modern LGBT organizations (Kollman and Waites 2009, 3). Even the first official American organization for homosexuals, the Society for Human Rights, was founded by Hirschfeld protégé and Berliner Henry Gerber in Chicago in 1924 (Dececco and Bullough 2002, 25). Especially after German reunification, "Berlin has developed ... into a gay Mecca in which the richness of ideas and diversity is hardly able to be surpassed" (Gmünder 2003, 323). In 2001, the newly elected then-mayor, Klaus Wowereit, ended speculation by saying, *"Ich bin schwul und das ist auch gut so"* ("I am gay, and it's alright that way"). In sum, the LGBT issue is highly visible, both socially and politically.

Warsaw, the center of gay life and activism in Poland, and Berlin are sharply different in terms of social spaces and organizational capacity (see Figure 3.3 and Figure 3.4). I use 15 years of issues of *Spartacus*, an international gay travel guide, to measure the number of gay social spaces and organizations leading up to the 2005 Equality March. The Spartacus guides have appeared yearly since 1970 and provide a systematic way to

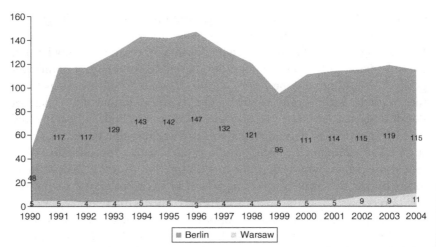

FIGURE 3.3. Number of LGBT social spaces (restaurants, cafes, bars, and clubs) in Berlin and Warsaw, 1990–2004.

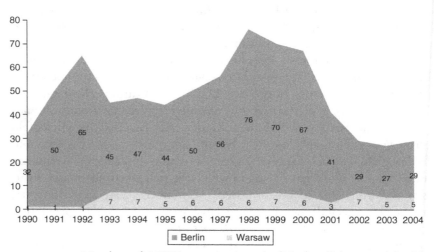

FIGURE 3.4. Number of LGBT organizations (political, religious, and health groups) in Berlin and Warsaw, 1990–2004.

measure the presence of gay life across cities in more than 160 countries because they use the same categories to list the presence of LGBT organizations and businesses. For Figure 3.3, I coded "LGBT social spaces" by counting the presence of LGBT restaurants, cafes, bars, and clubs in each city. For Figure 3.4, I coded "LGBT organizations" broadly by counting all political, religious, and health/counseling LGBT organizations and groups in each city.[12]

The figures show the cleft between two European member states – one open, one closed – in terms of potential for LGBT mobilization.[13] In the last twenty years, Europeanization has made this cleft less relevant by increasing the mobility of European citizens and by providing new channels to access foreign contexts within the EU's institutional framework. As a result, the above variables – available social spaces and organizational capacity in some member states – helped establish the necessary personal networks that brought together a new group of transnational actors involved in Polish LGBT activism.

Norm entrepreneurs

I define *transnational activists* as those individuals and groups who work across national borders to advance a cause. They mobilize resources and work on behalf of people in other countries, against opponents in other countries, or with people in other countries to advance common goals (Tarrow 2005b, 8–9). While European institutions have established norms on LGBT rights, these norms do not diffuse freely; they need actors and channels to carry them. Transnational activists – who typically fit the definition of norm entrepreneurs – have aided this process across channels that function vertically and horizontally. Different channels mobilized different types of actors involved in the Equality March. In this section, I first discuss actors who were mobilized horizontally (primarily between Germany and Poland), including expatriate Poles and German activists,

[12] While Figure 3.4 highlights the discrepancy in the number of organizations between Berlin and Warsaw, it is also worth noting that the number of organizations in Berlin has declined over time. There are three reasons for this. First, German reunification consolidated organizations and centers that had counterparts on the other side of the wall. In this sense, the drop in the number of organizations did not reduce the mobilization capacity of LGBT activists. Second, LGBT organizations have also been absorbed by and institutionalized through powerful national LGBT organizations (such as KPH in Poland, which both established and absorbed smaller organizations in some Polish cities). This process has influenced activism, privileging certain types of claims (e.g. same-sex marriage over queer politics) and modes of organizing. The third factor is the general trend of mainstreaming gay culture and assimilation across Western gay capitals, which has led to a reduction in the number of specifically LGBT spaces and organizations.

[13] Spaces for LGBT activism and LGBT organizations certainly also existed in Poland (Chetaille 2011), but they existed in far smaller numbers than in Germany (and many other EU member states). Other EU member states had more resources, experience, and openly LGBT publics that could be used to work with local activists in a closed context like Poland. Polish accession to the EU enabled access to these mobilizing structures.

celebrities, and ordinary citizens. I then discuss actors who were mobilized both horizontally and vertically, including European and German parliamentarians.

Especially among the nonpolitical elite actors, the transnational activists interviewed cited the importance of horizontal spaces and resources, because they connect European LGBT people, solidifying a transnational dimension of their identity.[14] Openly LGBT people share, at least in part, a common experience – such as coming out to family – that connects them across borders (Altman 1996; Tremblay, Paternotte, and Johnson 2011). At times, this connection can rival national identity to connect otherwise disparate actors. According to this line of thought, an openly gay German may identify more with an openly gay Pole than with a heterosexual German. However contested the social construction of identity across contexts may be, the transnational horizontal opportunities described above are important for giving LGBT people, who remain invisible in many domestic contexts, a space for interaction.

German activists and Polish rooted cosmopolitans

Expatriate Polish activists discussed the strength and inspiration they felt to become politically active after leaving Poland. According to one activist from the Fundacja Równości/Stiftung für Gleichberechtigung (Equality Foundation),[15] she now holds hands with her girlfriend when she visits Warsaw, which she attributes to socialization in Berlin and the comfort she takes in knowing that she can "escape" back to Berlin. "When you leave a country, you suddenly feel more brave [pause] to show yourself" (interview no. 5). Mobility has been important for much of LGBT history, in part because it has removed LGBT people from the constraints of family life (Chauncey 1994, 9).[16] Like the Polish activist, many of the actors involved were migrant and expatriate Poles who used

---

[14] Jon Binnie and Christian Klesse (2013) in particular have critically engaged and problematized notions of solidarity in network ties. I wish to note that while the activists mobilized do refer to moral shock and solidarity as a motivation for their activism, such an explanation alone does not produce a mobilization outcome. Indeed, the moral outrage associated with the Kaczyński government's treatment of LGBT Poles was widely publicized in Europe and resonated with people in many contexts. Yet moral shock does not explain why some locals become more involved than others, which is why I privilege the social spaces and organizational resources that my interviewees cited in actually mobilizing those who felt connected to LGBT Poles.

[15] The Fundacja Równości was funded by three Polish organizations (interview no. 129).

[16] The emancipatory experience the Polish activist described was reminiscent of the author Christopher Isherwood's account of Berlin decades earlier. The city's openness in the late

mobilizing structures available to them in Berlin. They make the dividing line between external and internal actors porous, occupying a hybrid ground that bodes well for norm brokerage. The role of migrant and expatriate Poles in their interactions with German allies is crucial because they provide a competent understanding of the Polish domestic context (through their personal experiences, language competence, and associational ties to Polish activists) and draw attention to the Polish situation by putting it on the agenda of German LGBT organizations.

In line with my argument that horizontal opportunities mobilize a distinct type of actor, I use Sidney Tarrow's (2005a, 1–8) definition of rooted cosmopolitans. He says:

> the special characteristic of these activists is ... their relational links to their own societies, to other countries, and to international institutions ... What is "rooted" in the concept ... is that, as individuals move cognitively and physically outside their spatial origins, they continue to be linked to place, to the social networks that inhabit that space, and to the resources, experiences and opportunities that place provides them with ... Most rely on domestic resources and opportunities to launch their transnational activities and return home afterwards.

One such activist, Bączkowski, came to Berlin in the 1990s to continue his studies in economics, international relations, and European law. At this time, the NGO field in Poland was weak and offered little in terms of LGBT rights (interview no. 125). By contrast, the visibility of LGBT life in Berlin fueled his engagement there, with "the background thought that these skills can be ... transported to Poland later" (interview no. 124). His partner, a volunteer at Maneo (a local Berlin LGBT organization that focuses primarily on community issues), introduced Bączkowski to the organization's president. At this point in the late 1990s, Maneo's president – who had previously worked as part of a transnational campaign to combat violence in Northern Ireland – was hoping to deepen the organization's political cooperation abroad, and Bączkowski's volunteer work brought Poland to the forefront of the discussion (interview no. 125). In 1998, Maneo organized its first roundtable meeting in Warsaw with Polish activists, establishing a lasting transnational network of LGBT organizations in five European capitals, called Tolerantia.[17]

1920s allowed him to explore his sexuality and embrace a newfound identity – a freedom Isherwood had lacked at home in 1920s London (Beachy 2014).

[17] Around the same time, Maneo established ties to France because of a Francophone colleague who was informed about the activist scene in Paris. Together, these ties led to Tolerantia, which brings together organizations in Berlin (Maneo), Warsaw (KPH and

As Maneo expanded its realm of activities to address Poland-related issues, it acted as a magnet for the involvement of Berlin's expatriate Poles. "Roughly 100,000 Poles live in Berlin and then, if roughly 5 to 10 percent are gay, there should be 5,000 to 10,000 gay Poles," Bączkowski joked, continuing, "As Maneo started having more contacts to Poland, expatriate Poles approached us wanting to be involved" (interview no. 124). What emerged in 2005 was Tolerancja po Polsku/ Toleranz auf Polnisch (Tolerance in Polish), a subsidiary of Maneo, which provided both a social space for expatriate Poles to gather and a mobilizing structure for using resources in Berlin to address LGBT politics in Poland. It encouraged "gays and lesbians from both countries to meet regularly to cooperate against violence and discrimination toward homosexuals in Germany and Poland, and to exchange information and develop projects" (Maneo-Tolerancja 2005).[18] Similar projects fostering transnational dialogue and cooperation between Germany and Poland have been organized since 1998. Alongside the personal and symbolic support expatriate networks provide, they generate material support for transnational activism. Through Maneo's organizational connections to Berlin's Gay-Lesbian Street Fair, for example, Fundacja Równości was given rent-free spaces to sell beverages and raise funds for the marches. This type of material support began in the 1990s and continues today.

Expatriate Poles were connected to allies in Germany. In 2006, an estimated 2,000 of the 5,000 participants at the Warsaw March were foreign nationals, of which most were German (Bączkowski 2008, 37). In Berlin, personal networks garnered the involvement of various German celebrities who aided Polish activism, such as the Warschauerpakt (Warsaw Pact) organization. This group was founded in 2005 by German media personalities – Thomas Herrmanns, Georg Uecker, Wolfgang Macht, and Holger Wicht – who knew the organizers through their personal networks and wanted to support their cause by increasing awareness and collecting funds for Polish demonstrations. Their mission statement reads:

The Warschauerpakt is a consortium of convinced Europeans, who volunteer to support the Equality March in Warsaw. We stand for the emancipation of LGBT Poles, whose chartered rights are continually ignored by the Administration.

Lambda-Warszawa), Paris (SOS-Homophobie), Madrid (COGAM), and soon Dublin (interview no. 125). Their mission statement reads: "We unite our power for the building of a civil society in Europe ... In the spirit of the European Human Rights convention we oppose hatred, violence and discrimination against social minorities ... We want to fight against discrimination and isolation of homosexuals in a unified Europe" (Tolerantia Declaration 2010).

[18] Translated from the German by the author.

Since 2005 we successfully support the Polish movement by building solid networks, which remain strong today. Through this network we foster the partnership and cooperative engagement of institutions between Germany and Poland. (Warschauerpakt 2007)[19]

From 2006 to 2009, the group grew to include the support of more than 300 German celebrities who sponsored activism in Poland through press work in the German media, fundraising for the Warsaw marches, organizing the participation of Germans at those marches, and collecting signatures for various petitions of solidarity with LGBT Poles (Warschauerpakt 2007). These efforts included printing T-shirts and hosting concerts to generate funds, as well as organizing buses to take Berliners to attend Polish marches. The group promoted their campaign to Berlin's LGBT community. Posters calling for involvement in Poland were visible in many of the social spaces described above, including in gay bars and clubs, LGBT health and social service centers, and at the yearly Gay-Lesbian Street Fair and the Christopher Street Day parade – where floats and information booths were adorned with fliers calling for action in Poland (interviews no. 2, 4, and 6). Figure 3.5, taken at the 2009 Berlin Christopher Street Day parade, captures this sentiment. It shows a man holding a poster calling in Polish for "*Solidarność Gejów*" (Gay Solidarity) below an image of side-by-side German and Polish flags encircled by the EU stars.

Berlin's LGBT community is also connected and accessible through free magazines, such as *Siegessäule*, which published interviews and press releases on the Polish situation. Such press releases, framed in a language of European solidarity, are explicit in their call for action. For example:

On the occasion of President Kaczyński's visit, we invite all brave and engaged persons who care about German–Polish relations and European solidarity in the struggle for equality for all, to come to Cracow and Warsaw with us. Polish NGOs are organizing CSDs [Christopher Street Day parades] and need international support. Marches will be held in Cracow on April 28, 2006 and in Warsaw on June 10, 2006. (Maneo-Tolerancja 2006)[20]

When asked what fueled the involvement of prominent Germans, and if they had connections to Poland, an organizer responded, "No, they were simply gay" (interview no. 124). Above, I emphasized that social spaces bring LGBT people together and, through generating interpersonal visibility, can introduce a political dimension to LGBT identity. The

---

[19] Translated from the German by the author.
[20] Translated from the German by the author.

FIGURE 3.5. "Solidarność Gejów," Berlin, 2009.
Photo taken by author at Berlin's Christopher Street Day parade, June 27, 2009.

space to broker such networks is central to transnational activism: "The most important role from my experiences is personal contacts, and in Poland they would not have been possible" (interview no. 124). These personal contacts resulted in funding opportunities and organizational ties between Germany and Poland.

Transnational activists and political elites

The organizers of the equality marches explained their connections to the prominent European politicians who supported them through networks of European LGBT organizations and friendships that were formed at social events in Germany (interviews no. 124 and 125). The organizers, who were based in Berlin and Warsaw, first established connections to German politicians, such as Claudia Roth, Volker Beck, Renate Künast, and Klaus Wowereit, because of their accessibility. According to Beck, a German Green Party parliamentarian who attended Warsaw marches in 2005, 2006, and 2010, he first became involved in the Polish equality marches after a friend at the German Lesben- und Schwulenverband in Deutschland (Lesbian and Gay Federation Germany, LSVD) contacted him (interviews no. 1 and 127). Activists said shared ideas on LGBT rights brought them into contact with Beck and Roth: "We have similar political ideas. They knew what [we were] working on … We became friends over beers and dinner" (interview no. 124).

In turn, these politicians had connections to sympathetic colleagues at the European level and in other EU member states. Alongside the German parliamentarians, representatives from Ireland, Norway, Sweden, and the United Kingdom attended the march. This support was organized through the contacts of German parliamentarians (for instance, Roth was active on LGBT issues as a member of the European Parliament from 1985 to 1998) and activists within the network of European LGBT organizations, such as ILGA-Europe's umbrella network (interview no. 124). ILGA-Europe regularly writes letters to authorities in states where marches will take place, to "point out safety problems and to let them know they will be watched from the outside" (interview no. 143). The European Parliament's Intergroup can also financially support the attendance of some MEPs at LGBT marches (interview no. 126). While groups connected to EU institutions are primarily involved in lobbying, they can be active in mobilizing a political elite – especially after the 2005 Equality March generated so much attention among LGBT organizations. By 2006, thirty-two representatives from fifteen different European parliaments attended the Warsaw Equality March (interview no. 124). An international presence has persisted in Warsaw, even as antigay violence at such events has waned. In 2014, twenty-seven ambassadors based in Warsaw signed a letter supporting the Equality March (Radio Poland 2014).

Mechanisms of change in Poland

Transnational and local Polish activists rely heavily on European frames, and on mechanisms of European socialization, to press for LGBT recognition in Poland. This section describes these tactical frames and socialization mechanisms and emphasizes that activists legitimized the LGBT issue through the constitutive effect of shared EU membership, not through their ties to leading member states.

Being "European": framing and norm brokerage

The actors involved in Polish LGBT activism had to develop innovative and appealing frames in order to deliver a coherent message on LGBT recognition to state and society (Kuhar 2011). For Polish LGBT activists, such appeal resided predominantly with the EU and the values it disseminates on LGBT rights. The literature assumes it is possible to make frames resonate with dominant cultural values or to "graft" the new idea to preexisting norms. While LGBT activists usually use agreed-upon human rights frames (Seckinelgin 2009; Waites 2009), finding resonance is exponentially more difficult with a norm that a large part of most societies considers "unnatural" (Nussbaum 2010). This critical distinction alters the strategies that LGBT activists use, since they have to be highly cognizant of the domestic context. The process requires the presence of LGBT activists with deeply rooted local knowledge working as brokers between the international and domestic ideas to make the norm fit locally.

Transnational activists involved in Poland faced a dual challenge. Because Polish nationalism is largely grounded in Catholic values and anti-German sentiment, both sexual deviance and German influence resonate poorly in Poland. According to organizers, "In 2005 and 2006 we were afraid that too many Germans would come. And we would again have the same propaganda, that the Germans want to come here and destroy [Polish] values" (interview no. 124). A central concern for LGBT activists is that transnational demonstrations bring those accustomed to transgressive visibility in their home states into societies where sexual minorities are largely invisible, which can be counterproductive. According to the chairman of Lambda-Warszawa, local activists were worried that Germans would bring the same level of public sexual expression to Warsaw that they were familiar with at the Christopher Street Day parade in Berlin (interview no. 139). In Poland, she says, "we are not looking to throw a party, but a political demonstration" (Götsch 2006). Open expressions of sexuality are easily stigmatized by right-wing political parties – for example, the League of Polish Families – and right-wing media, such as the Catholic Radio Maria (Ramet 2006); indeed, some Polish activists find such transgressive visibility works against their goals and fuels a debate about the effect of cultural misunderstandings between Poles and Germans (Götsch 2006).

Despite the usual right-wing critics, however, activists were able successfully to reframe the message as one of European responsibility, purposely shifting attention away from the fact that Germans were protesting for LGBT rights, by highlighting that Europeans were protesting for democratic values. The idea of the EU does not carry the same historical baggage as bilateral relations between Poland and its neighbors; instead, Poland's "return to Europe" is often associated with security and independence from communist oppression and a role as a modern partner within the society of EU states. European regulations are clear about how European societies "should" think about LGBT issues. While the topic is often domestically opposed as the imposition of foreign states' values, Poland's membership in the EU makes the issue less foreign. The ability to persuade is increased when "the socializing agency or individual is an authoritative member of the in-group to which the target belongs or wants to belong" (Checkel 2006, 364).[21]

When the Polish Right criticized Beck's involvement because he is German, his response was that Germany is a member of one of the most democratic clubs in the world and thus has an obligation to promulgate those values in a fellow EU member state (interview no. 127). Similarly, Roth says that conservative "governments [were] naturally critical of [her] traveling into their country to demonstrate for the equal treatment of LGBT people, which has [involved her] being denied a visa from Russia to attend a march in 2006" (interview no. 128). Within the EU, however, her engagement is about responsibilities associated with EU membership: "This has nothing to do with the German–Polish friendship; among friends one must say what does not work, especially among member states of the EU" (interview no. 128).

LGBT activism was framed in the language of "European" democratic values because those values resonated in Poland (interview no. 125). Examples of this frame include the Warschauerpakt T-shirts worn at demonstrations, which read "Europa = Tolerancja." The Warsaw marches' themes also strategically used vertical Polish and European frames. For example, the 2007 and 2008 themes have biblical references: "Love Your Neighbor" and "Culture of Love." Fittingly, Catholics were often directly engaged in LGBT marches in Poland (see Figure 3.6). The 2006 and 2010 themes were European: "Culture of Diversity" and "Wolność, Równość, Tolerancja" (Liberty, Equality, Tolerance [alluding to the French Revolution]). Figure 3.7, an image of Claudia Roth marching in Warsaw in 2006, illustrates the European framing. She is depicted walking in front of EU and rainbow flags and an LSVD banner reading "*Das*

[21] Similarly, psychologists have argued LGBT actors should make common group memberships other than sexual orientation salient (e.g. social, political, religious, and ethnic) to influence change among attitudes of the societal majority (Herek 2004, 14).

FIGURE 3.6. "Catholics We Love You," Warsaw, 2010.
Photo taken by author at Warsaw's EuroPride march, July 17, 2010.

FIGURE 3.7. European frames in Warsaw, 2006.
Claudia Roth walks in the Equality March in Warsaw, June 10, 2006 (AP Photo/ Alik Keplicz).

Fundament des Europarats sind die Menschenrechte" (Human rights are the basis of the Council of Europe). While European framing is effective in this Polish context, it should be noted that the frame is contingent on historically repeated phases of Euro-optimism and -skepticism – upward and downward trends in popular opinion toward European integration – and on context. The frame has less potency in Serbia, for example, which lacks a public majority eager to be part of the EU. Nonetheless, a vertical frame of LGBT issues as European, and thus indirectly also as Polish, is evident.

In consultation with their Polish counterparts, norm entrepreneurs use the same European frame in other states. Within Germany as well, activists framed the call for engagement in a language of human rights responsibility based on European citizenship. Leading up to former Polish President Lech Kaczyński's visit to Berlin in March 2006, Tolerancja po Polsku called on German Chancellor Angela Merkel, German Foreign Minister Frank-Walter Steinmeier, and all representatives of Germany's political parties to address the human rights situation in Poland, with the premise that the "EU is not only a federation of states, but also a community of citizens with equal rights" (Maneo-Tolerancja 2006).[22] While the group addressed only German politicians and citizens, it labeled their duties European: "For this reason it is imperative that all European politicians must protect and defend human and citizen rights – even if for those outside their national borders" (Maneo-Tolerancja 2006).

The tactics of LGBT activism in CEE have contributed to the process that Thomas Risse (2014, 10) and his collaborators argue connect the EU to the public, in that "European and EU issues, policies, and actors [become] sufficiently visible in the various public spheres." Local and Berlin-based Polish activists, in consultation with their foreign counterparts, predominantly called for mobilization of support and recognition of LGBT peoples in a language of European values and responsibilities. Aware of historical Polish sensibilities and domestic norms, they acted as norm brokers between different domestic contexts (contexts that were accustomed to incongruous types of LGBT expression), successfully framing the issue to manufacture local resonance.

Deliberation and learning through European socialization
Framing LGBT issues in a European discourse is part of a socialization mechanism that inducts actors into the norms of the EU community. In

---

[22] Translated from the German by the author.

large part, norm entrepreneurs undertake the effort of mobilization to generate a discourse about LGBT issues, which introduces members to EU norms and establishes their appropriateness. European institutions champion the norm of protecting sexual minorities, but these norms do not flow freely. They require actors – and the channels that connect them – to mobilize and to validate the norms that proponents feel ought to be learned. Communities learn when they reassess or question their beliefs and ways of doing things in light of new observations. The mobilization of actors in the EU framework – both horizontally and vertically – and the interaction of those actors with actors in the target state triggers the deliberation and learning mechanisms of socialization, which play a key role in this process by introducing new-adopter states to the LGBT issue. The remainder of the section explores the socialization engendered by the interaction between transnational actors and actors in the target state. In particular, I look at how the dialogue on LGBT issues engages Polish state authorities – politicians, police forces, and foreign officers – and the media.

Political elites and political parties

The presence of colleagues from EU institutions, other EU states, and political parties represented in the European Parliament aids the socialization of the Polish political elite and demonstrates the impact of transnational mobilization. European colleagues encouraged and supported the pioneering work of some Polish parliamentarians – such as early LGBT rights supporters Kazimierz Kutz (nonpartisan) and Izabela Jaruga-Nowacka (Unia Pracy)[23] – by marching with them and legitimizing their involvement. The emerging support of Poland's Democratic Left Alliance (SLD) for LGBT rights illustrates how socialization can work. About twenty SLD members marched in the 2010 EuroPride, which was puzzling because surveys showed that supporters of the party – many of whom live in rural areas – are more homophobic than the constituents of the conservative Law and Justice Party. Activists attribute the SLD position in part to EU socialization:

Outside influence [from institutions like the European Parliament] is motivational. These politicians read the outside stances of their parties, and whether or not they are convinced, they know what it means to be a Social Democrat [in

---

[23] While Jaruga-Nowacka was part of the Unia Pracy (not the SLD), she played an important role in Leszek Miller's government and attended the illegal march in 2005 as a vice-prime minister.

Europe], which includes being open to LGBTs ... [Polish political parties now] have to know about the topic not to embarrass themselves at international congresses. (interview no. 124)

This marks a change from "the early 2000s, [when] it was obvious that Polish politicians did not know how to talk about it" (interviews no. 8 and 124). Similarly, the new political party Ruch Palikota (Palikot's Movement, called Twój Ruch [Your Movement] after 2013) – which garnered 10 percent of the vote in the October 2011 elections on a platform of representing "modern Poland" – made LGBT issues a central theme of its campaign (group no. 206).

Police forces

The presence of international diplomats – from member states or the European Parliament – also attracts police protection for the protesters and international and domestic media attention. This was the case when German parliamentarians attended the illegal Warsaw march in 2005. The Polish government's secret service was obliged to protect the foreign parliamentarians, even though the illegal parade was originally denied any police protection. It should be noted that early mobilizations, when LGBT people first start occupying a visible space in the public sphere, often face violent attacks by countermobilizations. In contemporary CEE, marchers have been violently attacked and injured. Many interview participants described their experiences of physical violence. Even in the heavily policed events I participated in during my fieldwork, participants were pelted with eggs, dairy products (which smell at high temperatures), and vegetables. Yet the confirmed attendance of Beck, Roth, Künast, and others motivated the organizers because they knew "in advance that nothing terrible could happen" in terms of safety (interviews no. 124 and 132), safety being a common reason for canceled attempts at public LGBT mobilization. "The idea was having many parliamentarians there to *protect* [the march] ... [and] because embassies were present, the Polish government had to react to prohibit attacks on foreign diplomats" (interview no. 125, emphasis added). Beck describes the same process when he marched in Poland, Latvia, Lithuania, and Russia:

It is not just about creating media attention, but also about concrete support from the authorities. When the ambassadors from Sweden or France, for example, decide to join the march too – as was the case in Vilnius last year – the authorities at the local level have to react differently. Then they authorize Pride marches, and the police protect the participants instead of protecting counterdemonstrations organized by the extreme right. Of course the presence of prominent international figures also help[s] to create media attention for the causes of the gay and lesbian movement. (interview no. 127)

This human shield effect adds a transnational dimension to a process described by Doug McAdam (1988), which he illustrated with the example of white volunteers working on the Student Nonviolent Coordinating Committee campaigns in southern states during the American civil rights movement. Notwithstanding the troubling ethical issues surrounding the media fascination with Whites helping "poor" Blacks, White volunteers brought with them both media attention and police protection. Following this, countless FBI agents attended campaigns to ensure that "nothing bad" could happen (McAdam 1988, 39–40).

As police are authorities of the state, police protection bestows a shield of state legitimacy on LGBT mobilization. Horizontal socialization among European police forces – for example, the presence of London police forces at training sessions on protecting demonstrators' human rights in Warsaw – is an important outcome of cooperation that furthers future LGBT mobilization and visibility (interview no. 129).

The Foreign Ministry

Tactics of European socialization guided many of the decisions expatriate activists made outside Poland as well. Even demonstrations that took place in Germany were organized to create a diplomatic dialogue. In 2005, for example, Tolerancja po Polsku organized a demonstration in front of the Polish Embassy in Berlin to protest a repressed equality march in Poznan and call on the German government to condemn the Polish government's reaction to the march (Maneo-Tolerancja 2005). The 500-person equality march in Poznan had resulted in more than 100 arrests. The idea behind the demonstration, however, was not to attract large crowds or employ confrontational tactics – only 20 to 30 peaceful protesters attended and the Polish Embassy was informed three weeks prior (interview no. 124). Instead, the strategy was to generate a dialogue about Poland among high-ranking German political authorities that would then provoke a response by the Polish Foreign Ministry; if pressure came from external diplomatic authorities, it would be more likely to provoke a Polish reaction (Bączkowski 2008, 36). Connections between LGBT organizations and LGBT-friendly politicians created a platform to make issues public when they arose. Berlin activists described the process, which began when they contacted their allies in the German government, "first the ones that you know personally ... [who] formulate an official inquiry and send it to the party docket" (interview no. 124). Activists thought that the Polish administration would ignore grievances they themselves voiced but be obliged to react to inquiries from representatives of foreign governments.

In addition, the Polish Ambassador in Berlin brought up the demonstration and the issue it promoted with the Foreign Ministry in Warsaw (interview no. 124). Without an official protocol on the stance of the Polish government on LGBT public assembly, the Foreign Ministry had to formulate a response and articulate its general commitment to human rights and democratic values (interview no. 133). "So from the back door, [the activists] reached [their] goal, which was that everyone would know about the demonstration," generating public visibility even though the demonstration itself was unspectacular and ended with a friendly coffee invitation at the Polish Embassy (interview no. 124). The central motivation of such demonstrations "was not to demonstrate, not to riot, but simply to create the right environment through dialogue" (interview no. 124). Creating the right environment meant obliging the Polish Foreign Ministry to formulate a response, and transnational activists achieved this by involving the Polish ambassador and German political authorities (interview no. 133).

Domestic media

The presence of guest marchers also generated media attention, which made the issue visible publically. Domestically this engendered a discourse within Polish society, and internationally it drew outside attention to the social situation of LGBT Poles (interview no. 128). Polish LGBT organizations confirm that the LGBT issue has become increasingly visible in Poland since a series of campaigns began at the turn of the century, when the issue was virtually invisible (interviews no. 8 and 9). According to the former president of KPH, even the left-wing Polish media did not know how to write about homosexuality, and the media response to early campaigns was largely negative (interview no. 8). In newspapers across the political spectrum, a naive discourse questioned the campaign's break with "traditional" societal structures. This was "because there were no norms of conduct on the issue, there was no popular discussion of homosexuality before then" (interview no. 8). After a 2003 gay pride day in Warsaw, with an unprecedented 3,000 marchers, "the media largely ignored the event" (Pasek 2003). In the years following 2005, press reports have changed their discourse, and media have become more objective (interview no. 8).

The internal dialogue the equality marches started made LGBT issues publically visible domestically: "In Poland, the parades are just a symbol. We know we won't have a large [parade] in Poland. But we know that once a year we will have a discussion about tolerance, about homo-marriage" (interview no. 124). While this dialogue is often initially hostile, Polish LGBT activists say that the Polish media's reporting on LGBT issues has dramatically improved in the last ten years, in large part because of the visibility of the issue and the attention it generated in other EU member states. Internationally, press on the situation of LGBT Poles generates interest and heightens political pressure from the EU and other international institutions. It also increases awareness and further encourages the involvement of foreign LGBT persons, like those discussed above. International press coverage rose from a few dozen articles after the 2005 march to more than 300 articles after the 2010 march – with coverage ranging from *Gazeta Wyborcza* to *Al-Jazeera* (Equality Foundation Archives). According to Beck, "In Poland ... the debate on these issues has changed dramatically since 2005" (interview no. 127).

Summary and conclusion

The mobilization by and on behalf of LGBT people has become truly transnational in scope. In February 2013, a young organization of Balkan activists called Kampagne Solidarnost (Campaign Solidarity) hosted a meeting at the SchwuZ,[24] one of Berlin's social spaces that Polish activists plastered with fliers calling for mobilization in Poland in 2005 (group no. 210). Like their Polish counterparts before them, the activists of Solidarnost gathered sympathetic ears to draw attention to the situation of LGBT people in the Balkans and to discuss how to move forward after the violent repression of the 2012 Belgrade Pride event. Solidarnost is one of many illustrations of a cooperative transnationalism that has helped to unite disparate actors and to facilitate a movement that thinks outside of national and geographic boundaries.

After the 2005 Equality March, Bączkowski – along with four Polish-based activists – brought a case against Poland for prohibiting the protest before the ECtHR. With the help of a network of volunteer lawyers in Berlin and Warsaw, and legal resources provided by the

---

[24] SchwuZ is short for SchwulenZentrum (Gay Center). Founded in 1977, the center grew out of an initiative to create a meeting place for communication by the Homosexuelle Aktion West-Berlin – an organization symbolic of the birth of the German gay liberation movement in 1971.

Warsaw office of the Helsinki Human Rights Foundation, they filed the bilingual 500-page complaint. The court decided in their favor, making similar demonstrations legal and entitling them to police protection in all Polish cities. While the ruling applies to all demonstrations (including those by the extreme right), activists see it as a fundamentally important step for democratization in Poland. The ruling has further transnational implications, because Russian LGBT activists filed a similar complaint in Strasbourg. They worked closely with Bączkowski, who says the group recycled the successful complaint, "simply changing names and locations" (interview no. 124). Based on Russia's membership in the CoE and the Polish precedent, Russian activists won their case in 2011, though ILGA activists point out that implementation was always expected to be arduous in Russia, which is not subject to the norms of EU membership (interview no. 143).

I have argued that Europeanization offers both vertical and horizontal political opportunities for the political mobilization of transnational LGBT actors. Horizontal opportunities are particularly useful for non-institutionalized mobilization in a target state's public sphere and bring together a wide range of transnational actors. Vertical opportunities provide the legitimacy and institutional clout to mobilize European political elites to the target state. Alongside obliging governments to introduce some LGBT protections, they also provide the frames and socialization mechanisms that activists use to make their message resonate among state and media authorities in the target country.

It should be emphasized that cooperative transnationalism comes with cultural misunderstandings that trigger hostile reactions from some domestic groups, who see such activism as outside imposition from historically unwelcome neighbor states. Local activists, who work as norm brokers, compensate by framing the issue to resonate locally. In doing so, they play a critical role in framing and disseminating the norm, persuading international organizations to endorse it, and coaxing states into compliance, thereby fueling public deliberation and beginning the process of issue ownership (Keck and Sikkink 1998).

Serious challenges associated with sexual minority rights in Poland remain. Though the steps recounted in this chapter may be small, they are nevertheless fundamentally important, and it is clear that the debate in Poland on sexual minorities is changing. In recent years, the construction, burning, and reconstruction of a rainbow-colored arch on a prominent square in Warsaw embodies the contested nature of the struggle, but it also signifies the resilience of LGBT visibility in the public sphere. It is also worth noting that in 2011 Poland elected Robert Biedroń and Anna Grodzka, its first openly LGBT parliamentarians, both activists and former presidents of Polish LGBT organizations (KPH and Trans-Fuzja, respectively). Anna Grodzka is only the third openly trans parliamentarian I know of to have been elected to federal office at that point in history. (The first and second were in New Zealand and Italy.) In 2014, Robert Biedroń would be elected the mayor of Słupsk, a northern city by the Baltic Sea, achieving another milestone as the first openly gay mayor in Poland. Leading up to that victory, Biedroń optimistically remarked, "I see how fast Polish society has learned its lesson of tolerance. So I am very optimistic and happy with Polish society – and proud" (Gera 2014). In 2015, Poland overwhelming passed a gender recognition bill, but newly elected President Andrzej Duda did not sign it. The result of the October 2015 elections – which brought the conservative Polish Law and Justice Party (PiS) back to power – will surely limit progress in this area for four years.

While this chapter has not drawn a causal arrow between mobilization and broader social and legal developments in Poland, the following chapters do explore the link between channels of visibility and change. They investigate the effects of transnational channels and other domestic conditions on sociolegal change across European states. I turn first, in Chapter 4, to how the transnational activist networks and mechanisms just explored have changed the diffusion of LGBT legislation in both the new (EU-12) and old (EU-15) member states.

4

Complying with new norms: LGBT rights legislation

Gay rights are human rights, and human rights are gay rights.
    – *Hillary Clinton, 2011*

In 1948, Axel and Eigil Axgil and their colleagues founded Denmark's first gay rights organization, Kredsen af 1948 (The Circle of 1948). Inspired by the UN Declaration of Human Rights of that year, homophile organizations like Kredsen af 1948 began to lobby states for gay rights. For affluent democracies, the birth of the gay liberation movement and the dawn of the 1970s heralded a marked, albeit gradual, expansion in the legal protections that states provided gay and lesbian minorities. By October 1, 1989, the first same-sex couples – including the Axgils, who celebrated four decades as a couple and as human rights activists – had entered into registered partnerships in Denmark. Although progress has been slow and has often provoked countermovements intended to block progressive legislation and to promote anti-LGBT policies, the proliferation of LGBT-friendly legislation has amplified the voice of a once politically invisible group and has become a recurrent theme in modern European politics.

Legal recognition of LGBT minorities varies greatly across European states, however. In this chapter, I explore LGBT norm diffusion by examining legislative changes across states. Europe is distinctive in that it houses states at both ends of the global spectrum of LGBT egalitarianism, with wide discrepancies both in legislation, which this chapter examines, and in the social acceptance of LBGT minorities (Chapter 5). While some states (e.g. Denmark) quickly became the world's leading advocates for

LGBT rights and provided the most extensive legal measures to their citizenry, others have only recently decriminalized homosexuality (e.g. Romania in 2001). Furthermore, some states in the region have introduced or proposed legislation that retrenches the rights of LGBT minorities, such as bans on same-sex unions or bills banning gay propaganda. Figure 4.1 shows how EU member states have varied in adopting LGBT legislation over three decades. The 12-point LGBT legislation score counts various pieces of pro-LGBT legislation, described in detail in Table A.1 in the Appendix.[1]

Transnational activists have long publicized this imbalance in legal recognition of LGBT minority rights as a central concern for those working to achieve social equality across Europe. The observed variation also raises important questions for scholars of international relations and social movements: what accounts for such different levels of legal recognition of sexual minorities across European states? Is change due to heightened cooperation with individuals and groups in states that have previously adopted the legislation? Under what domestic preconditions (of the recipient state) do international norms regarding legal rights for sexual minorities proliferate? Finally, who are the agents who spread these norms, and what are the channels of norm diffusion? Few norms incite as much controversy in contemporary world politics as sexual minority rights, yet a growing number of states are adopting these norms into their legal frameworks. These rapid and sweeping changes have been unexpected, particularly in countries that have not historically recognized human rights and sexual diversity. Understanding the differential rates and timing of adoption brings to light the channels – both transnational and international – and domestic conditions of diffusion. Furthermore, understanding how the state responds to contentious norms offers important insights on normative change in world politics.

This chapter examines why LGBT rights legislation is introduced sooner and more frequently in some cases, and later and less frequently

---

[1] The overall legislation score is a count of the following provisions: anti-discrimination in employment, goods and services, and constitutional recognition; hate crimes based on sexual orientation recognized as an aggravating circumstance and/or incitement to hatred based on sexual orientation prohibited; same-sex partnership recognized for cohabitation, registered partnership, and marriage; same-sex couples' parenting rights for joint adoption and second-parent adoption; and sexual offenses provisions for equal age of consent and same-sex activity legal (cf. Table A.1 in the Appendix for the five categories that these 12 measures comprise).

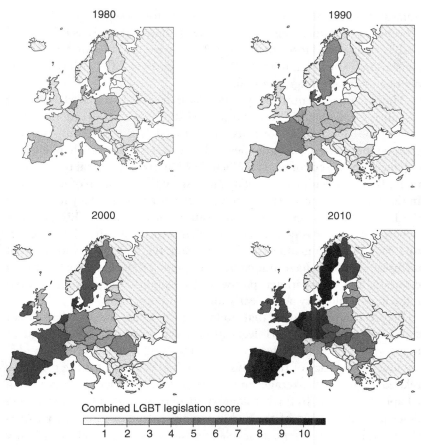

FIGURE 4.1. Mapping the introduction of LGBT rights legislation in EU states, 1980–2010.

in others. I focus on pieces of LGBT legislation because they constitute an observable consequence of norm diffusion, and one that is easily identifiable and evident (to varying degrees) in all the cases studied. Building on the efforts of international relations, social movements, and Europeanization scholars, I seek to explain the diffusion of LGBT rights policies by bridging theories of cognitive change among social actors and relational channels between states. I identify areas for further research by systematically exploring the (non)diffusion of five categories of LGBT legislation (both protective and equality measures) in multiple domestic contexts, and by specifying the transnational channels, domestic actors, and conditions responsible for change. To address the aforementioned questions, I employ a cross-national analysis of changed LGBT rights legislation in Europe. I compare the adoption of LGBT legislation by newly admitted EU member states in CEE with that of EU member states of longer standing.

This chapter's central proposition is that transnational channels of visibility, tying together new and old EU states, can accelerate the diffusion of LGBT norms in contexts where LGBT issues have only recently become politicized (i.e. the new EU-12 states). These channels can enhance the salience of norms. When they have transnational ties, domestic LGBT organizations can act as catalysts in the adoption of legislation. In the absence of these organizations, societies are more likely to perceive the LGBT norm as an external imposition. By contrast, in EU-15 states (where the norm was politicized earlier), it seems likely that domestic factors have played a greater role in increasing the likelihood and speed of diffusion than they have among new adopters. I thus distinguish between domestic and transnational pathways to visibility, suggesting that their influence should vary across early and new adopters.

Before examining data that address both when and to what extent states introduce pro-LGBT legislation, I elaborate on my argument of norm visibility as it relates to the diffusion of law. I continue by discussing the findings of the analysis, providing evidence for the processes related to norm brokerage and sociopolitical channels I described in Chapters 2 and 3. To further contextualize these findings, I close with a descriptive discussion of the highly symbolic issue of same-sex partnerships, explaining the important role of transnational channels of visibility in that domain of LGBT rights adoption.

Split Europe: domestic versus transnational influence

The achievement of norm visibility in new EU member states requires a specific set of actors and channels connecting the transnational and the domestic. The states most likely to adopt LGBT legislation are those that are the most porous in terms of political and social connectedness to other states. Furthermore, the adoption of such legislation is more likely when transnationally embedded LGBT organizations – norm brokers – exist to manufacture a narrative that can resonate with domestic norms. As I demonstrated with Poland, these actors help to interpret the norm, and send a clear signal to the state that norm compliance is necessary if the state is to fulfill its role in international society. Thus, my theoretical expectations here link back to the argument outlined in Chapter 2 and the mechanisms presented in Chapter 3, emphasizing the socialization processes created by visibility through the mechanisms of framing, brokerage, and social learning.

We should also expect systematic differences between contexts in which the LGBT norm was politicized during the 1970s (e.g. many old EU-15 states), and contexts in which the issue has only recently gained widespread public visibility (e.g. the new EU-12 states).[2] Many new member states have long and rich histories of LGBT life (Chetaille 2011; McCajor Hall 2009), but LGBT identity was expressed less openly in public than in many EU-15 states. The diffusion and institutionalization of norms may be a two-stage process, with the first, more internal stage occurring in a set of leading states where local communities respond to domestic political problems and crystalize a norm. In the second stage, other states may adopt the norm as they seek external legitimacy.[3] As a panel of LGBT activists explained, on issues like same-sex partnerships, "Eastern Europe has often skipped the domestic steps that Western states went through in their domestic developments" (panel no. 212). I expect greater norm diffusion in new EU member states as domestic LGBT organizations are connected to and furthered by transnational networks, and as states become more permeable to transnational and international influences.

To make that case, I combine several theoretical approaches and add insights from the contentious politics literature. Existing explanations characterize rights legislation as diffusing to states: when authorities fear the costs associated with international pressure (i.e. political conditionality and economic incentives); when they become convinced of the norm's appropriateness (typically via socialization); when their preexisting domestic norms resonate with an international norm (e.g. high levels of democracy and modernization); and when their advocacy organizations are embedded in transnational networks. I consider multiple dimensions of diffusion in a complex, multilevel, interactive environment, following Rudra Sil and Peter Katzenstein's (2010) call to move beyond grand narratives (see also Lloyd, Simmons, and Stewart 2012).

---

[2] A distinction between first movers and new adopters is often overlooked. An exceptional study on the diffusion of same-sex unions by Juan Fernández and Mark Lutter (2013), for example, finds that both international and domestic theoretical factors matter, but does not take into account the subregional and state identities that others have found to privilege some diffusion factors over others (Gurowitz 2006).

[3] See also Pamela Tolbert and Lynne Zucker (1983), David Strang (1990), and Sarah Soule (1997).

Transnational LGBT organizations as norm brokers

I suspect that domestic LGBT activist organizations will experience greater success in the EU-12 states when they have the benefit of external resources. This may be particularly true for minority movements, since they can gain valuable resources for mobilization if they look outside the state. Domestic LGBT movements are deemed radical in many societies, and ties to transnational advocacy networks enhance their effectiveness in channeling grievances and affecting policy. Transnational networks can multiply opportunities for the mobilization of marginalized people – who may not have sufficient resources at home – and increase their political potential by connecting groups across borders (Montoya 2013). As I demonstrated in Chapter 3, these ties with transnational networks can yield expertise, financing, and access to political actors who can apply pressure to state authorities.[4] The Latvian group Mozaika is a typical example. It receives its core funding from the Open Society Foundations and has a strategic partnership with Amnesty International (interview no. 138). Other external actors have supported several of Mozaika's initiatives. The Belgian, Canadian, Danish, Dutch, German, Swedish, and US embassies have, for example, financed LGBT film festivals, and some have attended pride parades and pressured local police forces to protect marchers.

Levels of LGBT resources vary among EU member states, and the results of my Transnational LGBT Organizations Survey (described in detail in the Appendix) suggest that LGBT organizations in the EU-12 are resource poor and far more reliant on external grants to finance their projects than such organizations in EU-15 states. External funding sources are broadly conceived and can refer to international organizations, the governments of other countries, or foreign civil society organizations (see question 13 in the Survey Details section in the Appendix).

Alongside external resources, the local knowledge and life experiences of activists in local organizations provide actors with a valuable understanding of the domestic realm. This understanding allows them to act as brokers between the international and domestic norms, framing the issue to resonate with the policymakers in their respective contexts (Tarrow 2005b). These actors actively select foreign ideas and adapt them to local norms and practices, and I suspect that this process – more

---

[4] Resource mobilization theorists have emphasized the importance of such resources, in terms of funds and coalitions with other organizations, for the mobilization and effectiveness of movement actors (McCarthy and Zald 1977).

TABLE 4.1. *European LGBT organizations' reliance on external funding sources*

EU-12	EU-15	
83%	32%	Part of budget comes from transnational and international sources
56%	5%	Majority of budget comes from transnational and international sources
40%	42%	Entirely volunteer based

Source: Author's Transnational LGBT Organizations Survey (for questions, see Appendix), *n* = 140

than the initial fit between international and domestic norms – explains success. Thus, I look at domestic actors who are also embedded in transnational networks of change and examine how they target their own governments.

Political and social channels of visibility

In addition to the presence of domestic organizations, I also expect social and political channels to influence norm diffusion, in that they prime the contexts within which activists function by making the LGBT rights norm visible. Indeed, it is the interaction of globalization and internationalization that enhances the porousness of states. I use the terms *internationalization* – "a process that refers to territorially based exchanges across borders" (Katzenstein 2005, 22)[5] – and *transnationalization*, which emphasizes the involvement of nonstate actors in these exchanges. Countries with the highest levels of social transnationalization and political internationalization, which connect them to larger communities of states, are more likely to have channels of access to the LGBT issue. This, in turn, yields visibility. Political and social channels prime the context by allowing the aforementioned transnational actors to send a clear and legitimate signal to both society and the state. These actors can harness those ideas and adapt them, manufacturing resonance in their domestic contexts, even when such ideas do not openly exist

---

[5] Globalization refers to "a process that transcends space and compresses time" (Katzenstein 2005, 13). The process I describe falls somewhere between internationalization and globalization. Since I argue that processes of diffusion for LGBT norms are highly contingent on various regional-institutional factors, I prefer to use the term *internationalization* rather than *globalization*.

locally. The more porous the context, the easier it is for actors to frame the norm as legitimate.

These channels lead to elite- and mass-level interactions between new-adopter and leading states that make the LGBT norm visible in domestic realms. *Political internationalization* creates channels of influence by embedding states in the international communities within which the LGBT issue receives more attention. *Social transnationalization* – particularly the flow of ideas and images – taps into the international awareness of the state's society and its exposure to complex issues and norms in first-mover states. Put simply, social and political channels expose states to "the world out there" and to European norms on LGBT rights. I expect these channels of visibility to explain more than the direct impact of EU conditionality (associated with EU accession), which should only be effectual in the limited area within which it has competences. The theoretical emphasis here is on channels of visibility and the centrality of mechanisms of socialization over the hard-law mechanism of EU conditionality.[6]

The primary mechanisms at work in this process of state-level change are brokerage, framing, and social learning. Transnational actors act as brokers between the international and the domestic norms, framing (or packaging and presenting) new ideas so that they resonate with a specific audience (Khagram, Riker, and Sikkink 2002; Tarrow 2005b). Once new repertoires of practices are introduced, political channels lead to social interactions between elites that fuel a process of social learning (Haas 1991). These pathways for learning operate by sending a visible signal that promotes state support of the issue. Information flows provide visibility and give actors a framework within which to make their case. The arguments LGBT organizations advance tend to have greater currency in states that are more familiar with the images that represent and the ideas that are associated with LGBT rights. Even if this visibility is negatively perceived, it is still effectual by virtue of creating a discourse.

Explaining how rights legislation spreads

The argument outlined above builds on a vast literature that analyzes how and when states alter their positions in response to international

---

[6] In a related article that uses this data (Ayoub 2015a), I elaborated on another theoretical aspect of the findings, arguing that new-adopter states are more reliant on international sources of change and that they have more to gain – in terms of state reputation and image – by adopting higher levels of LGBT rights legislation. While that same finding is apparent in the analyses presented below, the theoretical focus is different.

ideas and norms. Previous scholarship explaining the international diffusion of social policies has generally fallen into one of three camps (or a combination of them), wherein successful diffusion is linked to the presence of: (1) advocacy networks connecting international and domestic politics, (2) transnational and international channels of socialization and/or sanctioning pressure, and (3) bottom-up domestic resonance. These frameworks inform the core hypotheses in this analysis.

Transnational advocacy networks

My analysis suggests that relational channels of diffusion have an effect on LGBT politics in new-adopter states. Transnational advocacy groups play an important role in influencing the international diffusion of rights and anti-discrimination legislation, as these groups are particularly experienced at channeling a social group's grievances to the relevant authorities.[7] In particular, ILGA-Europe contributes to making legal norms visible by lobbying European institutions, providing local groups with resources and expertise, reporting movement activity and state-sponsored discrimination to the press, and calling on political authorities to address states when they deem their actions to be out of sync with EU standards. Evelyne Paradis, executive director of ILGA-Europe, sent a video message to the 2013 Minsk Pride (in this case outside EU borders) that provides an example of these dynamics:

Dear friends from Belarus, I am speaking to you today on behalf of ILGA-Europe to express our full support to the Pride organizers and to the LGBTI community in Belarus. The Minsk Pride ... is you exercising your right to freedom of assembly, and it is a huge step forward, an important step forward, in gaining *visibility* for your rights and your issues. It is also a hugely important moment to raise awareness about the rights of LGBTI people, and to gain solidarity and support from many people hopefully inside your country but certainly well beyond. ILGA-Europe considers that it is a very, very courageous step on the part of human rights defenders in Belarus, given the very difficult situation for civil

---

[7] Much scholarship has charted the capabilities of transnational advocacy networks (e.g. Keck and Sikkink 1998; Roggeband 2010). Following an important study on liberalization of sex by David Frank and Elizabeth Mceneaney (1999), Soule's work on minority rights legislation offers substantial evidence that social movement activity affects the introduction and diffusion of rights legislation for various minorities, including LGBT groups, in the United States (Soule 2004b; Soule and King 2006). On a global scale, and using the case of the feminist movement, Htun and Weldon (2012) have found the same strong effect of movements on social policies to combat violence against women. Focusing particularly on LGBT rights, David Paternotte and Kelly Kollman (2013) emphasize both a number of domestic factors and the centrality of advocacy networks that organizations like ILGA-Europe foster.

society organizations in your country, and we commend you for that very courageous step. We express our full solidarity with the Pride organizers, and we wish [them] strength, determination, and faith that this will be a positive step forward. In the past year, neighboring countries to Belarus, Ukraine, and Moldova, have seen authorities properly protect Pride marchers. We hope that your authorities will follow in these footsteps and provide you with the adequate protection you deserve. We send you our sincerest wishes for a wonderful and safe Minsk Pride, and may it be a huge step forward in your struggle for the recognition of your rights. Best wishes![8]

To accompany the message, ILGA-Europe formulated a letter that referenced the rights of Pride participants, as stipulated by the UN and the CoE.

I predict that the transnationalization of a new-adopter state's LGBT organizations will provide the movement with resources that, in combination with the domestic movement's ability to tailor the message to localities, promote greater domestic visibility. These messages send a clear and appropriate signal to policymakers while supporting successful diffusion of the norm.

> HYPOTHESIS 1a: The likelihood of introducing LGBT legislation increases when domestic LGBT organizations become embedded in the transnational activist networks Europe provides.

Sanction and socialization

Direct and indirect channels can engender change through socialization based on interactions across borders, a process I described in detail in Chapter 3.[9] Interactions between states in an international community lead to different cognitive understandings of what is acceptable via mechanisms of learning and deliberation (Risse 2000). A state's participation in international organizations can lead to a series of socialization outcomes

---

[8] December 9, 2013, emphasis added. Source: http://ilga.org/ilga-europe-support-letter-to-minsk-pride-2013/.

[9] World polity and constructivist scholars focus on such informal processes of influence, arguing that international norms exert an influence on states by defining the contours of appropriate behavior (Finnemore and Sikkink 1998; Ingebritsen 2002; Klotz 1995; Legro 1997; J. W. Meyer *et al.* 1997). For many international relations scholars, rights legislation diffuses to states when those states are convinced of the norm's social appropriateness (socialization) or when they fear the costs of international pressures (political conditionality and economic incentives). These theories – one linked to socialization; the other, to material incentives – posit logics of consequences and appropriateness, respectively.

on human rights, including changes in a state's self-perception of its role in the international community, as Brian Greenhill (2010; 2015) has demonstrated. When states are members of international organizations, their representatives are often required to confront the LGBT issue and take a stand.

Consider the sharp media criticism that British Tories faced when they and PiS formed the European Conservatives and Reformists Group (ECR) in the European Parliament. While their cooperation was based on anti-federalist Euroskepticism, the media criticized the Tories (at home and abroad) for cooperating with the PiS, because many PiS members espoused homophobic rhetoric around the time of heightened politicized homophobia in Poland (Helm 2010). The international media's negative portrayal was so severe that some group members went to great lengths to prove that they were not homophobic; for example, Tory politicians attended gay pride parades in Warsaw. A further illustration of such political socialization is the fact that foreign embassies now actively support LGBT visibility by backing the local activist campaigns with rhetorical and financial support and by organizing floats for LGBT pride parades and marches across the continent (interviews no. 117 and 132). While this can provoke the same type of negative reactions described in Chapter 3 (for instance, the British Embassy was accused of meddling in Polish internal affairs when it raised the rainbow flag in Warsaw in 2008 [interview no. 8]), it nonetheless furthers the perception that LGBT rights are among the norms that define European international society.

Other indirect channels of diffusion are social – for example, television shows imported from cultural powers in Western Europe and North America have, since the 1990s, featured increasing numbers of gay characters. Studies show that, in the United States, exposure to media with gay themes positively influences social attitudes and policymakers' actions regarding LGBT issues (Cooley and Burkholder 2011; Garretson 2015). In Europe, social channels reconfigure the threat associated with minorities by making them familiar. Such channels of interaction lead to social learning, providing images and understandings of what it means to be a member of a European political and social community.

HYPOTHESIS 2a: The likelihood of introducing LGBT legislation increases when the state's level of political porousness is higher.

HYPOTHESIS 2b: The likelihood of introducing LGBT legislation increases when the state's level of social porousness is higher.

Rational institutionalists attribute domestic change to the incentives provided by international organizations and focus on the costs associated with norm adoption (Martin and Simmons 1998; Mastenbroek 2003). According to this perspective, political leaders weigh the costs and benefits of adopting a norm. In the EU, not adopting the LGBT norm can mean lost material benefits linked to economic and security cooperation at the European level. Scholars have emphasized the unique and direct role of EU conditionality in the adoption of new laws in the EU member states, with sanctioning and competition representing the central mechanisms by which this type of process occurs (Toshkov 2008; Vachudova 2005).

For several reasons, I expect that states will adopt LGBT rights legislation in part through these mechanisms. First, in the late 1990s the EU required applicant states to decriminalize homosexuality and to adopt employment anti-discrimination measures in their legal frameworks. Second, economic competition – in terms of attracting foreign investment – is increasingly impacted by a state's position on LGBT rights. For example, in its Legalize Love Campaign targeting Asia and parts of Europe, Google has formed alliances with partners (e.g. Citigroup and Ernst & Young) to pressure states wishing to retain their business to make advances in LGBT rights. Google sharply criticized the ban on same-sex partnerships in Poland, where it has three offices and regularly participates in Pride and Equality marches. Similarly, in response to the Russian Duma's extension to the national level of St. Petersburg's 2012 law banning propaganda by gays, one of Europe's largest theater companies, the Friedrichstadt Palast GmbH, severed ties with its Russian affiliates (interview no. 145). The company canceled meetings, shows, and its cultural collaboration with Russia until the Duma rejects the law. In the United States, industry leaders increasingly use this strategy to pressure states to rethink legislation that limits the rights of sexual minorities. In 2015, more than seventy technology industry executives sent a strong signal by signing a statement that criticized Indiana's Religious Freedom Restoration Act and urged Governor Mike Pence to add anti-discrimination protections for LGBT minorities. Numerous transnational and international currents of sanctioning and competition surround the LGBT issue.

HYPOTHESIS 2c: The likelihood of introducing LGBT legislation increases when the state's level of economic porousness is higher.

HYPOTHESIS 2d: The likelihood of introducing LGBT legislation increases when a state accedes to join the EU.

Finally, while this analysis assumes that the adoption of LGBT policies is connected to diffusion, I also include a variable to measure diffusion related to emulation of individual types of legislation. My rationale is that policymakers will adopt laws if they feel compelled to do so and when they observe the trend in their society of states (Meyer *et al.* 1997).

> HYPOTHESIS 2e: The likelihood of introducing LGBT legislation increases when other EU member states pass similar laws.

Domestic resonance

Certain domestic characteristics can also make some adopters more amenable or susceptible to the diffusion of norms than others. The bottom-up aspect of my analysis emphasizes the domestic political and cultural variables that condition the reception of contentious new international ideas.[10] Several domestic factors may influence the receptivity of norms concerning social minorities. Higher levels of democracy and affluence tend to correspond with a state's readiness to legislate on minority rights issues (Inglehart and Norris 2003). Domestic social spaces for LGBT identities and culture may also affect the reception of legal norms by helping minorities form associational ties and mobilize counterhegemonic identities. While Chapter 3 made the case that LGBT norm entrepreneurs gain access to social spaces in foreign contexts (which may also give individuals enough distance from their roots to come out), this part of the analysis also tests the value of access to such spaces domestically. Scholarship has also noted that Catholic and Orthodox states have been especially resistant to EU standards on sexuality (Ramet 2006, 126). While I focus on the dominant religion of states here, I distinguish it from religiosity of peoples in the following chapter.[11] Finally, policymakers may be less likely to adopt LGBT legislation in domestic contexts where countergroups actively mobilize, though I question the validity of this assumption by recognizing that resistance also contributes to the visibility of norms (as I elaborate on in Chapter 6). In general, I suspect that such domestic factors are more critical for state compliance in first-mover states than they are for new adopters.

---

[10] The literature in this tradition focuses on the congruence between international norms and elements of the domestic context (Cortell and Davis 1996; Seybert 2012; Zürn and Checkel 2005). Relatedly, diffusion scholars have argued that some adopters are more "susceptible" to the norm than others (Soule and Earl 2001).

[11] Isabelle Engeli's (2011) work has also challenged the effect of religiosity on the passage of family rights for same-sex couples.

HYPOTHESIS 3a: The likelihood of introducing LGBT legislation increases when domestic social spaces for LGBT people exist.

HYPOTHESIS 3b: The likelihood of introducing LGBT legislation increases when a state is not predominantly Catholic or Orthodox.

HYPOTHESIS 3c: The likelihood of introducing LGBT legislation increases when a state's level of democracy is higher.

HYPOTHESIS 3d: The likelihood of introducing LGBT legislation increases when a state is wealthier.

HYPOTHESIS 3e: The likelihood of introducing LGBT legislation decreases when conservative or nationalistic groups mobilize.

The following analysis tests these hypotheses to explore the statistical explanations for why the LGBT norm diffuses rapidly and abundantly to some states rather than others.

Analysis of the introduction of pro-LGBT legislation

I have compiled panel data to explore changes in the rate of LGBT legislation adoption across states over time. The data set includes data on the passage of LGBT legislation in the EU-27 between 1970 and 2010.[12] It combines data collected on LGBT legislation (the dependent variable) with other country contextual data by year (the independent variables). I collected the independent variable data from an original LGBT organizations survey, organizational membership lists, and existing cross-national data sets containing information on levels of globalization (KOF Index of Globalization[13]), democracy (Polity IV[14]), GDP (Penn World Table[15]),

---

[12] With special thanks to Lena Renz for her research assistance in building the data set, to Kees Waaldijk for his pioneering research and indicators on LGBT legislation in the EU, and to the various LGBT organizations that helped us clear up discrepancies. Sources used to compile the data set include ILGA-Europe (Bruce-Jones and Itaborahy 2011), FRA Reports, Kees Waaldijk (2009), Amnesty International, The Palm Center, and GayLawNet. Discrepancies were cross-checked with local experts.

[13] See http://globalization.kof.ethz.ch for data (Dreher 2006; Dreher, Gaston, and Martens 2008).

[14] See www.systemicpeace.org/inscr/inscr.htm for data (Marshall, Jaggers, and Gurr 2010).

[15] See http://pwt.econ.upenn.edu/php_site/pwt_index.php for data (Heston, Summers, and Aten 2011).

and LGBT social spaces.[16] Table A.1 and Table A.2 in the Appendix provide information on coding and the descriptive statistics for the variables in this chapter. The survey data came from the author-conducted online expert survey of 291 transnationally embedded LGBT organizations in Europe that I describe in the Appendix.

I limit my analysis to the twenty-seven states that had joined the EU by 2010, because all states are embedded in the EU's institutional structures, and to the years 1970–2010. I begin the analysis in 1970 because it roughly coincides with the 1969 Stonewall Rebellion – the first broadly publicized instance of LGBT resistance – and the birth of the gay liberation movement, which arguably began in the United States in 1965 and found its way to Europe by 1971 (Adam, Duyvendak, and Krouwel 1998). As I describe in greater detail below, I analyze new and old EU member states separately because they have differing political histories. As such, I expect that different conditions hold for these distinct subsets. The data set includes 886 observations across 40 years in 25 countries.[17] The following sections explain the substantive meaning of the dependent and independent variables.

Dependent variable: LGBT-friendly legislation
Governments select from a set of legislative measures that grant LGBT people state-sanctioned recognition (in terms of equality and protection) in their respective states. This study focuses on five of these measures: anti-discrimination (employment, goods and services, constitution), criminal law (incitement to hatred prohibited), partnership (cohabitation, registered partnership, marriage equality), parenting rights (joint- and second-parent adoption), and equal sexual offense provisions (age of consent and legality of same-sex relations).[18] First, the analysis uses a five-category

---

[16] Special thanks to David Frank and his colleagues for suggesting this measure for an early paper and for sharing some of their Spartacus Travel Guide data with me (Frank, Camp, and Boutcher 2010).

[17] Data for Malta and Luxembourg are missing in the Polity IV Project data set, limiting the analysis to 11 of the new EU-12 states, and 14 of the old EU-15 states. Observations for countries that have not existed continuously for forty years, such as the Czech and Slovak Republics, will be coded as having missing data for the years prior to their formation.

[18] While trans people are affected by some of the pieces of legislation mentioned above, my coding is absent of legislation pertaining specifically to trans people. Though I had hoped to include this component in the analysis, developing a reliable and valid measure for trans legislation that could be used across cases was problematic for several reasons during the time period I analyze. For example, some states that afford legal recognition to trans persons require them to undergo compulsory sterilization or divorce, which many LGBT organizations view as a violation of individual rights. Such cases inform my decision to refrain from

LGBT legislation dependent variable, based on the key legislation components described above and in Table A.2 of the Appendix. Thinking of the adoption of LGBT legislation on an ordered scale has important theoretical justifications. Exploring only the legalization of sexual relations – which is linked to the global spread of individual rights (Frank *et al.* 2010) – tells us less about the extent of LGBT-friendly legislation achieved by states.[19] Moreover, it fails to capture fully the impact of LGBT activism, which has a rich multi-issue agenda that extends beyond legislation on sodomy. For example, Italy made same-sex activity legal in 1890 and Poland did so in 1932, yet this had little to do with concern for the well-being of LGBT people. While both states are coded as successes in anti-sodomy data sets, they are laggards on other measures of LGBT legislation. Second, recognizing that unique pieces of LGBT legislation may diffuse differently, this chapter explores the various understudied categories of LGBT legislation separately. Doing so enables me to examine better the time to adoption, while observing the emulation of specific pieces of the understudied policy types across time provides a better measure of diffusion.

The dual measurement of the dependent variable is based on two questions: what explains the extent to which states adopt LGBT rights legislation, and what explains the differential diffusion and timing of certain types of LGBT legislation? To answer these questions, I use ordered logit and discrete time logit regression models, respectively.[20] Let me now turn to the operationalization of the independent variables derived from the aforementioned theoretical approaches (see the Appendix for descriptive statistics).

coding a uniform trans rights measure across states. Since legal progress for trans people has taken place after the period I study here, this regrettable omission should not affect the results of the analysis. Instead, this progress can be the subject of future studies.

[19] The wave of decriminalization started with liberalization in France, two years after the 1791 revolution. Many Catholic countries followed by abandoning anti-sodomy legislation, which explains decriminalization in Spain, the Netherlands, and Belgium, as well as in many Italian and Catholic German states (e.g. Baden, Bavaria, and Württemberg) before unification (Hekma 2015). Sodomy provisions remained in force in many countries, including in England (until 1967), Germany (1968/9), and the United States (2003).

[20] The dependent variable in the ordered logit model is a combined indicator of the five categories of LGBT legislation, ranging from 0 to 5 (cf. Table A.2 in the Appendix). In this case, the dependent variable is ordinal and consists of six categories. A state might score 0 in 1990, but it will score 2 in 1991 if two pieces of legislation, falling under two separate categories (e.g. "adoption" in the parenting category and "marriage" in the partnership category), are passed that year. Next, the absence or presence of a particular type of LGBT legislation in a given year (e.g. partnership) represents the dependent variable in the discrete time logit model. Prior to a state's passage of legislation in a particular

Independent variables: transnational and international channels

A central variable in this analysis operationalizes the embeddedness of states' LGBT organizations in transnational LGBT networks. The transnationalization of domestic LGBT organizations refers to the number of domestic organizations that are members of transnational LGBT umbrella organizations in any given year. Using membership lists of ILGA-Europe and ILGA-International, I have collected data on all transnational LGBT organizations in Europe, including the year they joined the European LGBT umbrella organizations. The variable is coded in four categories, with countries having zero to three transnational organizations.[21]

Four additional variables operationalize the concepts of social, political, and economic channels, and the year of EU accession. The first three variables are based on the theory that porousness leads to LGBT norm visibility. Distinguishing between different forms of transnationalization and internationalization reflects Susan Olzak's (2011) call to differentiate between channels in terms of who and what they bring to interaction across borders and the (in)direct nature of their effect. I also run the models using an index – *combined channels* – that combines all three measures, which serves as both a measure of robustness and a measure of the overall porousness of a state (Asal, Sommer, and Harwood 2013).

The KOF Index of Globalization data set (Dreher, Gaston, and Martens 2008) provides measures for the concepts of social, political, and economic channels. *Political channels* measure the extent to which a country is a member of international organizations, has signed bi- and multilateral treaties (since 1945), hosts embassies and high commissions, and is involved in UN peace missions (KOF Method 2013). This measure should indicate a state's self-perception as a member of the international community (KOF Method 2013). *Economic channels* are measured as an index of actual economic flows (i.e. trade, foreign direct investment, and portfolio investment) and the breakdown of restrictions to trade and capital (e.g. revenues on tariffs) (KOF Method 2013).[22] To measure

category, each year is scored as a 0. The year that a state passes legislation in that particular category, it is coded as 1, and the state drops out of the risk set.

[21] Some countries have four or more organizations, but for 87 percent of the data points, countries have fewer than four organizations. I collapsed countries with more than three organizations into the highest "three organizations" category. There is little theoretical reason to expect that additional organizations will make a difference in the ability to signal to state authorities (based on the logic of diminishing returns).

[22] This measure captures the concept of transnational pressure through mechanisms of sanction and competition. That said, John D'Emilio, in his powerful work on capitalism

social channels, I use a subindex measure on information flows, which "is meant to measure the potential flow of ideas and images. It includes the number of internet hosts and users, cable television subscribers, number of radios (all per 1,000 people), and international newspapers traded (in percent of GDP). All these variables to some extent proxy people's potential for receiving news from other countries – they thus contribute to the global spread of ideas" (KOF Method 2013, 2). I also include a dummy variable that distinguishes the years before and after a state joins the EU. Finally, in the duration models, I include a diffusion variable to tap into the concept of emulation. This measure is a yearly count of the number of other EU states that have adopted the given policy.

While I expect political and social channels to matter most for the spread of an idea, all variables are conceptually similar in that they measure a state's connection to the international community. States with fewer channels are inherently less likely to have the LGBT norm become visible in their domestic contexts. As direct and indirect channels between transmitter and receiver increase, so should the diffusion of international norms (Soule 2004a).

Independent variables: domestic conditions

Next, a series of measures captures the concept of resonance in the domestic realm: the presence of domestic social spaces, the level of democracy, the level of state wealth, the type of religion, and the countermobilization of anti-LGBT rights groups. To measure the presence of domestic social spaces, I use the data and coding schema developed by David Frank and colleagues (Frank, Camp, and Boutcher 2010). Social spaces are scored on a six-point scale, ranging from 0 (no activity) to 5 (widespread gay social life) (cf. Table A.3 in the Appendix).[23] I include additional domestic variables to account for a state's level of democracy and wealth in a given year. The Polity IV Project database provides a measure for the degree to which a state is a consolidated democracy, using a 21-point

and gay identity, has attributed the development of gay and lesbian identities to spaces created by capitalism – because capitalism's labor system based on wages helps individualism to flourish, which subsequently allows gay and lesbian identities to form. He has also suggested that homophobia is at the root of capitalism (D'Emilio 1983). Though the embeddedness of states in international markets also contributes to the spread of ideas, I argue that it does so differently than the social mechanisms that accompany political internationalization and social transnationalization.

[23] Research on the American context has used similar measures of LGBT spaces (using the Gayellow Pages) to identify preexisting movement ties in the 50 states (Kane 2003, 320),

scale ranging from institutionalized autocracies to democracies. Next, I use the Penn World Table for the GDP per capita measure, which I log to obtain a more normal distribution and to alleviate heteroscedasticity. Finally, I include a measure of the state religion, separating states into four groups: Mixed Christian, Protestant, Catholic, and Other (Andersen and Fetner 2008, 947).

A final domestic condition is the ability of opposition groups to countermobilize. Here, *countermobilization* is defined as the presence of anti-LGBT groups. The responses are drawn from the survey question: "In your opinion, to what degree are opposition groups (domestic and foreign) active and effective in mobilizing in your country?" The scores of organizations in each new EU member state were averaged to form this macrolevel variable.[24]

Methods

I test my hypotheses using two statistical techniques. First, I employ ordered logit regression models to explore the determinants of the successful passage of legislation when the dependent variable is ordinal. The analysis assigns an ordered value according to the extent to which a state introduces LGBT legislation, taking into account that some states go much farther (e.g. legalizing LGBT partnerships) than others (e.g. decriminalizing same-sex sexual relations). Depending on the subset of states being analyzed, the models include between 306 and 886 yearly observations in 11- or 25-country clusters.

Second, I use a discrete time logit model, also known as a "duration" or "event history" model, to explore change within states. Duration models are useful for analyzing a question of differential diffusion of policies across time and states and have been used, for example, to examine related questions concerning the decriminalization of sodomy laws and the introduction of hate crimes legislation in the United States (Kane 2003; Soule and Earl 2001). This type of estimation allows us to calculate a hazard rate, or the likelihood that an event occurs at a particular time. When a state introduces a piece of LGBT legislation – for example,

or to study the inclusiveness of constituent ties in 218 counties (Negro, Perretti, and Carroll 2013).

[24] While this is the only cross-national data on countermobilization available to me, some will rightly argue that this is a weak measure. As such, I limit my use of the variable to one model (Table 4.2, Model 4) below, to demonstrate that its inclusion does not change the signs or significance of the other variables. Chapter 6 offers a qualitative analysis of countermobilization.

anti-discrimination legislation – it drops out of the hazard set because it is no longer "at risk" for introducing anti-discrimination legislation.

The models in Table 4.2, Table 4.3, and Table 4.4 test the three sets of independent variables in relation to the dependent variables – an ordinal variable in Table 4.2 and a set of dichotomous dummy variables in Table 4.3 and Table 4.4. Table 4.2 shows the results of the ordered logit models, which reflect the extent to which states adopt LGBT legislation. It provides the results for the combined analysis of EU-27 states (Models 8–10) and also explores differences between new adopters and first movers by dividing the results into two groups, according to the subset of states: the twelve new EU member states (Models 1–4) and the fifteen old EU member states (Models 5–7). All Models reported in Table 4.2 are run with either the *economic* or the *social channels* variables (Models 1, 2, 5, 6, 8, and 9). I separate these variables because they have a relatively high correlation coefficient at 0.76.[25] Furthermore, Models 3, 7, and 10 are rerun with only the combined channels variable. Model 4 also includes the variable measuring the level of countermobilization.

The extent to which states adopt LGBT-friendly legislation

In analyzing the adoption of LGBT legislation in Europe, my models provide a measure of support for the hypothesis that social channels and combined channels influence the extent to which LGBT-friendly policies diffuse into new-adopter states (Table 4.2). Consistent with my expectations, the *combined channels* variable is significant ($p \leq 0.05$) across contexts, controlling for all other variables in the models.[26] The results suggest that states are likely to pass LGBT legislation at higher rates if combined channels of visibility are more extensive, and it reflects the assertions made by many members of the movement: "The growing

---

[25] To test for multicollinearity, I generated a correlation matrix (see Table A.2 in the Appendix). In this test, two variables (economic and social channels) appear to be highly correlated, with a correlation coefficient of 0.76. The *combined channels* variable is also naturally highly correlated with its component parts (political, social, and economic channels). I thus report a series of reduced models in the analysis. In models 3, 7, and 10, I use the *combined channels* variable to ensure that the signs of the coefficients of my other predictors did not change.

[26] Following Stephen Ziliak and Deirdre McCloskey (2008), I opt not to distinguish between the significance levels of 0.05, 0.01, and 0.001. I find little theoretical value in making a distinction between these levels of statistical significance, and so I will report all of these significance levels as $p \leq 0.05$. Henceforth, I will also not specify that I am "controlling for all other variables in the model" and will assume that the reader is aware that the result of one predictor is contingent on the others.

TABLE 4.2. *Predicting pro-LGBT legislation in Europe, 1970–2010*[†]

Variables	EU-12				EU-15			EU-27		
	(1)	(2)	(3)	(4)	(5)	(6)	(7)	(8)	(9)	(10)
Transnational and international channels										
Transnational LGBT organizations	0.88* (0.23)	0.70+ (0.44)	0.85* (0.32)	0.90* (0.38)	-0.30 (0.37)	-0.25 (0.33)	-0.16 (0.32)	0.46* (0.23)	0.55* (0.25)	0.56* (0.26)
Social channels	0.12* (0.02)				0.02 (0.04)			0.06* (0.03)		
Political channels	0.05* (0.02)	0.04* (0.02)			0.04 (0.03)	0.04 (0.02)		0.03+ (0.02)	0.02 (0.02)	
Economic channels		0.13* (0.05)				0.01 (0.02)			0.05+ (0.02)	
Combined channels			0.17* (0.07)	0.17* (0.07)			0.05* (0.02)			0.06* (0.01)
EU accession	1.27 (1.05)	1.09 (1.34)	1.43 (1.29)	1.46 (1.28)	0.18 (0.88)	0.11 (0.88)	-0.41 (0.98)	0.33 (0.68)	-0.07 (0.68)	-0.07 (0.70)
Domestic conditions										
GDP (log)	-0.13 (0.53)	-0.30 (0.46)	-0.34 (0.38)	-0.20 (0.51)	5.18* (0.87)	5.13* (0.82)	5.22* (0.82)	2.11* (0.92)	2.02* (0.89)	2.34* (0.82)
Democracy level	-0.12 (0.07)	-0.10 (0.10)	-0.12 (0.11)	-0.12 (0.10)	-0.27* (0.10)	-0.27* (0.10)	-0.22* (0.09)	-0.16* (0.06)	-0.16* (0.07)	-0.15+ (0.08)

(continued)

TABLE 4.2 (continued)

Variables	EU-12				EU-15			EU-27		
	(1)	(2)	(3)	(4)	(5)	(6)	(7)	(8)	(9)	(10)
Protestant					-1.18	-1.12	-1.06	-0.56	-0.70	-0.61
					(1.21)	(1.17)	(1.31)	(1.26)	(0.97)	(1.03)
Catholic	-0.43	-0.91	-0.91	-0.79	-1.64+	-1.55+	-1.04	-0.83	-0.81	-0.37
	(1.34)	(1.10)	(1.09)	(1.07)	(0.88)	(0.83)	(0.80)	(0.59)	(0.50)	(0.49)
Orthodox	-0.77	-1.79	-1.27	-1.24	-2.06*	-2.03*	-1.99*	-0.93	-1.05	-0.89
	(0.98)	(1.42)	(1.16)	(1.28)	(0.90)	(0.81)	(0.89)	(0.76)	(0.67)	(0.76)
LGBT social spaces	0.16	0.26	0.12	0.02	-0.18	-0.14	-0.23	-0.10	-0.08	-0.11
	(0.60)	(0.58)	(0.66)	(0.75)	(0.65)	(0.62)	(0.63)	(0.34)	(0.31)	(0.32)
Countermobilization				-0.61						
				(0.98)						
Constant	8.20*	4.19	3.90	2.95	43.48*	42.63*	42.44*	20.56*	18.50*	20.40*
	(3.17)	(3.91)	(3.31)	(4.33)	(7.83)	(7.32)	(6.75)	(5.39)	(6.03)	(6.12)
Observations	306	306	306	306	560	560	560	886	866	886
Clustered by nation	11	11	11	11	14	14	14	25	25	25

† Malta and Luxembourg not included (data limitations in Polity IV Project data set); ordered logit coefficients, robust z-statistics in parentheses;
* p < 0.05, + p < 0.1

visibility of LGBT individuals in everyday life improves the legal situation" (survey no. 54, Austria).

Aside from these general findings (and the mix of international and domestic factors apparent in the combined analysis of EU-27 states [Models 8–10]), the results are more complex, supporting different theoretical approaches according to the subset of states analyzed. What is prominent is the high measure of support that new-adopter states (Models 1–4) provide for the influences of norm brokers and transnational and international channels in the extent of the diffusion of LGBT-friendly policies. The variables *transnational LGBT organizations, social channels, political channels, economic channels,* and *combined channels* are all significant. An examination of Models 1–4 in Table 4.2 indicates that, on average, as states have more transnationally embedded LGBT organizations, they are more likely to adopt LGBT-friendly policies and to do so at higher rates. The findings related to transnational channels are also in line with the hypothesis that diffusion depends on channels of visibility through mechanisms of socialization and political sanction. The *EU accession* variable fails to reach significance, challenging explanations that rest predominantly on hard-law Europeanization via conditionality. As I demonstrate below, this is related to the fact that the EU's direct pressure mechanism only influences a minimal area of legislation. Contrary to common assumptions, the results do not show support for the influence of any of the domestic conditions variables – *LGBT social spaces, religious denomination, GDP wealth, democracy level,* or *countermobilization* – on higher levels of policy adoption in new EU member states.

Figure 4.2 illustrates the strong influence of *transnationally embedded LGBT organizations* on the adoption of LGBT laws in new EU member states. The y-axis indicates the expected change in the predicted probability that a state will reach various levels of LGBT legislation when such LGBT organizations are present in the domestic sphere. In the new EU states, three categories is the highest level of law that a state passed in 2010. When transnationally embedded LGBT organizations exist, the estimated change in the predicted probability of passing no laws decreases by 30 percent. The probability of reaching medium and high categories of law – levels two and three – increases by 19 percent and 29 percent, respectively. Interestingly, the probability that a state will enact one category of law is lower when transnational LGBT organizations exist. Low levels of legislation that have benefited LGBT people have spread without

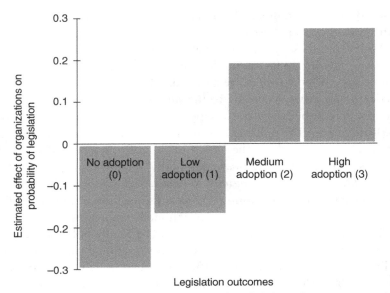

FIGURE 4.2. Expected change in the predicted probability of passing LGBT legislation when norm brokers exist in new EU states.

the necessary presence of LGBT movements. While we cannot interpret it directly from this analysis, the figure may reflect the finding established by David Frank and colleagues (2010) that traces the decriminalization of sex to the global cultural underpinnings of respecting individual rights – with or without movements. In general, the decriminalization of same-sex relations has come before the passage of protections against discrimination, which usually preceded the highly symbolic issue of relationship recognition and, ultimately, the most socially contentious issue of parenting rights (Waaldijk 2000). While new-adopter states have tended to skip some of the steps we have witnessed in first-mover states, destabilizing a sequential narrative, this general pattern played out in the past. My findings suggest that transnationally connected LGBT organizations influence the probability of moving beyond minimal thresholds of legal recognition in new-adopter states.

The image is somewhat different for the EU-15 states (Models 5–7), many of which were early movers (leaders) in the global expansion of LGBT rights. For this subset of states, two measures of domestic conditions are significant ($p \leq 0.05$). The results indicate that *economic wealth* is positively associated with high levels of an LGBT-friendly policy. For instance, the Nordic states and the Netherlands were the earliest first movers on many post-WWII issues of gender and sexuality. Substantively, the results suggest that the more affluent EU-15 states were particularly likely to adopt extensive LGBT legislation.

Interestingly, the level of democracy is negatively correlated with greater levels of LGBT policy adoption. It should be noted that this finding has been less stable in various analyses, some of which found the same significant and negative relationship in EU-12 states. While this finding applies to one of the most democratic groups of states in the world among this group (and the finding would likely be different if the analysis included states outside Europe), the strongest democracies are not always the most successful LGBT rights adopters. We might suspect the same outcome in North America, if the United States' once-laggard record on LGBT rights – which has improved tremendously in recent years (Ayoub 2015b) – provides any indication (Wilson 2013).

The negative relationship with democracy level might occur because more democratic states are more responsive to impassioned groups that oppose LGBT rights; or, most compellingly, it could be that states with strong democratic reputations need not worry about their international image to the extent that weaker democracies do (Towns 2010). For example, while the Danes were the first movers on registered partnership, they received no international criticism for waiting until 2012 to approve same-sex marriage. The newer democracies of Spain and Portugal moved sooner and went further when it came to adopting various pieces of LGBT legislation, despite being followers on LGBT rights in the early years (Denmark scores a perfect ten on democracy in all forty years of the analysis). France, Germany, and the United Kingdom, the centers of European power, are among the early leaders that – confident in their democratic and human rights stature – could comfortably wait longer to make advances. France and most parts of the United Kingdom legalized same-sex marriage in 2013 and 2014, respectively, while Germany has yet to move past registered partnership, despite increasing pressure from within and without to follow the European trend. The more recent visibility of trans rights is another example of this argument, with Catholic Malta and Ireland securing their newfound status on LGBT rights in 2015 by introducing far more open gender recognition procedures (based on self-identification without state or medical intervention), granting their trans citizens legal status. Indeed, Malta is now an "inspirational benchmark for other European countries" on trans rights, according to the president of ILGA-Portugal (Guilbert 2015). Malta and Ireland joined a small group of states – Argentina, Colombia, and Denmark – that have

similar measures in place. The Portuguese parliament added gender identity to its employment anti-discrimination code in 2015 (it also equalized
its adoption law that year).

Of the transnational channels, *combined channels* are significant and
positively correlated with higher levels of LGBT policy adoption, which
suggests that the porousness of states is paramount to the diffusion of the
LGBT norm across European cases. Aside from the consistent findings
concerning the effect of combined channels of diffusion, several explanations could account for the notable differences between the EU-12
and EU-15 states in the extent to which LGBT-friendly policies diffuse.
Domestic resonance is more important for diffusion in the EU-15 because
LGBT visibility came earlier in this subset of states, when international
norms concerning LGBT rights were less ingrained elsewhere. The null
effect for domestic LGBT social spaces does not necessarily diminish the
historical importance of these spaces in the development of the LGBT
movement. Social spaces brought together an invisible group of people
and helped to foment a movement in first-mover states; but, for several
reasons, these spaces mattered less for the passage of higher levels of
LGBT legislation, which generally came about much later. It may also
reflect the fact that, as was suggested in Chapter 3, Europeanization gave
actors greater access to established centers of gay life in foreign contexts.

Similarly, while GDP levels remain important for the extent of diffusion in EU-15 states, affluent modernity is not a significant predictor of
diffusion in EU-12 states. In line with modernization theory, wealth is
associated with policy adoption, but only in the leading EU-15 states. It
matters less for EU-12 adopters, where the diffusion of LGBT legislation
is influenced by a host of transnational and international variables. The
later timing of visibility – and the historically unprecedented magnitude
of LGBT rights in contemporary politics – may also explain why EU-12
states are more susceptible to transnational channels. Again, the ideas
and images that such channels carry today (and have increasingly carried
since the 1990s) are strikingly different, in terms of LGBT content, than
they were when the issue became visible in leading EU-15 countries.

The non-finding for the *countermobilization* variable is also interesting in light of studies predicting that greater countermobilization should
hurt movement effectiveness (Lipsky 1968). While I refrain from drawing
any conclusions on the non-significant finding here, it is worth noting
that many of my interviewees claimed that right-wing activism is counterproductive because its arguments verge on the extreme and are poorly
constructed, which can result in public sympathy for the LGBT cause

(see McAdam and Yang Su 2002; Minkoff 1994 on this process in other movements). An activist from Scotland summarizes fifty years of LGBT politics this way, a dynamic I elaborate on in Chapter 6:

Attitudes got better from the 1950s to 1970s, but then got worse again in the 1980s, thanks partly to a national conservative backlash ... in the 1970s and partly to HIV/AIDS ... [However, resulting from conservative countermobilization, the] law "Section 28" introduced in 1988, banning local public bodies and education authorities from "promoting homosexuality," caused a resurgence in lesbian and gay activism, and since 1994 onwards there have been many improvements to the laws affecting LGBT people, which have also contributed to an improvement in societal attitudes. (survey no. 107)

Introducing various types of legislation

I now consider what predicts the introduction of various types of legislation that go beyond the decriminalization of sex (sexual offenses). Decriminalization has been studied more extensively (Asal, Sommer, and Harwood 2013; Frank, Camp, and Boutcher 2010) and same-sex relations have been legalized across the EU. In Table 4.3 and Table 4.4, I report the results of models for each broad type of legislation (anti-discrimination, criminal law, partnership, and parenting). The models in both tables present the results of the discrete time logit regressions, which assess the relationships between the key explanatory predictors identified in Table 4.2 and the adoption-specific types of legislation.[27] The models in Table 4.3 and Table 4.4 also include the regional diffusion variable. Table 4.3 is an analysis of the new EU-12 states. Here, I omit parenting legislation from the analysis because no EU-12 state passed this type of legislation in the time frame considered.[28] Table 4.4 focuses on the EU-15 states and includes four legislation areas.

The diffusion variables perform strongly across both sets of states, which suggests that states do emulate other states in the region. Aside from the spread of partnership legislation in the EU-12 states, the results for the other types of legislation and across all subsets of states indicate that the introduction of LGBT rights in European countries increases the probability that other countries will adopt similar legislation. In other

---

[27] In Table 4.3 I also include the *EU accession* variable because there is strong reason to believe that this factor may play out differently on various pieces of LGBT legislation, since the EU has limited competency in this regard for the new EU-12 states.

[28] Slovenia became the first EU-12 state to introduce adoption, but not until 2011 (reversed by referendum in 2012). Comprehensive adoption rights passed in 2015, but were again reversed by a referendum later that year. Estonia introduced second-parent adoption in 2016.

TABLE 4.3. *EU-12 determinants of year passing anti-discrimination, criminal law, and partnership legislation, 1970–2010*[†]

Variables	Anti-discrimination	Criminal law	Partnership
	(1)	(2)	(3)
Transnational LGBT organizations	9.09*	−1.24	8.56*
	(2.19)	(1.96)	(3.26)
Combined channels	0.99*	0.19	3.18*
	(0.36)	(0.36)	(1.44)
EU accession	27.49*	0.23	−10.38+
	(7.58)	(4.34)	(5.71)
Democracy level	10.62*	−0.64	−4.88*
	(4.12)	(0.94)	(2.33)
GDP (log)	11.43	−3.84	11.76
	(9.22)	(8.15)	(16.19)
Diffusion anti-discrimination	2.82*		
	(0.44)		
Diffusion criminal law		2.61*	
		(1.16)	
Diffusion partnership rights			−0.69
			(1.02)
Constant	−359.49*	−22.49	−327.91*
	(77.39)	(53.60)	(105.03)
Observations	306	306	306
Clustered by nation	11	11	11

[†] Malta not included due to data limitations in Polity IV Project data set; discrete time logit models, robust z-statistics in parentheses; * $p < 0.05$, + $p < 0.1$

words, positive action by states in the region does promote diffusion, as states look for cues on what types of policy to adopt.

Table 4.3 shows that the effects of the focal predictors vary across legislation type in EU-12 countries. The data suggest that the *transnational LGBT organizations* and *combined channels* variables are significant, positive predictors of policy adoption in two of the three models. These variables have a positive effect on the passage of anti-discrimination and partnership legislation, but no effect on the passage of criminal law legislation. The results for the other variables are unsurprisingly less uniform. The *EU accession variable* is a significant and positive predictor of anti-discrimination, an expected finding since Article 13 of the Amsterdam Treaty focused specifically on employment anti-discrimination as an accession requirement. Its null effect in Model 2 and its reverse effect in Model 3 reflect the limits of hard EU conditionality. Some states, for example, responded to EU accession requirements by mounting strong opposition to same-sex marriage. Poland opted out of the EU's Charter on Fundamental Rights on the basis of a legally unwarranted fear that it might be compelled to accept same-sex partnerships and to legalize abortion (Barnard 2008). While they might come to adopt partnership legislation in later years (Poland came close to passing a partnership bill in 2012), it is often precisely at junctures like EU accession that state authorities seek to symbolically reaffirm their domestic sovereignty. The performance of the *EU accession* variable thus connects back to the discussion surrounding EU conditionality in Chapter 3, which emphasizes the limits to EU hard law. This may change somewhat in the future, as LGBT people are increasingly visible in EU accession negotiation talks (which was evident in 2007 surrounding negotiations with Croatia and Turkey) but it is important to emphasize that hard-law mechanisms for legal change have their shortcomings.

Furthermore, the results suggest that the initial introduction of partnership provisions is more likely in countries with lower democracy scores. The same surprising finding for *democracy level* that we saw in Table 4.2 (explained above) reappears in Model 3. At a time when the American movement's agenda has revolved around a marriage debate, some European states may see some form of partnership as a symbolically powerful way to signal that they are modern, especially if they feel that such a move may improve their democratic reputation. Activists have also referenced the unique role of same-sex marriage – one form of partnership – as a highly salient issue, whether or not it was seen as consequential to the movement domestically. They find it critical precisely because it generates so much visibility: "When you ask for marriage, you get everything in between, from media support to empowering LGBT people to come out to their families and get involved" (interview no. 100).

Table 4.4 shows the regression results explaining the introduction of individual pieces of legislation in EU-15 countries. As with Table 4.2, GDP represents a significant predictor of the introduction of individual pieces of LGBT legislation. In three of the four models, wealthier countries are more likely to pass LGBT legislation, regardless of legislation type. Likewise, the results indicate that *combined channels* represent a significant and positive predictor of policy adoption in all models. Transnational LGBT organizations have less influence on the initial introduction of legislation in the EU-15 states than they do in the EU-12 states.

TABLE 4.4. *EU-15 determinants of year passing anti-discrimination, criminal law, partnership, and parenting legislation, 1970–2010[†]*

Variables	Anti-discrimination	Criminal law	Partnership	Parenting
	(1)	(2)	(3)	(4)
Transnational LGBT organizations	−1.75	−1.17	0.88	−6.85
	(1.70)	(1.31)	(2.24)	(3.34)
Combined channels	0.88*	0.82*	0.34*	1.11*
	(0.17)	(0.29)	(0.16)	(0.38)
Democracy level	−0.46	−2.09	−2.92	−0.47
	(4.24)	(4.62)	(2.10)	(2.75)
GDP (log)	29.48*	11.87*	28.56*	16.80
	(10.50)	(5.62)	(11.95)	(10.65)
Diffusion anti-discrimination	2.48*			
	(0.53)			
Diffusion criminal law		1.57*		
		(0.38)		
Diffusion partnership rights			2.01*	
			(0.71)	
Diffusion parenting				3.24*
				(0.82)
Constant	−392.0*	−185.4*	−302.7*	−278.6*
	(106.4)	(70.87)	(113.3)	(121.6)
Observations	560	560	560	560
Clustered by nation	14	14	14	14

[†] Luxembourg not included due to data limitations in Polity IV Project data set; discrete time logit models, robust z-statistics in parentheses; * $p < 0.05$

The case of partnership legislation

To put these quantitative findings in context, I will now draw historical examples from a wide-ranging set of first-mover and new-adopter states in Europe in which transnational and international channels have fueled new developments in the category of *partnership legislation*. The diversity of the countries that have adopted same-sex unions challenges earlier scholarship that emphasized the domestic requisites to accelerate such rights – as Kelly Kollman (2007, 2013) and David Paternotte (2011) have shown, and as this book also demonstrates. The transnational channels of norm visibility – direct, indirect, and brokered – through which the politics of LGBT rights has long functioned have increased in the last two decades, especially in new-adopter states.

I should note at the outset that my broad category of partnership legislation is a simplification. Depending on the time and the context, activists have distinguished between registered partnerships and marriage. The claim for the former emerged in Western democracies around the late 1970s and gained momentum following the HIV/AIDS crisis of the 1980s and 1990s (Chauncey 2005; Paternotte 2015). The equality claim of same-sex marriage followed at the turn of the century. Furthermore, marriage is itself a contested issue within the LGBT movement, with some LGBT and queer groups viewing it as a conservative institution at odds with several tenets of queer liberation.

The broader idea of partnership recognition has a long history in Europe, with Denmark first granting legal status to same-sex couples in 1989. Eventually, same-sex partners there gained many of the same rights as married opposite-sex partners. This Danish model of registered partnership, as a distinct and separate union for same-sex couples, was emulated by the other Nordic states soon afterward. The Nordic domino effect was fueled in large part by the formation of the international Nordic Commission on Marriage to recognize same-sex unions from across the region (Kollman 2013, 66–8, 82; Rydström 2008), which cemented the influential norm-entrepreneurship played by Europe's smaller states on this issue (Ingebritsen 2002). By 1996, all the Nordic states except Finland (which followed in 2002) had implemented registered partnerships. Alongside its neighbors to the north, the Netherlands was an early mover on cohabitation laws and introduced a new form of registered partnerships in 1998 – one that was open to both opposite- and same-sex couples (Kollman 2013, 68). The other Benelux countries would follow suit, using this Dutch model in years to come. Within the course of two decades, variations of the Danish model have been emulated across the continent, including in Germany, Hungary, and Slovenia; and variants of the Dutch model in France, Andorra, and most Spanish regions (Paternotte 2015). These models can also be found in many North and South American jurisdictions.

In 2001, the Netherlands led again by becoming the first country in the world to pass same-sex marriage. Scholars have attributed the Netherlands' first-mover status in recognizing full marriage to a series of variables, emphasizing the strength of the domestic LGBT movement and the relatively weak status of mainstream Protestant and Catholic opposition to gay rights (Cox 2005, 7). In particular, the Cultuur en Ontspanningscentrum (COC) is the longest-functioning LGBT organization in the world and has been a major advocate of rights in the

Netherlands (Hekma and Duyvendak 2011). Again, the model spread, with the Netherlands' Benelux neighbor, Belgium, introducing same-sex marriage just two years later. Spain then turned heads in 2005, when the Catholic country became the third state to introduce same-sex marriage. In Spain, as in Belgium, adoption was predominantly a case of emulation. The Spanish parliamentary debates over partnership equality referenced foreign debates on the same topic as lawmakers drafted bills (Paternotte 2011, 137–41; Paternotte and Kollman 2013). In line with this chapter's earlier discussion on state hierarchies, Paternotte (2011, 37) also argues that European discourse, which often framed Spain as "backward" compared to other countries on a series of measures, motivated the trailblazing role the state would take on this issue. Transnational networks of activists and legal experts – especially Daniel Borillo, a French law professor – formed an epistemic community that was particularly influential in shaping this European discourse (Paternotte 2011, 146–53).

In the last decade, progress on partnership has indeed had the effect of boosting a state's image internationally, in this case in the European community, and arming other movements with the rhetoric to push for changes in their respective countries. The title of a 2005 press release by the LSVD read "Canada and Spain Are in the Passing Lane: Equality in Germany Is Long Overdue" (Kollman 2007, 341), and policy papers on marriage in Germany and Austria made numerous references to the recommendations of the European Parliament, as well as to the laws introduced in the Netherlands and Belgium. Indeed, Germany had invoked the Danish model in making its demands for registered partnership in the past (Kollman 2013, 124–5). While full marriage has yet to come to Germany and Austria, the Spanish move was crucial internationally, serving as a model not only for Sweden, France, Italy, and Portugal, but also for several Latin American states (Paternotte 2015). This occurred through both indirect emulation of Spain in some cases, and direct networks of norm brokerage from Spain in others (especially in Portugal and Argentina [Friedman 2012]).

Direct, indirect, and brokered transnational channels of visibility coalesce in various constellations depending on the case. For example, not much of a domestic LGBT movement existed when the Albanian Prime Minister Sali Berisha unexpectedly expressed his support for same-sex marriage in 2009, and he clearly geared his rhetoric on same-sex marriage to the international community, using European standards to justify the position to his domestic audience (Michels 2012). The local movement flourished in the years that followed. Yet while new-adopter states also emulate foreign examples, direct and brokered involvement by transnational activists plays an important role in both the dissemination and interpretation in many cases, as Table 4.2 shows. To take just one example, COC has in recent years been a strong advocate for the issue by specifically targeting new-adopter states – despite its complex relationship to the issue of partnership, which has been actively debated within the organization in the past. According to Ronald Holzhacker (2012, 27), COC sees transnational engagement as a component of its mission and has campaigned to export Dutch models of LGBT rights to CEE and Asia. It does so by financing the campaigns of domestic LGBT organizations in foreign countries, as well as by supporting international organizations like ILGA-Europe. The Dutch model is thus transmitted via various transnational channels across cases. The Dutch government's leadership in supporting LGBT rights, in collaboration with its domestic and European LGBT organizations, has given it international standing on human rights. For Dutch activists, working on LGBT issues in contexts where LGBT rights are more limited also motivates their organizations to mobilize new constituents (Holzhacker 2012, 42). It serves as a reminder that work remains to be done, echoing the sentiment of Swedish activists that we encountered in Chapter 2.

Even in the many cases that do not include the active involvement of external norm entrepreneurs (e.g. Spain adopted the Dutch marriage model without active Dutch involvement), norm brokers in new-adopter states can select from an array of international and transnational resources, seeking out the most suitable models and know-how, applying for grants to fund campaigns, and strategically framing their claims to persuade policymakers that adopting various LGBT rights norms would improve the standing of their state. In some cases, diffusion is less purposive, with policymakers picking up on the issue to signal their state's modernity to external observers.

Though partnership laws are less prevalent among the new EU-12 states, domestic movements are addressing this issue, and a handful of states have passed such policies. These movement actors almost always use a language that includes references to European examples – often vertically drawing upon EU frames, but sometimes also horizontally referencing the policies of specific states. Partnership is now salient among the bundle of LGBT rights norms from which European states choose, and many states who are addressing it later than others are in effect "skipping" some of the standard requisite steps on the path to LGBT rights. Hungary was among the first countries to introduce cohabitation in 1996, followed by registered partnership in 2009. In that country, where societal acceptance of sexual minorities was particularly low, norm brokers primarily advocated for partnership using political lobbying instead of grassroots mobilization. They framed same-sex partnership as a broader human rights issue, in a way that suggested: "just look at the world around you and the progress being made ... join the club!" (interview no. 109). In particular, Hungarian activists used the Spanish case as an example of a "Catholic country that somehow made it work" (interview no. 109). Slovenia, which I discuss at length in Chapter 6, passed registered partnership in 2005. The Czech Republic also moved early – in 2006 – to implement the Act on Registered Partnership (*Zákon o registrovaném partnerství*), which permitted homosexual couples to have a form of partnership with some of the same rights as marriage (FRA 2009c).

The years 2012–2015

The speed at which nations legalized same-sex unions only accelerated with time. In the twelve months after US President Barack Obama first expressed his support for same-sex marriage in May of 2012, five countries introduced such legislation: Brazil, Denmark, France, New Zealand, and Uruguay. England, Luxembourg, Scotland, and Wales had legislation in progress. In the United States, the District of Columbia and six additional states also legalized same-sex marriage that year: Delaware, Maine, Minnesota, Maryland, Rhode Island, and Washington. In June 2013, with *Windsor v. United States*, the US Supreme Court struck down Section Three of the Defense of Marriage Act, which was suddenly portrayed as an archaic vestige of the past, even though it was only introduced in 1996; two years later, the Court legalized same-sex marriage nationwide. With such progress in the United States, even established democracies with strong LGBT rights records felt compelled to address the issue further. It became a campaign issue in France, which passed same-sex marriage legislation in 2013, and in Germany. In Germany, same-sex marriage had not traditionally been at the center of the movement's agenda, but within days of President Obama's initial announcement, transnational LGBT organizations like All Out staged protests in front of the Chancellery in Berlin referring to Germany, which had a stronger LGBT rights record than the United States, as a laggard.[29]

---

[29] In 2013 the German Constitutional Court expanded civil unions to include second-parent adoption.

Chancellor Merkel and her Union of Christian Democrats (the Christian Democratic Union of Germany [CDU] and the Christian Social Union of Bavaria [CSU]) had to address the issue at their party congress. They declined to make it a platform issue at the time, and the party was banned from the 2013 Christopher Street Day parade in Berlin, an event that the CDU had supported and to which it had long contributed a float.

Even more recently, and much as Spain's legislation had reverberated earlier, the legalization of marriage in Ireland and the United States served as an impetus for deliberation across the globe. Ireland's historic "Yes" vote made it the first country to pass same-sex marriage by popular vote (62.4 percent in favor). While some activists rightly balk at a precedent for granting minority rights via referenda, the resounding result again proved that the most unexpected cases can achieve astonishing change in compliance with new norms. Indeed, the Irish "Yes" vote came after a low point for the Catholic Church, whose reputation had been tarnished by sex-abuse scandals. Knowing that its authority to lead on sexual mores was lost, the church hierarchy "left most of the organization of opposition to a relatively small [and weak] network of religious conservatives and their allies" (Farrell and Hardiman 2015, 1). To further complicate matters, several prominent religious and political figures backed marriage, which "made it harder for No campaigners to portray themselves as defenders of mainstream Irish values" (Farrell and Hardiman 2015, 1). Irish citizens from around the world also boarded flights to vote. Importantly, a strong Irish social movement campaign that involved the presence and support of activists from across Europe paved the way to the historic referendum.

The international repercussions were clear immediately afterward, with newspaper headlines such as, "'We're next' says Italy" and "The Pressure is on Italy" (Vogt 2015). As Italian Prime Minister Matteo Renzi's Democratic Union Party renewed its push for civil unions, party leader Roberto Speranza said, "Now it is Italy's turn," and Chamber of Deputies speaker Laura Boldrini tweeted, "Being European means recognizing rights" (Vogt 2015). Even in countries that had been confident in their standing, pressures increased as more and more countries adopted marriage. In Germany, activists again mounted a campaign to highlight the irony that Catholic Ireland preceded them in legalizing same-sex marriage. In perfect symbolism, Figure 4.3 depicts a stunned Chancellor Angela Merkel doomed to catch the bouquet from a newly wed Irish couple.

While Chancellor Merkel remained firm in her opposition to same-sex marriage, others both inside and outside her party vocally disagreed with

FIGURE 4.3. International dynamics of "passing" same-sex marriage.
Used with permission of artist Jürgen Tomicek. In German soccer lingo,
"Steilvorlage" refers to a perfect pass that the receiving player ought to turn into
a goal. The bouquet's banner reads "Gay Marriage," and an Irish (IRL) couple is
tossing it to the German (D) chancellor.

her. CDU politician Jens Spahn said, "You would think what the Irish
Catholics can do, we could do, too" (Terkel 2015, 1). Volker Beck, of the
Green Party, was more blunt, saying, "If the US Supreme Court rules soon
on gay marriage the way the Irish people have, that will raise the question of why Germany is living in the twentieth century on this issue and
not the twenty-first" (Scally 2015, 1). External voices joined the chorus.
Luxembourg's openly gay prime minister, Xavier Bettel, expressed support for marriage during a visit to Germany. The 2015 Berlin Christopher
Street Day parade was showered with Irish and American flags. Actually,
the American Embassy's float was in the shape of a massive wedding
cake. Later, in July 2015, Brian Sheehan and Sandra Gowran – prominent activists behind the Irish "Yes" Campaign – accompanied the Irish
president, Michael Higgins, to a state dinner hosted by the German president, Joachim Gauck. Before the dinner, Sheehan wrote on social media,
"And so we shall go to the ball ... to explain to the German President

that marriage equality would be great for Germany too!" In sum, the international momentum has led some to predict that even the "Iron Chancellor" will have to change her position in this area.

The visible symbolism of Ireland's and the United States' decisions is not unique. These political developments have coincided with remarkable changes across Europe, with Malta and Estonia passing registered partnership policies in 2014. Lawmakers in Malta voted 37–0 (with some lawmakers abstaining) to legalize both same-sex unions and joint adoption by same-sex couples. After Malta's votes, Prime Minister Joseph Muscat said, "Malta is now more liberal and *more European*," before adding that the legislation also gives "equality to all its people" (Nielsen 2014, emphasis added). In 2015, after a fierce domestic debate, Estonia passed a law that opened civil partnership to same-sex couples in 2016 – as well as second-parent adoption. In Cyprus, the Parliament approved a similar gender-neutral civil partnership in 2015. Greece also introduced civil partnerships that year, followed by Italy in 2016. Finally, the Slovenian parliament passed same-sex marriage legislation in 2015, though it was overturned in a referendum later that year.

While this history is admittedly only a brief overview that touches on just one category of LGBT rights, the case of partnership legislation demonstrates the increasing importance of transnational and international sources of change. While domestic politics are crucial to how the issue is received, put on the agenda, and interpreted, the channels of visibility I discuss in this book tell us much about when and where the norm has spread. At this moment of unprecedented LGBT visibility, these channels have currency in explaining the proliferation of LGBT rights.

Summary and conclusion

This chapter has sought to contribute to, and to test, the theoretical explanations for diffusion of contentious pieces of legislation. Four dominant theoretical expectations informed this investigation: rights legislation diffuses to states when those states fear the costs of external pressure, when they become convinced of the norm's appropriateness, when their preexisting domestic norms resonate with international norms, and when their advocacy organizations are embedded in transnational networks. I hypothesized that the presence of transnationally embedded LGBT organizations and other channels of transnationalization would lead to diffusion – especially in new-adopter states – because they make the issue visible in the domestic realm.

The results of the analysis suggest that transnational channels represent powerful explanations for the extent to which LGBT legislation diffuses to various domestic contexts. In particular, transnational channels of socialization are the most powerful predictors of LGBT rights diffusion across cases. In contrast to popular perception, in Europe new-adopter states with predominantly Catholic and Orthodox populations are not significantly less likely than Protestant states to adopt LGBT legislation. Our thinking in scholarly research about religion as a factor in diffusion of LGBT rights must become more sophisticated (see Chapter 6). Religious denomination is not a solid predictor for the contemporary diffusion of LGBT rights, nor was it a particularly compelling predictor in the past. Catholic France scrapped its sodomy prohibition in 1791, roughly 170 years before the Protestant United Kingdom. The strength and rise of countermovements in new EU member states is also not statistically correlated with the passage of LGBT legislation.

A comparison between the EU-12 and EU-15 member states also suggested different processes and mechanisms of diffusion in new-adopter and first-mover contexts, and that mediated transnational channels of activism matter more in the context of new EU-12 member states. In particular, transnationally embedded activist organizations appear to be highly effective for diffusion in new-adopter states. All other transnational channels – social, political, and economic – also proved significant for diffusion in these states, which underlines the importance of transnational linkages in this region (see also Way and Levitsky 2007). This finding coincides with my qualitative interviews, including those with opponents of the LGBT movement. When asked what could most erode values in Poland, one anti-LGBT activist responded, "Poland and the EU are in permanent moral confrontation concerning social issues. The only thing we fear could change that is the increasing outside imagery of this deviant [sexual] lifestyle as something commonplace, normal, or even appealing for Poland" (interview no. 141).

Because some of the EU-15 states were first movers in passing extensive LGBT rights legislation, they do not rely as heavily on transnational ties for influencing state authorities on LGBT legislation. But transnational channels did impact diffusion in EU-15 states, as is made evident by the strong and consistent significance of combined channels of visibility on the process of LGBT rights diffusion across all subsets of states. What is unique about the EU-15 states is the role that domestic variables, such as affluence and democracy level, play in predicting high rates of LGBT rights.

I have also tested dominant theoretical approaches across various pieces of LGBT legislation. While anti-discrimination in employment may be tied to EU conditionality, for example, hard-law conditionality may not be the best predictor of diffusion for various other pieces of LGBT legislation. By looking across separate types of policies and comparing them to an overall scale of LGBT-friendly legislation, I can make inferences about when, where, and under what conditions rights legislation is most likely to diffuse. Here again, the findings that states tend to emulate the specific types of LGBT policies that other states in their region are passing at any given time supports the importance of transnational channels.

In sum, this chapter builds on the discussion of mechanisms in Chapter 3 by providing a systematic, large-*n* analysis of various national contexts and by detailing the complexity of legislative diffusion across two sets of states and across various pieces of legislation. I examined the nuances of diffusion by using methodologically driven scope conditions and by closely examining a region that actively purports an LGBT norm but exhibits variation across member states. I discovered how the factors that explain the initial introduction of legislation vary, and the extent to which a state continues to pass LGBT legislation after the opportunity is created. Large-*n* studies that look across the globe often overemphasize certain variables, such as the importance of state wealth for the introduction of LGBT rights, taking for granted that the LGBT issue remains invisible in many of the contexts under study (Inglehart and Norris 2003). I want to emphasize that porousness to transnational channels may operate in the other direction. Contemporary Europe is unique, in that the systems of knowledge at the regional level privilege the issue of LGBT rights, and this posture toward LGBT rights is not yet necessarily global in orientation.

Finally, the results support the notion that state decision makers are drawn to internationally visible issues, even if the national debate concerning these issues is not resolved. States care about their image on the world stage and are willing to take risky policy decisions when they receive strong signals that their international community expects it of them. These findings thus expand on arguments that have emphasized various domestic prerequisites, including social acceptance of homosexuality among the majority population (Badgett 2009; Reynolds 2013, 270);

indeed, the next chapter shows that LGBT rights can also lead to greater social acceptance in some states. The shifts we observe are thus also about timing. The later timing of LGBT visibility surely plays a role in explaining why new EU-12 states are especially susceptible to international political and social channels. Early adopters operated in a less connected world, with fewer transnational pressures, but the game has changed over the last three decades, such that state decisions on LGBT rights can no longer be made in a vacuum.

The next chapter explores the hypothesis that societies, like their state decision makers, are also aware of and respond to international norms on LGBT rights. For example, the Warsaw EuroPride in 2010 – an international event with extensive media coverage – drew 15,000 participants. Agata Chaber, a co-organizer, said:

But this is Poland! Normally we get 6,000 people, max. And it's not just the foreigners. Because it's EuroPride, more Poles are coming. They don't want to be seen as homophobic. (Cragg 2010)

Chapter 5 elaborates on how awareness of international norms has affected attitudes toward homosexuality in Europe.

5

Internalizing new norms: Attitudes toward sexual minorities

Changing society required a revolution in thought.
— *Angelo Pezzana, 2011*

When the Berlin Wall fell, CEE societies had unprecedented exposure to norms concerning LGBT people, which were developing more rapidly in other parts of the continent. Pathways for the exchange of ideas opened tremendously as the continent again re-examined its understanding of "Europe," and as increased transnational channels supplemented the internal dynamics that led to such striking changes in CEE. While political scientists generally analyze the diffusion of policies across states, the abruptness and rapidity of European integration in the 1990s also exhibits value internalization among and across societies. Indeed, international norm diffusion theory suggests that accepted ideas spread from areas of high concentration (usually powerful states) to areas of low concentration; at its essence, this theory describes how social entities change their behavior (Florini 1996). Change in attitudes toward sexual minorities is thus a measure of norm internalization that goes beyond state compliance.

Surely, for most LGBT movements, legal recognition is deeply intertwined with the objective of sociocultural recognition. A "revolution in thought," as the Italian transnational activist Angelo Pezzana called it, is about fundamental shifts in behaviors, practices, and understandings that change lived experiences for sexual minorities. Activists like Pezzana understood that for minorities – who are so often deemed radical in their own domestic contexts – such changes have both domestic and transnational sources.

In this chapter, I focus on international norm diffusion pertaining to changing attitudes and perceptions of sexual minorities in an integrating Europe. Attitudes toward homosexuality are still largely negative in most countries around the world, including much of Europe, and only recently has there been a more rapid shift toward internalizing the norm of accepting homosexuality. In their "return to Europe," newly admitted member states were exposed to similar EU norms and regulation, yet their societies display stark variations in value shifts (see Figure 5.1). For example, between the dissolution of the Warsaw Pact in 1991 and accession to the EU in 2004, nearly 60 percent of Slovaks positively shifted their opinion on homosexuality, while Hungarians saw no positive change at all.

This chapter returns to several core questions: why have societal attitudes toward lesbian and gay people been different across states?[1] Are these differences due to heightened exposure to EU norms and institutions? Under what domestic and transnational preconditions do international norms on sexual minority rights successfully diffuse to new member states? I address these questions using data on the EU-27 from 1990 to 2010. As in Chapter 4, I also compare the trajectories of these attitudes in the new EU-12 member states to those in the EU-15 member states. The data are drawn from the attitudes of individuals nested in their domestic realm (societies) and influenced by smaller subgroups within their states (social groups).

The analysis expands upon norm diffusion literature by looking at societal dimensions of international relations theory. Different societies and social groups respond to the external environment in different ways. I follow David Rousseau (2006, 212) to "open up the black box of the state" by exploring how differences in the domestic realm – and in domestic ties to the international community – influence norm diffusion among individuals. Observing cross-national variation in attitudes held by individuals is one avenue for analyzing the effect of international norms. As I have argued throughout, I expect states to differ in the degree to which LGBT norms become visible. The transnational and international channels that have contributed to the visibility of LGBT norms should influence individual perceptions of LGBT people. The attitudes of individuals – nested both in societies and in social groupings within the

---

[1] Since cross-national attitudinal data going back to the 1980s is limited to questions dealing only with "homosexuality," this chapter's results speak primarily to the gay and lesbian subgroups of sexual minorities. The question does tap into attitudes toward non-heteronormative sexual orientation, however, which may serve as a proxy for attitudes toward sexual minorities more generally.

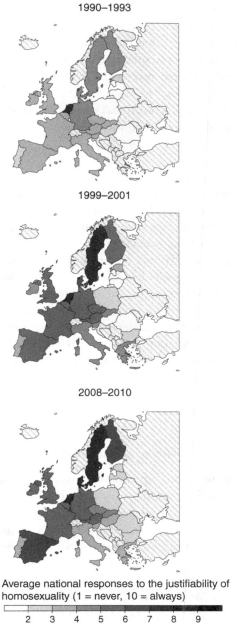

FIGURE 5.1. Mapping attitudes toward homosexuality in EU states, 1990–2010.

state – depend on the degree to which their societies are connected to the international community via channels of visibility. Attitudes depend also on the perceptions of threat that individuals' social groups associate with the norm. Within the domestic sphere, social groups that are more religious and more nationalist should perceive LGBT norms as more threatening, based on the assumption that LGBT rights challenge national identity and "traditional" values. In this sense, threat perceptions moderate the effectiveness of transnational channels and the diffusion of international norms to individuals.

I begin by surveying existing explanations for variation in attitudes toward gay and lesbian people. From this baseline, I build my theoretical propositions for explaining the variation recognized across individuals and elaborate on how I expect visibility and threat perception to function in this process. Thereafter, I describe the analysis with which I test my postulated hypotheses and present the results of my findings. The findings shed light on the data depicted in Figure 5.1. They explain the roles of visibility and threat perception in predicting tolerance among individuals (as well as the role of threat perception in moderating the effect of visibility), while also describing differences between process and outcome in EU-12 and EU-15 member states. In a third section, I connect back to Chapter 4, exploring the link between adopting pro-LGBT legislation and attitudes and providing the reader with illustrations of this relationship in both EU-12 and EU-15 states. I conclude by summarizing the arguments and their implications.

Explaining attitudinal change

My theoretical foundation explains the role of transnational channels of visibility – and the substantial variation across states in this regard – that shape how otherwise similar individuals might position themselves differently in relation to homosexuality. Recent cross-national research has linked changing attitudes on homosexuality to various demographic variables, but it has paid less attention to transnational sources of such change (Adamczyk and Pitt 2009; Andersen and Fetner 2008; Gerhards 2010; Hooghe and Meeusen 2013; Lax and Phillips 2009; T. W. Smith 2011; Takács and Szalma 2011).[2] The research puzzle presented here

---

[2] The studies by Judit Takács and Ivett Szalma (2011) and Robert Andersen and Tina Fetner (2008) enhance our understanding of the nuances behind positive and negative attitudes

encompasses both the transnational and internal domestic dynamics that enable international pressures to succeed or fail (see also Hadler 2012). By viewing states as differentiated entities that require disaggregation, my argument takes into account that transnational channels vary in breadth and scope across states and their societies. First, I argue that differences in transnational channels of visibility linked to LGBT norms are powerful determinants of normative change across societies. Second, I consider the differing potential the social groups to which individuals are tied have for associating threat with LGBT norms. Threat perception can augment the thesis that norms diffuse through transnational channels, and it plays an important role in the success or failure of norm internalization. Therefore, I suggest that different groups within the domestic sphere construct norms based on different levels of threat perception with regard to homosexuality, that these norms socialize individuals, and that these norms can resist or facilitate the internalization of "imported" norms.

Linking threat construction to the norm diffusion literature provides a useful starting point to understand the variation. The construction of threat differs across social groups, with domestic players competing to define "self" and "other" according to their distinct perceptions of what is acceptable and what is threatening. As Chapter 6 elaborates, my interviews with proponents of LGBT rights have emphasized that resistance movements found supporters when those movements recast LGBT identities as external and antithetical to domestic values and practices. If LGBT rights norms are portrayed as inherently external, then the degrees to which individuals are socialized in their national identities and a discourse of traditional values will influence reactions to the norm. Thus, not all individuals will find the imported norm equally threatening. Individuals embedded in groups where they will be socialized to perceive the LGBT norm as threatening – based on the logic that it challenges traditional values and national identity – will be more likely to reject it. The reverse is also true: individuals in groups less wedded to discourses of nation and tradition will be more likely to incorporate a well-framed international norm. Within the domestic

toward homosexuality. The former finds evidence that same-sex marriage legislation leads to increasingly favorable attitudes toward homosexuality. The latter is theoretically rooted within the post-materialist thesis, demonstrating that the effect of modernization on pro-LGBT attitudes is moderated by economic inequality. Jürgen Gerhards (2010) finds evidence for both modernization and secular arguments associated with more positive LGBT attitudes. I draw on this literature in discerning which variables, especially control variables, to include in the models used in this chapter.

realm, the social underpinnings of individual attitudes are effectual in light of international norms.

In sum, my expectations in this chapter are twofold. First, I expect that transnational channels of visibility will shape outcomes in attitudes across societies. Second, I expect the effect of these channels will vary across the social groups to which individuals are connected depending on the level of threat perception in those groups. The causal argument is simple: (1) individuals nested in the societies of more porous states will be more likely to internalize the norm but (2) individuals whose values align with social groups that are more nationalistic and religious will perceive norms associated with foreign contexts as external and, subsequently, as "threatening." Individuals with these "high-threat-perception" traits should be systematically less likely to internalize the international norms that their societies are adopting.

Analysis of attitudes toward LGBT minorities

In this chapter, I test theories of norm diffusion on both the transnational and the domestic level. At the transnational level, EU conditionality on governments and increasing contacts across various European societies should change conceptualizations of the "self" and the "other" (Rousseau 2006, 211). Because the *acquis communautaire* – the accumulated body of EU law that states must adopt to join the Union – and other EU conditions do not vary across my cases, I measure both the individual's geographic proximity to, and the European identification with, first-mover states. As in Chapter 4, I also explore the extent of a state's political, social, and economic channels to the international community, as a test of international norm diffusion. Furthermore, I look at characteristics of the individual that denote the levels of perceived threat they may associate with the norm.

I utilize data collected by the European Values Study (EVS) between 1990 and 2010 (EVS 2011).[3] I am careful to stipulate that the survey responses I use validly capture the concepts I put forth, and I demonstrate this below. I also expand the EVS data set by using a series of state-level

---

[3] During the designated period, the EVS researchers surveyed more than 43,000 respondents in my countries of interest in three waves (1990–1991, 1999–2000, and 2008–2010). They controlled for sampling bias and measurement error by using random selection and uniform measures, and they asked the same questions to all respondents, in the same way, and using the same response scale.

variables, and by coding for the geographic proximity of individuals to Western Europe. For state-level variables, I use data from the *KOF Globalization Index* and the legislation data set I used in Chapter 4. To measure geography, I corresponded the EVS regional codes in the EVS data with *Nomenclature of Units for Territorial Statistics* (NUTS) data, to add two proximity variables to the EVS data set. These variables measure the distance from each individual's residence in the new EU-12 states to Western Europe.[4] These additional measures supplement the EVS data that I employ to demarcate attitudes toward gay and lesbian people. Table A.3 and Table A.4 in the Appendix describe the data sources and all variables in detail.

The study explores the determinants of attitudes toward homosexuality in all twenty-seven EU member states. In several models, I again limit the analysis to the twelve member states that joined the EU during the EU-25 and EU-27 enlargements.[5] Consistent with my theoretical proposition, I select these states on the basis of two criteria: all states (1) experienced greater exposure to more developed norms surrounding homosexuality after 1989, and (2) were successful in gaining membership to the EU. I also compare these EU-12 models to others limited to the EU-15 states.[6]

Dependent variable: attitudes toward gay and lesbian people
The indicators for the dependent variable tap into one dimension of norm internalization: change in the attitudes of individuals within society. The variable is constructed from responses to this EVS survey prompt: "Please tell me for each of the following whether you think [homosexuality] can always be justified, never be justified, or something in between." Responses were coded on a scale of 1 (never justifiable) to 10 (always justifiable). Since the distribution of the data points on this

---

[4] This coding process was a large endeavor that involved able research assistance by Jakob Tesch and helpful communication with Dr. Inge Sieben, a researcher with the EVS study. We took the regional variable (x048) in the EVS data set and corresponded the regions with NUTS data. Because of coding discrepancies across different EVS waves, we needed to combine two different codes in the EVS. The codes underlying the x048 variable were not the same as the codes underlying the coding for the NUTS variables in the subsequent EVS waves, and the codes underlying the NUTS variables by the EVS do not correspond to the NUTS codes used by the European Union. In the end, we managed to use NUTS3 data to code for most individuals in EVS Waves 3 and 4, but only for seven of twelve countries in Wave 2.

[5] Cyprus, the Czech Republic, Estonia, Hungary, Latvia, Lithuania, Malta, Poland, Slovakia, and Slovenia (EU-25 enlargement); and Bulgaria and Romania (EU-27 enlargement).

[6] The differences in the variability of the independent variables between EU-12 and EU-15 member states are unsubstantial; they have a similar spread in terms of range and mean.

variable is slightly skewed to the left, I transformed the variable using the natural logarithms.[7]

The dependent variable indicator above has been used in recent research on attitudes toward homosexuality (Andersen and Fetner 2008; Takács and Szalma 2011), but general concerns about the use of single-item measures remain, in that such variables are more prone to measurement error.[8] To address this concern, I also created a composite measure that integrates the dependent variable data above with a question on unwanted neighbors. EVS respondents were also asked: "On this list are various groups of people. Could you please sort out any that you would not like to have as neighbors?" Among the fifteen identified groups, respondents could select "homosexuals" as one of their unwanted neighbor groups. While the previous dependent variable question on attitudes illuminates whether or not respondents feel homosexuality is acceptable, this second measure also might uncover respondents' willingness to practice intolerance by placing themselves in a scenario in which they single out gay and lesbian people for discrimination. In any respect, the composite index serves as a robustness check of the findings using the original variable on homosexuality as justifiable.

Independent variables: domestic variation in transnational channels

I again employ the indicators of social, political, economic, and combined transnational and international channels – all measured at the state level – to discern transnational channels of diffusion. Each respondent is thus linked to their state's macro-level score at the time of the survey. As presented in Chapter 2, these channels of diffusion are theoretically important because they produce the transnational interactions that expose individuals to new norms, making them visible and open to deliberation in the domestic sphere.

---

[7] I also ran each model with the original variable, and the sign and significance levels of the predictors did not change.

[8] Beyond the issues with single-measure survey items, there remain limits to using attitudinal survey data to capture norm internalization. A critical concern is that respondents might consciously moderate their actual positions when they respond to survey questions, as research on symbolic racism in political psychology has shown (McConahay and Hough 1976; Sears 1988). The bimodal nature of the survey responses used here – showing that respondents generally take extreme positions on either end of the spectrum, and with a majority still feeling comfortable in expressing negative feelings toward homosexuals – alleviates this concern only somewhat. I have taken steps (described above) to improve on previous studies that use this data, which is the best we have to address the topic of this chapter.

If norms spread through channels of transnational interaction, then we might also expect that geographic proximity to the states west of the Iron Curtain – where homosexuality was politicized earlier – can predict successful diffusion. Political scientists and sociologists have already demonstrated through empirical applications that distance is a politically and socially salient variable in explaining, for example, the democratization and market-Europeanization of post-communist states (Kopstein and Reilly 2000) and the positive attitudes of citizens toward the EU (Berezin and Diez-Medrano 2008). This is especially true after the sociopolitical boundaries of the Cold War broke down. I thus view geography as an indicator of a direct channel between transmitter and receiver of a norm (Givan, Roberts, and Soule 2010), and I create two indicators of proximity to Western Europe. The first variable measures the distance to Vienna or Berlin, whichever lies closer, because these cities' locations along the Iron Curtain made them critical economic and cultural referents for the societies of the former socialist world (Kopstein and Reilly 2000, 10).

The second indicator measures the distance to Brussels, the political center of the EU and NATO (see Berezin and Diez-Medrano 2008). I measure the exact distance (in kilometers) between the residences of 14,910 individuals in more than 400 cities across CEE and their western counterparts (Berlin/Vienna or Brussels). If individual information flows and the spread of ideas constitute the goal, then we can assume that the citizens of the Polish city of Słubcie (historically connected to the German city of Frankfurt an der Oder) may be somewhat more familiar with norms in Germany than are the citizens of Cracow. In this regard, my measure is more accurate and careful in capturing the propositions put forth in previous scholarship. The same logic should make the *Iron Curtain* variable more valid than the *Brussels* variable (which may be one of the EU capitals but is not necessarily tied to the embodiment of EU norms). I test both measures as a robustness check, but I only report the *Iron Curtain* measure in my tables. The unreported *distance to Brussels* variable produces nearly identical results in terms of sign and direction, though with a slightly larger coefficient size.

Finally, I include an individual measure of shared identification with the EU that constitutes an indirect channel of diffusion (Zapryanova and Surzhko-Harned 2015). As discussed in Chapter 3, my qualitative research has shown that proponents of LGBT rights in the EU consciously frame the LGBT norm as one of European democratic values and responsibilities (see also Beger 2004; Kuhar 2011; Stychin 1998). The rights of sexual minorities are also clearly articulated in EU treaties (cf. Slootmaeckers and Touquet in press). Thus, I expect an individual's shared identification with European institutions to establish an indirect channel of diffusion, in that these individuals have a shared identification with an institution that purports the norm (Givan, Roberts, and Soule 2010). I use an EVS (2011) survey question that asks how much confidence individuals have in the EU ("a great deal," "quite a lot," "not very much," or "none at all"). Whether or not individuals are originally convinced of the content of the norm, if they have strong confidence in the values of the EU, then they may be more likely to embrace the norm as part of their European identity.

> HYPOTHESIS 1a: Positive attitudes toward homosexuality increase if the state is more porous to the international community (state-level variable).

- Positive attitudes toward homosexuality increase if the state is more *socially* porous to the international community.
- Positive attitudes toward homosexuality increase if the state is more *politically* porous to the international community.
- Positive attitudes toward homosexuality increase if the state is more *economically* porous to the international community.

> HYPOTHESIS 1b: Positive attitudes toward homosexuality increase if the individual is geographically closer to Western Europe (direct channel) (individual-level variable).

> HYPOTHESIS 1c: Positive attitudes toward homosexuality increase if the individual identifies with the EU (indirect channel) (individual-level variable).

Independent variables: perceived threat

The main variables of interest in this category of independent variables are related to religion and nationalism. As Jeff Checkel warns, top-down understandings of Europeanization "will interact with additional types of bottom-up processes in new member states, where historical memory and religion may craft a different sense of [European] identification" (Checkel 2014, 239). Nationalism should matter for perceiving homosexuality as threatening, because the anti-LGBT opposition almost always frames LGBT norms as "external" and imposed by the periphery (see Chapter 6). Individuals who are deeply rooted in the imaginary of the nation will feel more vulnerable toward "external" LGBT norms, which they see as challenging their national identity. Churches – the original global institutions – also recognize international norms on homosexuality as threatening to important moral values. In post-socialist societies, the Catholic and Orthodox Churches have been especially opposed to the import of EU standards on sexuality (Ramet 2006, 126), and different religious institutions generally have unique relationships to EU integration (Katzenstein and Byrnes 2006).[9] Finally, individuals who regularly practice their religions are more exposed to the messages of religious institutions (Adamczyk and Pitt 2009) and should be more likely to perceive "imported" norms as threatening to their values (Herek 1987).

I use four indicators – nationalism, religiosity, church authority, and religious affiliation – to distinguish individuals who have characteristics that I expect will lead them to perceive norms governing LGBT rights as threatening. People with these characteristics hold more traditional or national values, which should be more likely to associate the LGBT norm with external imposition. National pride is measured in four intervals, from not at all proud (1) to very proud (4). Church authority is a dichotomous measure in response to the EVS question: "Generally speaking, do you think that [your church is giving/the churches are giving], in your country, adequate answers to the social problems facing your country today?" To measure religiosity and religious doctrine, I use the EVS data on religious service attendance and religious affiliation. I predict that more frequent church attendance is negatively correlated with malleable attitudes to international norms. I remain ambivalent about whether religious doctrine should matter, since references to sexuality in the religious texts of different denominations do not vary greatly. That said, the structure and organization of religious institutions vary considerably, and Catholic and Orthodox hierarchies in Europe have been more vocally opposed to LGBT norms as a part of Europeanization (Ramet 2006), which is why I choose to include this measure. Religiosity is measured on an 8-point scale (1 = "never, practically never," 8 = "more than once a week"), and religious denomination is divided into four categories: Protestant, Catholic, Orthodox,

---

[9] Unlike the Catholic Church hierarchy, the Orthodox Church hierarchy is decentralized across national contexts (Philpott 2007). That said, it takes a strongly uniform position when it comes to issues of homosexuality (Gerhards 2010, 16).

and Other. These indicators tap into the likelihood that individuals will be embedded in groups where they will be socialized to perceive the LGBT norm as threatening.

> HYPOTHESIS 2a: Positive attitudes toward homosexuality will be lower among individuals who have higher levels of national pride (individual-level variable).

> HYPOTHESIS 2b: Positive attitudes toward homosexuality will be lower among individuals who believe churches have legitimate authority over answers to their state's social problems (individual-level variable).

> HYPOTHESIS 2c: Positive attitudes toward homosexuality will be lower among individuals who attend religious services more frequently (individual-level variable).

> HYPOTHESIS 2d: Positive attitudes toward homosexuality will be lower among individuals who are Catholic or Orthodox (individual-level variable).

Interaction among variables

Furthermore, I expect that the effect of transnational channels will vary across individuals, who are more or less likely to perceive the LGBT norm as threatening. In this sense, the state's level of norm visibility and individual-level threat perception interact in their effects on norm internalization. Specifically, the differences between individuals of low threat perception and high threat perception – in terms of religion and nationalism – should become more pronounced as the level of visibility increases.

> HYPOTHESIS 3a: Positive attitudes toward homosexuality will increase as channels of visibility increase, but more sharply among individuals who are less religious.

> HYPOTHESIS 3b: Positive attitudes toward homosexuality will increase as channels of visibility increase, but more sharply among individuals who are less nationalist.

Control variables

The models also control for a series of additional variables that previous research has found to explain attitudes toward lesbian and gay people.

In particular, scholars who have worked with societal values find that modernity is an important predictor of value change. For example, Ronald Inglehart's (1997) post-materialist theory stipulates that societies invest in social issues when they have the luxury to do so – after they have achieved high levels of industrialization, education, and wealth. To control for these factors, I use Ronald Inglehart and Pippa Norris' (2003) 12-point *post-materialist index* variable. I also include separate variables that control for gender, age, and education. These controls derive from consistent and robust findings across previous studies, which show that younger generations, educated people, and women are generally more accepting of homosexuality (Andersen and Fetner 2008; LaMar and Kite 1998; Lax and Phillips 2009). Age is measured in years (beginning at fifteen) and education is measured in years of schooling.

Next, I include a variable that measures the more contested finding that residents of urban areas are more tolerant toward homosexuality (Herek 2004; Takács and Szalma 2011). Urbanity is measured by a variable that accounts for the size of the municipality in which the respondent lives. It is coded according to Robert Andersen and Tina Fetner's (2008) four categories: "less than 5,000," "5,000 to 49,999," "50,000 to 499,999," and "greater than 500,000." This control variable also serves as a measure of social isolationism, the theory being that people in isolated rural communities are less likely to have interpersonal relationships with LGBT people. Finally, I include year dummy variables to control for time differences across survey waves.

Methods

I test my hypotheses using multilevel random intercept regression. The multilevel structure of the research design drives the selection of the method, which combines data at the level of respondents (individual-level data) and states (group-level data). This means that my data consist of observations at two analytical levels where one unit of analysis (43,296 individuals) is nested in another (27 states) (cf. Anderson and Tverdova 2003, 98). Multilevel models are useful when the researcher believes that the individuals in his or her data set are nested in unique groups that influence the outcome (Snijders and Bosker 1999, 43). The merits of this method include making inferences about the state's contextual influence over individual attitudes. Indeed, people "form attitudes and make choices in variable [social and political] environments ... that shape people's interpretations and actions" (Anderson 2007, 590). The method also addresses some of the concerns associated with hierarchical data resulting from random variance, clustering, and underestimating standard errors (Anderson and Tverdova 2003, 98). The baseline model I develop in the following tables can be econometrically expressed as:

> Attitudes toward Homosexuality = β_0+ β_1 *Transnational and International Channels (State-Level)* + β_2 *Geographic Proximity* + β_3 *EU Identification* + β_4 *National Pride* + β_5 *Church Authority* + β_6 *Religiosity* + β_7 *Denomination* + β_8 *Controls* + ε || *Country/Wave*

My expectation is that transnational channels predict more positive attitudes toward homosexuality. By contrast, I expect a significant and negative relationship between threat perception predictors and attitudes toward homosexuality. In Table 5.2 and Table 5.3, I test how these expectations bear out across different contexts (EU-12 and EU-15 states). A subsequent analysis then adds interaction terms to the above models, to explore the role of individual threat perception in internalizing norms among citizens of new-adopter states. In this analysis, my expectation is that transnational channels are moderated by the perceived threat variables in the model. If this is true, we should see two trends in the margins plotted below (Figure 5.3 and Figure 5.4). First, individuals in highly porous contexts should, on average, have more positive attitudes than people in not-very-porous contexts. Second, we should also see that the effect of transnational channels plays out differently across groups, with individuals in low-threat perception groups exhibiting a more positive and profound response to increased transnational channels. Individuals in high-threat perception groups, by contrast, should exhibit both lower scores and more modest slopes of change in response to transnational channels. Finally, the analysis in Table 5.3 adds a state-level pro-LGBT legislation variable to the analysis. This serves the purpose of exploring the effect of legislation on attitudes – connecting this discussion more firmly back to the one in Chapter 4.

Table 5.1 presents the results of the regression models for the state-level and individual predictors of tolerant attitudes toward lesbian and gay people. For each of the three sets of states (EU-27, EU-12, and EU-15) in Table 5.1, I estimate two separate models. The first model for each subset of states uses the logged measure of attitudes toward homosexuality, which the second model then re-estimates using the index measure of the dependent variable. All of these models include a state-level variable measuring the combined transnational and international channels (social, political, and economic) that tie a state to the international community. The EU-12 analysis subset also includes a measure of geographic proximity to Western Europe; this variable does not apply to the other subsets of states and is thus missing from those models.[10] Finally, the models throughout all of the tables in this chapter include unreported year dummy variables – they are almost always insignificant across models.

Visibility and threat

In the sample of all individuals in the EU, my models in Table 5.1 provide a measure of support for both the transnational channels and domestic threat approaches. The signs of the coefficients take the expected directions: they are positive when channels of visibility are high and negative when individuals have characteristics that may associate homosexuality with threat. For the channels variables, all three measures are significant ($p \leq 0.05$), controlling for all other variables in the model.[11] At the state level, increases in channels of visibility are positively correlated with more tolerant attitudes on homosexuality. As a Swedish LGBT organization bluntly reported, "As visibility has increased, societal attitudes have changed" (survey no. 100). And in Italy, where internalization has been far more challenging, activists noted, "Visibility certainly improved societal attitudes toward LGBT individuals. Suffice [to say that visibility only came in the form of] newspapers in the 1970s" (survey no. 123). The finding in Table 5.1 is in line with the hypothesis that the political, social, and economic embeddedness of the state in the international community facilitates successful norm internalization. The same is true for individuals in EU-12 states who reside closer to the former Iron Curtain border and identify with the EU.

Though they are difficult to calculate in a multilevel model with transformed dependent variables, the coefficient sizes are considerably large when taking into account that DV1 is on a scale of 0 to 2.3, and DV2 is on a scale of −1.2 to 1.5. When compared to individuals in countries with the lowest level of transnational channels, individuals in the countries with the highest level of transnational channels are, on average, expected to have more positive attitudes by 0.6 to 0.9 units (depending on the model). Similarly, the results support the hypothesis that individuals who identify with the EU generally hold more positive attitudes. Each unit increase in EU identification is associated with an increase of roughly 0.03 units in tolerant attitudes. Finally, geographic proximity

---

[10] Including this geographic proximity variable in the EU-12 models does not change the sign and direction of the other predictors.

[11] I do not distinguish between significance levels at $p \leq 0.05$, 0.01, and 0.001.

TABLE 5.1. *Predicting tolerance toward homosexuality in the EU*

Variables	EU-27		EU-12		EU-15	
	(1)	(2)	(3)	(4)	(5)	(6)
	DV(log)	DV (index)	DV(log)	DV (index)	DV(log)	DV (index)
Transnational and international channels						
Combined channels (state)	0.02*	0.02*	0.03*	0.04*	0.01*	0.01*
	(0.004)	(0.004)	(0.008)	(0.007)	(0.003)	(0.003)
Geographic proximity			0.0001*	0.0001*		
			(0.000)	(0.000)		
EU identification	0.03*	0.04*	0.04*	0.04*	0.03*	0.03*
	(0.005)	(0.005)	(0.007)	(0.008)	(0.006)	(0.006)
Threat perception						
National pride	−0.09*	−0.08*	−0.06*	−0.05*	−0.10*	−0.10*
	(0.005)	(0.006)	(0.009)	(0.010)	(0.007)	(0.007)
Church authority	−0.15*	−0.12*	−0.13*	−0.12*	−0.15*	−0.12*
	(0.008)	(0.008)	(0.013)	(0.015)	(0.010)	(0.010)
Religiosity	−0.04*	−0.04*	−0.02*	−0.02*	−0.04*	−0.04*
	(0.002)	(0.002)	(0.003)	(0.004)	(0.002)	(0.002)
Catholic	0.02	−0.01	−0.06+	−0.12*	0.04*	0.02
	(0.017)	(0.017)	(0.029)	(0.033)	(0.020)	(0.021)
Orthodox	−0.12*	−0.18*	−0.07*	−0.19*	−0.35*	−0.30*
	(0.030)	(0.031)	(0.037)	(0.040)	(0.073)	(0.072)
Other	−0.29*	−0.24*	−0.23*	−0.24*	−0.30*	−0.24*
	(0.024)	(0.025)	(0.046)	(0.050)	(0.028)	(0.028)

Controls						
Post-materialism	0.14*	0.14*	0.10*	0.10*	0.15*	0.16*
	(0.006)	(0.006)	(0.011)	(0.012)	(0.008)	(0.008)
Education	0.02*	0.02*	0.01*	0.01*	0.02*	0.02*
	(0.001)	(0.001)	(0.001)	(0.001)	(0.001)	(0.001)
Town size (5,000–49,999)	0.08*	0.09*	0.07*	0.07*	0.10*	0.11*
	(0.010)	(0.010)	(0.016)	(0.017)	(0.013)	(0.013)
Town size (50,000–499,999)	0.15*	0.16*	0.13*	0.14*	0.18*	0.18*
	(0.011)	(0.011)	(0.017)	(0.019)	(0.014)	(0.014)
Town size (500,000+)	0.22*	0.21*	0.22*	0.20*	0.24*	0.23*
	(0.014)	(0.014)	(0.025)	(0.027)	(0.017)	(0.017)
Age	-0.01*	-0.01*	-0.01*	-0.01*	-0.01*	-0.01*
	(0.000)	(0.000)	(0.000)	(0.000)	(0.000)	(0.000)
Gender (Women = 1)	0.21*	0.23*	0.11*	0.14*	0.26*	0.27*
	(0.007)	(0.008)	(0.013)	(0.014)	(0.009)	(0.009)
Constant	-1.03*	-2.31*	-0.58	-2.48*	-0.30	-1.38*
	(0.294)	(0.284)	(0.448)	(0.389)	(0.265)	(0.253)
Observations	43,296	42,348	14,598	14,060	28,386	27,976
Number of groups	69	68	28	27	40	40

Estimates for hierarchical linear models, standard errors in parentheses

$* p < 0.05, + p < 0.1$

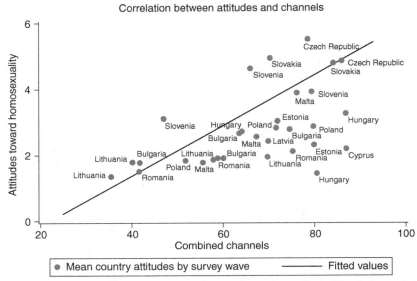

FIGURE 5.2. Correlation between aggregate attitudes and combined channels in new EU states.

is positively correlated with internalization, suggesting that the closer individuals live to the former Iron Curtain, the more likely they are to embrace the international norm. On average, every kilometer east is associated with a 0.0001 or 0.0002 unit decrease, depending on the model and indicator used. In Model 3, a resident of Bucharest is expected to hold a position toward homosexuality 0.11 units lower than a resident of Bratislava. All of these findings lend support to the expectations of the diffusion hypothesis.

The regression results suggest that transnational channels of visibility influence the extent to which individuals internalize norms concerning homosexuality. To demonstrate this visually, I present a scatter plot of the simple correlation with the fitted line of the slope. Correlations between aggregate-level variables are useful in visualizing this key relationship. Figure 5.2 plots the correlation between the primary predictor of state porousness (combined channels) and the dependent variable. Each state is shown at the three different time points. On average, EU-12 states with more developed transnational channels correlate with successful norm internalization (a similar trend is apparent for the EU-15 states). As the qualitative chapters suggest, these channels provided the foundation for a growing visibility of the

LGBT community, fostering more comfortable self-expression on the part of LGBT people as well as some erosion of misperceptions on the part of the society at large.

Across models, all of the perceived threat variables are also significant at the 0.05 level. Higher levels of national pride, church authority, and religiosity are all negatively correlated with positive attitudes. The results indicate that, on average, individuals who have higher levels of national pride, who see the church as an authority on social problems, and who attend religious services frequently are less likely to accept the norm. For example, the coefficient size – roughly 0.1 for each unit change on a 4-point scale of national pride in Models 5 and 6 – is substantial. Similarly, the findings suggest an average decrease of 0.04 with each unit increase in religious service attendance. This means that the relative rate of tolerance score for an individual who goes to church more than once a week will be 0.32 units lower than an individual who never goes to church. Finally, differences among denominations are more pronounced in EU-12 states, in which people of Catholic and Orthodox faith are on average less tolerant of homosexuality than their Protestant peers. In EU-15 states, I only observe a statistically significant difference between Catholics and Protestants in one model (Model 5). While I wish to make less of the significance of this finding, since the result is not stable across models (see Models 6, 9, and 10), it remains interesting that Catholics have a positive relationship with attitudes toward homosexuality, in comparison to Protestants in EU-15 states. It might be less surprising when we take into account the stark changes in opinion toward gay and lesbian people in predominantly Catholic countries such as Spain, Portugal, Belgium, and Ireland.

Although I do not discuss in depth the various control variables, for the purposes of this analysis they are consistent with previous findings on attitudes toward homosexuality: attitudes are more tolerant among women and among those who are younger, more educated, and more likely to possess post-material values. Post-materialism and the development of the welfare state played a fundamental role in the lives of LGBT people (Wilson 2013), as sexual minorities needed autonomy from the family unit to carve out a space to express themselves. Relatedly, attitudes become more positive as the size of the municipality increases. Urbanity is indeed a source of visibility, not only because LGBT people who have the means to do so often seek these places out, but also because these localities often offer a greater diversity of ideas.

The findings are consistent across models, regardless of the dependent variable I analyze. I report both indicators of the dependent variable in Table 5.1 to give the reader additional confidence in the measures. In terms of significance level and sign, both dependent variable measures produced nearly identical results, which holds true for the subsequent analyses presented here. Thus, I opt to report only the composite dependent variable hereafter. Moreover, in this section I report the calculated *R-squared* at two levels, using the equations put forth by Tom Snijders and Roel Bosker (1999) and Stephen Raudenbush and Anthony Bryk (2002). Across models the variance levels are quite substantial, and comparable to those reported in studies using a similar dependent variable (Gerhards 2010). For both dependent variables, the majority of the variance appears across states (about 70 percent). A smaller part of the variance occurs across individuals (about 30 percent).

Differences between EU-12 and EU-15 states

The models in Table 5.2 replace the *combined channels* variable to examine the differences between social, political, and economic channels among new-adopter (EU-12) and first-mover (EU-15) states. Social and economic channels are not run in the same model, to avoid issues associated with multicollinearity.[12] Since the substantive significance of the coefficient regressions is difficult to interpret and is also addressed carefully in the previous analysis, I limit this section to a brief non-substantial description of the findings. I highlight findings that differ between EU-12 and EU-15 states. As expected, the consistency of transnational channels as significant predictors of more tolerant attitudes is stronger among new EU-12 states. This corresponds to the notion put forth in Chapter 4 that, on average, new-adopter states are more influenced than first-mover states by transnational variables (Tolbert and Zucker 1983). Moreover, different types of transnational channels play distinct roles across contexts.

In new-adopter states, all three transnational and international channels are statistically significant. The results suggest that individuals in

---

[12] I control for multicollinearity by evaluating the correlations among my predictors (cf. Table A.4 in the Appendix). I also ran an ordinary least squares regression and calculated the variance inflation factors (VIF) for my independent variables. The mean VIF is low (1.1), and none of the VIF are above 1.18. The only correlations that are somewhat concerning are economic and social channels, with a correlation coefficient of 0.65. To deal with this, I report the reduced models in the analysis. The *combined channels* variable is naturally highly correlated with its component parts (social, political, and economic channels), and is thus not run in the same models as those that include social and political channels.

TABLE 5.2. *Predicting tolerance toward homosexuality in
new and old EU states*

Variables	EU-12		EU-15	
	(7)	(8)	(9)	(10)
	DV (index)	DV (index)	DV (index)	DV (index)
Transnational and international channels				
Social channels (state)	0.04*		0.00	
	(0.007)		(0.004)	
Political channels (state)	0.01+	0.01*	0.00	0.00
	(0.003)	(0.004)	(0.004)	(0.003)
Economic channels (state)		0.02*		0.01*
		(0.007)		(0.003)
Geographic proximity	0.0001*	0.0001*		
	(0.000)	(0.000)		
EU identification	0.04*	0.04*	0.03*	0.03*
	(0.008)	(0.008)	(0.006)	(0.006)
Perceived threat perception				
National pride	−0.05*	−0.05*	−0.10*	−0.10*
	(0.010)	(0.010)	(0.007)	(0.007)
Church authority	−0.13*	−0.13*	−0.12*	−0.12*
	(0.015)	(0.015)	(0.010)	(0.010)
Religiosity	−0.02*	−0.02*	−0.04*	−0.04*
	(0.004)	(0.004)	(0.002)	(0.002)
Catholic	−0.12*	−0.11*	0.02	0.02
	(0.033)	(0.033)	(0.021)	(0.021)
Orthodox	−0.18*	−0.18*	−0.31*	−0.30*
	(0.040)	(0.040)	(0.074)	(0.073)
Other	−0.23*	−0.24*	−0.24*	−0.24*
	(0.051)	(0.051)	(0.028)	(0.028)
Controls				
Post-materialism	0.10*	0.10*	0.16*	0.16*
	(0.012)	(0.012)	(0.008)	(0.008)
Education	0.01*	0.01*	0.02*	0.02*
	(0.001)	(0.001)	(0.001)	(0.001)
Town size (5,000–49,999)	0.08*	0.08*	0.11*	0.11*
	(0.017)	(0.017)	(0.013)	(0.013)
Town size (50,000–499,999)	0.14*	0.14*	0.18*	0.19*
	(0.019)	(0.019)	(0.014)	(0.014)

(continued)

TABLE 5.2 *(continued)*

Variables	EU-12		EU-15	
	(7)	(8)	(9)	(10)
	DV (index)	DV (index)	DV (index)	DV (index)
Town size (500,000+)	0.20*	0.20*	0.23*	0.23*
	(0.027)	(0.027)	(0.017)	(0.017)
Age	−0.01*	−0.01*	−0.01*	−0.01*
	(0.000)	(0.000)	(0.000)	(0.000)
Gender (Women = 1)	0.14*	0.14*	0.27*	0.27*
	(0.014)	(0.014)	(0.009)	(0.009)
Constant	−3.09*	−2.47*	−1.07*	−1.30*
	(0.568)	(0.481)	(0.320)	(0.282)
Observations	14,060	14,060	27,976	27,976
Number of groups	27	27	40	40

Estimates for hierarchical linear models, standard errors in parentheses, $* p < 0.05, + p < 0.1$

EU-12 states who are more socially, politically, and economically connected through such channels are on average more likely to adopt more tolerant attitudes toward homosexuality. Of the three channels, the softer social channels are the most robust across EU-12 models and have a larger coefficient size (0.04) than the political (0.01) or economic channels (0.02). On average, individuals in more porous EU-12 countries evaluate homosexuality less negatively.

The picture is again somewhat different among EU-15 countries, in which economic channels are the only significant subcomponent of state porousness. This finding not only reflects differences among diffusion to new-adopter and first-mover states (Tolbert and Zucker 1983), it also limits the economic narrative of homosexuality as linked to capitalism (D'Emilio 1983), suggesting that this narrative may have currency for the development of homosexual identity in first-mover states but is only one of several factors for its spread. Other notable differences in the predictors of attitudes between respondents in EU-12 and EU-15 states are the aforementioned findings for Catholicism in EU-15 states. The data in Table 5.2 suggest that Catholics are distinct from Protestants in their attitudes toward homosexuality in EU-12 states but not in EU-15 states. Indeed, as I have mentioned, some Catholic countries are leaders in LGBT rights, and, as I show in Chapter 6, distant national experiences of church–society relations play a more fundamental role than denomination in predicting resistance to LGBT norms. The fact that the Catholic Church, and especially Pope John Paul II, viewed the integration of post-communist states in the EU as an opportunity for returning Christian values to Europe is consequential for the strong political role that this church played in some EU-12 states (Katzenstein and Byrnes 2006). Finally, while women are more likely than men to approve of homosexuality in both contexts, the difference in coefficient size between men and women is greater in EU-15 states (0.27) than in EU-12 states (0.14). As is the case with the previous section, the signs of the coefficients of the other variables take their expected directions.

Perceived threat and moderating transnational channels

I now explore differences across distinctly situated individuals within and across EU-27 states. In particular, I expect the positive effect of visibility to be less pronounced among individuals who are prone to perceive LGBT individuals as threatening. In additional models, which are unreported here for reasons of space, I add interaction terms to test the hypothesis that individuals who are more inclined to perceive the norms as "an external threat" are likely to exhibit more gradual shifts in their attitudes as channels increase.

Figure 5.3 and Figure 5.4 illustrate that individuals in groups with "low threat" characteristics hold substantially more positive attitudes as norm visibility heightens. I report the untransformed dependent variable (on a scale of 1 to 10) for ease of interpretation. As expected, in low-visibility contexts – contexts with few transnational channels – I do not observe substantial differences among groups of individuals. As channels heighten, the fitted lines representing the attitudes of individuals in low-threat groups show a strong upward trend. While this trend also exists among high-threat groups of individuals (reported here as individuals who are more religious and who are more nationalistic), it is much less pronounced. For example, in Figure 5.3 individuals who attend religious services most avidly (lower third of the sample) are marginally different from their group peers in low- or high-visibility contexts (from 2.6 to 4.1), while the individuals least likely to attend services show improvement in their attitudes by over one point more (from 2.4 to 5.2). In fact, the attitudes of the high-threat-perception group are initially more negative as channels increase from low to medium levels (from 2.6 to 2.4), which may hint at the argument I make about the initial likelihood of backlash among such groups as norms become visible. By contrast, individuals in groups who rarely attend religious services internalize norms of tolerance toward homosexuality more rapidly. They are arguably also

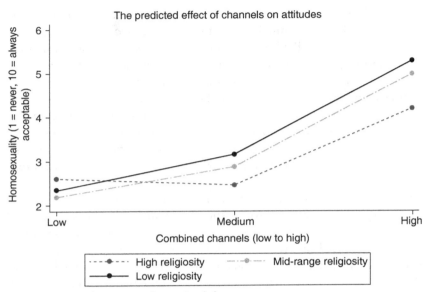

FIGURE 5.3. Religiosity and perceived threat.

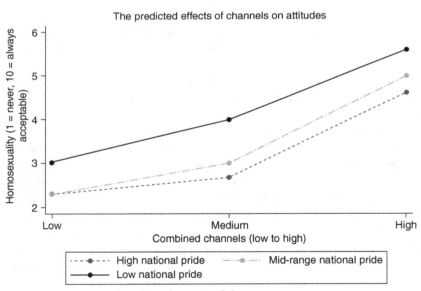

FIGURE 5.4. National pride and perceived threat.

more likely to see added value in adopting norms of legitimate behavior according to international scripts, compared to their peers who perceive international pressures as threatening. A second threat-perception variable, national pride, shows similar trends as the context of visibility heightens. Individuals who are less nationalistic exhibit more substantially and more rapidly improved attitudes toward homosexuality than do their peers in the highest-perceived-threat group. These findings support the idea that various social groups in the domestic realm respond to international norms governing LGBT rights differently. They indicate that individuals in high-threat groups will internalize such norms more cautiously, often resisting them along the way.

Legislation as visibility

Finally, Table 5.3 adds another state-level variable to explore the effect on attitudes of introducing pro-LGBT legislation. This final step of the analysis thus ties back to Chapter 4 and contributes to previous studies by exploring the links between legislation – a commonly studied indicator of diffusion – and internalization at a societal level. Judit Takács and Ivett Szalma's (2011) work modeled this effect, finding that the introduction of partnership legislation correlated with more positive attitudes (see also Hooghe and Meeusen 2013). In this interpretation, the state leads and society follows. In Table 5.3, I use the five-category legislation index as a predictor to show that Takács and Szalma's finding holds in first-mover EU-15 states (Model 13). If I break down the analysis to explore its effect in new-adopter states, however, I lose the positive effect of legislation on attitudes (Model 12).

Survey results and my interviews show that the effect on attitudes of legislation was always more pronounced in first-mover states. While organizations in new-adopter states all said they believed that legislation would ultimately help their cause, they qualified its effect, noting that legislation could be responsible for temporary "backlashes" in attitudes toward LGBT peoples – especially if opponents perceived it as "forcibly imposed" (interview no. 141). Hungarian activists all noted backlashes after their successful movement introduced legislation (interviews no. 109 and 123). Similarly, an LGBT activist in Latvia, which has a dubious record on LGBT rights and is arguably the most socially conservative of the Baltic States, noted:

We want to pass legislation because it is good and creates a discussion, but [with discussions] suddenly the issue begins being talked about shamelessly, even in

TABLE 5.3. *Predicting the effect of pro-LGBT legislation on tolerance toward homosexuality*

Variables	EU-27	EU-12	EU-15
	(11)	(12)	(13)
	DV (index)	DV (index)	DV (index)
Legislation			
Legislation score	0.18*	−0.11	0.11*
	(0.037)	(0.105)	(0.028)
Transnational and international channels			
Combined channels (state)	0.01*	0.04*	0.01*
	(0.004)	(0.008)	(0.003)
Geographic proximity		0.0001*	
		(0.000)	
EU identification	0.04*	0.04*	0.03*
	(0.005)	(0.008)	(0.006)
Perceived threat perception			
National pride	−0.08*	−0.05*	−0.10*
	(0.006)	(0.010)	(0.007)
Church authority	−0.12*	−0.13*	−0.12*
	(0.008)	(0.015)	(0.010)
Religiosity	−0.04*	−0.02*	−0.04*
	(0.002)	(0.004)	(0.002)
Catholic	−0.01	−0.12*	0.02
	(0.017)	(0.033)	(0.020)
Orthodox	−0.18*	−0.18*	−0.25*
	(0.031)	(0.040)	(0.071)
Other	−0.23*	−0.23*	−0.23*
	(0.025)	(0.050)	(0.028)
Controls			
Post-materialism	0.14*	0.10*	0.16*
	(0.006)	(0.012)	(0.008)
Education	0.02*	0.01*	0.02*
	(0.001)	(0.001)	(0.001)
Town size (5,000–49,999)	0.09*	0.08*	0.11*
	(0.010)	(0.017)	(0.013)
Town size (50,000–499,999)	0.16*	0.14*	0.19*
	(0.011)	(0.019)	(0.014)
Town size (500,000+)	0.21*	0.20*	0.23*
	(0.014)	(0.027)	(0.017)
Age	−0.01*	−0.01*	−0.01*
	(0.000)	(0.000)	(0.000)
Gender (Women = 1)	0.23*	0.14*	0.27*
	(0.008)	(0.014)	(0.009)

TABLE 5.3 *(continued)*

Variables	EU-27	EU-12	EU-15
	(11)	(12)	(13)
	DV (index)	DV (index)	DV (index)
Constant	-1.91^*	-2.50^*	-1.18^*
	(0.256)	(0.382)	(0.218)
Observations	42,348	14,060	27,976
Number of groups	68	27	40

Estimates for hierarchical linear models, standard errors in parentheses
$^*p < 0.05, + p < 0.1$

Parliament. Here shameless arguments are still [legitimate] that are [no longer acceptable] in other countries. (interview no. 138)

The answer to the same question with Spanish and Portuguese activists yielded far less cautious responses. For example, according to representatives from both countries, same-sex marriage (introduced in 2005 in Spain, and in 2010 in Portugal) came with rapid and dramatic increases in societal attitudes (interviews no. 100, 104, and 135–7). According to the president of ILGA-Portugal:

In 2010 we had a turning point, because same-sex marriage is the large, key issue that opens all types of doors or closes all types of doors. So in a sense we had an issue that the whole society is able to discuss or willing to discuss. It let in a lot of visibility and removed the silence that usually impedes LGBT issues. In our case, Spain's successful move on the issue in 2005 paved the way for a smooth transition delegitimizing opposition. Legislation had an important social impact. Since the start of the marriage campaign in 2005 [Portuguese] support for marriage has risen from 20 to 50 percent. (interview no. 100)

The null finding for the LGBT legislation variable in EU-12 states, as opposed to the strong statistical significance present in the EU-15 states, supports the qualitative and organizational survey data presented in Figure 5.5. In response to the question, "In your opinion, what has been the effect of your country introducing legislation that strengthens the rights and protection of LGBT people?" the representatives of 46 percent of transnationally connected LGBT organizations across EU-15 states said that introducing LGBT legislation had a substantial positive influence on people's attitudes in their country. Another 46 percent said it had some effect. Only 1 percent said it had a null effect, and

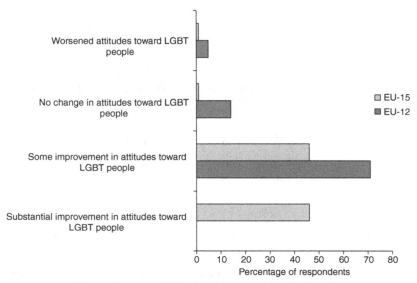

FIGURE 5.5. Effect of pro-LGBT legislation on societal attitudes.
Source: Author's Transnational LGBT Organizations Survey (for questions, see Appendix), *n* = 168.

1 percent said it had a negative effect. The reaction of organizations in EU-12 states was far more tempered: while 71 percent said legislation had some effect on attitudes, no organizational representative ventured to say it had a substantial effect. Another 14 percent said it had no effect, and 5 percent said it had a negative effect.

These findings suggest that legislation is an important source of deliberation, but its positive effect on internalization is often on a non-linear and extended time horizon. In states with no prior widespread discourse surrounding LGBT people, the introduction of legislation can be perceived as imposition by large segments of society, and fuel a societal backlash – even if such a backlash is temporary. Importantly, it is the mechanism of deliberation behind the legislation that has the most effect. Juris Lavrikovs of ILGA-Europe made this clear when he said, "As we see in many countries, only with openness ... can [we] win the situation[,] because the laws, however important they are, [are] only one particular element in changing public opinion. But it's about being open[,] about speaking" (*Euronews* 2012). Even the cautious Latvian activist cited above went on to note that backlash is not a permanent outcome, as deliberation has positive long-term effects: "My guess would be that those homophobic statements in parliament eventually led to a more positive attitude in general. Many were shocked over the kind of language used by politicians" (interview no. 138). Her colleague, also from Latvia, concurred:

The only legislation ever adopted in Latvia is the labor code prohibiting discrimination on the grounds of sexual orientation. This caused a lot of media attention and homophobic debate in Parliament ... In a broader sense [such visibility, also in the form of] Riga Pride parades, stirs a lot of emotion, both positive and negative. My belief is that while the initial reactions were very negative and loud, a positive change is noticeable in the long run. Today, media and the general public are more capable of speaking about LGBT issues in a calmer and more factual way than five to six years ago. (survey no. 23)

This is certainly true of more recent discourses, both domestically and in Latvia's international community. Responding to a historic first among Latvian politicians, diplomats from around Europe applauded the coming out of Foreign Minister Edgars Rinkēvičs in 2014 (Mackey 2014). German parliamentarian Michael Roth responded by tweeting, "Dear @edgarsrinkevics, I'm proud of you! Our united #Europe stands for freedom, diversity and respect to all minorities." Estonian President Toomas Hendrik, EU Foreign Policy Commissioner Federica Mogherini, and multiple European foreign ministers joined Roth's enthusiastic reception. Rinkēvičs' coming out also opened the door to another discussion within Latvia. In fact, a former local politician of Rinkēvičs' governing Unity Party, Inga Priede, provoked outrage shortly afterward by suggesting that Nazi eugenicists were right to kill gay people to improve fertility in society. Her comments led many "embarrassed" Unity members to clarify their own position toward LGBT rights, with the general secretary of Unity, Artis Kampars, insisting that Priede's views were "categorically unacceptable and contrary to the position of Unity" (Public Broadcasting of Latvia 2014). Similar sentiments were echoed in survey and interview statements from across the region.[13]

---

[13] For example, Bulgarian activists also described an indirect effect of legislation on activism: "The [anti-discrimination] law gave LGBT people a chance to start legal action against people who perform or promote by their speech LGBT discrimination and harassment. It did not directly affect people's attitudes toward LGBT minorities, but it created an enabling environment for targeted strategic litigation and LGBT activism to change attitudes" (survey no. 61). Likewise, in Slovakia, the visibility of LGBT people came around the time of EU accession, from 2003 to 2006. During that time, the first proposal on a registered partnership bill came before parliament. While it took the parliament less than an hour to dismiss the bill, in a discussion shrouded in homophobic language, activists claim that these institutional dynamics were effective in influencing

Summary and conclusion

This chapter has described European societies' responses to norms governing LGBT rights by combining state-, group-, and individual-level analyses and comparing their relative effects. Alongside the commonly theorized variables at the individual level, such as gender and age, I have shown that relational and non-relational channels that connect the state to the international community also explain much of the variation in attitudes among people who live within those states. States with greater transnational channels differ from less porous ones in how their societies internalize norms.

These channels have varying effects on distinct subgroups of individuals, however. Individuals who perceive LGBT norms as threatening have more negative attitudes toward lesbian and gay people, and they also alter their positions more gradually than their peers. In some cases, the attitudes of individuals in high-threat groups worsened in a phase of backlash – as the channels of visibility increased. Indeed, individuals who hold more nationalistic or traditional values are systematically less likely to internalize LGBT norms. It is then not surprising that, in Latvia, mobilized resistance to LGBT rights centered around a conglomeration of "religious groups, priests, nationalists, and a group, No Pride, specifically opposed to LGBT people," all of which used a singular argument resting on the intersection of religion and the nation: "LGBT rights are not Christian and not Latvian" (interview no. 138). Based on the qualitative research, which I elaborate on in the following chapter, the mechanism through which this process functions is threat perception. Individuals who are oriented to national and traditional discourses are more likely to think of LGBT norms as external and imposed.

Finally, the results do not suggest that internalization proceeds in a steady linear fashion. Instead, the basic descriptive statistics in Figure 5.1 show a common occurrence of small dips in attitudes that come with heightened resistance in response to "outside" norms – this is especially true in new-adopter states. Levels of perceived threat vary across states and across individuals, and these variables can fuel resistances that produce a nonlinear path to internalization among societies. That said, twenty years after the fall of the Berlin Wall, all societies in the EU took a more favorable position toward homosexuality than

a domestic debate, which has motivated LGBT groups to push forward a more active agenda (interviews no. 119 and 120). In 2015, a referendum to ban same-sex marriage in Slovakia failed decisively.

they had done in 1990. Most basically, the results support the intuition of an ILGA-Europe activist who said confidently, "The LGBT movement has turned challenges into opportunities. The visibility of coming out – which can be very dangerous – is a successful practique in changing hearts and minds, not just changing legislation" (panel no. 215). Chapter 6 develops our understanding of perceived threat by exploring how it is fomented and how resistance is mobilized differently in two cases: Poland and Slovenia.

6

Poland and Slovenia's responses to international norms

Braving sweltering summer temperatures, 15,000 people gathered in Warsaw to celebrate LGBT visibility on a July weekend in 2010. Everything about that weekend in Warsaw – from the 90-degree temperatures to the parade of rainbow colors – seemed atypical as marchers from Poland and beyond assembled for the annual EuroPride parade. Hosting the regional event was a first for Poland and also for CEE. The European Pride Organizers Association, a group that included Tomasz Bączkowski, wanted the event to come to Warsaw after the 2007 ECtHR decision that had made it illegal to ban public assembly in Poland. This was a moment to reflect on the progress that domestic and transnational activism had made in Poland, and for activists from across Europe to gather and discuss the achievements and obstacles ahead. Yet the parade was met with strong resistance, as an estimated eight counterdemonstrations took place alongside it.

That same month, roughly 300 participants attended the tenth annual Ljubljana Pride, where "there have never been large masses of counter-demonstrations" (interview no. 154).[1] The Ljubljana Pride, whose theme that year was "Enough Waiting on Equal Rights," proceeded as usual. It received political endorsements from the president of the national assembly, Pavel Ganta, and Ljubljana's mayor, Zoran Janković – who has attended in years since. The minister of the interior, Katarina Kresal of the Liberal Democracy of Slovenia party, again marched alongside participants. Novel to the 2010 event was the attendance of several Slovenian

---

[1] Three hundred is a common attendance figure at the Ljubljana Pride, though around 500 to 600 participants took part in the 2012 parade (interview no. 154).

celebrities who expressed their support for expanding additional rights to the LGBT community. As had been the case every year since 2001, the Ljubljana Pride looked and felt like a celebration.

The Warsaw and Ljubljana Pride parades employed similar tactics and made related claims. Yet the striking difference between the events lies in the forms and extent of local resistance they provoked. Even the academic panels at the Warsaw "Pride House" in the week leading up to the event drew demonstrators. In Slovenia, political leaders were responsible for the sober public statements in reaction to the parade, but in Poland the stage was left open for religious leaders to respond. Although the EuroPride program included encouraging messages of support from mayors of other cities, such as London and Berlin, Warsaw's mayor, Hanna Gronkiewicz-Waltz of the center-right Civic Platform Party, remained silent. However, the Archbishop of Warsaw, Kazimierz Nycz, gave a statement echoing the sentiments of a vocal Polish opposition: "No one can force us to support, promote or sponsor this parade" (Cragg 2010).

The central theme of the counterdemonstrations that week in Warsaw was the commemoration of the battle at Grunwald, where Poles and Lithuanians had defeated the Teutonic knights in 1410, exactly 600 years earlier. This nationalist frame harped on unwanted external influences – German Teutonic knights returning as European crusaders for "sexual deviance" – entering into the domestic sphere to destroy something sacred: Polish values as defined by the Roman Catholic Church. According to Robert Winnicki, organizer of the Marszu Grunwaldzkiego (Grunwald March), "We feel that the situation today is similar [to the year 1410] ... EuroPride is some kind of ideological aggression: the knights from the West want to force us to think that gayness is normal" (Cragg 2010). In defense of the Catholic nation, counterprotesters waved flags, rallied, chanted, fired rockets, and disseminated leaflets citing the alleged wrongs of nonheterosexuality. Tomasz Andryszczyk, from the Warsaw city hall, contextualized the reaction (so different to the one in Ljubljana), saying, "You can point to the background in attitudes ... the role of the church here is different; history is different" (Cragg 2010).

This chapter explores the varied nature of domestic responses – such as those typified by Poland and Slovenia – to new norms, and examines how these responses interact with the politics of visibility. While previous chapters have highlighted the powerful effect of the transnational channels that make such norms visible, domestic understandings shape how these norms are received and interpreted by the public. The findings in the previous chapters raise three important questions about domestic and transnational mechanisms and the relationship between politics and social change. First, how do the processes of Europeanization – so fundamental to the diffusion of LGBT rights in Europe – interact with domestic institutions and norms? Second, why does the same norm mobilize an active resistance in some cases but not in others? Finally, how does resistance influence norm internalization? Using a paired comparison design, I answer these questions by tracing the different trajectories of norm reception in Poland and Slovenia. These cases show different rates of change on both indicators of the two dependent variables of interest: social attitudes and laws toward sexual minorities.

Specifically, different domestic perceptions of threat moderate the effect of transnational channels on norm internalization. The chapter's core compares the link between national identity and religion in Poland and Slovenia. The varied constitutive effects of secularism and nationalism in different country contexts influence responses to norms concerning sexual minorities. I find that the historical antecedents of the popular idea of the nation can enable religion to fuel the process of countermobilization. This is particularly relevant if we consider the distinct roles played by the Catholic Church and the related impact on the strength and longevity of the anti-LGBT response.

The argument – that norms governing LGBT rights diffuse according to transnational channels but are moderated by the perception of their threat domestically – is presented in four sections. First, I conceptualize the differing perceptions of threat that derive from the ties between religion and nationalism in Europe. Next, I trace these differences – both in LGBT visibility and in threat perception – in the cases of Poland and Slovenia. I then explore the different trajectories of mobilized resistance that such threat produces in each case. Finally, I examine the effect of resistance on LGBT visibility.

Differing perceptions of threat across Europe

Threat perceptions

My central premise is that successful norm diffusion is moderated by differing perceptions of threat across national contexts. Sociologists of sexuality and queer theorists have long argued that new forms of sexuality threaten national identity because they destabilize the narrative of nation. This argument builds on the work of Carl Stychin (1998), Jon Binnie (2004), and Anna Marie Smith (1994), who trace a long history of national policies intended to categorize and repress unreproductive forms of sexual intimacy, homosexuality being historically "linked to conspiracy, recruitment, opposition to the nation, and ultimately a threat to civilization" (Stychin 1998, 9). Sexuality, like gender, is threatening to national narratives because it is not confined to national borders.[2] This is not to say, as Binnie (2004) also notes, that the relationship between national identity and sexuality is determined and unchangeable. National narratives of sexuality do change, for better or for worse, across time and place.

In international relations scholarship, one understanding of national security is the absence of threat to acquired societal values (Bajpai 2000, 8). Understanding societal security requires studying situations – and the behaviors triggered (Búzás 2013) – when a group reacts to the perception that its identity is under threat (Waever 1993, 23). Indeed, some state actors do interpret the imposition of the EU's norms on sexual minorities as a threat that requires "self-defense" (Cârstocea 2006, 216). This is especially true if our understanding of societal security "concerns the sustainability ... of traditional patterns of language, culture, and religious and national identity and custom" (Buzan 1990, 2). Paradoxically, the security of LGBT individuals – who seek protection from the state and the social collective – is often framed as threatening to the security of nations.

Religion and the popular nation

Religion connects to nationalism because national narratives often invoke a return to the purity of an imagined past, one that is rooted in religious tradition (Hayes 2000). In many European countries, religion is still a defining feature of the nation and has a dominant, authoritative voice on issues of sexuality and societal security. As previous chapters have shown, however, religion and modernization on their own do not explain the diffusion of norms concerning social issues. More secular states are not necessarily the first to adopt LGBT norms. Championing a complex

---

[2] According to Kathryn Conrad (2001, 125), "Homosexuality in particular threatens the stability of the narrative of Nation: the very instability and specific historical contingency of the definition of homosexuality makes the category more fluid than most, and thus brings into question the fixity and coherence of all identity categories." National narratives are related not only to sexual minorities but also to traditional gender roles and the status of women – often simultaneously. Importantly, Jasbir Puar's (2007) work has also explored the reverse construction, of *homonationalism*, in which gay and lesbian subjects become intertwined with national ideology. This construction has occurred in some states, allowing them to obscure other forms of their own injustices by purporting to be "gay friendly" (pinkwashing), as well as problematically disciplining other states and peoples to render them as uncivilized or not "modern."

understanding of religion's effect on politics, I show that religion plays a role in moderating the effect of international LGBT norms, but only in contexts where it has become linked to the popular nation.[3] As Agnieszka Graff (2010, 601) has demonstrated so well, the instrumentalization and politicization of homophobia in Poland is not just about religious morality; it is also about "a discourse of wounded pride characteristic of the postaccession period ... At stake are not the actual attitudes of Poland's citizens toward sexual freedom but the position of Poland as a state and a nation." The role of religion varies not only across national contexts but also across time, as the relationship between religion and nation changes, and as the LGBT issue is deliberated and co-opted by various social actors. These factors have shaped the discourse and the extent of the opposition to norms concerning LGBT rights.

In post-socialist European states, the fusion between religion and nation has been established in part by democratic transition (Grzymała-Busse 2014), where "the church" has played vastly different roles across states. By looking at Poland and Slovenia, two Roman Catholic countries, I hold constant the separate effect that denomination could play. Catholicism is deeply transnational in its institutional structure, and yet, as Daniel Philpott (2007, 506) has warned, "religions do not usually act singly or comprehensively in their politics," which is true of the role religion plays in LGBT politics across states. As I will demonstrate, Roman Catholicism – a religion that is both transnational and hierarchical – has an influence on politics that varies greatly across contexts, depending on the intricacies of church–society relations and the church's role in processes of meaning-making concerning national identity. Poland and Slovenia demonstrate the divergent trajectories of the church's political legitimacy and ties to national identity.

The historical ties between religious nationalism and LGBT rights in Poland and Slovenia indicate the general trends and illuminate the diffusion processes of other states in the region.[4] As one LGBT activist

---

[3] Among scholars who challenge the secularization argument, Peter Berger (1993) and José Casanova (2009) offer a nuanced argument that explores the varied root factors of religious demise and revival across contexts. Conor O'Dwyer and Katrina Schwartz's (2010) comparative study of party politics has also emphasized that illiberal LGBT politics is a product of nationalism in Latvia and Poland. Safia Swimelar (in press) charts a similar trend in the Balkans. Finally, Anna Grzymała-Busse (2014) articulates the political importance of the ties between religion and national identity.

[4] Poland and Slovenia have unique features that relate to several elements of the argument. During the communist period, travel, experimentation, and innovation were more

explained, "We [new EU member states] all have the post-Soviet syndrome, a lack of trust in social partners, [and we're] skeptical of NGOs and often homophobic and socially conservative. The difference [in processes of change] is the ties between the church and the nation. At any political event [in Poland], there are always ten bishops in the first row" (interview no. 140). Another activist also challenged the post-communist explanation: "We cannot blame it all on the communist past, which explains part of it, but clearly not all of it, if we compare [Poland] to other post-communist countries. It's the role of church nationalism mostly" (interview no. 129).

While I wish to treat generalizations cautiously, the weak role of the Catholic Church in Slovenia is comparable to that of the church in Slovakia and the Czech Republic, two states that have internalized the international norms governing LGBT rights at similar rates to Slovenia (see Figure 1.1). In these cases, the unpopularity of the Catholic Church dates back to the Reformation – when the Habsburgs suppressed a nationalist Protestant uprising – and a particularly weak relationship with the Czechoslovakian state during the Cold War (Philpott 2007, 508), which resulted in relatively few church ties to democratic opposition groups in the 1980s (Ramet 1998). Similar dynamics also play out in earlier democratizers such as Spain and Portugal, within which the Catholic Church had long and sustained ties to authoritarian rule, and their late role in democratization processes did little to restore the church's authority (Philpott 2007, 509, 512). Four decades of international isolation ended in 1975, and Spain now has among the most far-reaching legal protections and rights for sexual minorities in Europe (including full marriage rights), and social attitudes have become more favorable since 1990 (a more than 60 percent positive change). Similar successes are apparent in Portugal, where an optimistic activist stated "religion is no longer really an identity" (interview no. 100). Czechs and Slovaks linked the church to state socialism in Czechoslovakia, Spaniards linked it to Franco's regime, and the Portuguese tied it to the Estado Novo (Second Republic) (interviews no. 100, 104, 135, 136, and 137). One activist eloquently compared Spain and Poland: "The main difference ... is Solidarity and the role the Catholic Church played [during transition]. The church collapsed

developed in Slovenia (then part of Yugoslavia) than in other states in the region, and Slovenia's openness to the West has allowed transnational channels to affect the situation there. In Poland, religion has arguably resonated more deeply in people's lives than elsewhere in Europe.

with Franco in Spain. Here [in Poland] the Catholic Church gave people energy, strength" (interview no. 140).

The authority the Catholic Church wields in Poland is most similar to that it holds in Lithuania, where it also played an active role in civil society resistance to state socialism (Linz and Stepan 2011). In both cases, the church maintained deep ties to the nation and remained autonomous from the socialist state (Philpott 2007, 511). In domestic responses to LGBT norms, Lithuania followed a similar trajectory to Poland. Likewise, the Protestant Church played the central role in fueling civil society opposition to the socialist state in Estonia, Latvia (mixed Christian), and East Germany (Philpott 2007, 514; Stepan 2000). Estonia, Latvia, Lithuania, and Poland were among the laggards in furthering the rights of LGBT people. The German Democratic Republic (GDR) (East Germany) is a unique case because of the dynamic that a divided Germany produced between the church and the state – the result was a "church from below" that unexpectedly sheltered and supported the lesbian and gay movement (Hillhouse 1990; Kellogg 2001).

In this exceptional case, the more than twenty lesbian and gay groups in the GDR orchestrated much of their activism under the church's umbrella in the 1980s (group no. 205, interviews no. 19 and 20). There are two key reasons (one internal and the other external) for this development: the competition between the church and the state in the GDR, and the competition between East and West Germany. First, despite some aversion to homosexuality, the church in the GDR provided a safe space for new social movements generally (e.g. also pacifist, environmental, and disabled people's groups) to maintain their legitimacy and relevance within GDR society (Hillhouse 1990, 593). Second, the state was troubled by the church's close ties to its Protestant counterpart in the West and the outflow of its citizens to the Federal Republic. As a consequence of competition with West Germany, and the disproportionate number of gay and lesbian people applying to leave the GDR, the state enacted some minimal liberal government policies on homosexuality (Hillhouse 1990, 592). The unique role of divided Germany was fundamental to the special relationship between the movement and the church, which is evident because only 10 percent of the lesbian and gay groups under church patronage identified as Christian, and because most of these groups severed their ties to the church after reunification (Hillhouse 1990).

Among the EU-15 member states, laggard cases (until recently) such as Greece, Italy, and Ireland have had religious institutions with close ties to national identity. Ken Wald (2013) has emphasized the powerful role of the Greek Orthodox Church in both the Greek state and nation, tracing its influence back to four centuries of Ottoman occupation. Similarly, LGBT activists refer to Italy as the "last bastion" of the Vatican (interviews no. 104 and 134). The conflict in the Republic of Ireland and Northern Ireland sustained religion as a beacon of national identity, the result being initially sluggish protections toward sexual minorities. Northern Ireland decriminalized homosexuality fifteen years after Great Britain, and only after legal intervention based on ECtHR principles. The Republic of Ireland's astounding embrace of LGBT minorities, notably its popular vote to legalize same-sex marriage in 2015, has been linked to the waning authority of the Roman Catholic Church (Hakim and Dalby 2015). For a country that decriminalized homosexuality only in 1993, the vote in favor of same-sex marriage "would have been unthinkable" not long ago (Hakim and Dalby 2015, 1). The ample transnational channels of visibility in Ireland, and a strong movement, accelerated the pace toward norm internalization as the tie between church and nation weakened. According to the co-president of the European Forum of LGBT Christian Groups,[5] the historical ties between religion and nation that I trace in the cases below largely explain European resistance to the transnational movement for LGBT rights (interview no. 104).

Visibility and threat perception

LGBT visibility in Poland and Slovenia

Poland and Slovenia exemplify the importance of the differences in LGBT visibility described in the previous chapters, with Slovenia developing deeper, earlier, and more abundant transnational ties to first-mover states. As part of the emerging civil rights movement that helped topple communism in Yugoslavia, the first two Slovenian gay and lesbian organizations, Magnus and Lesbian Group (ŠKUC-LL), were founded in 1984 and 1987, respectively. These were the first gay and lesbian groups not only in Yugoslavia but also in Eastern Europe (Greif 2005, 150). In Slovenia, the LGBT movement was transnationally oriented very early on; by 1991, three groups had applied for membership in ILGA, a relatively high number of transnationally linked LGBT organizations for a

---

[5] In 2010, the forum included thirty-nine LGBT groups from twenty European countries. It has a double mission: representing Christians in the LGBT world, and representing an LGBT voice among ecumenical communities.

small country of two million people.[6] The organizations maintained a healthy relationship with international bodies, obtaining a large part of their annual budgets from transnational and international sources, along with support from the state and the city of Ljubljana. In 2010, external funding made up 60 percent and 80 percent of the annual budget for Magnus and ŠKUC-LL, respectively (Survey Data).

Poland has also established the channels that enhance the visibility of LGBT rights, but these changes came later. The presence of LGBT groups has grown rapidly since around the time of EU accession, with six groups developing transnational ties to EU-15 states and beyond by 2009.[7] The "Let Them See Us" campaign and the Cracow March of Tolerance, in 2003 and 2004, were the earliest key moments for gay and lesbian visibility in Poland (Gruszczyńska 2007, 99). These events were primarily organized by KPH, the largest and most transnationally connected group in Poland, which had emerged in 2001 as a politically oriented LGBT organization focused on attaining LGBT rights from the state. KPH joined ILGA-Europe in 2002, and 80 percent of its funding came from external sources in 2010 (Survey Data).

The data in Table 6.1 offer statistics describing the differences in transnational channels of socialization and the presence of norm brokers (transnationally linked LGBT organizations) in Poland and Slovenia. These channels contributed to the earlier politicization of LGBT rights in Slovenia. The results of my organizational survey support this correlation; experts answered questions about LGBT visibility by selecting a year using a sliding bar from 1950 to 2011 (or selecting "not applicable") in response to the question: Do you recall approximately when newspapers and other mass media started to cover stories related to the question of sexual minority rights? (cf. Survey Question 6 in the Appendix). The mean year Slovenian and Polish experts selected was 1993 and 2004, respectively.

The Polish experience with state-sponsored homophobia (Chapter 3) stands in contrast to Slovenia's history of accelerated change in social attitudes and legislation. In 2000, about 60 percent of Poles said that

---

[6] ŠKUC-LL joined in 1987, followed by Magnus and Roza Klub in 1991.
[7] For example, ILGA-Europe; International Lesbian, Gay, Bisexual, Transgender, Queer Youth and Student Organization; Open Society Foundations; COC in the Netherlands; Maneo in Germany; RFSL in Sweden; Homotopia in Britain; and the embassies of Denmark, Sweden, the Netherlands, the United Kingdom, Luxembourg, and, following the 2008 election, the United States.

TABLE 6.1. *Transnational social channels and norm brokers*

	Poland			Slovenia		
	1991	2000	2009	1991	2000	2009
Channels of information (0–100)[a]	66.1	79.8	89.7	80.1	85	95
Channels of social contact (0–100)[a]	57.6	56.9	57.3	70.1	74.2	77.1
Transnationally linked LGBT organizations[b]	0	1	6	3	4	5

Source: [a]KOF Index, [b]Transnational LGBT Organizations data set

homosexuality was never justifiable, while only about 40 percent of Slovenians agreed (EVS 2011). Slovenia also enacted some of the most far-reaching LGBT rights laws in CEE, including protections that surpass those of many older EU member states. No European state ensures that sexual minorities enjoy full human and civil rights and privileges. However, the frameworks of different states incorporate LGBT minorities to different degrees, which the cases of Poland and Slovenia demonstrate. Table 6.2 illustrates this comparative difference.

These differences persist even though both states have a majority-Catholic population, with more than 90 percent of both Slovenians and Poles self-identifying as Catholic in 1990 (Conway 2009). However, Poles are far more likely to attend religious services. In 1990, 71 percent of Slovenians considered themselves adherent to the Catholic faith. In both countries, the Catholic Church observes the Vatican's moral opposition to nonheterosexual relations. Both countries are also ethnically and linguistically homogeneous relative to their European counterparts. Finally, the two post-communist countries attained independence at roughly the same time, joined the EU in May of 2004, and are among the countries Freedom House ranked as having the most successful democratic transitions (Bunce 2003, 172). In what follows, I trace the distinctions between them back to different perceptions of threat.

Threat perception in Poland

In Poland, national identity is linked to a long history of being deprived of nationhood and to the collective memory of foreign intrusion and oppression (Borowik 2002, 240). The Polish Catholic Church "was a church that, through a century and a half of fending off invaders from

TABLE 6.2. *Legal framework for LGBT people in Poland and Slovenia*

	Poland	Slovenia
Same-sex sexual activity legal/equal age of consent	Yes (1932)[8]	Yes (1977)
Sexual orientation can be a grounds for granting asylum	Yes (2007)	Yes (2007)
Partnership rights	No	Yes (registered partnership 2006, marriage passed in 2015 but reversed by referendum)
Freedom of assembly (no bans in last ten years)	No	Yes
Comprehensive anti-discrimination	No (only in employment, passed in 2004)	Yes (beginning in 1994)
The incitement of hatred, violence, or discrimination on grounds of sexual orientation is a criminal offense	No	Yes (2008)[9]
Homophobic intent is an aggravating factor in common crimes	No	Yes (2008)
Equality body to address discrimination on grounds of sexual orientation	No	Yes
Parenting rights	No	Pending (second-parent adoption passed in 2011; joint-adoption passed in 2015 but reversed by referendum)

Sources: ILGA-Europe (Bruce-Jones and Itaborahy 2011); FRA Reports, (Krzeminski 2008; Kuhar 2008); Kees Waaldijk (2009)

---

[8] Homosexuality remained legal during the communist period, but police kept files on gays and lesbians and there were no registered LGBT organizations or press (Mizielińska 2010). Same-sex relations were first criminalized in Poland in the nineteenth century, under German, Russian, and Austro-Hungarian laws.

[9] Article 297 of the Slovenian constitution refers explicitly to sexual orientation. Criminal law provisions, in Article 300, had existed more generally since 1994, but were not always upheld for sexual minority cases. Thanks to Roman Kuhar for pointing this out to me.

Prussia, Russia, and the Austro-Hungarian Empire, had established a strong autonomy from the state, fortified by a deep identification with the popular nation" (Philpott 2007, 511). As part of this narrative, the church hierarchy kept alive memories that linked unwanted external interventions to other churches, such as German Protestantism and Russian Orthodoxy. Similarly, the members of the anti-LGBT opposition I interviewed emphasized the overlap between national identity and Catholicism in Poland, without dismissing the prominent role that Catholicism has played across Europe. In their view, Polish Republican tradition is uniquely linked to the Roman Catholic Church, unlike French Republican tradition (which is "anti-Christian") and Anglo-Saxon Republican tradition (which is liberal) (interviews no. 141 and 150). This is, in part, because Poland experienced neither a reformation nor a social revolution against the church or the monarchy to which it was tied, because the country lost independence before the monarchy could be overthrown. Instead, the church in the last two centuries adopted most of the functions of a political organization. It "gave people faith and power to struggle against invaders: the Germans, the Russians, and the Austrians," and it became a defining feature of Polish nationhood and identity (interview no. 141). In due course, the church in Poland began to wield tremendous influence in shaping the national narrative. It strove to embed its legitimation in the past (stating the church had always served the nation), to respond to criticism in the name of the nation, and "to affirm that nobody can teach the church how to understand the nation, including the nation itself" (Borowik 2002, 248–9).

The German-Soviet occupation of Poland during WWII and the subsequent population transfer and redrawing of geographic borders only strengthened the role of the church in popular memory as resistant to external power. During the postwar period, the WWII narrative of "bad" Germans was expanded into a "dualistic societal structure" that included "bad" communists, linked to the Communist Party, and "good" patriot Poles, linked to the church (Borowik 2002, 239–41). For Philpott (2007), Poland is the ideal type of a "high-differentiated" context, in which the church was severed from the nondemocratic state for decades. Soured relations between church and state date back to the internment of priests, including the Primate of Poland, Cardinal Stefan Wyszyński, in response to church resistance in the 1950s and 1960s (Philpott 2007, 511). In 1981, after the state imposed martial law and imprisoned Solidarity activists, the church again assumed its role as a symbol of truth and freedom against political censorship (Borowik 2002, 241). The church became not only an increasingly important political actor, but also a symbolic force equated with autonomy and democracy.

Before and after democratic transition, Karol Józef Wojtyła, later Pope John Paul II, played an exceptional role in the church's relationship to Poland, Europe, and LGBT people. Born in Wadowice in the south of Poland, Wojtyła maintained close ties to the Polish people through papal pilgrimages, thus commanding unparalleled respect from Polish society and exercising great symbolic influence over Poland's political role in Europe. He wanted the EU to reunify the entire continent to enable "a new evangelization flowing from East to West" (Katzenstein and Byrnes 2006, 684). As part of Poland's special role in Europe, Wojtyła articulated strong views on nonheterosexuality. In 1986, as Pope John Paul II, he issued his first official statement on the issue, written by Cardinal Joseph Ratzinger (later Pope Benedict XVI):

[The homosexual inclination] is a more or less strong tendency ordered toward an intrinsic moral evil; thus the inclination itself must be seen as an objective disorder. Therefore special concern ... should be directed to those who have this condition, lest they be led to believe that the living out of this orientation in homosexual activity is a morally acceptable option. It is not. (Ratzinger 1986)[10]

Indeed, the charismatic Pope's own brand of visibility politics, which tied the Catholic Church firmly to the Polish political opposition to communism, also informed a position antithetical to LGBT rights. It was a powerful position that singled out certain issues, such as abortion and homosexuality, as profoundly contradictory to Polish and European identity. According to Tony Judt, "what John Paul II lacked in soldiers he made up in visibility" (2006, 587).

Polish LGBT activists regularly referred to the influence that the "Polish Pope effect" exercised on society, even after Wojtyła died. It was an influence attached to the charisma that inspired a nation during a period of political transition ("Even Polish atheists cried at the Pope's funeral" [interview no. 8]), but one that was attached to philosophy

---

[10] Aside from some limited rhetoric in 2013, in which Pope Francis said the church should limit its preoccupation with the homosexual issue, the church hierarchy's position has remained unchanged. Before resigning as head of the church in 2013, Pope Benedict XVI again deplored the global diffusion of same-sex unions, calling them a threat to "human dignity and the future of humanity itself" (Colbert 2013). Pope Francis spoke out in favor of the Slovakian Alliance for Family's initiative, intended to prevent the granting of new rights to gay and lesbian people. The Catholic Church was the strongest backer of the resulting 2015 referendum, which nonetheless failed to contract the definition of family and ban the adoption of children by same-sex couples.

that held serious obstacles for LGBT activists. A KPH activist lamented, "while Ireland and Spain, for instance, also had Catholics, the Poles had the Pope" (interview no. 9). She echoed the scholarship that has cited the Pope's political vision for a new East to West evangelism, and the responsibility bestowed upon Polish society to maintain and spread Catholic values via their return to Europe. In her view, the obstacle behind this philosophy for the LGBT movement is that "'saving the world' is already a difficult enough task, and doing it with 'fucks' [LGBT people] is impossible, so you had to kick 'fucks' out of the country [to realize the Pope's political role for Poland]" (interview no. 9). The ramifications of this philosophy played out politically when the socially conservative coalition of the PiS, the League of Polish Families (LPR), and the Self-Defense of the Polish Republic (SRP) came to power in 2005. In 2007, the then president of KPH, Robert Biedroń, said to a reporter, "the brothers Kaczyński want to export their moral revolution to Europe, trapping us in a civilization of death instead of the civilization of love endorsed by Pope Wojtyła" (Sandro 2007, 13).[11]

As Joseph Burns (2009) has noted, the Polish church hierarchy found itself in a precarious position leading up to European accession. It was concerned that any identity shift among Poles toward Europe could threaten its own power, which rested on Polish national identity. Furthermore, while most of Polish society backed accession, the church's staunchly supportive agrarian constituency opposed the EU's Common Agricultural Policy. But this national view stood in sharp contrast to pro-EU aspects of the church, such as the church hierarchy's traditional skepticism of the state, the European Christian-Democratic parties' historically strong support of European integration, and the Pope's own strategic plan for Poland in Europe (Katzenstein and Byrnes 2006, 682).[12] By way of compromise, the Polish church officially supported EU accession, but "church leaders at the highest levels peppered their public statements with caveats about Poland's membership. From the pulpit, priests' statements were even more skeptical – presenting scenarios of lost cultural identity"

---

[11] Translated from the Italian print version by the author.

[12] According to Pope John Paul II, "The church in Poland can offer Europe as it grows in unity, her attachment to the faith, her tradition … and certainly many other values on the basis of which Europe can become a reality endowed not only with higher economic standards but also with a profound spiritual life" (Katzenstein and Byrnes 2006, 684). Others took a more pragmatic stance: according to Archbishop Józef Życiński, "Even if Poland remained outside EU structures the younger generations will seek patterns of living foreign to Christianity, following a lifestyle taken from the media or learned abroad" (KAI, 8 August 2000).

(Burns 2009, 169). In this process, LGBT politics and abortion became an especially easy – even if materially insignificant – target with which to distinguish "Europe" from Poland. In sum, church leaders saw a role for Poland in Europe but greatly questioned the role of Europe in Poland. The frame of the LGBT actors was exactly the reverse, as expressed in the fliers for a 2011 LGBT equality march in Poznan, which read: "Equality in Europe, Equality in Poland." The Polish anti-LGBT opposition, which is almost always anti-EU, echoed the church's sentiments, claiming that EU institutions adhered to a liberal-left consensus that was inherently incompatible with national values. In their view, "Europe" became synonymous with LGBT rights, framed as inseparable sides of the same coin.

Threat perception in Slovenia

In stark contrast to Poland, the Roman Catholic Church in Slovenia failed to become a consolidating social force either before or after democratic transition. The opportunity presented by a "return to Europe" did little to restore the political legitimacy of the church, and Slovenians placed minimal emphasis on it as a vehicle for evangelizing the "West":

> Contrary to common sense expectations ... issues related to Slovenia's national consciousness have not been dominant in the wake of the country's international recognition in 1991. Thus, in all its intensive efforts to restore the power and prestige that has been taken from it over five decades of socialist rule, the Roman Catholic Church has not been able to draw on a widely accepted concept of nationalism. (Črnič and Lesjak 2003, 361)

Coming out of WWII, the state successfully attributed the early postwar tensions between itself and the church – which involved the expropriation of church properties, prosecution of priests, and removal of religious curricula from schools – to the wider punishment for the church's collaboration with Nazi occupiers and its failure to support the Resistance (Radeljić 2011, 179; Ramet 1982, 257). Society's skeptical attitude toward the church thus dates back to this time and is in contrast to the Polish collective memory, where the church was heralded for its great resistance to outside forces. In the postwar Yugoslav context, the essence of nation did not depend on the church. Instead the state succeeded, at least in part, in linking the church – not LGBT norms – to external political powers. As one activist explained, "When it comes to the church, it was really strong until World War II but then began a history of missteps and misfortune that came with the change of the system" (interview no. 108).

While the church was generally suppressed under communism in CEE, neither interactions between church and state nor the level of suppression were uniform across the Eastern Bloc. State suppression of the Catholic Church was substantially weaker in Yugoslavia than in other communist countries (Ramet 1998). For example, Aleš Črnič and Gregor Lesjak (2003) list a series of incidents exemplifying what they call a tolerant relationship between the church and the Yugoslav state (the only socialist country to sign a protocol with the Vatican in 1966, Yugoslavia re-established relations with the Holy See in 1970). But this history did not win the church popular sympathy after the regime changed, and the Slovenian church does not have the social pull of the church in Poland. As one LGBT activist recalled, "We had a long communism, but it was not such a hard communism as in Poland. Today when people go to church, they don't listen" (interview no. 111).

During the dissolution of Yugoslavia, Slovenia was spared the process of political identification that homogenized all Serbs as Orthodox, Croatians as Catholic, and Kosovars as Muslim: "Despite the fact that most Slovenes *were* Catholic, this did not need to be a defining aspect of their identity *qua* Slovenes" (Črnič and Lesjak 2003, 350). In Croatia, the link to nationalism was made devastatingly clear at the 2011 Split Pride, with many of the 10,000 counterprotesters chanting both "Kill Fags" and "Kill Serbs" (panel no. 205). This became a phenomenon of nationality politics within Croatia, Serbia, and especially Bosnia. It was the war in Bosnia that forced religious identity to the fore, even when majorities were nonbelievers or from multiethnic families. Slovenia's brief, ten-day involvement in the war did not cement religion – which was used to differentiate the other republics and justify militarism – with the national philosophy. A Croatian LGBT activist confirmed the importance of this distinction for LGBT people: "Slovenia had an experience with war unlike the other republics. This was important [for the Slovenian movement] because then nationalism and religious fundamentalism did not become so developed there" (interview no. 102). The church tried but failed to seize the opportunity to restore its role in politics in the 1990s, which LGBT activists say made it less of a factor in their work:

After Slovenia separated from Yugoslavia, the church tried to become more visible in the 1990s, but it did not succeed in entering mainstream politics. The church existed – and it was not necessarily a bad thing – but certainly not as a political institution. The government made sure to emphasize the separation between church and state, and the [societal] attitude is that the church should not be involved in politics. If you asked the population, 90 percent would agree with that. (interview no. 108)

Historical experiences had political consequences for the Slovenians' collective memory of church–state relations. Contrary to the widely accepted suppression narrative in Poland, Slovenians do not remember the church as a victim of the socialist state. The results of the Aufbruch survey showed that 25 percent of respondents "believed that the church was not persecuted at all during this [40-year socialist] period" and another 45 percent said the church was only occasionally persecuted during that time (Črnič and Lesjak 2003, 357). Similarly, 84 percent of Slovenians believed that individual Catholics were not at all (43 percent) or only occasionally (41 percent) discriminated against (Črnič and Lesjak 2003, 357). Historical legacy has diminished the role of the church in its ability to influence societal thinking on LGBT politics: "People have a critical attitude toward the church and they believe strongly in the separation of church and state. People do not take church messages seriously anymore" (interview no. 107).

By way of comparison, the descriptive statistics in Table 6.3 demonstrate the gap between Polish and Slovenian aggregate responses to the EVS question on the legitimacy of the church in the face of social problems. Legitimacy dropped in both cases after transition, but it did so more rapidly in Slovenia. While the Polish church's legitimacy is also decreasing, largely because the church is entrenching itself as an institutional actor and concurrently relinquishing its command on the discourses of civil society (Borowik 2002, 251), the difference remains clear. In 2008, the Polish score of .60 (compared to Slovenia's 0.39 that year) is approximately what it was seventeen years earlier in Slovenia (0.64). The data also show differences in Polish and Slovenian perceptions of their national identity's vulnerability.

When asked why Slovenia's trajectory in accepting LGBT rights developed relatively more smoothly than in other new EU member states, one activist said:

Slovenia is somehow a strange country. I think it has to do with the fact that it's a small country and that the nationalist movement and the nationalist mentality is not as influential or strong as in other countries. The intolerance and nonacceptance of differences is not so transparent. We were the first republic in former Yugoslavia to decriminalize homosexuality in 1977. We often have these types of extreme situations, like this year [2010] we elected the first Black mayor in Eastern Europe. I didn't expect this, but this is Slovenia. Sometimes we are the first in good things, and as I see it, that is because we are a small country and we want to prove ourselves. (interview no. 101)

TABLE 6.3. *Church authority and national vulnerability in Poland and Slovenia*

Year	Poland (*n* = 3,587)	Slovenia (*n* = 3,407)
Generally speaking, do you think that the churches are giving, in your country, adequate answers to the social problems facing our country today? Country means on a scale of 0 to 1 (Yes)		
1990–1991	0.80	0.64
1999	0.66	0.45
2008	0.60	0.39
Perception of the EU as threatening to national identity, on a scale of 0 to 1 (very threatening)		
2008	0.64	0.43

Source: EVS 2011

A Polish activist responded similarly when I asked him if he could compare the two countries: "It is different to Slovenia. They are Catholic too but, unlike Poland, they are small and have experienced living with diversity. They are far less ideological. I have never heard about a nationalist problem in Slovenia" (interview no. 140).

Religious institutions gain the most political traction when their messages are used to define national identity in the popular discourse, and norms governing LGBT rights meet the most resistance in countries where national identity hinges on religious scripts. The next section examines how these different degrees of threat perception influence the makeup and mobilization of the anti-LGBT resistance in both countries, resulting in the varied discourses and frames of mobilization used by the opposition. In Poland, more than in Slovenia, heightened threat perception initially stifled the reception of LGBT norms, to which state and society responded with vigorous resistance.

The manifestation of threat

Dissimilar perceptions of threat manifest themselves in different rhetoric and forms of resistance.[13] Those who resist LGBT rights frame their grievances differently in Poland and Slovenia, and they mobilize in different

[13] Here I look at domestic responses to the visibility of LGBT norms and demonstrate how a perceived threat to domestic norms from "external" norms mobilizes opposition. The threat is not to the material benefits of the state (Ayoub 2010; Davenport 1995; Tilly 1978), but to the nation's values and identity. I thus expand on social movement

FIGURE 6.1. The "defend the nation" frame.
Translations (clockwise from left): "These are Fascists?"; "These are Poles?"; "Gay is OK".
Source: DlaPolski TV [online], November 8, 2011, used with permission. Available from: www.dlapolski.pl/faszysci-polacy [Accessed December 1, 2012].

public arenas. Like LGBT groups, opposition groups also package information for their respective audiences, but these messages vary greatly in theme and intensity. In both cases, they initially ground their frames in morality and "the laws of nature," and they portray LGBT rights as a threat to the family, and thus also to the nation.

In Poland, the threat that nonheterosexuality poses to the nation begins with the family but then makes a large leap to become associated with the invasion, occupation, and repression of the nation by outside forces. I call this the "defend the nation" frame, because it is rooted in a philosophy of defensive moral nationalism. The frame is so potent because it harps on the idea that the nation is under attack – as depicted in Figure 6.1, in which wholesome Poles waving the Polish flag are juxtaposed with "the

concepts of threat, which have viewed it as the flip side of opportunities for movement mobilization (Tarrow 2011, 160). By instead focusing on how threat is perceived by the reactionary movement (Fetner 2008), I thus also put forward the idea that collective threat can create opportunities for opposition group identity formation and for subsequent mobilization (Almeida 2003; Zepeda-Millán 2011).

external other" waving the EU, rainbow, and (ironically) Soviet flags. Thus, as Richard Mole (2011) has also shown in the case of Latvia, threat is framed as external and presented in a way that suggests norms on sexuality can dismantle the many attributes of national identity. The Polish frame of resistance creates an artificial binary between Polish values and the imagined European queer periphery.

In Slovenia, nonheterosexuality is framed as a threat to children and reproduction. Adopting Roman Kuhar's (2011) term, I use the phrase "the well-being of children" to define the Slovenian countermovement's frame. The frame links LGBT rights to societal frustrations with change in social structures, such as that provoked by lower birth rates. While the "well-being of children" frame is also inherently about the nation, the argumentation is not extrapolated to threat via invasive external power – it is not about the occupation of the Slovenian nation.

In Slovenia, the opposition has less public visibility, and nationalist and religious groups do not always rely on the same narrative. In Poland, the threat attributed to LGBT norms sparked a vocal call to "defend the nation" and presence by groups that define themselves as both national and religious. In what follows, I explore how anti-LGBT actors employed these frames and the types of actors who mobilized in response to LGBT visibility in four arenas: conventional political debates, the streets, the media, and the education system.

Conventional politics: the Roman Catholic Church(es)

The FRA's reports on sexuality exemplify the different political roles that the Catholic Church plays across contexts:

Slovenia: The church adheres to the Vatican's moral condemnation of homosexuality. It stresses, however, its human standpoint toward homosexuals and says that the church is not going to turn its back on them, but they must purify themselves. Bishop Kramberger of Maribor stated in an interview with Radio Slovenia, "The Church cannot accept homosexuals, but it may never sentence them." (FRA 2009b, 8)

Poland: The Catholic Church has considerable cultural and political influence and actively takes part in the public debate regarding LGBT issues. Their stance is very much against granting LGBT persons equal rights ... There are numerous incidents where Church officials have expressed homophobic hate speech ... For example, homosexuality has been called a disease, and/or a disorder, which needs to be cured and that homosexual persons need to be isolated from society. Similarly, it has been argued that homosexuality is in opposition to the 'European civilization.' (FRA 2009a, 10)

According to Slovenian LGBT activists, the church did not play a politically pivotal role in opposition to the movement, and it only entered the public debate on LGBT issues concerning registered partnership and adoption. The message broadcast by the church revolved around the family. Even then, "some representatives of the Roman Catholic Church did not condemn the legal regulation of homosexual partnership [but said it] should not be made equal to marriage" (Kuhar 2008). In opposition to the partnership legislation, the church "held press conferences on this issue, saying that [LGBT people] are going to corrupt family values ... But on the other side [LGBT organizations] formed a strong campaign which connected all existing LGBT groups, called the 'Campaign for All Families'" (interview no. 101).[14] Activists were ambivalent about the church's effectiveness in public debates on sexuality: "Whenever it comes to something that conflicts with their values, they'll issue a statement, but I am not sure how effective those statements are. They are not taken very seriously, and the media does not reflect on every statement" (interview no. 107).

Slovenian LGBT organizations began demanding partnership rights in 1997, achieving success in 2005 with registered partnerships. Initially, three Slovenian LGBT organizations (ŠKUC, Magnus, and ŠKUC-LL) and other experts (academic, legal, and psychiatric) brought the initiative to the government and established a working group for the draft law on registered partnership (interview no. 101). The eventual 2005 bill (implemented in 2006), which allows for registered partnerships, was drafted and passed following the 2004 election, which brought the conservative Slovenian Democratic Party (SDS) to power. While activists were disappointed with the inferiority of these partnerships to marriage (as in most cases where partnerships have been granted), it is worth noting that the governing SDS that passed the bill is the only party with ties to the church.

The church contributed to the public debate more actively later on, as activists demanded that the benefits of registered partnership be expanded. When asked if his group faced structured opposition, the president of one Slovenian LGBT organization said, "No, not really. Until the Family [Code], there were no organized opposition groups" (interview no. 108). The *Družinski zakonik* (Family Code) sought to expand the registered partnership legislation and give same-sex registered partnerships the same legal rights as those of heterosexual partnerships,

---

[14] LGBT activists recognized and reacted to the "well-being of children" frame. The 2012 Ljubljana Pride theme was "Day of Families" and the logo showed the silhouettes of six children walking together.

including the right to second-parent adoption. In this case, the Catholic and minority Islamic hierarchies in Slovenia together spoke out against the Family Code, exemplifying the church's willingness to use a frame that invoked a heterogeneous national identity. One LGBT activist noted the irony of the new union between Catholicism and Islam: "It was the first joint statement of the Christian Church and Muslims in Slovenia. After 2,000 years of wars among themselves they finally united against gays ... I guess we brought them together" (interview no. 107).[15]

Among the Slovenian opposition, the Institute for Family Life and Culture (KUL), founded in 2009, was the most vocal and organized. KUL's campaign embodied the "well-being of children" frame, which activists linked to emulating the initially successful 2008 campaign by the Mormon Church against Proposition 8 in California (interviews no. 107 and 108).[16] The organization cited social issues related to marriage, childbirth, abortion, suicide, alcoholism, and poverty as their rationales for opposing the Family Code. Tadej Strehovec (2012), KUL's founder and secretary of the Commission for Justice and Peace at the Slovenian Bishops' Conference, ironically referenced the high birth rates in other EU countries (those that have same-sex unions) as grounds for preserving the traditional family in Slovenia. Despite Strehovec's role as the most vocal opponent of the Family Code, he wrote only about the societal structure of family and child, making no reference to unwanted outside forces or inherently Slovenian values. Interestingly, the Slovenian opposition has often used European frames, but for the purpose of distinguishing their nation from the more "uncivilized" Balkans (panel no. 215).

The relationship between the Slovenian Church hierarchy and KUL also exemplifies the backseat role the church has taken. Despite ideological ties, the church consistently denied its involvement with the institute, and KUL claims it is privately funded. LGBT activists created some controversy, however, when they exposed a direct connection: the church's server hosted KUL's website (interviews no. 107, 111, and 151):

The Catholic Church was the most active party against the Family Code, but they did it quietly, setting up an independent lobbying group that says it's separate

---

[15] Transreligious collaboration of this type did not occur in Poland, as most members of the opposition feared it would challenge their attempt to frame the issue as a threat to the homogeneous nation.

[16] Proposition 8 was the 2008 California referendum that reversed the legalization of same-sex unions. It remains unclear whether there were any formal ties between the Mormon Church and KUL, though the interviewees who mentioned the connection assume it was informal emulation.

from the Catholic Church. Yet, their website server can be traced back to the church, and funds were funneled from the church to [KUL]. (interview no. 111)

Despite these efforts, in 2015 the Slovenian parliament adopted – with a large majority – a bill to grant same-sex couples marriage and adoption rights. The Family Code's more encompassing partnership and adoption bill had also been passed in 2011, only to be reversed by small majority in a subsequent referendum. A request by opposition groups to hold a referendum on the 2015 bill was initally denied, but later the Constitutional Court granted an appeal. The referendum held in December of that year was successful, blocking the bill's implementation. To the detriment of LGBT activists, turnout was low at 36 percent and consisted primarily of people in demographics that typically oppose LGBT rights. Despite this serious setback, activists remain optimistic for the future in light of a new government proposal for enhanced partnerships and polls showing 60 percent of Slovenians in favor of same-sex marriage (Kearney 2015; Novak 2015).

Unlike in Slovenia, the church in Poland has not shied away from vocally trying to influence Polish politics through debates on social issues. The church maintains close ties with Polish political parties and parliamentarians, and the Episcopate has approached voters directly, sending them letters that support candidates who defend the inviolable and natural rights of man, from conception to death (Borowik 2002, 244). The 2005 campaign of former President Lech Kaczyński produced a document called "Catholic Poland in Christian Europe," listing the 2004 and 2005 bans on the Warsaw Equality Marches as successes (Gruszczyńska 2007, 100). And the church leadership has been vocal in implementing political roadblocks to public assembly by LGBT groups. Cracow Old Town's roughly thirty churches always posed an obstacle to the organizers of LGBT marches, since the city originally requested that march routes not pass in front of any church.[17]

In 1997, the same year Slovenian activists and their government established a working group on same-sex unions, Article 18 of the Polish constitution defined marriage as a union between a man and a woman. Pope John Paul II's visit to Poland in 1995 emphasized the role he thought the Catholic Church should play in the new Polish politics; he highlighted the issues fundamental to nourishing the Christian nature of the

---

[17] Outside the formal political sphere, members of the clergy have occasionally protested LGBT demonstrations on the streets. Grażyna Kubica (2009, 133) notes that at the 2004 Cracow Festival a Benedictine monk would appear from a church on the march route to sign the cross and perform an exorcism.

state: opposition to both abortion and same-sex partnerships (Burns 2009, 166). The visit was a direct attempt to oversee and shape the country's new legal foundations, including the constitution (Burns 2009, 166).[18] Several LGBT activists ascribed the obstacles they faced surrounding partnership and other movement goals to the role of the church in politics:

Belgium is very Catholic, and the church didn't agree with [same-sex] marriages, and a year later they got it. In Poland it's different, the church is involved in different aspects of life, especially politics. They talk too much about politics. They have religion in schools and feel legitimate in telling politicians how to lead. Here the church has a super position. (interview no. 140)

With the support of thirty-six senators and various LGBT representatives, in November 2003 Senator Maria Szyszkowska submitted to parliament a motion to allow same-sex partnership, but no legislative procedure was started, and the draft bill was never sent to a parliamentary committee to take a final form (Mizielińska 2010, 331). In January 2013, after a few failed proposals and just over a year after electoral wins by former presidents of LGBT organizations, a partnership bill had a real chance in parliament, but it lost by seventeen votes (228 to 211).[19] A gender-neutral civil partnership bill failed for a third time in 2014, by fifty votes (235 to 185). Though the initiatives in 2013 and 2014 unleashed typically harsh homophobic rhetoric in parliament, the sizeable support for some form of partnership exemplifies the shift LGBT politics has taken since domestic and transnational activism made the issue visible at the turn of the century. Nevertheless, compared to Slovenia, the ability of the church to influence political responses to LGBT norms is far greater in Poland.

Resistance on the streets

The "well-being of children" frame in Slovenia has also not spurred public mobilization the way the "defend the nation" frame has in Poland. Since independence in 1991, the Slovenian state has not banned freedom of assembly, which is protected by Article 42 of the constitution (FRA 2009b, 5). LGBT activists only note one incident, where the proprietor of the Ljubljana Castle withdrew a reservation to use the venue to celebrate

---

[18] Article 25 of the constitution stipulates that "relations between the Republic of Poland and the Roman Catholic Church shall be determined by [the] international treaty concluded with the Holy See, and by statute."

[19] The partnership, which was also presented as an alternative for heterosexual couples, was inferior to marriage. The strongest backing came from the PO (146 of 206 votes) and from two opposition parties, the anti-clerical RP and the left SLD, with 42 and 23 votes respectively. The other three parties, with 137 Law and Justice votes, were unanimously opposed.

the tenth anniversary of the LGBT movement when the nature of the event was revealed (FRA 2009b, 6). Furthermore, as Table 6.4 shows, there are no anti-LGBT demonstrations on record (FRA 2009b, 6).

The situation was different in Poland, where "various groups and politicians organize marches of normalcy, especially around the time of gay pride marches" (interview no. 129).[20] Among the most active groups in mobilizing demonstrations is the Stowarzyszenie Kultury Chrześcijańskiej im. Ks. Piotra Skargi (Father Piotr Skarga Association for Christian Culture), founded in Cracow in 1999 (Mizielińska 2010, 333). This group organized the annual Marsz dla Życia i Rodziny (March for Life and Family) from 2006 to 2008, for which participants donned crosses, waved the typical Polish national symbols, and carried banners saying "Stop Perversion" and "Marriage is One Man, One Woman." As is typical in Poland, chants often took a nationalist bent: "Lesbians and faggots are ideal citizens of the EU" and "Healthy Poles are not like that" (Gruszczyńska 2007, 100). Around this time, the Skarga Association published anti-homosexual propaganda leaflets and sent letters to citizens in Cracow, Poznan, and Warsaw that encouraged recipients to contact local authorities. In 2006 it also disseminated to schools a fifty-page brochure, "Hidden Problems of Homosexuality," which, among other things, linked homosexuality to pedophilia (Mizielińska 2010, 333). The group has ties to the American Society for the Defense of Tradition, Family, and Property (TFP), a transnational Catholic organization that activists suspect funds the "wealthy" organization's fliers (interviews no. 129 and 139). The secretary at TFP confirmed the "sister-organization" status of the Skarga Association but denied having transferred funds to Poland (interview no. 147).[21] Another Catholic organization, the Fundacja Mamy i Taty (Foundation for Mothers and Fathers) is vocal in the public sphere and lobbies conservative politicians (interviews no. 129 and 141). Before EuroPride in 2010, it paid for a full-page newspaper advertisement outlining the homosexual threat and, together with the Catholic magazine *Fronda*, organized an online petition and counterprotest (Redakcja Fronda.pl 2010). All three groups have a Catholic mandate, but they deploy a clearly nationalist discourse around the defense of uniquely Polish values.

---

[20] "[These demonstrations] are never very big, but they do happen and they have politicians marching with them, so it is not that niche" (interview no. 129).

[21] He says that there are ample opportunities for networking and knowledge transfer (e.g. on organizing pro-life marches) at conferences, but that cross-border financial transfers happened strictly through tax-deductible, private donations and were minimal at best (interview no. 147).

TABLE 6.4. *Slovenian mobilization in the public sphere, 2000–2009*

	2000	2001	2002	2003	2004	2005	2006	2007	2008	2009
# of LGBT demonstrations and parades	0	1	1	1	2	2	2	2	2	2
# of demonstrations against tolerance for LGBT people	0	0	0	0	0	0	0	0	0	0

Source: Table recreated from 2009 FRA Report (FRA 2009b)

Several activists identified their early opposition as Młodzież Wszechpolska (All Polish Youth), a far-right nationalist and Catholic youth organization founded in 1922 and revived after independence in 1989. In response to Cracow's Festival of Culture for Tolerance in 2004, the group formulated their "Declaration of Ideas" as follows: "The Nation is the most important worldly value. First, after God, service is deserved by our own nation. [The Roman Catholic Church] creates and strengthens Polish national identity" (Kubica 2009, 130). A former president of All Polish Youth justified the strong Polish opposition more broadly, based on three core Polish values that he said were contrary to the goals of the LGBT movement: power of the country (legal sovereignty over international influences), Christian values (a Christian concept of mankind and human dignity), and the common good of the Polish community (against modern individualism and liberalism) (interview no. 141). The organization, which had direct ties to the PiS, was most active against LGBT mobilization from 2004 to 2007 but lost influence after the vocal anti-LGBT governing coalition of PiS, LPR, and SRP dissolved in 2007.

Other Polish nationalist groups also mobilized against LGBT rights, making LGBT politics the focus of their "defense of nation" rhetoric (see Figure 6.1). The Narodowe Odrodzenie Polski (National Rebirth of Poland, NOP) describes its mission as "spiritually motivated" nationalism, with the first two points of their 10-point declaration specifically referencing the Christian faith: "We, the Polish nationalists concentrated in the ranks of the NOP, contribute to the development of the Polish national community. Our actions will be based on the teachings of the Catholic Church" (NOP 2011).[22] As depicted in Figure 6.2, the organization's logos include a series of religious, anti-EU, anti-American, and antigay symbols that represent the "defend the nation" frame. The opposition at Polish LGBT marches commonly displays an antigay symbol that depicts two stick-figure men in a sexual position encircled by the phrase "Zakaz Pedałowania" (Ban Faggots). Similarly, the group Obóz Narodowo-Radykalny (National Radical Camp, ONR) lists "the development and revival of national and Catholic values" as their central objective and takes an identical position vis-à-vis the LGBT movement.[23] Finally, LGBT activists listed the informal fringe group that runs a website called Redwatch Polska among those that organize violent counterprotesters at LGBT events. The website also created an online list

---

[22] Translated from the Polish by the author.
[23] Translated from the Polish by the author.

FIGURE 6.2. NOP symbols.
Translations (left to right, top to bottom): "Protected, registered symbols of the NOP," "Hand with sword, aka. Phalanx," "Ban fags," "Celtic cross," "White-red flame," "The EU – you choose, you lose," "Cross and sword," "Eagle in crown with cross, fasces, and ax".
Source: NOP 2011.

targeting individuals from leftist groups and LGBT and other minority groups.[24]

In practice, these groups mobilize extremists from around the country to gather and block LGBT marches. Often these forms of recruitment are informal, for example, through soccer fan forums that bring together hooligans opposed to LGBT rights. In 2011, before the first LGBT pride march in the city of Lodz, organizers at KPH-Lodz created their own accounts on soccer fan forums to gain information on how the extremist opposition

---

[24] The three men responsible for coordinating the website were arrested, and their website was blocked by the Polish government due to the illegal xenophobic content; the group responded by using an international server to make it accessible (interview no. 139). Redwatch Polska has links to other Redwatch websites in Germany, New Zealand, and the United Kingdom. The first Redwatch website was started by supporters of the British People's Party.

was organizing (interviews no. 130 and 131). Because nationalist groups often use violent tactics, organizers planned accordingly, informing themselves and the police about numbers and locations and potentially making alterations to the route (interviews no. 130 and 131). Describing the Lodz march, an LGBT activist who traveled in for the event from Warsaw, recalled:

> We saw it clearly. We were on the road lined with police, and [the counterprotesters] were in the park. We had 150 people and they had plenty, around 400. They threw plastic bottles [filled] with water, and potatoes, eggs, and tomatoes. Eggs and tomatoes are popular. They are very aggressive and shout, "Go to the gas chambers." And alongside the nationalists we also see church people, with crosses, with Bibles, they throw holy water and say things like, "Oh, Holy Father, bless them." They don't come with the nationalists but they are there next to each other. (interview no. 139)[25]

The recollection paints a vivid picture of the ties between religion and nationalism in the Polish countermovement.

In contrast, Slovenian far-right groups remain poorly organized. The two opposition groups that activists sometimes, though rarely, mentioned in interviews and surveys are Tukaj je Slovenija (Here is Slovenia) and the Slovenian branch of Blood and Honor. The former makes a reference to the church on its website, but religion is not mentioned among its three fundamental goals, which are patriotism, bonds of friendship among Slovenians, and activism to draw attention to the Slovenian nation's right to exist. The latter, Blood and Honor, is a group that has promoted fascist ideals through rock music concerts since 2001 (Trplan 2005, 231). Neither group has organized counterprotests, but they are responsible for sporadic violence directed at individuals and for vandalizing the facades of LGBT organizations' buildings. In 2010, for example, affiliates of Here is Slovenia attacked three men after the Pride parade, for which they were sentenced to a year and a half in prison.[26] According to an activist from the LGBT group Legebitra:

---

[25] One of the organizers of the event listed the attendance figures as 200 for the LGBT activists and 350–400 for the opposition (interview no. 131).

[26] These attacks were also related to the vandalizing of Café Open, a popular gay-friendly Ljubljana cafe that has been damaged several times since 2009. Three perpetrators were found guilty of a crime of incitement to hatred, violence, and intolerance. Such acts of "physical violence or interference by third parties with the rights of LGBT people has won severe and unanimous condemnation from the highest Slovenian officials" (FRA 2009b, 23).

The attacks after Pride were not organized. They see someone on the street and say, "He's a faggot, let's kick him." They only organized after the arrests were made [to protest the sentence]. There was a protest of maybe 100 [people], dressed in black with masks, in front of the court. The [hate crime] sentence was high, which they [found to be exaggerated] because "a kick is a kick, just a bit of fun." Now they say they are not against the gays, but against the system. They graffitied the house of the judge that ruled in the case. (interview no. 107)

The difference between Slovenia and Poland in public sphere opposition to LGBT rights is that while Slovenian "nationalist groups are anti-religious, and quite strongly anti-religious" (interview no. 108), Polish religious and nationalist groups both use the "defend the nation" frame in response to LGBT rights, even though the Polish church hierarchy is far removed from many of the groups described above.

Education and the media

The ramifications of threat perception are also apparent in other spheres of public life, such as education and the media. In Poland, schools are among the most conservative elements of society. Either a religion or ethics course is mandatory, and the overwhelming majority of students (around 90 percent) opt for religion. This is in part because priests who are employed by the schools encourage students to enroll and, more generally, because "being the 'other' is not popular for young people" (interview no. 130). The curriculum is also conservative: sex education is limited and, in many cases, uses archaic biology textbooks that refer to the need to "cure" homosexuality (Bączkowski 2010).[27] The previous PiS/LPR/SRP government banned curricula addressing sexuality altogether and the "family life" curriculum only refers to traditional heterosexual families (Krzeminski 2008). In 2006, Roman Giertych, Polish Minister of Education, dismissed the director of the Service Teacher Training Center, Mirosław Sielatycki, for promoting homosexuality (Biedroń and Abramowicz 2007). Sielatycki had simply

---

[27] The Church is also involved in "curing" homosexuality in the private sphere. Father Francis Blachnicki and Ruchu Światło-Życie (Light and Life Movement) founded the treatment center Odwaga (Courage!) in Lublin. Supported by several Polish bishops and priests, the center uses controversial psychotherapy techniques "to help people with homosexual tendencies to achieve purity and rejection of the homosexual lifestyle" ("ODWAGA" 2012). LGBT actors say that financing tied to the Ex-Gay Watch and to the American National Association for Research & Therapy of Homosexuality brought at least two American speakers to Poland in the last ten years (interviews no. 8 and 129). In 2011, however, NARTH's Joseph Nicolosi was obliged to move the venue of his talk from a medical school in Poznan after the *Gazeta Wyborcza* published a damning front-page critique of gay-to-straight therapy preceding the event.

published the European Council's recommended guidelines for teachers, *Compass–Education on Human Rights* (FRA 2009a).[28] Polish "teachers are very reluctant to talk about homosexuality for fear of losing their jobs," reported the FRA (2009a, 9). In 2010, the Polish Equality Minister, Elżbieta Radziszewska, argued that EU law allows Catholic schools to discriminate against LGBT teachers, and then asked that opinions contrary to hers be censored, provoking startled and reproachful responses from MEPs (European Parliament 2010).

By contrast, the nine-year curriculum of the Slovenian education system requires fifth-grade schoolchildren to learn about sexual diversity, and in some cases textbooks do mention sexual orientation and same-sex families (Kuhar 2008). While LGBT advocates argue that the issue deserves more prominence in the education system, there have been no state bans on discussing homosexuality, and LGBT activists have sent representatives to lecture at a number of public schools (Kuhar 2008).

As is the case with education, the domestic media uses two different narratives in the two states. Polish members of the LGBT movement highlight ultra-conservative Catholic media sources as a well-organized source of resistance. Prominent Catholic media sources, including Radio Maryja and the magazine *Fronda*, made homosexuality a household issue among clerical communities by tying issues of sexuality to the vast array of social topics they cover (interview no. 129, see fronda.pl and radiomaryja.pl). Similarly, scholars have described Radio Maryja as its own social movement with an action frame that postulates: "Any attack on Polishness is perceived as an attack on the church and vice versa. In this perspective ... the nation is not history's but God's creation" (Bylok and Pędziwiatr 2010). Both networks publicize LGBT demonstrations and call for people to oppose them. The church hierarchy has distanced itself from the extreme perspectives voiced by Radio Maryja, but their parallel deployment of the "defend the nation" frame has given them influence in the national discourse against LGBT rights.

Other researchers also note the "dubious quality" of Polish mainstream journalism on LGBT issues at the turn of the century (Kubica 2009, 134). Grażyna Kubica (2009) gives examples from journalism across political leanings, all of which were naive in their reporting of the 2004 Cracow Festival of Culture for Tolerance, an event that some have

---

[28] A Warsaw district court later ruled that Sielatycki was discriminated against, and he was paid 5,700 euros in damages.

called the "Polish Stonewall" (Gruszczyńska 2007). She notes that the press generally mischaracterized these early events as a provocation – for example, the media used images of drag queens from the Berlin Love Parade, which would be perceived as radical in Polish society, instead of actual images from Polish LGBT events (Kubica 2009, 135). A public statement by a *Gazeta Wyborcza* journalist – an authority among the Polish press – exemplifies the media's ignorance: "No newspapers, at least the important ones, wrote about [KPH] or about the festival, unjustly. They only portrayed the dominant Polish feelings" (Voxerbrant 2004). On most occasions, reporting on "dominant Polish feelings" gave little or no voice to the supporters or organizers of LGBT events. While the Catholic media has not changed its tone, LGBT organizations' ties to the mainstream media have improved considerably in Poland since 2007 (interview no. 8).[29] Several activists also point to some working relationships with journalists of the mainstream media that result in a more "neutral" depiction of LGBT people (FRA 2009a).

According to proponents of LGBT rights, the mainstream Slovenian media attained fluency on LGBT issues much earlier than did the media in Poland. Kuhar's (2003) study on Slovenian print media concluded that its representation of homosexuality was favorable or neutral. The Slovenian media also actively reports on hate crimes toward LGBT people (Kuhar 2008). LGBT activists cited partners and contact points in the media to whom they have access for fair reporting. By contrast, the opposing Institute for Family Life and Culture is motivated in large part by what they say is underrepresentation by the media: "[Our] main purpose is to acquaint visitors with ... the values that touch on family, culture, life, and solidarity that the mainstream Slovenian media ignore" (24kul.si 2013, para. 3).[30] While activists did remark on the Slovenian media's tendency to stereotype LGBT people, Slovenian journalists do not display the aggressive homophobia large segments of the Polish media do.

Across the board, in conventional politics and on the streets, Poland's opposition has outpaced its Slovenian counterpart in degree and intensity. The church in Poland confidently worked to marginalize LGBT people by

[29] Activists attribute this improvement to domestic activism and to the transnational and international attention given to the situation of LGBT Poles. These factors have infused the discourse with new frames of reference and more complex, nuanced understandings of sexuality. While contingents of Polish society already had these understandings, they were often ignored by the domestic media. Transnational visibility has influenced the debate by giving such arguments legitimacy and credibility in the broader framework of modern European society.

[30] Translated from the Slovenian by the author.

branding them a threat to the Polish nation and to European civilization. The "defend the nation" frame in Poland mobilized a fervent opposition, uniting diverse actors under a narrative of nation that equated LGBT rights with an invasion of the domestic sphere. In Slovenia, the perceived threat was lower, and the "well-being of children" frame could not mobilize or unite a fragmented domestic opposition. Slovenian LGBT actors commanded a discourse that maintained that LGBT rights were part of what it meant to return to Europe, and the church was not in a position to "adopt the powerful rhetoric of being a 'traditional,' 'national' or 'state-Constitutional Church' " (Črnič and Lesjak 2003, 361).

Resistance as visibility?

Yet what effect do the forms of resistance described above have on the ability of LGBT movements to generate social and political change in their respective contexts? Paradoxically, movements of resistance also enhance the visibility of LGBT norms and can strengthen the chances of LGBT movement success in contexts where strong transnational channels are established. As one activist noted: "Conservative backlashes have finally opened a possibility for a real dialog on an everyday level" (survey no. 80). In most cases, resistance follows the initial visibility of the LGBT norm, in a period of protracted discourse surrounding its legitimacy. Conor O'Dwyer's (2012, 344–8) discussion of the role of anti-LGBT backlash in Poland presents a similarly powerful idea: that backlash can benefit LGBT movements. The argument here echoes an element of radical flank theory: that movements generate negative attention when they employ an extreme repertoire, which can, in turn, benefit the groups from which they are distinguishing themselves (Haines 1984; Minkoff 1994).[31] Through a process in which it fuels deliberation, resistance benefits the cause of the LGBT rights movement by making the issue more salient.

---

[31] While radical flank theory usually looks at this process within one movement, examining how one "flank" interacts with another, the radicalization of a movement can also make the opposing movement's position seem more moderate. My argument corroborates Doug McAdam's findings that disruptive countermovement activity, including violence aimed at opposing demonstrators, can lead to favorable policy outcomes and enhance societal sympathies for the movement (McAdam 1999; McAdam and Su 2002). It is also in line with the work of Michael Dorf and Sidney Tarrow (2014), who show that the religious right created a legal opportunity for the American LGBT movement. See also the work on backlash by Benjamin Bishin, Thomas Hayes, Matthew Incantalupo, and Tony Smith (2015).

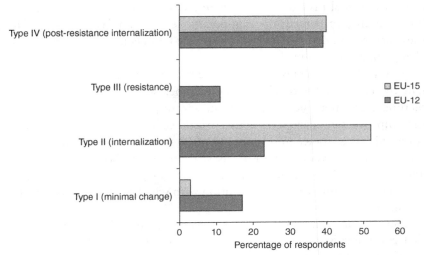

FIGURE 6.3. Type of norm reception process described by respondents (%).
Source: Author's Transnational LGBT Organizations Survey (see Appendix), *n* = 125.

Data derived from my survey of transnationally connected LGBT rights organizations show that resistance is preferable to invisibility over time. Expert respondents from each organization described the effect of "visibility" on change, which I then coded according to the four different processes theorized in Chapter 2 and depicted in Figure 6.3. Among the organizational representatives in new EU-12 states, 39 percent describe a nonlinear Type IV process, where some improvement followed an initial backlash. In this process, transnationally embedded domestic actors publicize resistance and international attention grows, which in turn fuels visibility and active deliberation in the target state. This process suggests a strategic relationship where resistance leads to more international visibility, but only if transnationally embedded domestic groups exist. Another 22 percent of survey respondents said that visibility leads to a Type II process, whereby the LGBT norm generates deliberation once visible, making it salient. In these cases, norm brokers highlight historical narratives of LGBT people in their own respective countries, resistance is minimal, and states conform to the standards of a community to which they belong. Of the respondents, another 11 percent described a Type III process that involved an intensification of anti-LGBT politics by religious and nationalist sectors of society. In these cases, the absence of activist networks and few channels of transnational pressures fail to counter the arguments of the opposition. Finally, 17 percent of respondents described a Type I process. In these cases, no adequate levels of visibility had been reached and, thus, change had not occurred.

Among EU-12 member states, an active resistance has occurred in half the cases analyzed. The EU-15 member states paint an optimistic picture: more than 90 percent of survey respondents described eventual improvement, even if an active resistance had mobilized in the past. A mobilized resistance in response to norm visibility is common; indeed, it precedes improvement in most cases. These results, both among EU-12 and EU-15 LGBT organizations, are quite staggering, especially when taking into account the general caution with which LGBT activists measure success.

The predominant theme in the survey and interview data suggests that resistance is partly self-defeating because it contributes to making the issue visible. I substantiate these findings with a discussion of the deliberative process and discursive advantage that LGBT actors have in the European context. According to actors for and against LGBT rights, there are several plausible explanations for this phenomenon, all of which rest on the theme of visibility via deliberation. In general, the respondents' explanations centered around two themes: (1) "defend the nation" frames used by anti-LGBT groups mobilize an extreme, sometimes violent, demographic that eventually drifts out of sync with the sensibilities of the general population; and (2) anti-LGBT movements have weaker ties to, and less support from, transnational contexts than the LGBT movements themselves.

Radical tactics

According to LGBT activists, anti-LGBT activism often fails because it employs extreme arguments (emotional, rooted in the past, aggressive, and ideological), which can result in increased public sympathy for the LGBT cause. While the opposition can construct counterarguments to claims made by the LGBT movement that some find compelling (e.g. that LGBT rights are against natural design) (Bob 2012), opposition actors who are granted attention on the street and in the media generally use provocative antigay arguments. This is especially so in cases where the church has delivered a "defend the nation" response that the far right can appropriate. These arguments, though they find receptive ears in most national contexts, do not fare well in European public sphere discourse. Resistance has made the issue visible to the general public because it provokes a strong reaction when there are LGBT groups who can publicize it in the European polity.

This was the case in Poland when the nationalist NOP trademarked an aforementioned homophobic symbol (a red circle crossing out two male stick-figures in a sexual position) as their logo in 2011. While rightist counterprotesters have often used the symbol at LGBT events, the NOP's decision to trademark it backfired when a subsequent court case prohibited its use, further legitimizing LGBT groups. Before the court banned the trademark, Polish LGBT organizations publicized the story widely, and various European institutions and the Polish and international press reported on it. In another political arena, one interviewee referred to an instance in the Polish parliament in the fall of 2011, where newly elected and openly gay parliamentarian Robert Biedroń was told he was "punching below the belt," a reference to his sexuality that brought the parliament, especially members of PiS and the Civic Platform Party, to laughter. This disrespectful reaction drew the attention of European institutions and media sources. One of the activists who contributed to KPH's press release following the incident said, "My feeling is that after MPs laughed at Robert, all media felt sympathetic to him. Now even the newspapers called it homophobic! The PO is embarrassed" (interview no. 140). Finally, at Ruch Palikota's postelection party, which also celebrated Poland's first gay and trans parliamentarians, KPH's policy coordinator jokingly whispered, "And what exactly am I going to tell our [international] sponsors now? Gross homophobia is definitely an easier sell for sympathy than the world's only transgender parliamentarian" (event no. 206).

These examples suggest how LGBT actors can engage and strategically interact with countermovement mobilization when they are well connected transnationally – even in a context of highly mobilized political homophobia. And this process is not limited to Poland; a Hungarian activist and academic described a similar process:

The right-wing has become very strong in the past four years. But I think there was a [favorable] shift in the public discourse in response. In 2008, when the Gay Pride happened it was very violent and that was a bit too much for a lot of people ... even for people who thought that Gay Pride shouldn't happen. It was so violent and so aggressive and damaging – even to the road and to historical monuments! It was too much, you know. There were between 1,000 and 2,000 marchers and, like 5,000 riot police. It was horrible. *But that horror made the whole thing more visible.* By the "whole thing" I mean both extremist violence and gay people. And it was not the gay people anymore who were seen as violating public morals, but the extremists. In this case, the discourse created by left-wing intellectuals drew more sympathy. (interview no. 123, emphasis added)

Seven years later, the scene in Budapest looked quite different. Despite the rule of the far-right government, the 2015 Pride in Budapest, which was described as "safe" and "even joyful," went largely unopposed on the street (Gessen 2015). The dynamic also holds in potential EU member states. According to a scholar-activist from Bosnia-Herzegovina, violence against LGBT people peaked in 2014; yet, while violence peaked, "activism blossomed," and the constitutional court felt compelled to pass legislation protecting minorities (panel no. 215).

The bizarre group of (in)voluntary bedfellows, from xenophobic nationalists to traditional Catholics, results in a fractured and uncoordinated opposition that has little impact on the formation of a compelling frame or network beyond initial mobilization. For initial mobilization, frames resting on religion and nationalism were effective, but then became too radical to sustain, especially when "the whole world" – or at least all of Europe – was watching. By contrast, LGBT groups have found a balance by using both local and European frames that connect the norm to democratic values and human rights responsibilities in an international society of states. Pointing to other states in their club, they can also employ frames of inevitability that destabilize a countermovement if its members feel their chances of winning are low (Tarrow 2011). LGBT groups make the norm salient by connecting activists and grafting international ideas to domestic ones, thereby framing the message to fit locally – especially when domestic contestation heightens.

Transnational ties

LGBT activists also have a critical advantage, in that they are embedded both vertically and horizontally in enduring cross-border constellations through European institutions and networks of activists, both formal and informal. Many conservative resistance movements often fail to activate a similar identity or establish equivalent ties across borders because their philosophies are rooted in nationalism. Despite the Catholic Church's transnational nature, for example, its opposition to nonheterosexual acts often becomes deeply bound up with a popular nationalism that precludes the use of transnational scripts and channels for legitimate meaning-making. This is in large part because the nationalist nature of the opposition actors leads them to worry that an external presence could diminish the dominant frame, which revolves around rejecting outside influences (interviews no. 141 and 150). The notion of collaboration between like-minded outsiders perplexed one member of the resistance: "You mean having some foreigners, like Germans, demonstrate? Why would we have Germans with us? We don't want Germans here. We are doing this for Poland" (interview no. 150). Leftist groups dramatically outpace their opposition in transnational presence at these events – and not just LGBT groups. On Poland's Independence Day in 2011, for example, ninety-two German anarchists and communists were arrested in Warsaw for protesting against a demonstration organized by the All Polish Youth and the ONR (Polskie Radio 2011).[32]

Although transnational networks for anti-LGBT counterprotesters do exist, in most of the European cases I analyzed they are sporadic and do not last.[33] Those LGBT actors that mentioned the opponents' potential transnational ties admitted that "they are not well organized and the coalition is weak. The only thing they have that unites them is 'us' [LGBT people]" (interview no. 140). Sexual identity creates an intrinsic solidarity that ties LGBT groups across borders. The opposition has the disadvantage of finding it difficult to activate a similarly uprooted identity: in many cases, they do not want to. In sum, LGBT and anti-LGBT groups differ in terms of transnational material resources, the transmission of know-how, and human capital.

Networks of homophobia do play a role globally (Bob 2012; Weiss and Bosia 2013), but they are often delegitimized in regions where the systems of knowledge have an LGBT rights mandate. According to the president of KPH, "Many American Christian groups are active in Africa and elsewhere, but in Europe I think they no longer believe [having an impact] is possible" (interview no. 140). While opposition groups can craft competing claims in the domestic realm (Bob 2012), they nonetheless introduce a discourse that evokes a reaction from state authorities, as various sides of the electorate request it of them. When these authorities

---

[32] "'For years, the right-wing government and the Catholic Church have promoted a racist, anti-Semitic and homophobic atmosphere in Poland,' the German website antifa.de declares, adding that last year, Polish anti-fascists got 'inspired' by the German left-wing blockade of a march in Dresden" (Polskie Radio 2011).

[33] For example, the NOP lists ties to groups in Italy (Forza Nuova), the United Kingdom (British National Party), Spain (Movimiento Social Republicano), Greece (Χρυσή Αυγή), Cyprus (ELAM), and Sweden (Svenskarnas Parti). LGBT activists claim that transnational ties to religious groups, mainly to American evangelical communities, have helped fund some campaigns (such as the Skarga Association's fliers linking homosexuality to pedophilia), but further research established that these transfers are minimal (interview no. 147). Transnational guests have been present at some anti-LGBT demonstrations, as in Latvia, where American evangelicals spoke at counterdemonstrations surrounding LGBT Prides (interview no. 138, Film Baltic Pride) or at Polish conferences on reparative therapy. Concrete examples like these are, however, not abundant in Europe.

look to the international level for templates with which to respond to LGBT issues, those they find in Europe align with those of LGBT activists.

Summary and conclusion

Six hundred meters from the 2010 EuroPride parade route in Warsaw, conflict brewed. Calling themselves the "Defenders of the Cross," supporters of the late Polish President Kaczyński had placed a 13-foot-high cross in front of the Polish parliament and sparked a heated debate about the separation of church and state in Poland. The two demonstrations – one of Poles with crosses and Polish flags, and one of LGBT people with European flags – is symbolic of a broader conversation in Poland about the place of the church and of LGBT people. For instance, Polish university professors sent an open letter distancing themselves from the misuse of science in the January 2013 parliamentary debate on same-sex partnership, calling the debate degrading to all nonheterosexual and trans people.[34] Former president and iconic Solidarity activist Lech Wałęsa boldly stated in March 2013 that Anna Grodzka and Robert Biedroń should sit outside the walls of the parliamentary chamber for being trans and gay. The two parliamentarians responded by sitting in the chamber's front row, and Wałęsa's son, another parliamentarian, publically distanced himself from his father's statement. This discourse, despite its strong homophobic element, is an intrinsically important element of social change.

Threat perception concerning LGBT norms depends largely on the degree to which the political and moral authority of religious institutions is tied to the histories of political transition and national identities. The argument thus places importance on the situational politicization of religion in national identity. It is the role of religion in people's identities that matters for LGBT politics, and distinctive political manifestations for LGBT resistance can result across states. In Poland, the intense collective reaction in society of a perceived threat from LGBT rights, linked to the church's historically deep ties to the popular nation, resulted in zealous resistance – a resistance that could frame LGBT norms as an external threat to nation. Comparatively, in Slovenia, the weaker credibility of the church hampered its ability to bring together an opposition around a national and moral narrative, which in turn limited its mobilizing

---

[34] LGBT people "deserve the respect recommended by the Catechism of the Catholic Church's principles on human rights." Translated from the Polish by the author.

potential against LGBT rights. The goal of this analysis is not to paint Slovenia as a success story; as in most countries, homophobia is present in the everyday lives of gay and lesbian Slovenians (Greif 2005). Instead, the goal is to explore the relative accomplishments of two increasingly well-organized and well-connected LGBT movements, looking at factors that distinguish domestic responses to LGBT norms.

In the analysis, threat perception based on religious-nationalism traveled further than alternative explanations; for example, explanations rooted in political party power. While rightist parties have contributed to anti-LGBT mobilization, these patterns are not consistent across cases. In Poland, for example, the conservative PiS coalition years from 2005 to 2007 coincided with a heightened resistance to LGBT rights – this was a time when the resistance felt particularly legitimized, during a phase of illiberal politics following EU accession. Yet resistance to LGBT rights had emerged earlier, following a series of events organized by LGBT activists that gave LGBT rights visibility leading up to EU accession. Furthermore, a party power explanation does not hold in Slovenia: no resistance movements mobilized after LGBT activists pushed same-sex partnerships through parliament in 2005, when the conservative SDS party governed. This phenomenon is not unique to Slovenia; it is, for example, the center-right Cameron government in the United Kingdom that pushed for same-sex marriage. In the Czech Republic, societal attitudes were "improving when the registered partnership bill was still a visible issue up to 2006 ... then improvement slowed down, before again gaining momentum in these days with a right/conservative government" (survey no. 66). In France, despite elite support for LGBT rights, a fierce mobilized resistance emerged with the election of socialist President François Hollande and his government's introduction of same-sex marriage.[35] Resistance (in degree and scope) depends on the context, and is linked to the nation's perception of a possible threat.

Whether resistance is effectual, however, is a separate question. The pathway to LGBT rights in Slovenia has been smoother than it has been in Poland, but the active resistance in Poland will not necessarily yield success for opponents of these rights in the long term. In fact, Slovenian

[35] While the French Revolution may have severed the church from the state (and only 5 percent of the French population regularly attends church), the state's attempt to establish a single creed of nation embedded Catholicism in the nation (Zaretsky 2013). Zaretsky cites Tocqueville in his comparison of American pluralism to French nationalism, arguing that the church is paradoxically more relevant for resistance to LGBT rights in France.

attitudes, though they have far outpaced Poland's, did not improve between 2000 and 2008. On the contrary, Poland continued making gains, however small, in the year following an active period of aggressive resistance. In Poland, resistance helped activists make the issue "mainstream" (interview no. 140). The less polarizing formal approach of opposition in Slovenia, grounded in pseudoscientific rational language ("protecting the child") proved slightly more effective for the opposition than did Polish mobilization on the streets (interview no. 151). Slovenians narrowly rejected the Family Code that parliament approved in 2011. They did so again after the passage of marriage and adoption in 2015. Even these setbacks need to be contextualized. The Slovenians were voting on marriage and adoption privileges, which the publics of most states would still reject in 2015. Popular resistance in Poland has contributed to the norm's newfound degree of societal and political attention.

In contexts like post-Cold War Europe, invisibility is more detrimental to the objectives of the LGBT movement than active deliberation fueled by resistance, as the latter destabilizes the state's historical role of keeping LGBT people socially invisible and publically scandalized (Seidman 2004, 247; Weeks 2000). Instead of keeping the issue hidden, the mobilization of an anti-LGBT resistance indirectly puts it on the agenda as something that needs to be deliberated in terms of appropriateness. Paradoxically, when resistance movements occupy the public sphere, they themselves reaffirm and cement the notion that being European is equivalent to respecting LGBT rights.

7

Visibility in movement and transnational politics

The tide of history only advances when people make themselves fully
visible.
                              – Anderson Cooper, 2012

During the opening days of the 2014 Winter Olympics in Sochi, Russia,
activists from a group called the Gay Folks' Movement cunningly
beamed their logo onto the facade of the Russian embassy in Berlin.
This visible act of solidarity was in response to a lengthy campaign by
Russian and transnational activists that voiced concerns about Russia's
draconian state ban on gay "propaganda." So was Google's home page,
which depicted various winter sports in the bright rainbow colors commonly associated with the LGBT movement. Beneath the design, Google
quoted statements on human rights and anti-discrimination from the
Olympic charter. Acts like these, which make the LGBT norm publicly
visible, have gained unparalleled momentum in recent years. And more
and more frequently, prominent figures across the globe, including a
British diving star (Tom Daley), an Icelandic prime minister (Jóhanna
Sigurðardóttir), a Latvian foreign minister (Edgars Rinkēvičs), and a
Polish Catholic priest (Krzystof Charamsa), are coming out. The notable
actor Wentworth Miller came out in 2013 by referencing his Russian
heritage while declining to take part in the annual St. Petersburg film
festival. "I cannot in good conscience participate in a celebratory occasion," he wrote, "hosted by a country where people like myself are being
systematically denied their basic right to live and love openly" (Miller
2013). Shortly afterward, the retired German soccer professional Thomas
Hitzlsperger came out, saying that he did so because "gay football players

so far don't exist officially" (Agence France Presse 2014). The attention Hitzlsperger's coming out attracted in Europe suggests that he has indeed helped to lift the veil of silence he decried. By September 2014, following campaigns by various LGBT rights organizations, the International Olympic Committee added non-discrimination based on sexual orientation to the Olympic charter. The addition sent a strong signal to potential host countries that have laws discriminating against LGBT people. As the visibility of the transnational LGBT community grows, it reshapes our understanding, and indeed our imaginations, about the place of LGBT people in international society.

This book has explored the effect of this increasing visibility on state and societal recognition of LGBT people across states in the European region. I set out to answer two broad questions: how do international norms spread, and why do societies and states embrace change in some cases and not others? The conclusion of my empirical analysis is simple but matters a great deal: norm visibility increases the political efficacy of marginalized groups and their ability to place demands on their states. This notion of visibility explains how minority-group rights diffuse across borders: visibility empowers social groups on the political margins; it moves them to the center of political debate and public recognition, and helps them claim their rights. Before the terms "lesbian," "gay," "bisexual," and "trans" can become politically salient identity markers, the people they describe must first become visible. When people openly identify as lesbian, gay, bisexual, or trans, that visibility mobilizes actors, and it affects minority groups' ability to assert themselves and to demand recognition from their societies and states. As LGBT rights spread to new states, this necessary visibility comes from both domestic and transnational sources. People are empowered to act because of the transnational channels that make new norms visible – a particularly important process in places where LGBT rights are not already part of the popular discourse.

I substantiated this visibility argument with empirical evidence demonstrating that differences in the transnational channels of visibility yield differing degrees of LGBT recognition across states and societies. Since there is an asymmetry in political will and information between first-mover states and new-adopter states, these transnational channels of visibility have become critical for the diffusion of LGBT norms: when activated, direct, indirect, and brokered channels can make hidden political issues visible. And this visibility allows international norms to resonate within domestic politics, leading to compliance with, and then gradual internalization of, the new norms. A state's openness to international organizations and social information flows has consistently demonstrable effects on diffusion, because that openness enables the entry of new ideas into the domestic discourse, fueling deliberation and learning in the domestic sphere.

The speed and direction of diffusion of LGBT norms are also shaped by the degree to which domestic actors are embedded in transnational advocacy networks. These domestic LGBT advocates – or norm brokers – who tie new-adopter states to advocacy groups in first-mover states are of central importance due to variability in domestic societal interpretations of new LGBT norms. Norm brokers make the norm salient by connecting activists to one another and by grafting international ideas to domestic ones, framing the message to fit locally. Not only do they redistribute resources and know-how across borders, they also unite with external elites that have the power to sanction states for noncompliance. My findings make a strong case that these transnational actors, and the movements they substantiate, affect the likelihood of norms becoming visible and salient in domestic discourse.

In sum, an international norm may exist, but its felt intensity varies across contexts due to (in)visibility. States differ in the degree to which norms become visible, and this variation depends in large part on the channels that connect across a given state's borders. Indeed, for LGBT people in many closed and unresponsive domestic contexts, transnational channels provide the only real avenue for initial political influence at home. The transnational channels of LGBT visibility have been effective. Sociopolitical channels, in combination with local LGBT actors embedded in transnational networks, signal to state and society that compliance with the visible norm is part of what it means to be a member of their international community (in this case, European society). And these successful increases in LGBT visibility and rights have occurred in the most unexpected of cases; we are witnessing a rapid, unmistakable shift in both attitudes toward and legislation concerning LGBT people across parts of Europe, Latin America, and North America.

In addition to its discussion of the effects of norm visibility, this book has also examined how perceived threats moderate norm reception. Since different domestic contexts and social groups attach different degrees of perceived threat to the incursion of external norms into domestic space, threat perceptions play an important role in the success or failure of norm internalization. This variable perception of threat may help to explain why the diffusion of international norms is often nonlinear: norms perceived as originating externally meet the heaviest resistance in states where societal identities are rooted in religious nationalism. In these cases, domestic opponents of contentious norms frame their rejection as based on the norms' objectionable challenges to national identity. This process reveals a great deal about resistance and backlash, responses which are most likely to appear where there is perceived threat. Paradoxically, however, the same domestic opposition that resists these norms also increases their visibility. LGBT movements in Europe have, in most cases, found that waves of resistance are often followed by some success.

Proponents of both sides of the LGBT issue have emphasized the importance of visibility – of "coming out," not just as individuals, but as a collective – to the LGBT movement's ability to influence change. The AIDS Memorial Quilt has commemorated the victims of the virus in several massively visible displays (the first in 1987 on the National Mall in Washington); it is one of the most successful campaigns to raise awareness of the HIV/AIDS epidemic and the funding of research to combat it. Coming out, a process for making the invisible visible, takes advantage of the human rights and dignity movement that has marked European and world politics since 1945. And while coming out is often associated with the LGBT experience, it is not limited to that domain. The 1960s American antiwar movement benefited greatly from the visibility and felt intensity of many American families' personal experiences with the draft. In contrast, the new century's Afghanistan and Iraq wars are detached from the public and far more invisible. For example, the Obama administration has banned images of the caskets of fallen American soldiers from being broadcast on television – just one way in which the contemporary antiwar movement has faced invisibility. For the animal rights organization People for the Ethical Treatment of Animals, "the *image* of [animal] abuse is the most powerful tool they have" – indeed, "it is what [a movement] can show people [that] has the potential to change the world" (Galkin 2007, emphasis added).

Visibility has always been central to mainstream recognition of movements mounted by subordinate groups: consider an example from recent American history, when undocumented immigrants used the term "coming out" to mobilize historic waves of immigrant protest. Long silenced by fears of deportation, immigrants now campaign for their rights and have gained a prominent position on the policy agenda (Zepeda-Millán 2011). Similarly, Europe's highly stigmatized Roma population has begun to organize Roma Pride parades to challenge negative stereotypes and affirm group identity (McGarry, forthcoming). Visibility has also had marked success in the arena of women's rights. Women's entry into

the paid labor force and exit out of the invisibility of the home provides another example of the power of visibility, as do the transnational
dynamics behind the politicization of violence against women (Htun and
Weldon 2012).[1] This transnational process of coming out as a group
empowers marginalized people, mobilizing actors to demand change and
influencing the spread of norms. The LGBT movement is just one aspect
of this larger process of social change.

Invisibility, by contrast, has caused marginalized groups either not to
initiate or effectively to halt their movement toward recognition. We can
observe a politics of invisibility in the "poor people's movement" in the
United States, in which the state over the last forty years has moved from
regulating, to disciplining, and finally to incarcerating the poor – thus making them, and their grievances, largely invisible (Piven and Cloward 1977;
Soss, Fording, and Schram 2011). Scholars have compellingly argued that
the disproportionate incarceration of Hispanic and African American men
is a strategy to make these groups less visible and ultimately to control them
(M. F. Katzenstein, Ibrahim, and Rubin 2010; Pattillo, Weiman, and Western
2004). Similarly, what Myra Marx Ferree (2004, 95–6) has called the "deaf-
ening silence" of pro-choice abortion discourse in Germany between 1970
and 1994 helps to explain why the German movement was less successful
than its contemporary counterpart in the United States. The difference lay
not in the quality or quantity of women's mobilization in each place, but
in the very different levels of visibility the media granted them. Visibility
awakens a discourse that moves us away from the impotence of invisibility's
silence. Differing degrees of invisibility also explain the differential power
dynamics between subgroups within minority categories (Beltrán 2010;
Strolovitch 2007). For example, Polish parliamentarian Anna Grodzka
describes the relative invisibility that trans people continue to face as a
group, both within society at large and within the LGBT movement:

High visibility illustrates a strange paradox that we as transgender people experience daily. We are highly visible [physically] and yet almost invisible [politically]
at the same time. Individually you often can't miss us. On a bus or in the street
many trans people stand out, even if we would like to pass as a woman or a
man. And because we are easy to spot, we are easy to bully. I have lost count
of the number of times I have been shouted at in the street or felt threatened by
unwanted attention from drunk men who think it's funny to ridicule someone
who looks different from the norm ... I think this is because... as a social group
our voice is rarely heard. (Grodzka 2013)

[1] Deondra Rose (2012) finds that increased educational attainment for women in higher
education leads to enhanced citizenship in terms of equitable treatment by the state, social
inclusion, and political incorporation.

While Grodzka alludes to the high day-to-day visibility of individuals, her emphasis is on the vast invisibility that trans people experience as a group. This invisibility mutes the group's ability to assert itself politically; only recently has the *T* been added to the acronyms of many LGBT groups.[2] Recall the anecdote of Judith Butler speaking at the Brandenburg Gate to a colorful and highly visible crowd of LGBT people with which this book opened; the dynamics of invisibility now characterize not LGBT people as a group, but LGBT people of color and LGBT migrants, who remain targets of discrimination and who are often disproportionately powerless – for example, the popular perception in several European countries that Muslim immigrant communities are more homophobic than white majorities has rendered LGBT immigrants largely invisible (Mepschen, Duyvendak, and Tonkens 2010): if immigrants are homophobes, there remains no space for the existence of LGBT immigrants. The same dynamic is true in the United States, where the artificial construction of African and Latin Americans as homophobic erases the existence of LGBT people of color (Flores and Ramakrishnan n.d.). The 2015 trailer to the Hollywood feature Stonewall – which features a young white protagonist as instigating the riots – is a striking example of the whitewashing of LGBT people: most historical accounts link the instigation of the riots to trans activists of color.

The general underrepresentation of women and racial minorities in the American and European leaderships of the LGBT movement indicates how difficult it is to combat this exclusion (Strolovitch 2007). The processes of invisibility have hampered the development of the foundational elements of rights attainment: forming interpersonal relationships within societies, mobilizing actors for change, and establishing ties to the sympathetic elites who might help further a group's cause. In the end, this book speaks to the politics of (in)visibility and how it can hasten or impede social change on many fronts.

LGBT rights and the reconceptualization of diffusion

The case of LGBT norms offers both theoretical and empirical novelties that further our understanding of change in world politics. Indeed, the empirical realities surrounding the spread of LGBT rights modify existing theoretical accounts of diffusion and social change. To answer the

---

[2] Similarly, the International Day Against Homophobia (IDAHO) only added "and Transphobia" (IDAHOT) in 2013.

questions I posed at the outset, I built on conventional explanations – which have focused on differences in international pressures, the fit between domestic and international norms, modernization, and low implementation costs – to explain the timing and patterns of diffusion I observed in the examined cases. For instance, scholars of international relations have argued that international norms diffuse when they fit with domestic norms. In a review of the field, Richard Price (2003, 593) provocatively asked whether "transnational advocacy is [then] likely to work best where it is needed the least." This book has shown that transnational advocacy can work where it is needed (see Evangelista 1999). Despite the norm's contentious nature, some societies change against expectation, as when religious Catholic countries become leaders on LGBT rights. In secular countries, where we might expect more rapid adoption, we observe drastically divergent outcomes; and some strong democracies have struggled to adopt basic measures protecting the rights of LGBT minorities, while newer democracies have done so smoothly.

Rational institutional models rooted primarily in cost-benefit logic also fail to explain the variation in the spread of LGBT norms. The expectation that human rights norms are more easily transmitted when they come with carrots (such as access to the bundle of economic benefits accompanying EU membership) is clearly challenged by the active opposition to formal EU demands to protect LGBT people. In fact, Poland opted out of the European Charter of Fundamental Rights under the guise of protecting the state from having to implement same-sex unions, even though the Charter did not require state recognition of same-sex unions.

While isomorphism, path dependencies, and post-communist syndromes have affected the spread of LGBT rights in different ways, the extensive variation that I have charted points to more complex and contingent causality. At least in a region as receptive to transnationalism and norm diffusion as Europe, there is considerable room for optimism. Under the right transnational conditions, the most unexpected cases can change on this issue.

Bridging insights from different fields of knowledge, the visibility argument develops our theoretical understanding of diffusion processes and social change by emphasizing the agency of norm brokers and the mechanisms of framing, deliberation, and learning. It encompasses both relational and non-relational channels of norm diffusion and considers the internal domestic dynamics that moderate that diffusion, such as the presence of LGBT advocates as norm brokers, resistance, backlash, and relationships between movements and countermovements. By considering both compliance and internalization, I expand the potential of any analysis of transnational change, for international norms concerning marginalized people are clearly intended to influence both state and society. Finally, my focus on resistance and social change contributes to an important new line of inquiry into contending movements and contested norms that commonly engender backlash (Fetner 2008).

The transnational mobilization of LGBT people and the development and spread of LGBT rights norms together offer a unique platform from which to study processes of change in contentious politics and international relations. Not only do sexual minorities exist in all societies, but the contemporary LGBT movement lets scholars systematically isolate and analyze the observable consequences of norm diffusion. Their rights have become the symbol of modernity on the world stage and a defining issue in geopolitical struggles over lost cultural identity. Yet despite the extensive research on transnational activism and the human rights regime, few political scientists have studied the transnational movement or normative changes concerning sexual minorities (Kollman and Waites 2009, 8). I hope that, by combining in-depth case studies with the quantitative analysis of multiple states, I have generated a bridging dialogue within the burgeoning field of LGBT politics.

Implications of the visibility argument

The various components of this book's central argument have broad implications for scholarship in contentious politics, international relations, and comparative politics, as well as practical implications for advocates of LGBT rights. Not only do the findings chart the empirical developments related to the LGBT movement in Europe, they also have far-reaching implications for theory building related to key concepts in the field. I use this section to reflect on fundamental aspects of the argument as they relate to political opportunities, transnational actors, diffusion, state compliance, societal internalization, threat perceptions, and domestic resonance.

Political opportunities and transnational actors
Europeanization impacts the mobilization of marginalized people. LGBT activism relies on transnational resources – especially social spaces and organizational capacity, which are scarce in some EU member states but

readily available in others – to mobilize. Cross-border mobility in Europe has given sexual minorities access to glimpses of LGBT life as it is lived in other countries; though LGBT expression and identity are rooted in distinct domestic experiences, some experiences travel. Multilevel opportunities (horizontal across states, and top-down, vertical ones provided by the European polity) served as mobilizing structures that united distinct groups of transnational actors, mediating new transnational channels of visibility for LGBT rights. The key actors include the political elites often seen in studies of Europeanization, along with the rooted cosmopolitans and foreign publics that work with and engage local actors in targeted states.

When domestic organizations join transnational LGBT networks, they become connected to actors in states with advanced resources. These networks are crucial, because they channel know-how, financial resources, avenues for political pressure, a voice with which to attract media attention, and foreign publics that can be mobilized for action in various contexts. Marginalized groups have established ties to first-mover states, and this kind of transnational cooperation can open access to political opportunities outside of the nation state.

In addition, transnational cooperation alters the tactics that movement actors use when they engage authorities and society in the target state. In the case of Europe, norm brokers tactically framed their demands by fusing the issue of LGBT acceptance with the democratic responsibilities associated with membership in the European polity. Strategically packaging ideas for a given audience was imperative when taking into consideration the strongly held views in opposition to the LGBT norm. Having "European" frames at their disposal, norm brokers could borrow from international scripts and graft this highly contentious norm into the domestic context.

In this process, states have rapidly attained a high level of fluency on LGBT issues, despite closed domestic political opportunities and minimal popular visibility of the LGBT issue at the turn of the century. According to the president of KPH in Poland, even the Polish language had signaled LGBT invisibility: "My first activity with KPH in Krakow was producing a leaflet and distributing it in the main square. I realized only later that [Microsoft] Word in Polish didn't recognize the word 'homophobia' and autotranslated it incorrectly on every leaflet" (interview no. 140). The situation has changed remarkably in the years since transnational activism began to increase LGBT visibility, fomenting domestic deliberation. Similar dynamics played out across the region as the LGBT issue moved from invisibility to visibility.

Interpersonal and public visibility

In addition to signaling to states that acceptance of LGBT norms is connected to membership in international society, LGBT visibility highlights the central role of interpersonal relationships in states' social acceptance of LGBT minorities.[3] While these relationships vary tremendously across states (for example, 3 percent of Romanians report having interpersonal contact with LGBT people, compared to 69 percent of the Dutch [CoE 2011]), transnational processes can help such ties form, both relationally and non-relationally. First, they connect sexual minorities across borders. These cross-border networks include rooted cosmopolitans who mobilize and organize in foreign contexts and return home to demand change; they also include LGBT people who are mobilized in solidarity to march in foreign contexts. Second, the public visibility of international norms dispenses ideas and images about novel identities, which offer models that can be invoked by people coming out in their own respective contexts. Such visibility engages societal majorities. The American ambassador to Albania, Alexander Arvizu, described the importance of visibility for LGBT acceptance:

> Change in Albania, I believe, will come when families and friends are able to put faces to the term "LGBT." I am always impressed at how people's impression of LGBT individuals changes, when they have an opportunity to get to know them, when they discover a good friend is gay or lesbian, or when they work with them. LGBT individuals in Albania are their own best ambassadors. We are looking merely for ways to support them and their message of tolerance. (Pinderi 2013)

As Arvizu points out here, LGBT visibility (and the visibility of norms governing LGBT rights) provides the foundation for the interpersonal relationships found by psychological and sociological studies to play an important role in tolerance for LGBT people. And these movements toward visibility are an often-overlooked source of empowerment for the participants themselves. Many of the activists I interviewed explained how their involvement in the movement has reshaped their outlook on the world, experiencing their identities as increasingly shared and fluid across borders. Increasing interpersonal relationships with LGBT people, coinciding with heightened public debate about LGBT rights in many

---

[3] Individual-level Eurobarometer surveys have consistently shown that knowing LGBT people has a tremendous effect on the political landscape for LGBT people. Europeans with LGBT friends are much more likely to feel comfortable with an LGBT person attaining the state's highest elected office (8.5, on a scale of 10) compared to those without LGBT friends (5.5) (European Commission 2009, 119).

parts of contemporary Europe, are affecting the way people – within and without the movement – think and feel about this group.

Compliance and internalization

I also tested the effects of nonbrokered relational and non-relational transnational channels – political, social, economic, geographic, and shared identification channels. In examining sociolegal change for LGBT people across states, these transnational channels, to different degrees, foster the visibility of international norms that can lead to compliance and eventual internalization in domestic politics. Especially in new-adopter states, the channels most effective in influencing change are those that function through mechanisms of socialization; while sanctioning mechanisms for change are also active, their effects are generally more limited. In the case of LGBT rights, the latter were only strongly influential before EU accession, and they could spawn resistance and signify paternalism in domestic contexts where they find little resonance. In line with queer theorists that critique the power relations inherent in the disciplining of states, my findings lead me also to doubt such sanctioning top-down processes. By contrast, the social channels connecting transnational and domestic spheres were highly effective throughout the periods analyzed here. They empowered local minority actors with legitimacy and resources (discursive, human, and material). While activists note that "the influence of the EU is huge" (interview no. 138), they emphasize that the EU's influence is transmitted through the social mechanisms of learning and deliberation, and indirectly through aid to domestic and transnational civil society. "What you get with the EU is dialogue," a dialogue that is new and requires interpretation in many of the contexts analyzed in this study (interview no. 126).

Specifically on compliance, more porous states were more likely to adopt pro-LGBT legislation; and different processes of norm diffusion are evident in first-mover and new-adopter states. The findings demonstrated that states generally depend on transnational channels to influence them to adopt pro-LGBT legislation, and that new-adopter states are more dependent on these channels than first-mover states. While only the combined measure of transnational channels had a strong and consistent effect in first-mover states, several domestic variables (religious denomination, democracy level, and economic affluence) were also robust predictors of how likely that state was to adopt pro-LGBT legislation. In new-adopter states, all transnational channels of visibility were highly beneficial to the diffusion of higher levels of rights legislation, but the domestic variables (religion, affluence, and level of democracy) were not.

Broadly speaking, authorities – especially in new-adopter states – are attracted to internationally visible issues, even if domestic LGBT-rights debates remain unresolved. States care about their image on the world stage and are likely to make changes when their international society softly encourages them to do so. This was particularly apparent in the robustness of the diffusion variables in the event history models, which showed that European states emulate each other's policies toward LGBT people across various issue areas. For better or for worse, the visibility of the marriage issue has brought it to the forefront of the political agenda, even in countries where LGBT movements did not prioritize advocating for same-sex marriage. While the analysis focused on LGBT legislation, there is reason to believe that the results are relevant to several other issues concerning marginalized groups in international politics. The findings also, for example, have broad implications for research on the spread of pro-woman policies against domestic violence (Montoya 2013) and sexual harassment in the workplace (Roggeband 2010), and for the (de)criminalization of sex (e.g. adultery and abortion) (Frank, Camp, and Boutcher 2010) and the introduction of gender quotas (Towns 2012); state behaviors toward women are linked to both domestic and international politics, such as transnational networks for brokerage, emulation, and hierarchies in international society.

The results also suggest that the societal internalization of norms governing LGBT rights is, like state compliance with pro-LGBT laws, largely rooted in a process of transnational socialization. For example, before the successful 2015 referendum turned heads, a 2012 survey in Ireland indicated that 75 percent of Irish citizens would vote "yes" on a referendum to legalize same-sex marriage (Kennedy 2013). Of those supporters, most used an international frame of reputation, followed by a more general will to promote tolerance:

> Two out of three people said they felt Ireland's *reputation as a modern society* will be strengthened by allowing same-sex couples to have civil marriages, while three out of five people agree that allowing same-sex couples to have civil marriages will promote a more tolerant environment in Ireland. (Kennedy 2013, emphasis added)

Societal majorities are aware of and respond to international cues of appropriateness concerning norms on minority rights. The channels of visibility tying porous states to the international community were responsible for much of the change in societal attitudes toward gay and lesbian people; they also helped to fuel processes of societal deliberation and learning in the domestic realm. But transnational visibility influences various social groups differently. Individuals embedded in groups that socialize them to perceive the new norm as threatening – often because it challenges their religious and national identities – are consistently more reluctant to adopt favorable attitudes toward homosexuality. Among these "high threat perception" groups, change is more gradual; increased transnational channels can lead to a phase of worsening attitudes toward LGBT people. In these times of heightened international visibility of LGBT people, we should thus expect more positive attitudes among European societies in states that are more closely tied to the international community, and we should expect to see variation in the degree to which individuals will change their positions, based on the levels of perceived threat that their social groups ascribe to the norm.

A practical implication of the visibility argument is that the implementation of laws like Russia's ban on gay propaganda seriously impedes diffusion because such laws criminalize visibility, blocking both deliberation and learning. As an activist from ILGA-Europe notes, "It's about being open about speaking, and that's why exactly these laws in Moldova, Ukraine, and Russia are very dangerous because they would prevent the debate" (Euronews 2012). Furthermore, if visibility matters for change and acceptance, then local and norm-brokered activism that targets the public sphere – like Pride parades – should be supported by proponents of LGBT rights, even when they initially produce a societal backlash. Proponents should also proceed carefully so as not to overinstitutionalize LGBT activism and thereby remove the issue from local public debates (Lang 2013).[4]

Threat perceptions and domestic resistance

The visibility argument required that I establish systematic differences between transnational channels (both relational and non-relational) and the diffusion of norms governing LGBT rights. Relatedly, states – like the social groups within them – also differ from one another in terms of their own internal responses to new norms. Even the effects of strong transnational channels are moderated by differing domestic perceptions of threat (especially when the threat, as in the LGBT case, is perceived to

---

[4] As the issue becomes more transnationalized, movement actors might also be cautious of steps leading toward the "NGO-ization" (Lang 2013; see also Paternotte in press) of LGBT activism. Lang (2013) refers to an institutionalization process that increasingly furthers a disconnect between activists and their grassroots constituents, privileges urban, cosmopolitan, "Western"-oriented activists, and sidelines transgressive politics.

be at the intersection of national identity and religion). Comparing socio-legal outcomes for LGBT people to the mobilized resistance against LGBT norms, I found that when religion is deeply rooted in national identity, resistance to outside norms is heightened. While I analyzed Europe, other regions demonstrate a similar dynamic. In Latin America, for example, the history of the Catholic Church in Argentina – including its close ties to the dictatorship before democratic transition – has deflated its legitimacy to effectively lead the opposition to LGBT norms. In Chile, where the Catholic Church was officially and explicitly against the dictatorship, the Church has been a more legitimate and formidable opponent to the LGBT-rights movement (Schulenberg 2013).

Furthermore, domestic resistance to LGBT norms is, ironically, also an instigator of issue visibility and the political salience of norms. European anti-LGBT movements have two critical handicaps when compared to their LGBT movement counterparts. First, resistance movements generally include a broad spectrum of societal actors, including those who use radical tactics that can alienate certain segments of society. Second, the agendas of core segments of these resistance movements have been rooted in a nationalist philosophy that has often precluded any desire to establish transnational ties. Many members of the anti-LGBT resistance willingly dismiss the cross-border vertical and horizontal constellations that have done so much for channeling support and framing the arguments of LGBT movements.

While proponents of LGBT rights can remain optimistic that the effect of popular backlash in the streets can benefit LGBT rights, the newer and more concerted efforts by the Catholic Church and socially conservative political parties to orchestrate opposition behind closed doors is worrying for the LGBT movement. These new strategies could break down the nationally defined boundaries that have stifled their progress, by instead lobbying and funding antigay politics in ways that do not involve the street. Unlike the strategies of the past, these back-door and professionalized politics may not make LGBT people more visible. More research is needed on the newer strategies of opposition groups and their transnational networks in Europe.

In sum, these findings not only substantiate the importance of visibility for the spread of LGBT rights, they also highlight the often nonlinear nature of internalization. The development of societal responses to international norms depends both on the norm's visibility and on the nature of domestic perceptions of threat associated with the norm. While the analogy of diffusion (from the field of biology) has been useful to this study, it does have a flaw: while it assumes that molecules diffuse into an empty space, "empty spaces" do not exist in topics studied by political scientists or sociologists, certainly not in the context of contentious norms.[5] The findings should, thus, encourage scholars of diffusion to attend to the internal domestic dynamics of the state that moderate diffusion: the norm brokers that tie the domestic and the transnational context, the differing levels of threat perception and their potential for politicization (defined in part by the unique relationships between the church, the state, and the nation), and the varying degrees of resistance in domestic realms and their relationships to the movement under consideration.

This book has another general takeaway: social movements matter. Making claims about the "effects" of movements remains tremendously challenging, even though scholars have spent decades trying to explain the elusive questions of why, when, and how movements actually produce change (D. S. Meyer 2003). I, too, will continue to grapple with these questions, but I close this book confident that activism, alongside broader changes in international norms, is indeed affecting outcomes related to compliance with and internalization of norms governing LGBT rights. In the multifaceted ways illustrated in this book, these activists do so by making the norm visible and helping states and societies interpret it. To be sure, transnational LGBT movements are thus making sexual minorities visible and fueling a discourse of legitimization around their place in society. Even those who disagree with the movement's goals still have to decide why they disagree (Goodwin and Jasper 2009, 412–13), acknowledging the presence of a once-invisible group – a tremendously powerful transformation in and of itself (Brysk 2013).

Moving forward

Beyond Europe: the regional and global dynamics of norm diffusion

Though I have described and explained norm diffusion in the European experience, Europe offers a solid foundation for understanding more general processes. With the spread of various types of LGBT rights and increasingly evolved societal attitudes, we observe some similar dynamics at play across some parts of the globe. For example, since Denmark introduced same-sex civil unions in 1989, dozens of countries have followed suit, and nineteen now recognize same-sex marriage at the federal

---

[5] Thanks to Rahul Rao for this analogy.

level. In the order in which they have taken this step, they are: the Netherlands, Belgium, Spain, Canada, South Africa, Norway, Sweden, Portugal, Iceland, Argentina, Denmark (and Greenland), Brazil, France, Uruguay, New Zealand, Luxembourg, Ireland, Finland, and the United States. Some subnational jurisdictions, for instance within Mexico and the United Kingdom, afford same-sex couples marriage rights. Colombia and Australia are on the cusp of implementing marriage legislation. In Asia, commentators expect that Taiwan and Vietnam may have the support of enough delegates to introduce same-sex marriage to the legislative agenda in coming years (Maresca 2013).[6] In Japan, a Tokyo district's (Shibuya) local government began issuing marriage certificates to same-sex couples in 2015 and several Japanese cities followed suit (Murai 2015); the federal government will debate introducing the nation's first employment anti-discrimination law in 2016. South Korea, Nepal, China, and the Philippines are debating the partnership issue. Nepal also added anti-discrimination protections for LGBT people to its constitution in 2015, as well as introducing a third gender passport.

Perhaps most impressively, Latin America has made rapid and pronounced changes on several forms of LGBT rights in recent years. Aside from the domestic advances just mentioned, Spanish and Latin American norm brokers have played a successful role – particularly in Argentina – in spreading ideas about how to promote LGBT rights and how to obtain the resources necessary to do so, as Elisabeth Friedman (2012) has demonstrated. She also taps into the dynamics of network ties and diffusion between first-mover states and new-adopter states. Mexico, Colombia, Chile, Brazil, and Uruguay are all deliberating extensively on the LGBT rights norm. The extent of the advances in LGBT rights – and not just in the "liberal West" – signals a period of momentum in which the international community is showing a remarkable degree of responsiveness to a new and unanticipated frontier in human rights.

But the processes of change are not monolithic. However widely parts of this book's argument might travel, other parts remain limited to Europe. Considerable questions still remain about the degree to which

---

[6] While they remain unrecognized, the Vietnamese government abolished a ban on same-sex marriage in 2015. The ministries of health and justice have supported such a measure. Some have attributed Vietnam's receptiveness to LGBT norms – despite its generally poor human rights record – to the presence of established LGBT activist organizations and the muted influence of religion in Vietnamese politics (Maresca 2013). The nation hosted its first Pride parade in 2013, and LGBT groups are petitioning to end employment discrimination.

LGBT rights norms have "global" weight (Langlois and Wilkinson 2014). Uganda and Russia represent two cases that have displayed a different dynamic – in both countries, what has diffused has been a heightened level of politicized homophobia (Weiss and Bosia 2013) and a global trend toward norm polarization (Symons and Altman 2015). I turn now to these difficult cases to discuss aspects of the visibility argument that hold in these contexts and to point out avenues for further study.

Pride and prejudice in Uganda and Russia
The introduction of sharpened antigay legislation in Uganda and the murder of David Kato, a Ugandan LGBT activist, have placed Africa – and Uganda in particular – on the radar of LGBT activism and scholarship, most of which follows a narrative about the export of political homophobia (Weiss and Bosia 2013). Scholars are correct to highlight what they see as a double-edged sword of diffusion: transnational homophobia, in the African case largely linked to western evangelical communities, is used to inhibit progress on LGBT rights even as some other parts of the globe experience one of the most rapid shifts toward the social and legal recognition of LGBT minorities in history. In February 2014, Ugandan President Yoweri Museveni succumbed to pressure to sign a bill into law that expanded the grounds for imprisonment related to homosexuality, including suggestive touching by members of the same sex in public. A similar bill was passed in Nigeria, where homosexuality was also already illegal, around the same time. In the face of international condemnation, Museveni first held off on signing the popular bill, but he eventually agreed to do so after his scientific board could not establish a genetic basis for homosexuality. Archbishop Desmond Tutu and the European Parliament both condemned the bill, and United States President Obama sharply criticized Museveni's intention to sign it into law, saying, "This will complicate our valued relationship." Museveni went forward even though Norway, Denmark, and the Netherlands canceled twenty-six million dollars in aid, and the World Bank almost immediately put a ninety-million dollar healthcare loan on ice (Ring 2014).

On a regional level, Africa is distinct from Europe, in that its regional structures do not have a normative consensus on LGBT rights, even though it includes South Africa, which has been a trailblazer in passing LGBT legislation. The African Union institutions do not moderate this domestic debate in the same way as the European Union does. There is also a historically rooted suspicion in many African countries related to adopting "un-African" and "Western" ways of doing things (Currier 2012). This provides the conservative opposition with strong ammunition with which to resist LGBT norms, even though the grassroots African LGBT movement has long worked without the support of – and often in opposition to – powerful states of the Global North. While in Europe opposition to European norms highlights national frames, in Africa opposing forces also draw upon pan-regional frames that denounce meddling in African affairs. These critical factors dispel the unfounded notion that domestic politics are reactionary while transnational politics are progressive. Furthermore, they highlight that we must take caution in describing the "global" successes of LGBT rights.

At the same time, this book's findings do contribute to the debate in contexts extending beyond Europe, including Africa. First, transnational diffusion – be it linked to homophobia or to LGBT norms – has strong transnational and domestic components. It is clear that the domestic developments made in these contexts cannot be separated from transnational processes. Scholars are correct to attribute the politicization of homophobia in Uganda to heightened transnational involvement by American conservatives, but they would be wrong to ignore the numerous domestic factors, also closely connected to identity and religion, that contribute to Ugandan homophobia. Second, a fundamental reason why Uganda has captured scholarly and popular attention is that channels tie an active and engaged Ugandan LGBT activist community to a transnational network of pro-LGBT groups. In some ways, Uganda mirrors Poland. Though other European states scored equally poorly on measures of LGBT recognition, Poland became an exemplar of LGBT oppression in Europe because Poland's norm brokers, like Uganda's, were well connected across borders. Ugandan norm brokers and the American missionaries who involve themselves in Ugandan politics may be equally responsible for the issue's visibility. In fact, like their European counterparts, Ugandan and transnational LGBT activists may be more responsible, because they captured the world's attention by publicizing the issue.

Despite domestic repression, LGBT Ugandans are marching in the streets more than they did before, and observers on the ground note that "the dynamics of being gay in Uganda have changed" (Okeowo 2012). Some activists view this wave of contestation as linked to the Ugandan movement's success. At the 2012 ILGA-International conference in Stockholm, representatives of African LGBT organizations were frustrated by the attention Uganda was granted: "American and European donors were focused almost exclusively on Uganda, because of the visibility LGBT politics have attained there" (interview no. 155). And observers also note the paradox inherent in this oppressive backlash to public visibility. According to the South African constitutional court judge Edwin Cameron:

> The most interesting thing going on here is what I call an "unstable transition." It explains the force of the backlash just as African gays and lesbians are starting to come out. It releases hatred and rage, but what is happening is irreversible. Gays and lesbians are coming to consciousness, organising themselves and speaking out. (D. Smith 2013)

Indeed, the backlash in Africa has generated deliberation on the commonly held perception that LGBT people are un-African. The coming out of Binyavanga Wainaina, an acclaimed Kenyan author widely read across the continent, is an example of visibility that helps localize the issue. He spoke up in January 2014, just as the debate surrounding antigay legislation heightened in Uganda. Archbishop Desmond Tutu also restated his commitment to carving out a space for LGBT people in the African identity, drawing parallels between LGBT oppression and the struggle against racist laws that had mobilized hearts and minds during apartheid. In 2015, Mozambique decriminalized homosexuality when it removed Portuguese colonial anti-sodomy legislation from 1886. A year later, following a decision not to enforce the country's colonial-era sodomy law, Malawian President Peter Mutharika's government stated that LGBTI "rights should be protected" (Gwede 2016). Five months after Museveni signed it into law, the Ugandan constitutional court annulled the anti-homosexuality act. In 2015, former Ugandan Prime Minister and presidential candidate Amama Mbabazi made a declarative statement against homophobia (McDonald 2015). African LGBT politics highlights regional differences to Europe; yet there, too, a combination of domestic and transnational currents factor into new discourses on LGBT rights.

Russia is a case marred by low LGBT visibility – only 11 percent of Russians claim to have homosexual friends or relatives (Moscow Times 2013) – and high threat perception regarding LGBT norms. Like the tie between the Catholic Church and the notion of "Polishness" that heightened threat perception in Poland, "Russians today view [Orthodox] Church affiliation as a way to reaffirm their 'Russianness'" (Khazan 2013). While rates of religiosity are strikingly low in global comparison, much of the Russian population supports the Russian Orthodox

Church as a national symbol of pride, and the church wields considerable political might as a close ally to President Vladimir Putin's government (Stoeckl 2014). Russia differs from Poland in that transnational
pressures have not yielded socialization successes during the country's
era of zealous, anti-LGBT backlash. In June 2013, the Russian Duma
extended various city ordinances banning LGBT "propaganda" – the
ordinances that had aroused ample international attention in 2012 – by
unanimously passing a federal bill that fines individuals or organizations up to $31,000 for promoting homosexuality (Khazan 2013). The
Russian government remains undaunted by international efforts to push
back on this trend, even provocatively warning France and the United
Kingdom that their moves to institute same-sex marriage could dis-
qualify their citizens from adopting Russian children. LGBT rights also
found a central place in the contemporary geopolitics of the region, most
notably in the recent Ukrainian crisis, when Russia portrayed its antigay
stance as a feature of the cultural paradigm – distinct from the decadent
West – that it can offer the world (Riabov and Riabova 2014; Wilkinson
2014). At the societal level, recent polls show similarly disapproving
positions toward LGBT people. For example, more than 80 percent of
Russians oppose same-sex marriage and adoption rights, and gay pride
parades (Sansalone 2013).

The response is unsurprising in the sense that resistance is common
when LGBT issues are new and when high threat perception is politicized. The more states perceive these issues to be "external," the more
resistance they will provoke. While some Russian activists – including
those the state has formally labeled "foreign agents"[7] – remain optimistic that this new struggle is better than silence, they face far greater difficulty combating domestic resistance amid a protracted opposition that
has made their very visibility illegal. International condemnation and
worldwide demonstrations against state-sponsored homophobia have
had minimal effects politically in Russia (group no. 208).[8] This is surely
linked to key differences that remain between the cases of Russia and
those within the EU. While Russian LGBT activists are well connected
to their European counterparts (one of the few established channels of

---

[7] In 2013, a St. Petersburg court formally referred to the Russian LGBT organization
Выход as a foreign agent.

[8] A key example is the case filed by Russian activists, following *Bączkowski and Others
v. Poland* at the ECtHR. While Strasbourg lifted Poland's bans on LGBT assembly, St.
Petersburg quickly introduced gay-propaganda bans, and the city of Moscow banned
LGBT parades for precisely one century.

LGBT visibility), they have not had at their disposal the same in-group frames that being "European" provides. Only 13 percent of Russians considered themselves "European" in a 2011 study by the Russian Academy of Sciences, and just 7 percent felt Russia should step "into the common European home" (Riabov and Riabova 2014). Russia's political isolation from the international organizations, such as the EU and NATO, that house many first-mover norm entrepreneurs has greatly limited the socialization mechanisms of norm diffusion.[9] The unresponsiveness to international critique underscores the importance of regional differences and the limits of globalization, highlighting the argument that being in an in-group is immensely important to the spread of such norms (Checkel 2005; Deutsch 1957). As Oleg Riabov and Tatiana Riabova (2014) compellingly suggest, Russian attitudes toward sexual minorities are likely to correlate strongly with their attitude to the "West" for the foreseeable future.

Indeed, the international debate surrounding LGBT rights prompted by the Russian laws and the Sochi Winter Olympics may have had more immediate and empowering effects outside Russia. As the media extensively reported on the situation of LGBT Russians, and as foreign leaders reprimanded Russia for its antigay laws, they were also compelled to highlight their own states' hypocrisies, furthering a rhetoric that can be effectual for change.[10] Furthermore, social media users suddenly linked Olympic sponsors like McDonalds and Visa with homophobia: "Shame on @McDonalds sending #CheersToSochi while gay activists are attacked by Olympic officials" and "Visa: It's everywhere you want to be. Unless you're LGBT." The German Olympic team's rainbow-colored uniforms made headlines, as did the 2,000 Swedes who gathered in Stockholm's Olympic Stadium to sing the Russian national anthem in solidarity with LGBT Russians. According to the assistant director of an internationally oriented UK-based LGBT rights group, Kaleidoscope Trust, "One of the reassuring things that has come out of the response to the Russian laws ... is a growing international apprehension. One of the last great undone pieces of the civil rights movement is to address the rights of

[9] We are left to wonder if the "historic opportunity" to include Russia as an associate member of NATO in the 1990s (Shevtsova 2007) may have paved a different path for LGBT recognition.

[10] Protests and boycotts were organized around the globe to generate public visibility. Even gay online social networks such as PlanetRomeo and Grindr attempted to generate interpersonal visibility and politicize their communities to protest Russian antigay laws. PlanetRomeo surveyed their Russian members and reported back to other members on the severity of local LGBT repression.

LGBT people, and there does seem to be a growing international support for change" (Saner 2013, 3).

Even within Russia, proponents of LGBT rights might hope that protracted backlash also introduces new, positive ideas and images regarding LGBT people into the debate. The tropes the opposition uses are not uncontested in Russia. For example, the blasé naivety with which LGBT people had been made invisible locally – and often the irony of it – was tellingly captured in a news article entitled, "20 Photos from Sochi's Biggest Gay Club: The One the Mayor Claims Doesn't Exist" (Ippolito 2014). Protests against the draconian laws that limit public expression by LGBT people continue, and some report that they are growing (Morgan 2014). As this book has shown, resistance does not suggest that change is unattainable or that states will remain locked in a state of politicized homophobia. Elsewhere, resistance has been part of a process of internalization that involves deliberation and learning. Future research will have to chart whether that will be the situation in Russia. The question remains whether contesting the norm will lead to socialization in a state that defines itself outside the international community that champions the norm. For Russian LGBT activists, as for their counterparts in many corners of the globe, the challenges that remain are formidable.

Open questions

How transnational channels play out in other world regions should challenge and fascinate scholars of world politics for years to come, as norms governing LGBT rights continue to spread and to meet resistance in various corners of the globe. Current developments in cases like Russia, Uganda, and Nigeria hold implications for future research, which needs to explore the effects of antigay domestic and transnational activism, acknowledging that standards of appropriate behavior concerning sexual minorities remain hotly contested and smack to many of outside imposition. It also seems quite clear that strong regional currents are at play, and that we should not expect any global homogenization of LGBT recognition. In this sense, a central task for future study is to explore how distinct regions – their institutional structures, domestic understandings, and political histories – mediate the effects of transnational channels of visibility.

Other questions related to the global frames for LGBT recognition arise. What is the effect of the LGBT activists' approach to framing the debate on the global level – for example, having Latin American states propose pro-LGBT resolutions at the UN to remove the "Northern" or "Western" tinge of LGBT rights? How do activists navigate contexts in which "Western" norms are especially suspicious, and alternative frames for activists are few? Finally, what types of risks does visibility – in terms of its valence – entail in contexts that have a high threat perception domestically and that lack identification with international communities of first-mover states? I suspect that the degree to which states are embedded in international systems of knowledge that define LGBT rights as a norm affects the possibility for visibility to lead to positive outcomes for norm diffusion. The level of consensus at the macro level impacts the norm's legitimacy, and subsequently how deliberation in the domestic realm proceeds. For the spread of LGBT rights, it is important that states identify as part of a larger community in which the issue is championed. While for proponents of LGBT rights it is a welcome development that positive etymologies of LGBT people are now more plentiful and available for LGBT organizations to latch onto globally, future research must do more to determine the resonance of such ideas in specific states, depending on the prevailing regional norms in those states' particular international community.

This book also provides a point of departure for another area of study: the relative (in)visibility of subgroups within the LGBT categories and, more generally, the question of who is left out in the transnational diffusion of LGBT norms. Critical theorists (Binnie and Klesse 2013; Butler 2008; Kulpa and Mizielińska 2011; Weber 2015) have begun tackling these questions: are certain world regions (e.g. Africa), countries (e.g. Poland), subnational regions (e.g. the United States' South), religions (e.g. Islam), and groups (e.g. immigrants) "othered" and excluded as LGBT identities become recognized – and arguably "normalized" – by states? Do more radical queer forms of expression also diffuse, or are they precluded from transnational debates and identity categories that travel across borders? How do the norms and activism surrounding LGBT rights address intersectional identities and multiple marginalizations? As scholars are increasingly noting, "There is utility in identity politics, particularly for marginalized groups trying to forge new spaces and establish visibility, [but such politics] can overemphasize some categories while continuing to obscure others" (Irvine, Lang, and Montoya 2015, 5).

To give just one example of how important these questions are for LGBT politics, it is worthwhile to return briefly to the Berlin Christopher Street Day parade. Judith Butler's lament concerning the presence of homonationalism and pinkwashing has proven ever more justified in transnational activism. In more recent years, for example, the Israeli tourism board has distributed numerous Israeli flags at the festival, and their abundant presence – waved in the air or attached as stickers to clothing – reflects at least in part the complicity that frustrated Butler. What is often lacking is a sense of "intersectionally linked fate" (Dawson 1994; Strolovitch 2007, 63), and thus a disconnect exists between one's own experience of oppression and marginalization and that of others. By waving the Israeli flag, the marchers linked gay rights (consciously or unconsciously) with a state that has been criticized by activists for using those rights in an effort to justify its treatment of the Palestinians (Lind 2014, 602; Puar 2007). LGBT activists are often attuned to this terrain of multiple marginalizations, judging by the debates I have heard at many international LGBT activist conferences, but the issue ought to be even more evident in the popular narrative of LGBT liberation.[11]

Many of these open questions call for the continued development and application of intersectional approaches (Cohen 1997; Hancock 2007; Strolovitch 2012). It is my hope that (in)visibility arguments contribute to the scholarly call to move beyond rigid typologies that exclude certain groups. Such a move will be important for theory building in contentious politics and international relations alike.

In looking closely at an often invisible group and its transnational interactions, I have striven to extend and integrate existing scholarly agendas, while also illuminating important implications for the contemporary expansion of LGBT rights. The movement for these rights has in the last decade gained a momentum that is arguably unprecedented in speed and suddenness among human rights movements. This study thus joins both scholarly and popular debates, some of which have regarded recent global trends with awe.

---

[11] In his eloquent ethnography of the International Gay and Lesbian Human Rights Commission, Ryan Thoreson (2014, 61) challenges the portrayal of LGBT NGOs as a homogeneous gay international, a portrayal he argues has slighted their internal differences and also their sensitivity to many debates that critical theorists address. My fieldwork with European LGBT organizations supports Thoreson's assessment. For example, at the 2010 ILGA-Europe conference in The Hague – which the Dutch government generously sponsored, including an opening reception dinner at the Hall of Knights – the sociologist Meike Verloo gave a lecture critical of Dutch immigration policy. She lambasted the host state for using LGBT rights as a narrative with which to crack down on immigrant communities portrayed as homophobic. When concerning the promotion of LGBT rights, I thus emphasize that neither international advocacy nor states are monolithic. Furthermore, norm brokers negotiate their strategies and the identity categories they draw on in unique ways when they bring it into the domestic realm. The process is not simply top-down, and conceiving of it as such only strips local norm brokers of their own agency.

Was Victor Hugo right when he said in the nineteenth century that "nothing can stop an idea whose time has come"? And what does the LGBT movement tell us about Cesar Chavez's optimism about the civil rights movement: "Once social change begins, it cannot be reversed ... You cannot humiliate the person who feels pride. You cannot oppress the people who are not afraid anymore." As politics in Russia, Uganda, and many parts of Europe remind us, even at this historic moment for LGBT rights, these inspirational remarks ring true only for some sexual minorities in some contexts. Looking at the rapidity of change in some regions over the last two decades, it is tempting to end on a note of modest optimism, but such modest optimism should not overshadow the fact that the oppression of LGBT peoples across societies persists, that LGBT norms continue to provoke resistance, and that transnational advocacy is limited in many corners of the globe. This book has been both an effort toward a holistic understanding of how and why states embrace LGBT rights, and an acknowledgment that that does not always occur.

What do the findings of this book suggest about general trends of LGBT norm diffusion across the globe? In terms of a linear trajectory and a specific time frame, very little. Rather, my work has shown that visibility can provoke both recognition and resistance, and that in many cases resistance follows visibility and precedes recognition. Yet while the process will play out differently across contexts (with smooth processes of norm internalization most likely in contexts with low threat perception), there is little question that state and societal recognition of LGBT people will continue to spread in some world regions. And when it spreads, it will extend first to contexts within which norm brokers are active and to places that are highly connected to the international community through channels of visibility. In these contexts, LGBT people can achieve public recognition and move themselves from the margins to the center of political debate.

Methodological appendix

Research methods and data collection

Research methods

In my research design, I employed an eclectic multimethod (quantitative and qualitative) approach.[1] I used a nested analysis technique, which began with the large-n statistical test of correlation between variables and then, depending on the results, proceeded to either "model-testing" or "model-building" small-n analysis (Lieberman 2005, 436). The project included large-n analyses that used statistical methods to test correlations between predictors in all EU member states, and small-n analyses that used qualitative methods to trace channels of diffusion between carefully selected case studies. I thus used a triangular design in which the preliminary large-n analyses identified a set of ideal cases (on the regression line) for the small-n analysis, which I used to test the theory and to understand the mechanisms by which ideas diffuse.

I first constructed the data sets for preliminary quantitative analyses (final versions appear in Table A.1 and Table A.3). Next, I turned to qualitative methods in order to confirm or question the validity of the correlations I observed in the large-n analysis. This allowed me to answer open questions of causal order, measurement, and the heterogeneity of cases. I followed the principle that in triangulation "the best use of [small-n analysis] is to leverage its distinct complementarities with [large-n analysis], not to try to implement it with the exact same procedures as one would carry out regression analysis" (Lieberman 2005, 440).

[1] With permission, this section draws partially on portions of Ayoub, Wallace, and Zepeda-Millán (2014).

In this sense, the small-*n* analyses also allowed me to observe the mechanisms that connected the independent and dependent variables, aiding my understanding of historical sequence and causal process (McAdam, Tarrow, and Tilly 2001).

In a paired comparison, I chose Poland and Slovenia because my initial analysis revealed that, among new EU member states, these historically Catholic states were on opposite ends of the spectrum in terms of legal standing and societal attitudes toward LGBT people. Both cases had variation on the explanatory and dependent variables. I also studied Germany and the EU as "norm entrepreneur" cases, because I identified them as sources of horizontal and vertical diffusion, respectively. These cases served as mobilizing structures for activism in CEE. They illustrated how ideas diffused, with activists using resources available to them in one context to mobilize in another.

Data collection

Data collection in Europe involved over two years of on-site fieldwork from July 2010 to August 2012, as well as several weeks of preliminary fieldwork in 2008 and 2009 and follow-up fieldwork in 2013 and 2015. My methods included semistructured interviews, participant observation, and archival research in Berlin, Bratislava, Brussels, Budapest, Cracow, the Hague (host of the 2010 ILGA-Europe meeting), Madrid, Prague, Turin (host of the 2011 ILGA-Europe meeting), and Warsaw. I also conducted an organizational survey of transnationally linked LGBT organizations.

While the brunt of the qualitative research focused on actors from my case studies (Germany, Poland, Slovenia, and the European institutions), I interviewed nearly ninety actors representing European institutions and the following states: Belgium, the Czech Republic, Croatia, Estonia, Germany, Hungary, Ireland, Italy, Latvia, Malta, Poland, Portugal, Slovakia, Slovenia, Spain, and Turkey. Interviews ranged between forty-five minutes and four hours. Most interviewees were organizers at LGBT rights advocacy groups and policymakers who work with LGBT issues. I asked activists and politicians about their motivations and the strategies behind their mobilization, as well as their perception of the outcomes of that mobilization.

These interviews investigated several questions concerning transnational ties between actors and the types of local obstacles they face, for example: do domestic LGBT organizations focus on instigating change through their national governments, or do they look to Brussels to influence change from above? What percentage of their initiatives focus on each level? How much do actors rely on external aid and expertise? What are the various state responses to activism? Among which segments of society does resistance to LGBT rights originate? These questions shed light on the conditions that have led to divergent outcomes across the cases. My interviews explored the transnational ties between actors and the types of local obstacles that they face. The interviews also helped me to understand causal process. To deal with potential endogeneity concerns in the large-n analysis, I asked several questions geared at understanding the sequencing of external support in relation to domestic activism and change. I selected and interviewed organizers from transnationally linked LGBT rights organizations. Then, using snowball-sampling techniques, I identified a sample of opposition groups and individual policymakers who oppose the introduction of LGBT rights norms, whom I approached for further interviews. The purpose of this set of interviews was to observe the strategies and rationales underlying the opposition toward liberalization, and to supplement the information I obtained from LGBT rights groups.

Archival research uncovered qualitative and quantitative data for all EU member and applicant states, through the analysis of organizational documents, mission statements, grant applications, and press releases relating to transnational LGBT activism in Europe. This research allowed me to code LGBT legislation across states and by year (1970–2010), count LGBT social spaces across time in Poland and Germany, and compile a series of other rich contextual data. It also allowed me to identify the network ties of NGOs working on LGBT rights in Europe through the membership lists of key umbrella organizations. In sum, I used a combination of online archives (e.g. those of ILGA, the European Parliament, the European Council, and the FRA), as well as on-site archives in LGBT museums, centers, and organizations.

Participant observation centered around two types of events. First, I attended the strategic meetings and conferences of LGBT activists, including the 2010 and 2011 ILGA-Europe annual meetings, the 2011 OSCE meeting, the 2010 EuroPride Warsaw conference, a 2013 US State Department international videoconference on trans rights, and several activist workshops. Issues covered at these meetings included the tactics behind transnational LGBT activism in Europe, among them strategic litigation, organizing demonstrations, and creating synergy in transnational cooperation. At some of the meetings I observed (e.g. the OSCE meeting), anti-LGBT rights activists also participated and voiced their positions. Participant observation also informed my analysis by allowing me to listen to and interact with various representatives from states where I did not schedule formal interviews, thereby providing additional valuable information to contextualize the findings of the large-n analysis.

Second, I invested time in attending numerous political demonstrations for and against LGBT rights (both those that targeted their own states and those that drew attention to LGBT repression in foreign states), Pride parades/marches for LGBT rights, and nationalist demonstrations. For example, I attended a February 15, 2012, demonstration by LGBT activists and German parliamentarians at the Russian Embassy in Berlin that protested an anti-LGBT propaganda law in St. Petersburg (group no. 208). Specifically, participant observation at such events took place in Belgium, Germany, Italy, the Netherlands, Spain, and Poland, though I visited many other countries to conduct the interviews.

Finally, I sent out a survey (using Qualtrics Survey Software) to one expert at each of the 291 transnational LGBT organizations that my research identified in the 47 CoE countries (see below for survey questions). By transnational LGBT organizations, I refer to domestic organizations that are members of transnational umbrella organizations (i.e. ILGA-Europe and IGLYO). While the merits of organizational surveys are undisputed in the quantitative analysis of transnational activism, illuminating important patterns in movement dynamics, country contexts, and organizational characteristics, their limitations include low response rates and oversampling. In response to these concerns, I utilized features of the software to ensure that only invited respondents could take the survey and that each organization could respond only once. Of the 291 organizations I surveyed, 180 responded, bringing the response rate to 62 percent. While there is no standard response rate, compared to previous research that employed organizational surveys, a 62 percent yield is substantially above the average (Baruch and Holtom 2008; Hager *et al.* 2003).

The data collection, coupled with data derived from existing databases (described in Table A.1 and Table A.3), resulted in three data sets for analysis: a Europe-wide data set of 5 different pieces of LGBT legislation across states and time, the survey of the 291 transnational LGBT organizations in Europe, and an international survey of attitudes toward LGBT people. The quantitative large-n analysis compares diffusion across all EU member states using various statistical modeling techniques: ordered logistic, event history, and multilevel random intercept iterative generalized least squares regression models (Chapters 4 and 5). The qualitative component uses process-tracing techniques to study the change in the selected case studies described above (Chapters 3 and 6). Moreover, the combination of state-, group-, and individual-level analyses, and the comparison of their relative effects, should advance our understanding of the diffusion processes more generally. For example, I have theorized how transnational diffusion is mediated through attitudes of individuals organized in social groups, compared that mediation to other mechanisms identified by scholars, and measured the relative impact of these mechanisms.

This "analytically eclectic" research design follows a pragmatic, problem-driven approach to scholarship, in which the pursuit of understanding complex realities drives the selection of methods – even if they are rooted in ostensibly incompatible academic traditions (Sil and Katzenstein 2010). Combined, the various methods I employ shed light on the processes behind the adoption of and resistance to LGBT rights norms in various domestic contexts. In calling for multi-method research designs that explore both "why" and "how," the fields of political science and contentious politics have taken great strides; my hope is that this book's application, of a design that takes seriously both variables and mechanisms, is a step in the direction of the field's future. While this appendix describes the methods used for this study, a more elaborate discussion of the benefits and constraints of the mixed-method approach can be found in a methodological chapter I coauthored (Ayoub, Wallace, and Zepeda-Millán 2014), wherein I describe the methods used for this project with greater attention to the method of triangulation and how it has been applied in social movement research.

Survey details

I administered the survey from October to December 2011. I sent one survey to each of the 291 LGBT organizations that were members (in 2010) of European LGBT umbrella organizations – ILGA-Europe and IGLYO. To generate the data set, I obtained the contact information for each organization's president or next highest representative through archival fieldwork at ILGA-International and IGLYO.

Survey questions

1. How many paid employees work for your organization?
   [Select: 0–99]

2. How many volunteers work for your organization?
   [Select: 0–100]
3. In your opinion, how much influence do European-level institutions –
   that is, institutions like the European Commission, the European
   Parliament, the European Court of Justice, or the European Court
   of Human Rights – have on your country's politics and policies
   related to the rights of sexual minorities? (O'Dwyer 2010)[2]
   3 – A lot of influence
   2 – Some influence
   1 – Not much influence
   9 – No answer or don't know
4. In your opinion, how much influence do European-level
   institutions – that is, institutions like the European Commission,
   the European Parliament, the European Court of Justice, or the
   European Court of Human Rights – have on what people in your
   country think about the rights of sexual minorities?
   3 – A lot of influence
   2 – Some influence
   1 – Not much influence
   9 – No answer or don't know
5. Do you recall approximately when newspapers and other mass
   media started to cover stories related to the question of sexual
   minority rights?
   [Survey had a sliding bar with years marked 1950–2010]
   9 – No answer, not applicable, or don't know
6. In your opinion, what best explains why these stories started to be
   covered at that time?
   a – EU pressures or EU accession
   b – Other international pressures
   c – Domestic activism
   d – National legislation dealing with LGBT issues
   e – Other [space for free recall]
   9 – No answer or don't know
7. In your opinion, what has been the effect of your country introducing legislation that strengthens the rights and protection of sexual
   minorities?
   4 – Substantial improvement in peoples' attitudes toward LGBT people
   3 – Some improvement in peoples' attitudes toward LGBT people
   2 – No change in peoples' attitudes toward LGBT people

---

[2] This question is adapted from a question first formulated by Conor O'Dwyer (2010, 236–7) for his survey of Polish activists and politicians.

      1 – Worsened peoples' attitudes toward LGBT people

      9 – No answer or don't know

8. Please comment on your perception of the process of change in societal attitudes toward LGBT individuals. For example, did attitudes improve/worsen immediately after LGBT issues became visible? Or did improved attitudes follow an initial backlash in attitudes when the issue was first introduced?

      [Comment box for text]

9. In your opinion, how does the rate of social and political change that has occurred in your country over the last twenty years compare to that of neighboring European countries?

      [Comment box for text]

10. In your opinion, how well defined is the LGBT movement in your country, in terms of its organization and the clarity of its goals? (O'Dwyer 2010)[3]

      3 – Well-defined movement with clear, shared goals

      2 – Somewhat defined with some goals, but little consensus about them

      1 – Not very well defined and no clear goals

      9 – No answer or don't know

11. How closely does your organization cooperate with other L, G, B, and/or T organizations in your country?

      4 – Very close cooperation and shared goals

      3 – Some cooperation

      2 – No active cooperation

      1 – Disputes among organizations and contradictory goals

      9 – No answer or don't know

12. On average in the last five years, what has been your organization's approximate annual budget in Euros (please include grant money in your estimation)?

      1 – Under 5,000

      2 – 5,001–15,000

      3 – 15,001–30,000

      4 – 30,001–50,000

      5 – 50,001–100,000

      6 – 100,001–200,000

      7 – 200,001–300,000

      8 – 300,001–500,000

      9 – 500,001–1,000,000

[3] This question is adapted from a question first formulated by O'Dwyer (2010, 236–7), and used in his survey of Polish activists and politicians.

10 – Over 1,000,000
No answer or don't know

13. What percentage of your funding comes from international/foreign sources? (For example, from international organizations, the governments of other countries, or foreign civil society organizations.) What percentage comes from domestic sources? (For example, from the national government or domestic civil society organizations.)
    [Sliding bars for (1) International/Foreign funding sources and (2) Domestic funding sources. For example, if the respondent attributes 60 percent of funding to foreign sources, the survey software will automatically attribute the remaining percentage (40 percent) to the domestic funding source bar.]

14. Please name the top five organizations/institutions/states that provide funding for your organization:
    [Five spaces for free recall]

15. What percentage of your organization's activities involves cooperation with international organizations?
    [Sliding bar ranging from 0 to 100 percent]

16. Please name the top five foreign civil society organizations with which you work most closely, in order from 1 (most) to 5.
    [Five spaces for free recall]

17. What five groups would you say provide the strongest *domestic* opposition to the LGBT movement in your country? Please indicate whether any of the groups are religious or nationalist organizations as well as your perception of how well organized they are. (For example, a domestic organization that organizes counter-demonstrations at pride parades.)
    [Five spaces for free recall]
    [Following each space, respondents could select from a list of the organization's motivations and attributes: "Motivation of the organization (check all that apply): religious, nationalist, other" and "Organization attributes (check all that apply): well-organized, high membership, well-funded, successful"]

18. Are there any *foreign* opposition groups to the LGBT movement active in your country? If so, which would you say provide the strongest source of foreign opposition? Please indicate whether they are religious or nationalist organizations as well as your perception of how well organized they are. (For example, the financial support from an American Evangelical group to Polish organizations that disseminate school pamphlets linking homosexuality to pedophilia. This American group would qualify as a foreign opposition group.)

[Five spaces for free recall]

[Following each space, respondents could select from a list of the organization's motivations and attributes: "Motivation of the organization (check all that apply): religious, nationalist, other" and "Organization attributes (check all that apply): well-organized, high membership, well-funded, successful"]

19. In your opinion, to what degree are opposition groups (domestic and foreign) mobilized in your country?

    3 – Strong, well-organized

    2 – Somewhat organized

    1 – Weak, unorganized

    9 – No answer or don't know

Quantitative research summaries

TABLE A.1. *Dependent and independent variables summarized (Chapter 4)*

Concept	Mechanism	Coding, notes or examples	Source
Dependent variable			
Legal status			Author's
Combined DV		Combination of the five categories (see below)	legislation data set
Anti-discrimination legislation refers to sexual orientation		One point for any: employment, goods and services, constitution	
Criminal law refers to sexual orientation		One point for: hate crimes based on sexual orientation an aggravating circumstance and/or incitement to hatred based on sexual orientation prohibited	
Partnership recognition of same-sex couples		One point for any: cohabitation rights, registered partnership, marriage equality	
Parenting rights of same-sex couples		One point for any: joint adoption, second-parent adoption	
Discriminatory sexual offenses provisions		One point for any: equal age of consent, same-sex sexual activity legal	

(continued)

TABLE A.I *(continued)*

Concept	Mechanism	Coding, notes or examples	Source
Independent variables			
Transnational and international channels			
Transnational LGBT organizations	Brokerage, framing	# of domestic LGBT orgs with membership in transnational organization, by year	Author's network membership data set
Social channels	Learning	Information flows: Internet users (per 1,000 people), television (per 1,000 people) and trade in newspapers (percent of GDP)	KOF index of globalization
Political channels	Learning, sanctioning	Embassies in country, membership in international organizations, participation in UN Security Council missions, international treaties	KOF index of globalization
Economic channels	Competition, sanctioning	Actual flows: trade, foreign direct investment, portfolio investment, and income payments to foreign nationals (all as percentage of GDP) Restrictions: hidden import barriers, mean tariff rate, taxes on international trade, and capital restrictions	KOF Index of Globalization
Combined channels	Learning, sanctioning, competition	Combined index of political, economic, and social channels	KOF Index of Globalization
EU accession	Learning, sanctioning	Year state joined EU	
Diffusion variables	Emulation	Yearly measure of the number of other states that have previously adopted a given policy	

Concept	Mechanism	Coding, notes or examples	Source
Domestic			
LGBT social spaces		0 – Nothing going on 1 – Mention of some activity but not explicitly gay or lesbian (e.g. bars, restaurants, cafes) 2 – Activity mentioned in one main city 3 – Some gay life in more than one city (this could be little activity in each city but dispersed across multiple locations) 4 – Gay social life in multiple cities 5 – Widespread gay social life	Spartacus Travel Guides, using method of David Frank *et al.* (2010)
Dominant religion		Categorical variable for Mixed Christian (baseline), Protestant, Catholic, and Other	
Counter-mobilization		Average score reported in reference to domestic opposition in expert survey: *In your opinion, to what degree are opposition groups (domestic and foreign) active and effective in mobilizing in your country?* 1 – Weak, unorganized, and ineffective 2 – Somewhat organized and somewhat effective 3 – Strong, well organized, and very effective	Transnational LGBT Organizations Survey
Level of democracy		Polity2 Measure (cf. Polity IV codebook)	Polity IV Data
GDP (log)		Real GDP per capita and components are obtained from an aggregation using price parities and domestic currency expenditures for consumption, investment, and government	Penn GDP Data

TABLE A.2. *Descriptive statistics and correlations (Chapter 4)*

Variable	Mean	S.D.	Min.	Max.	(1)	(2)	(3)	(4)	(5)	(6)	(7)	(8)	(9)	(10)
Legal status	1.52	1.28	0	5	1.00									
(1) Transnational LGBT organizations	0.98	1.27	0	3	1.00									
(2) Social channels	74.38	12.02	34.8	98.37	0.63	1.00								
(3) Political channels	76.95	19.84	12.3	98.56	0.35	0.30	1.00							
(4) Economic channels	68.56	16.89	28.7	98.88	0.58	0.76	0.46	1.00						
(5) Combined channels	67.50	15.98	24.5	92.84	0.50	0.65	0.57	0.79	1.00					
(6) EU accession	0.51	0.50	0	1	0.38	0.41	0.50	0.64	0.63	1.00				
(7) LGBT social spaces	3.72	1.17	0	5	0.24	0.26	0.64	0.40	0.48	0.63	1.00			
(8) Dominant religion	2.85	1.01	0	4	-0.18	-0.28	-0.33	-0.32	-0.41	-0.30	-0.43	1.00		
(9) Democracy level	7.81	5.16	-9	10	0.32	0.54	0.38	0.59	0.50	0.44	0.41	-0.32	1.00	
(10) GDP (log)	9.32	0.83	6.4	11.51	0.68	0.68	0.57	0.76	0.69	0.61	0.51	-0.38	0.60	1.00
(11) Countermobilization	2.18	0.57	1	3	0.04	-0.23	-0.27	-0.36	-0.40	-0.23	-0.24	0.39	-0.15	-0.15

TABLE A.3. *Dependent and independent variables summarized (Chapter 5)*

Concept	Measure	Coding, notes, sources, or examples
Dependent variable		
Societal attitudes	Individual level	Question F118: "Please tell me for each of the following whether you think it [homosexuality] can always be justified, never be justified, or something in between." Scale of 1 (never) to 10 (always). Source: EVS 2011
Societal attitudes (log)	Individual level	As above, but scale 0 to 2.3
Societal attitudes (Index)	Composite measure, individual level	Question F118 combined with Question: "On this list are various groups of people. Could you please sort out any that you would not like to have as neighbors?" Homosexuals (1). Scale: −1.2 to 1.5. Source: EVS 2011
Transnational and international channels		
Social channels	State level	Information flows: Internet users (per 1,000 people), television (per 1,000 people), and trade in newspapers (percentage of GDP). Range 34 to 98. Source: KOF Index
Political channels	State level	Embassies in country, membership in international organizations, participation in UN Security Council missions, international treaties. Range 12 to 99. Source: KOF Index
Economic channels	State level	Actual flows: trade, foreign direct investment, portfolio investment, and income payments to foreign nationals (all as percent of GDP). Restrictions: hidden import barriers, mean tariff rate, taxes on international trade, and capital restrictions. Range 23 to 99. Source: KOF Index
Combined channels	State level	Combined index of political, economic, and social channels. Range 24 to 92. Source: KOF Index
Geographic proximity	Individual level	Interval variable measures distance in kilometers from respondent's residence to Berlin or Vienna, whichever is closer. Range 66 to 2,024. Only EU-12 states. Sources: EVS 2011 and NUTS Level 3
Shared EU identification	Individual level	Question: "Please look at this card and tell me, for each item listed, how much confidence you have in them, is it a great deal, quite a lot, not very much or none at all? The European Union" Scale of 1 (none at all) to 4 (great deal). Source: EVS 2011

(continued)

TABLE A.3 *(continued)*

Concept	Measure	Coding, notes, sources, or examples
Threat variables		
National pride	Individual level	Question: "How proud are you to be a: [nationality]?" Very proud (4), quite proud (3), not very proud (2), not at all proud (1). Source: EVS 2011
Church authority	Individual level, dummy	Question: "Generally speaking, do you think that [your church is giving/the churches are giving], in your country, adequate answers to the social problems facing our country today?" Scale of 0 (no) to 1 (yes). Source: EVS 2011
Religiosity	Individual level	Question: "Apart from weddings, funerals, and christenings, about how often do you attend religious services these days?" Scale of 1 (never) to 8 (more than once a week). Source: EVS 2011
Religious doctrine	Individual level, categorical variable	Protestant (1/Reference), Catholic (2), Orthodox (3), Other (4). Source: EVS 2011
Legal status		
Combined	State level	Combination of the five categories (see Table A.1). Range 0 to 5
Controls		
Post-materialism	Individual level	Inglehart and Norris 4-point index. Materialist (1), mixed (2), post-materialist (3)
Education	Individual level	Question: "What age did you complete your education?" Range 0 (no formal education) to 96. Source: EVS 2011[4]
Town size	Individual level	Size of town. 1 = less than 5,000, 2 = 5,000 to 49,999, 3 = 50,000 to 499,999, and 4 = 500,000 or greater. Source: EVS 2011, following Andersen and Fetner (2008) coding
Age	Individual level	Range: 15 to 108. Source: EVS 2011
Gender	Individual level, dummy	Women = 1. Source: EVS 2011
Year	Dummies	Year survey was conducted (1990/reference, 1991, 1992, 1993, 1999, 2000, 2001, 2008, 2009). Source: EVS 2011

[4] The education measure is the only consistent measure of education across waves. According to Dr. Inge Sieben of the EVS, it is commonly used in studies based on the EVS data set. Robert Andersen and Tina Fetner (2008) also based their education variable on this question.

TABLE A.4. *Descriptive statistics and correlations (Chapter 5)*

Variable	Mean	S.D.	Min.	Max.	(1)	(2)	(3)	(4)	(5)	(6)	(7)	(8)	(9)	(10)	(11)	(12)	(13)	(14)
Attitudes (index)	0.15	0.98	-1.23	1.58														
Attitudes (log)	1.02	0.94	0.00	2.30														
(1) Social channels	77.46	13.54	34.87	98.37	1.00													
(2) Political channels	80.02	19.15	12.33	98.56	0.21	1.00												
(3) Economic channels	73.45	15.83	23.07	98.88	0.74	0.36	1.00											
(4) Combined channels	74.04	14.07	24.48	92.84	0.72	0.68	0.89	1.00										
(5) EU identification	2.53	0.85	1	4	-0.01	0.00	-0.04	-0.03	1.00									
(6) National pride	-1.75	0.79	-4	-1	0.05	0.02	0.00	0.01	-0.08	1.00								
(7) Church authority	0.31	0.46	0	1	0.00	-0.09	-0.06	-0.07	-0.09	0.09	1.00							
(8) Religiosity	-5.09	2.51	-8	-1	0.02	-0.12	-0.05	-0.10	-0.10	0.13	0.29	1.00						
(9) Denomination	2.01	0.74	1	4	-0.03	0.03	-0.19	-0.17	-0.02	-0.02	0.07	0.18	1.00					
(10) Post-materialism	1.87	0.63	1	3	-0.06	0.03	0.03	0.04	-0.02	-0.10	-0.06	-0.07	-0.08	1.00				
(11) Education	18.22	5.19	0	93	0.04	0.03	0.05	0.04	-0.02	-0.11	-0.08	-0.09	-0.04	0.15	1.00			
(12) Town size	2.21	0.99	1	4	-0.07	0.10	-0.01	0.04	-0.01	-0.08	-0.03	-0.09	0.05	0.07	0.15	1.00		
(13) Age	45.68	17.63	15	108	0.10	0.04	0.08	0.09	0.02	0.12	0.13	0.13	-0.02	-0.14	-0.26	-0.04	1.00	
(14) Gender	0.54	0.50	0	1	0.02	0.00	0.01	0.00	0.03	0.01	0.04	0.11	0.01	-0.05	-0.04	0.03	0.00	1.00
(15) Geographic proximity*	625	453	66	2024	0.09	-0.32	0.16	-0.03	-0.03	0.06	0.07	0.12	0.32	-0.02	-0.07	0.13	0.02	0.01

Selected list of interviewees

I have redacted the names of interviewees to comply with institutional review board approval. I have also redacted any specific information related to the interviewee's role in the organization to which they are associated (e.g. president, director, policy coordinator, advisor to commissioner, legal representative, Pride organizer, parliamentarian, etc.). Instead, the roles have been compressed under the following categories: activist, politician, organizational representative, and academic. This is a far too general way to describe the nuance of the varied work my interviewees do, but it is necessary to protect their identities.

1. Lesben und Schwulen Verband Deutschland (LSVD) (Lesbian and Gay Federation in Germany) (translated from German), Activist, June 20, 2009
2. Initiative Queer Nations e.V. (translated from German), Academic and Activist, June 15, 2009
3. Initiative Queer Nations e.V. (translated from German), Activist, June 23, 2009
4. Berliner Christopher Street Day e.V. (translated from German), Activist, June 15, 2009
5. Fundacja Równości (Equality Foundation) (translated from German), Activist, July 2, 2009
6. Bündnis 90/Die Grünen (Green Party in Germany) (translated from German), Politician, June 22, 2009
7. Center of Transnational Relations, Free University Berlin (translated from German), Academic, June 29, 2009
8. KPH, Activist, July 17, 2009
9. KPH, Activist, July 17, 2009
10. EU Commission, Office of the Commissioner for Employment, Social Affairs, and Equal Opportunities, Representative, July 8, 2009
11. EU Commission, Directorate, Representative, July 8, 2009
12. EU Commission/Alliance of Liberals and Democrats for Europe, Civil Liberties, Justice, and Home Affairs, Politician, June 8, 2009
13. ILGA-International, Activist, July 9, 2009
14. ILGA-Europe, Activist, July 9, 2009
15. EU Commission, Agency on Fundamental Rights, Representative, July 9, 2009
16. EU Commission, Agency on Fundamental Rights, Representative, July 9, 2009
17. Lambda: Berlin-Brandenburg (translated from German), Activist, July 10, 2009

18. Lambda: Berlin-Brandenburg (translated from German), Activist, July 10, 2009
19. Lambda: Berlin-Brandenburg (translated from German), Activist, July 10, 2009
20. Center for the Study of Discrimination Based on Sexual Orientation (CSDSO) (translated from German), Academic, June 29, 2009
21. CSDSO (translated from German), Academic, June 29, 2009
100. ILGA-Portugal, Activist, October 28, 2010
101. Lesbian Section ŠKUC-LL, Activist, October 28, 2010
102. Lesbian Group Kontra and Iskorak, Activist, October 29, 2010
103. Ogólnopolskiego Porozumienia Związków Zawodowych (OPZZ) (The All Poland Alliance of Trade Unions), Activist, October 29, 2010
104. European Forum of LGBT Christian Groups, Activist, October 29, 2010
105. NGO Estonian Gay Youth, Activist, October 29, 2010
106. Mozaika: Alliance of LGBT and their Friends, Activist, October 30, 2010
107. DIC Legebitra and formerly with IGLYO, Activist, October 30, 2010
108. DIC Legebitra, Activist, October 30, 2010
109. Háttér Társaság a Melegekért (Hatter Support Society for LGBT People in Hungary), Activist, October 30, 2010
110. Gay and Lesbian Equality Network (GLEN), Activist, October 31, 2010
111. Drustvo DIH/Association DIH, Activist, October 31, 2010
112. Malta Gay Rights Movement, Activist, November 1, 2010
113. Fundacja Równości (Equality Foundation) (translated from German), Activist, July 2, 2009
117. United States Embassy to Germany, Human Rights Portfolio, Representative, April 17, 2013
118. International Group of Trans Activists Bratislava, Activist, January 25, 2011
119. Inakost, Activist, January 25, 2011
120. Inakost, Activist, January 25, 2011
121. Informal Group of LGBT Christians (Slovakia), Activist, January 25, 2011
122. Rainbow PRIDE Bratislava, Activist, January 26, 2011
123. Labrisz, Activist, January 29, 2011
124. Fundacja Równości (Equality Foundation) (translated from German), Activist, February 21, 2011

125. Maneo/LSVD: Berlin-Brandenburg (translated from German), Activist, March 24, 2011
126. European Parliament's Intergroup on LGBT Rights, Representative, April 26, 2011
127. Bündnis 90/Die Grünen (written interview), Politician, April 4, 2011
128. Bündnis 90/Die Grünen (written interview), Politician, June 1, 2011
129. KPH, Activist, October 12, 2011
130. KPH Łódź, Local Chapter Activist, October 23, 2011
131. KPH Łódź, Local Chapter Activist, October 23, 2011
132. United States Embassy to Poland, Representative, October 24, 2011
133. Foreign Ministry of the Republic of Poland, Representative, October 25, 2011
134. Associazione Radicale "Certi Diritti" (Radical Association "Certain Rights"), Politician and Activist, October 28, 2011
135. Comisiones Obreras Spain (The Worker's Commission in Spain), Activist, October 28, 2011
136. European Gay and Lesbian Sports Federation (EGLSF), Activist, October 28, 2011
137. EGLSF, Activist, October 28, 2011
138. Mozaika/ILGA-Europe, Activist, November 12, 2011
139. Lambda-Warszawa, Activist, November 15, 2011
140. KPH, Activist, November 16, 2011
141. Młodzież Wszechpolsk (All Polish Youth), Activist, November 25, 2011
142. European Parliament, Human Rights Unit, Representative, March 6, 2012
143. ILGA-Europe, Activist, March 3, 2012
144. IGLYO, Activist, March 8, 2012
145. Friedrichstadt Palast GmbH, Representative, May 4, 2012
146. Lambda Istanbul, Activist, July 16, 2012
147. American Society for the Defense of Tradition, Family, and Property (TFP) (phone interview), Representative, March 18, 2013
148. European Commission, Unit on Human Rights and Democratisation, Representative, April 8, 2011
149. Chancellery of the Federal Republic of Germany, Representative, July 5, 2011
150. Anonymous, November 29, 2011

151. The Peace Institute (Slovenia), Academic, April 23, 2013
152. US Embassy to Germany (invited to participate during videoconference meeting with the US State Department and others on transgender rights), Human Rights and LGBT Portfolio, Representative, April 17, 2013
153. Transgender Europe (TGEU) (invited to participate during videoconference meeting with the US State Department and others on transgender rights), Activist, April 17, 2013
154. DIC Legebitra (email interview), Activist, May 6, 2013
155. Associazione Radicale Certi Diritti, LGBT Rights Mandate, Politician, January 31, 2014
156. CCOO (email interview), Activist, April 10, 2015
157. ILGA-Portugal (email interview), Activist, March 24, 2015
158. ŠKUC-LL (email interview), Activist, March 10, 2015
159. Hatter Support Society for LGBT People (email interview), Activist, March 10, 2015
160. Malta Gay Rights Movement (email interview), Activist, March 9, 2015
161. COC Nederland (email interview), Activist, February 20, 2015
162. International Gay and Lesbian Human Rights Commission/formerly Swedish Federation for Lesbian, Gay, Bisexual, Transgender, and Queer Rights (RFSL) (email interview), Activist, March 10, 2015
163. ILGA-Europe, Activist, February 26, 2015
164. Parliamentary Office of Anna Grodzka, Representative, March 28, 2015
165. Human Rights Campaign (email interview), Activist, March 17, 2015
166. KPH (email interview), Activist, February 27, 2015
167. European Parliament Intergroup on LGBT Rights (email interview), Representative, March 9, 2015
168. Associazione Radicale "Certi Diritti" (email interview), Politician, February 21, 2015
169. Open Society Foundations, Representative, March 6, 2015

Selected participant observation and informal interviews at activist panels and political events

200. ILGA-Europe Workshop: National Government Focal Points on LGBT Equality Mainstreaming Policies in Europe;

Participants: Polish Ministry for Human Rights in Foreign Affairs and Dutch Company Pride Platform: Gays in Work Place, October 28, 2010

201. ILGA-Europe Workshop: Developing a Coherent and Comprehensive Approach to Strategic Litigation at European Level; Participants: Human Rights Law King's College London, ILGA-Europe, CoE, October 28, 2010

202. ILGA-Europe Workshop: How to Create Synergy in International Cooperation; Participants: COC, RFSL, Norwegian LGBT Organization (LLH), October 29, 2010

203. ILGA-Europe Workshop: How to Create Synergy in International Cooperation Brainstorming Session; Participants: NGO Estonian Gay Youth, Homosexuelle Initiate (HOSI) Wien, ILGA-Europe, The Norwegian LGBT Organization (LLH), The Norwegian LGBT Organization (LLH), October 29, 2010

204. ILGA-Europe Workshop: Expressing Our Differences, Challenging Our Prejudices, Developing Our Alliances; Participants: MEP Denmark, Dutch Institute for Gender Studies, European Commission Against Racism and Intolerance, October 29, 2010

205. Human Dimension Implementation Meetings and Panels in Warsaw, Organization for Security and Co-operation in Europe (OSCE), September 26–October 7, 2011

206. Political Speeches at Election Night Celebration of the Ruch Palikota Party, October 9, 2011

207. Warsaw Pride House Panels and Events, associated with EuroPride 2010, July 15–17, 2010

208. Politicians Speaking on Solidarity with Russian LGBT People, Demonstration against Antigay Propaganda Bill at Russian Embassy Berlin, February 15, 2012

209. Panel with GDR Activists at Berlinale Premiere of the Documentary "Out In Ost-Berlin: Lesben und Schwule in der DDR," February 17, 2013

210. Kampagne Solidarnost Activist Panel and Meeting in SchwuZ Berlin, February 11, 2013

211. United States State Department Panel [invited to participate during videoconference from US Embassy Berlin], Stakeholders Discussion on Protecting Transgender Persons from Violence, April 17, 2013

212. ILGA-Europe Panel: Towards Partnership Legislation in the Rest of Europe; Participants: LGBT group of CCOO (Spain), ŠKUC-LL

(Slovenia), Kontra (Croatia), KPH (Poland), Mozaika (Latvia), October 27, 2011

213. ILGA-Europe Panel: Traditional values – an international perspective; Participants: former MEP and former government representative on women issues (Netherlands), ARC International, Russian LGBT network, October 28, 2011

214. Political Panel on Gay Rights Preceding the 2009 German Election: Liberale Schwule und Lesben (LiSL-FDP) [Gays and Lesbians of the Liberal Party], Arbeitsgemeinschaft der Lesben und Schwulen in der SPD (Schwusos) [Working Group of Lesbians and Gays in the Social Democratic Party], Lesben und Schwulen in der Union (LSU-CDU/CSU) [Lesbians and Gays in the Christian Democratic Union], Die Linke.queer [Left Party Queer Group], Bundesarbeitsgemeinschaften Schwulenpolitik Bündnis 90/Die Grünen [Federal Working Group for Gay Politics in the Green Party], June 30, 2009

215. Conference on EU Enlargement, Democracy, and the Politics of Sexual Orientation and Gender Identity, European Parliament, February 4, 2015

References

24kul.si. 2013. "Institute for Family Life and Culture." http://24kul.si/zavod-kulsi.

Abdelal, Rawi, Yoshiko M. Herrera, Alastair Iain Johnston, and Rose McDermott. 2006. "Identity as a Variable." *Perspectives on Politics* 4(4): 695–711.

Acharya, Amitav. 2004. "How Ideas Spread: Whose Norms Matter? Norm Localization and Institutional Change in Asian Regionalism." *International Organization* 58(2): 239–75.

Adam, Barry, Jan Willem Duyvendak, and Andre Krouwel. 1998. *Global Emergence of Gay & Lesbian Politics.* Philadelphia: Temple University Press.

Adamczyk, Amy, and Cassady Pitt. 2009. "Shaping Attitudes about Homosexuality: The Role of Religion and Cultural Context." *Social Science Research* 38(2): 338–51.

Agence France Presse. 2014. "Thomas Hitzlsperger, Gay German Soccer Player, Says Homophobia Now Has an 'Opponent.' " *Huffington Post.* www.huffingtonpost.com/2014/01/09/thomas-hitzlsperger-homophobia-_n_4566999.html.

Allport, Gordon W. 1954. *The Nature of Prejudice.* Reading, MA: Addison-Wesley.

Almeida, Paul D. 2003. "Opportunity Organizations and Threat-Induced Contention: Protest Waves in Authoritarian Settings." *The American Journal of Sociology* 109(2): 345–400.

Altman, Dennis. 1996. "Rupture or Continuity? The Internationalization of Gay Identities." *Social Text* 14(3): 77–94.

——— 1999. "Globalization, Political Economy, and HIV/AIDS." *Theory and Society* 28(4): 559–84.

Amar, Paul. 2013. *The Security Archipelago: Human-Security States, Sexuality Politics, and the End of Neoliberalism.* Durham: Duke University Press Books.

Amt fuer Statistik Berlin-Brandenburg. 2011. "Über 457 000 Ausländer Aus 190 Staaten in Berlin Gemeldet." www.statistik-berlin-brandenburg.de/pms/2011/11-02-04.pdf.

Andersen, Robert, and Tina Fetner. 2008. "Economic Inequality and Intolerance: Attitudes toward Homosexuality in 35 Democracies." *American Journal of Political Science* 52(4): 942–58.

Anderson, Christopher J. 2007. "The Interaction of Structures and Voting Behavior." In *Oxford Handbook of Political Behavior*, eds. Russell Dalton and Hans-Dieter Klingemann. New York: Oxford University Press, 589–609.

Anderson, Christopher J., and Yuliya V. Tverdova. 2003. "Corruption, Political Allegiances, and Attitudes toward Government in Contemporary Democracies." *American Journal of Political Science* 47(1): 91–109.

Andrews, Bruce. 1975. "Social Rules and the State as a Social Actor." *World Politics* 27(4): 521–40.

Asal, Victor, Udi Sommer, and Paul G. Harwood. 2013. "Original Sin: A Cross-National Study of the Legality of Homosexual Acts." *Comparative Political Studies* 46(3): 320–51.

Ayoub, Phillip M. 2010. "Repressing Protest: Threat and Weakness in the European Context, 1975–1989." *Mobilization* 15(4): 465–88.

2013. "Cooperative Transnationalism in Contemporary Europe: Europeanization and Political Opportunities for LGBT Mobilization in the European Union." *European Political Science Review* 5(2): 279–310.

2014. "With Arms Wide Shut: Threat Perception, Norm Reception, and Mobilized Resistance to LGBT Rights." *Journal of Human Rights* 13(3): 337–62.

2015a. "Contested Norms in New-Adopter States: International Determinants of LGBT Rights Legislation." *European Journal of International Relations* 21(2): 293–322.

2015b. "Thematic Review: LGBT Rights and Movements in Comparative and International Politics." *Politics & Gender* 11(1): 218–30.

Ayoub, Phillip M., and David Paternotte, eds. 2014. *LGBT Activism and the Making of Europe: A Rainbow Europe?* Basingstoke, UK: Palgrave Macmillan.

Ayoub, Phillip M., Sophia J. Wallace, and Chris Zepeda-Millán. 2014. "Triangulation in Social Movement Research." In *Methodological Practices in Social Movement Research*, ed. Donatella della Porta. Oxford University Press, 67–96.

Bączkowski, Tomasz. 2008. "Diese widerwärtigen Päderasten." *Berliner Debatte Initial* 19(6): 33–41.

2010. "Spór O Sobotnią Paradę Równości W Warszawie." *Rzeczpospolita*. www.rp.pl/artykul/9157,509229-Spor-o-sobotnia-Parade-Rownosci-w-Warszawie.html.

Badgett, M. V. Lee. 2009. *When Gay People Get Married: What Happens When Societies Legalize Same-Sex Marriage*. New York University Press.

Bajpai, Kanti. 2000. *Human Security: Concept and Measurement*. New Delhi, India: Kroc Institute Occasional Paper No. 19:OP:1.

Balzer, Carsten, and Jan Simon Hutta. 2014. "Trans Networking in the European Vortex: Between Advocacy and Grassroots Politics." In *LGBT Activism and the Making of Europe: A Rainbow Europe?*, eds. Phillip M. Ayoub and David Paternotte. Basingstoke, UK: Palgrave, 171–92.

Barnard, Catherine. 2008. "The 'Opt-Out' for the UK and Poland from the Charter of Fundamental Rights: Triumph of Rhetoric over Reality?" In *The*

Lisbon Treaty: EU Constitutionalism without a Constitutional Treaty?, eds. Stefan Griller and Jacques Ziller. Austria: Springer Wien New York, 257–83.

Baruch, Yehuda, and Brooks C. Holtom. 2008. "Survey Response Rate Levels and Trends in Organizational Research." *Human Relations* 61(8): 1139–60.

Baumgartner, Frank R., and Bryan D. Jones. 2009. *Agendas and Instability in American Politics*. 2nd edn. University of Chicago Press.

Beachy, Robert. 2014. *Gay Berlin: Birthplace of a Modern Identity*. New York: Knopf Doubleday Publishing Group.

Beger, Nico J. 2004. *Tensions in the Struggle for Sexual Minority Rights in Europe: Que(e)rying Political Practices*. Reprint. Manchester University Press.

Beissinger, Mark, and Stephen Kotkin, eds. 2014. *Historical Legacies of Communism in Russia and Eastern Europe*. New York: Cambridge University Press.

Beltrán, Cristina. 2010. *The Trouble with Unity: Latino Politics and the Creation of Identity*. Oxford University Press.

Benford, Robert D., and David A. Snow. 1999. "Alternative Types of Cross-National Diffusion in the Social Movement Arena." In *Social Movements in a Globalizing World*, eds. Donatella della Porta, Hanspeter Kriesi, and Dieter Rucht. New York: St. Martin's Press, 23–9.

Berbec-Rostas, Mariana. 2013. "Homophobia in Romanian Football Receives a Red Card from European Union Court." *Open Society Foundations*. www.opensocietyfoundations.org/voices/homophobia-romanian-football-receives-red-card-european-union-court.

Berezin, Mabel, and Juan Diez-Medrano. 2008. "Distance Matters: Place, Political Legitimacy and Popular Support for European Integration." *Comparative European Politics* 6(1): 1–32.

Berger, Peter L. 1993. *A Far Glory: The Quest for Faith in an Age of Credulity*. New York: Anchor.

Bernstein, Mary. 2002. "Identities and Politics: Toward a Historical Understanding of the Lesbian and Gay Movement." *Social Science History* 26(3): 531–81.

Bernstein, Mary, and Renate Reimann. 2001. *Queer Families, Queer Politics: Challenging Culture and the State*. New York: Columbia University Press.

Biedroń, Robert, and Marta Abramowicz. 2007. "The Polish Educational System and the Promotion of Homophobia." In *The Situation of Bisexual and Homosexual Persons in Poland 2005 and 2006 Report*, ed. Marta Abramowicz. Warsaw: Campaign Against Homophobia and Lambda Warsaw Association, 51–5.

Binnie, Jon. 2004. *The Globalization of Sexuality*. London: Sage Publications.

Binnie, Jon, and Christian Klesse. 2013. "'Like a Bomb in the Gasoline Station': East-West Migration and Transnational Activism around Lesbian, Gay, Bisexual, Transgender and Queer Politics in Poland." *Journal of Ethnic and Migration Studies* 39(7): 1107–24.

Bishin, Benjamin G., Thomas J. Hayes, Matthew B. Incantalupo, and Charles Anthony Smith. 2015. "Opinion Backlash and Public Attitudes: Are Political Advances in Gay Rights Counterproductive?" *American Journal of Political Science*. http://dx.doi.org/10.1111/ajps.12181.

Blumenfeld, Warren J., and Diane Christine Raymond. 1988. *Looking at Gay and Lesbian Life*. Boston: Beacon Press.

Bob, Clifford. 2012. *The Global Right Wing and the Clash of World Politics*. Cambridge University Press.

Borowik, Irena. 2002. "The Roman Catholic Church in the Process of Democratic Transformation: The Case of Poland." *Social Compass* 49(2): 239–52.

Broqua, Christophe. 2015. "AIDS Activism from North to Global." In *The Ashgate Research Companion to Lesbian and Gay Activism*, eds. David Paternotte and Manon Tremblay. Farnham: Ashgate Publishing, 59–72.

Bruce-Jones, Eddie, and Lucas Itaborahy. 2011. *ILGA Report: State-Sponsored Homophobia*. ILGA-Europe. www.europarl.europa.eu/meetdocs/2009_2014/documents/droi/dv/4_04ilgareport_/4_04ilgareport_en.pdf.

Bruce, Katherine McFarland. in press. *Parading Toward Equality*. New York University Press.

Brysk, Alison. 2000. *From Tribal Village to Global Village*. Palo Alto: Stanford University Press.

2013. *Speaking Rights to Power: Constructing Political Will*. New York: Oxford University Press.

Bunce, Valerie. 2003. "Rethinking Recent Democratization: Lessons from the Postcommunist Experience." *World Politics* 55(2): 167–92.

Burns, Joseph R. 2009. "The Laying of Hands: Pope John Paul II and the Catholic Church's Political Role in Poland Pre- and Post-1989." In *The Rhetoric of Pope John Paul II*, eds. Joseph Blaney and Joseph Zompetti. Lexington Books, 151–73.

Butler, Judith. 2008. "Sexual Politics, Torture, and Secular Time." *The British Journal of Sociology* 59(1): 1–23.

Buzan, Barry. 1990. "The Case for a Comprehensive Definition of Security and the Institutional Consequences of Accepting It." *Working Papers* 4(0): 1–17.

Búzás, Zoltán. 2013. "The Color of Threat: Race, Threat Perception, and the Demise of the Anglo-Japanese Alliance (1902–1923)." *Security Studies* 22(4): 573–606.

Bylok, Katarzyna, and Konrad Pędziwiatr. 2010. "The Family of Radio Maryja and One of Its Activists." Presented at Tischner European University.

Carlson-Rainer, Elise. 2015. "LGBT Pride: Marching on the Front Lines." *E-International Relations*. www.e-ir.info/2015/07/01/lgbt-pride-marching-on-the-front-lines/.

Carpenter, R. Charli. 2011. "Vetting the Advocacy Agenda: Network Centrality and the Paradox of Weapons Norms." *International Organization* 65(1): 69–102.

Carrillo, Héctor. 2007. "Imagining Modernity: Sexuality, Policy and Social Change in Mexico." *Sexuality Research & Social Policy* 4(3): 74–91.

Cârstocea, Sinziana. 2006. "Between Acceptance and Rejection: Decriminalizing Homosexuality in Romania." In *The Gays' and Lesbians' Rights in an Enlarged European Union*, eds. Anne Weyembergh and Sinziana Cârstocea. Brussels: Editions de l'Université de Bruxelles, 216–22.

Casanova, José. 2009. "The Religious Situation in Europe." In *Secularization and the World Religions*, eds. Hans Joas and Klaus Wiegandt. Liverpool University Press.

Chabot, Sean, and Jan Willem Duyvendak. 2002. "Globalization and Transnational Diffusion between Social Movements: Reconceptualizing the Dissemination of the Gandhian Repertoire and the 'Coming Out' Routine." *Theory and Society* 31(6): 697–740.

Chauncey, George. 1994. *Gay New York: Gender, Urban Culture, and the Making of the Gay Male World, 1890–1940*. New York: Basic Books.

2005. *Why Marriage: The History Shaping Today's Debate Over Gay Equality*. New York: Basic Books.

Checkel, Jeffrey T. 1997. "International Norms and Domestic Politics." *European Journal of International Relations* 3(4): 473–95.

2001. "Why Comply? Social Learning and European Identity Change." *International Organization* 55(3): 553–88.

2005. "International Institutions and Socialization in Europe: Introduction and Framework." *International Organization* 59(4): 801–26.

2006. "Tracing Causal Mechanisms." *International Studies Review* 8(2): 362–70.

2014. "Identity, Europe and the World beyond Public Spheres." In *European Public Spheres: Politics Is Back*, ed. Thomas Risse. New York: Cambridge University Press, 227–46.

Chetaille, Agnes. 2011. "Poland: Sovereignty and Sexuality in Post-Socialist Times." In *The Lesbian and Gay Movement and the State*, eds. Manon Tremblay, David Paternotte, and Carol Johnson. Surrey, UK: Ashgate Publishing, 119–34.

Cohen, Cathy J. 1997. "Punks, Bulldaggers, and Welfare Queens: The Radical Potential of Queer Politics?" *GLQ: A Journal of Lesbian and Gay Studies* 3(4): 437–65.

Colbert, Chuck. 2013. "LGBT Catholics React to Pope's Resignation." *Pride Source*. www.pridesource.com/article.html?article=58503.

Conrad, Kathryn. 2001. "Queer Treasons: Homosexuality and Irish National Identity." *Cultural Studies* 15(1): 124–37.

Conrad, Ryan, ed. 2014. *Against Equality: Queer Revolution, Not Mere Inclusion*. Oakland, CA: AK Press.

Conway, Brian. 2009. *Individual-Level Determinants of Religious Practice and Belief in Catholic Europe*. IRISS at CEPS/INSTEAD. IRISS Working Paper Series. http://ideas.repec.org/p/irs/iriswp/2009-14.html.

Cooley, Jonna, and Gary Burkholder. 2011. "Using Video and Contact to Change Attitudes toward Gay Men and Lesbians." *Journal of Social, Behavioral, and Health Sciences* 5(1): 83–90.

Cortell, Andrew P., and James W. Davis. 1996. "How Do International Institutions Matter? The Domestic Impact of International Rules and Norms." *International Studies Quarterly* 40(4): 451–78.

Council of Europe. 2011. *Discrimination on Grounds of Sexual Orientation and Gender Identity in Europe*. Strasbourg: Council of Europe Publishing.

Cox, Cece. 2005. "To Have and To Hold – Or Not: The Influence of the Christian Right on Gay Marriage Laws in the Netherlands, Canada, and the United States." *Law & Sexuality* 14: 1–50.

Cragg, Gulliver. 2010. "Gays Defy Traditionalists with Warsaw March." *New Zealand Herald.* www.nzherald.co.nz/relationships/news/article.cfm?c_id=41&objectid=10659619.

Crenshaw, Kimberle. 1991. "Mapping the Margins: Intersectionality, Identity Politics, and Violence against Women of Color." *Stanford Law Review* 43(6): 1241–99.

Crisp, Richard J., and Rhiannon N. Turner. 2009. "Can Imagined Interactions Produce Positive Perceptions?: Reducing Prejudice through Simulated Social Contact." *American Psychologist* 64(4): 231–40.

Črnič, Aleš, and Gregor Lesjak. 2003. "Religious Freedom and Control in Independent Slovenia." *Sociology of Religion* 64(3): 349–66.

Currier, Ashley. 2012. *Out in Africa: LGBT Organizing in Namibia and South Africa*. Minneapolis: University of Minnesota Press.

Darden, Keith, and Anna Grzymała-Busse. 2006. "The Great Divide: Literacy, Nationalism, and the Communist Collapse." *World Politics* 59(1): 83–115.

Davenport, Christian. 1995. "Multi-Dimensional Threat Perception and State Repression: An Inquiry into Why States Apply Negative Sanctions." *American Journal of Political Science* 39(3): 683–713.

Dawson, Michael C. 1994. *Behind the Mule: Race and Class in African-American Politics*. Princeton, NJ: Princeton University Press.

Dececco, John, and Vern L. Bullough. 2002. *Before Stonewall: Activists for Gay and Lesbian Rights in Historical Context*. Binghamton, NY: Routledge.

Deutsch, Karl W. 1957. *Political Community and the North Atlantic Area*. Princeton, NJ: Princeton University Press.

———. 1963. *The Nerves of Government: Models of Political Communication and Control*. New York: Free Press.

Dimitrova, Antoaneta, and Mark Rhinard. 2005. "The Power of Norms in the Transposition of EU Directives." *European Integration Online Papers* 9(16).

Dixon, John, Kevin Durrheim, and Colin Tredoux. 2005. "Beyond the Optimal Contact Strategy: A Reality Check for the Contact Hypothesis." *The American Psychologist* 60(7): 697–711.

Dorf, Michael C., and Sidney Tarrow. 2014. "Strange Bedfellows: How an Anticipatory Countermovement Brought Same-Sex Marriage into the Public Arena." *Law & Society Review* 39(2): 449–73.

Dreher, Axel. 2006. "Does Globalization Affect Growth? Evidence from a New Index of Globalization." *Applied Economics* 38(10): 1091–1110.

Dreher, Axel, Noel Gaston, and Willem Martens. 2008. *Measuring Globalisation: Gauging Its Consequences*. New York: Springer.

della Porta, Donatella, and Manuela Caiani. 2007. "Europeanization From Below? Social Movements and Europe." *Mobilization* 12(1): 1–20.

della Porta, Donatella, and Sidney Tarrow. 2005. *Transnational Protest and Global Activism*. Lanham, MD: Rowman & Littlefield.

D'Emilio, John. 1983. "Capitalism and Gay Identity." In *Powers of Desire: The Politics of Sexuality*, eds. Ann Snitow, Christine Stansell, and Sharon Thompson. New York: Monthly Review Press, 100–11.

1998. *Sexual Politics, Sexual Communities.* 2nd edn. Chicago, Ill: University of Chicago Press.

de Wilde, Pieter, and Michael Zürn. 2012. "Can the Politicization of European Integration Be Reversed?" *Journal of Common Market Studies* 50(S1): 137–53.

Easter, Gerald M. 1997. "Preference for Presidentialism: Postcommunist Regime Change in Russia and the NIS." *World Politics* 49(2): 184–211.

Economist. 2014. "Pride and Prejudice." www.economist.com/news/international/21595034-more-places-are-seeing-gay-marchesor-clever-substitutes-pride-and-prejudice.

Encarnación, Omar. 2014. "Gay Rights: Why Democracy Matters." *Journal of Democracy* 25(3): 90–104.

Engeli, Isabelle. 2011. "Citizens but Not Parents? Comparing Same-Sex Union Policies in Western Europe." Presented at the 18th Conference of Europeanists, Barcelona, Spain, June 21, 2011.

Euronews. 2012. "Hungary, Latvia, Lithuania Anti-Gay Criticism." www.euronews.com/2012/05/25/hungary-latvia-lithuania-anti-gay-criticism/.

European Commission. 2009. *Special Eurobarometer 317: Discrimination in the EU in 2009.* 119.

European Parliament. 2006. *European Parliament Resolution on Homophobia in Europe.* 2005/2666(RSP) www.europarl.europa.eu/sides/getDoc.do?type=TA&reference=P6-TA-2006-0018&language=EN&ring=B6-2006-0040.

2010. "Polish Minister for Equal Treatment Sends Censorship Requests to Organisations and Media." *The European Parliament's Intergroup on LGBT Rights.*

2015a. *European Parliament Resolution of 30 April 2015 on the 2014 Progress Report on Albania (2014/2951(RSP)).* www.europarl.europa.eu/oeil/popups/ficheprocedure.do?lang=en&reference=2014/2951%28RSP%29.

2015b. *European Parliament Resolution of 30 April 2015 on the 2014 Progress Report on Bosnia and Herzegovina (2014/2952(RSP)).* www.europarl.europa.eu/oeil/popups/ficheprocedure.do?lang=en&reference=2014/2952%28RSP%29.

European Values Study. 2011. *European Values Study 1981–2008.* www.europeanvaluesstudy.eu.

Evangelista, Matthew. 1999. *Unarmed Forces: The Transnational Movement to End the Cold War.* Ithaca, NY: Cornell University Press.

Evans, Sara M., and Harry C. Boyte. 1992. *Free Spaces: The Sources of Democratic Change in America.* Chicago, Ill: University of Chicago Press.

Farrell, Henry, and Niamh Hardiman. 2015. "Ireland's Voters Approve Same-Sex Marriage. Here's How That Happened." *Washington Post.* www.washingtonpost.com/blogs/monkey-cage/wp/2015/05/23/ireland-has-voted-yes-to-same-sex-marriage-how-did-it-happen/.

Fernández, Juan J., and Mark Lutter. 2013. "Supranational Cultural Norms, Domestic Value Orientations and the Diffusion of Same-Sex Union Rights in Europe, 1988–2009." *International Sociology* 28(1): 102–20.

Ferree, Myra Marx. 2004. "Soft Repression: Ridicule, Stigma, and Silencing in Gender-Based Movements." In *Authority in Contention (Research in Social Movements, Conflicts and Change, Volume 25)*, eds. Daniel Meyers and Daniel Cress. London: Emerald Group Publishing Limited, 85–101.

Fetner, Tina. 2008. *How the Religious Right Shaped Lesbian and Gay Activism.* Minneapolis: University of Minnesota Press.

Finke, Roger, and Amy Adamczyk. 2008. "Cross-National Moral Beliefs: The Influence of National Religious Context." *Sociological Quarterly* 49(4): 617–52.

Finnemore, Martha. 1996. "Norms, Culture, and World Politics." *International Organization* 50(2): 325–47.

Finnemore, Martha, and Kathryn Sikkink. 1998. "International Norm Dynamics and Political Change." *International Organization* 52(4): 887–917.

Flores, Andrew, and Karthick Ramakrishnan. n.d. "Restrictive Attitudes towards Same Sex Marriage: The Varying Importance of Gender by Race." http://karthick.com/wp-content/uploads/2013/11/AFKR-prop8-may2012.pdf.

Florini, Ann. 1996. "The Evolution of International Norms." *International Studies Quarterly* 40(3): 363–89.

Frank, David John, Bayliss J. Camp, and Steven A. Boutcher. 2010. "Worldwide Trends in the Criminal Regulation of Sex, 1945 to 2005." *American Sociological Review* 75(6): 867–93.

Frank, David John, and Elizabeth Mceneaney. 1999. "The Individualization of Society and the Liberalization of State Policies on Same-Sex Sexual Relations, 1984–1995." *Social Forces* 77(3): 911–43.

Friedman, Elisabeth Jay. 2012. "Constructing 'the Same Rights with the Same Names': The Impact of Spanish Norm Diffusion on Marriage Equality in Argentina." *Latin American Politics and Society* 54(4): 29–59.

2009a. *The Social Situation concerning Homophobia and Discrimination on Grounds of Sexual Orientation in Poland.* Available at http://fra.europa.eu/sites/default/files/fra_uploads/387-FRA-hdgso-part2-NR_PL.pdf.

2009b. *The Social Situation concerning Homophobia and Discrimination on Grounds of Sexual Orientation in Slovenia.* Available at http://fra.europa.eu/sites/default/files/fra_uploads/392-FRA-hdgso-part2-NR_SI.pdf.

FRA (Fundamental Rights Agency). 2009c. *The Social Situation concerning Homophobia and Discrimination on Grounds of Sexual Orientation in Czech Republic.*

Galkin, Matthew. 2007. *I Am an Animal: The Story of Ingrid Newkirk and PETA.* Stick Figure Productions. Documentary.

Garretson, Jeremiah J. 2015. "Exposure to the Lives of Lesbians and Gays and the Origin of Young People's Greater Support for Gay Rights." *International Journal of Public Opinion Research* 27(2): 277–88.

Gera, Vanessa. 2014. "Robert Biedron Becomes Poland's First Openly Gay Mayor." *Huffington Post.* www.huffingtonpost.com/2014/12/01/robert-biedron-poland-gay-mayor-_n_6248648.html.

Gerhards, Jürgen. 2010. "Non-Discrimination towards Homosexuality: The European Union's Policy and Citizens' Attitudes towards Homosexuality in 27 European Countries." *International Sociology* 25(1): 5–28.

Gessen, Masha. 2015. "In Europe, Pride Is a Key Political Barometer. Budapest's Was Safe, at Times Even Joyful." *Slate.* www.slate.com/blogs/outward/2015/07/13/budapest_pride_2015_did_kennedy_s_gay_marriage_decision_keep_hungarian_marchers.html?wpsrc=sh_all_dt_tw_ru.

Gillion, Daniel Q. 2013. *The Political Power of Protest: Minority Activism and Shifts in Public Policy*. New York: Cambridge University Press.

Givan, Rebecca Kolins, Kenneth M. Roberts, and Sarah A. Soule. 2010. *The Diffusion of Social Movements: Actors, Mechanisms, and Political Effects*. New York: Cambridge University Press.

Gmünder, Bruno, ed. 2003. *Spartacus: International Gay Guide 2002/2003*. Berlin: Bruno Gmünder Verlag GmbH.

Goodwin, Jeff, and James M. Jasper, eds. 2009. *The Social Movements Reader: Cases and Concepts*. 2nd edn. Malden, MA: John Wiley & Sons.

Götsch, Antonia. 2006. "Wenn Abartige Demonstrieren, Brauchen sie den Knüppel." *Spiegel Online*. www.spiegel.de/politik/ausland/0,1518,420206,00.html.

Graff, Agnieszka. 2010. "Looking at Pictures of Gay Men: Political Uses of Homophobia in Contemporary Poland." *Public Culture* 22(3): 583–603.

Graham, Erin R., Charles R. Shipan, and Craig Volden. 2013. "The Diffusion of Policy Diffusion Research in Political Science." *British Journal of Political Science* 43(3): 673–701.

Greenhill, Brian. 2015. *Transmitting Rights: International Organizations and the Diffusion of Human Rights Practices*. New York: Oxford University Press.

2010. "The Company You Keep: International Socialization and the Diffusion of Human Rights Norms." *International Studies Quarterly* 54(1): 127–45.

Greif, Tatjana. 2005. "The Social Status of Lesbian Women in Slovenia in the 1990s." In *Sexuality and Gender in Postcommunist Eastern Europe and Russia*, ed. Aleksandar Štulhofer. New York: The Haworth Press, 149–69.

Griffiths, Craig. 2015. "Gay Politics in 1970s West Germany." PhD Dissertation. Queen Mary, University of London.

Grodzka, Anna. 2013. "As the World's Only Transgender MP, I Want to Ensure Our Voices Are Heard." *Guardian*. www.guardian.co.uk/commentisfree/2013/may/17/transgender-mp-voices-heard.

Gruszczyńska, Anna. 2007. "Living 'La Vida' Internet: Some Notes on the Cyberization of Polish LGBT Community." In *Beyond the Pink Curtain*, eds. Roman Kuhar and Judit Takács. Ljubljana: Peace Institute, 95–115.

Grzymała-Busse, Anna. 2014. "Historical Roots of Religious Influence on Postcommunist Democratic Politics." In *Historical Legacies of Communism in Russia and Eastern Europe*, eds. Mark Beissinger and Stephen Kotkin. New York: Cambridge University Press, 179–201.

Guilbert, Kieran. 2015. "Surgery and Sterilization Scrapped in Malta's Benchmark LGBTI Law." *New York Times*. www.nytimes.com/reuters/2015/04/01/world/europe/01reuters-gay-rights-malta.html.

Gurowitz, Amy. 2006. "The Diffusion of International Norms: Why Identity Matters." *International Politics* 43(3): 305–41.

Gwede, Wanga. 2016. "Mutharika Wants Gay Rights Protected, Says Viola: Law Experts Question Legality of Moratorium." *Malawi Nyasa Times*. www.nyasatimes.com/2016/01/07/mutharika-wants-gay-rights-protected-says-viola-law-experts-question-legality-of-moratorium.

Haas, Ernst B. 1991. *When Knowledge Is Power: Three Models of Change in International Organizations*. Berkeley: University of California Press.

Hadler, Markus. 2012. "The Influence of World Societal Forces on Social Tolerance: A Time Comparative Study of Prejudices in 32 Countries." *The Sociological Quarterly* 53(2): 211–37.

Hafner-Burton, Emilie M. 2013. *Making Human Rights a Reality*. Princeton University Press.

Hager, Mark A., Sarah Wilson, Thomas H. Pollak, and Patrick Michael Rooney. 2003. "Response Rates for Mail Surveys of Nonprofit Organizations: A Review and Empirical Test." *Nonprofit and Voluntary Sector Quarterly* 32(2): 252–67.

Haines, Herbert H. 1984. "Black Radicalization and the Funding of Civil Rights: 1957–1970." *Social Problems* 32(1): 31–43.

Hakim, Danny, and Douglas Dalby. 2015. "Ireland Votes to Approve Gay Marriage, Putting Country in Vanguard." *New York Times*. www.nytimes.com/2015/05/24/world/europe/ireland-gay-marriage-referendum.html.

Hancock, Ange-Marie. 2007. "Intersectionality as a Normative and Empirical Paradigm." *Politics & Gender* 3(2): 248–54.

Harwood, Mark. 2015. "Adopting Same-Sex Unions in Catholic Malta: Pointing the Finger at 'Europe.'" *South European Society and Politics* 20(1): 113–31.

Hayes, Jarrod. 2000. *Queer Nations: Marginal Sexualities in the Maghreb*. Chicago, Ill: University of Chicago Press.

Hekma, Gert. 2015. "Sodomy, Effeminacy, Identity: Mobilizations for Same-Sex Loves and Practices before the Second World War." In *The Ashgate Research Companion to Lesbian and Gay Activism*, eds. David Paternotte and Manon Tremblay. Farnham: Ashgate Publishing, 15–29.

Hekma, Gert, and Jan Willem Duyvendak. 2011. "Gay Men and Lesbians in the Netherlands." In *The Lesbian and Gay Movement and the State*, eds. Manon Tremblay, David Paternotte, and Carol Johnson. Farnham: Ashgate Publishing Co., 103–18.

Helm, Toby. 2010. "Conservatives Ignored Secret Report on Extremist Polish Allies." *Guardian*. www.guardian.co.uk/politics/2010/apr/11/conservatives-report-extremist-polish-allies.

Herek, Gregory. 1987. "Religious Orientation and Prejudice: A Comparison of Racial and Sexual Attitudes." *Personality and Social Psychology Bulletin* 13(1): 34–44.

 2004. "Beyond 'Homophobia': Thinking about Sexual Prejudice and Stigma in the Twenty-First Century." *Sexuality Research and Social Policy* 1(2): 6–24.

Heston, Alan, Robert Summers, and Bettina Aten. 2011. "Penn World Table Version 7.0, Center for International Comparisons of Production, Income and Prices at the University of Pennsylvania." www.rug.nl/research/ggdc/data/pwt/pwt-7.0?lang=en.

Hilgartner, Stephen, and Charles L. Bosk. 1988. "The Rise and Fall of Social Problems: A Public Arenas Model." *American Journal of Sociology* 94(1): 53–78.

Hillhouse, Raelynn J. 1990. "Out of the Closet behind the Wall: Sexual Politics and Social Change in the GDR." *Slavic Review* 49(4): 585–96.

Holzhacker, Ronald. 2012. "National and Transnational Strategies of LGBT Civil Society Organizations in Different Political Environments." *Comparative European Politics* 10(1): 23–47.

Hooghe, Marc, and Cecil Meeusen. 2013. "Is Same-Sex Marriage Legislation Related to Attitudes Toward Homosexuality?" *Sexuality Research and Social Policy* 10(4): 258–68.

hooks, bell. 2001. *All about Love: New Visions*. New York: Harper Collins.

Htun, Mala, and S. Laurel Weldon. 2012. "The Civic Origins of Progressive Policy Change: Combating Violence against Women in Global Perspective, 1975–2005." *American Political Science Review* 106(3): 548–69.

Huber, Evelyne, and John D. Stephens. 2001. *Development and Crisis of the Welfare State*. University of Chicago Press.

Imig, Doug, and Sidney Tarrow. 2001. *Contentious Europeans*. Lanham, MD: Rowman & Littlefield Publishers, Inc.

Ingebritsen, Christine. 2002. "Norm Entrepreneurs Scandinavia's Role in World Politics." *Cooperation and Conflict* 37(1): 11–23.

Inglehart, Ronald. 1997. *Modernization and Postmodernization*. Princeton University Press.

Inglehart, Ronald, and Pippa Norris. 2003. *Rising Tide*. Cambridge University Press.

Ippolito, Nina. 2014. "20 Photos From Sochi's Biggest Gay Club – the One the Mayor Claims Doesn't Exist." *Mic*. http://mic.com/articles/80391/20-photos-from-sochi-s-biggest-gay-club-the-one-the-mayor-claims-doesn-t-exist.

Irvine, Jill, Sabine Lang, and Celeste Montoya. 2015. "Gendered Mobilization in an Expanding Europe." Presented at a conference workshop of the same name at the University of Washington, Seattle, WA, May 1, 2015.

Jackson, Julian. 2015. "The Homophile Movement." In *The Ashgate Research Companion to Lesbian and Gay Activism*, eds. David Paternotte and Manon Tremblay. Farnham: Ashgate Publishing, 31–45.

Johnson, Paul. 2012. *Homosexuality and the European Court of Human Rights*. New York: Routledge.

Jowitt, Kenneth. 1992. *New World Disorder: The Leninist Extinction*. Oakland: University of California Press.

Judt, Tony. 2006. *Postwar: A History of Europe Since 1945*. New York: Penguin Books.

KAI. 2000. "'Nie Lękajcie Się Europy!' – Przesłanie Przed Kongresem Kultury Chrześcijańskiej." *Katolicka Agencja Informacyjna*.

Kane, Melinda. 2003. "Social Movement Policy Success: Decriminalizing State Sodomy Laws, 1969–1998." *Mobilization: An International Journal* 8(3): 313–34.

Katzenstein, Mary Fainsod, Leila Mohsen Ibrahim, and Katherine D. Rubin. 2010. "The Dark Side of American Liberalism and Felony Disenfranchisement." *Perspectives on Politics* 8(4): 1035–54.

Katzenstein, Peter J. 1995. "Alternative Perspectives on National Security." *Items: Social Science Research Council* 49(4): 89–93.

1996. *The Culture of National Security*. New York: Columbia University Press.

1997. "United Germany in an Integrating Europe." In *Tamed Power: Germany in Europe*, ed. Peter J. Katzenstein. Ithaca, NY: Cornell University Press, 1–49.

2003. "Same War: Different Views: Germany, Japan, and Counterterrorism." *International Organization* 57(4): 731–60.

2005. *A World of Regions: Asia and Europe in the American Imperium.* Ithaca, NY: Cornell University Press.

Katzenstein, Peter J., and Timothy A. Byrnes. 2006. "Transnational Religion in an Expanding Europe." *Perspectives on Politics* 4(4): 679–94.

Kaufmann, Chaim D., and Robert A. Pape. 1999. "Explaining Costly International Moral Action: Britain's Sixty-Year Campaign against the Atlantic Slave Trade." *International Organization* 53(4): 631–68.

Kearney, Seamus. 2015. "Slovenia Becomes 11th EU Nation to Approve Gay Marriage." *Euronews*. www.euronews.com/2015/03/04/slovenia-becomes-11th-eu-nation-to-approve-gay-marriage/.

Keck, Margaret E., and Kathryn Sikkink. 1998. *Activists beyond Borders: Advocacy Networks in International Politics.* Ithaca, NY: Cornell University Press.

Kellogg, Michael. 2001. "Putting Old Wine into New Bottles: The East German Protestant Church's Desire to Reform State Socialism, 1989–90." *Journal of Church and State* 43(4): 747–72.

Kennedy, Jason. 2013. "75% Support Same-Sex Marriage: Poll." *Irish Times*. www.irishtimes.com/newspaper/breaking/2013/0128/breaking25.html.

Keuzenkamp, Saskia, and Julian Ross. 2010. *Steeds Gewoner, Nooit Gewoon: Acceptatie van Homoseksualiteit in Nederland.* The Hague: Sociaal en Cultureel Planbureau.

Khagram, Sanjeev, James Riker, and Kathryn Sikkink. 2002. *Restructuring World Politics: Transnational Social Movements, Networks, And Norms.* Minneapolis: University of Minnesota Press.

Khazan, Olga. 2013. "Why Is Russia So Homophobic?" *Atlantic*. www.theatlantic.com/international/archive/2013/06/why-is-russia-so-homophobic/276817/.

Klotz, Audie. 1995. *Norms in International Relations: The Struggle Against Apartheid.* Ithaca, NY: Cornell University Press.

KOF Method. 2013. "KOF Method 2013." http://globalization.kof.ethz.ch/media/filer_public/2013/03/25/method_2013.pdf.

Kollman, Kelly. 2007. "Same-Sex Unions: The Globalization of an Idea." *International Studies Quarterly* 51(2): 329–57.

2013. *The Same-Sex Unions Revolution in Western Democracies: International Norms and Domestic Policy Change.* Manchester University Press.

Kollman, Kelly, and Matthew Waites. 2009. "The Global Politics of Lesbian, Gay, Bisexual and Transgender Human Rights: An Introduction." *Contemporary Politics* 15(1): 1–37.

Kopstein, Jeffrey, and David A. Reilly. 2000. "Geographic Diffusion and the Transformation of the Postcommunist World." *World Politics* 53(1): 1–37.

Kriesi, Hanspeter. 2004. "Political Context and Opportunity." In *The Blackwell Companion to Social Movements*, eds. David A. Snow, Sarah A. Soule, and Hanspeter Kriesi. Oxford: Blackwell Publishing, 65–90.

Kristoffersson, Mattias, Bjoern van Roozendaal and Lilit Poghosyan. in press. "European Integration and LGBT Activism – Partners in Realizing Change?"

In *The EU Enlargement and Gay Politics*, eds. Koen Slootmaeckers, Heleen Touquet, and Peter Vermeersch. Basingstoke, UK: Palgrave Macmillan.

Krzeminski, I. 2008. *The Situation Concerning Homophobia and Discrimination on Grounds of Sexual Orientation in Poland*. European Fundamental Rights Agency.

Kubica, Grażyna. 2009. "A Rainbow Flag against the Krakow Dragon: Polish Responses to the Gay and Lesbian Movement." In *Postsocialist Europe: Anthropological Perspectives from Home*, eds. Laszlo Kürti and Peter Skalnik. New York: Berghahn Books, 119–49.

Kuhar, Roman. 2003. *Media Representations of Homosexuality: An Analysis of Print Media in Slovenia, 1970–2000*. Ljubljana: Mediawatch. http://pdc.ceu.hu/archive/00001509/.

2008. *The Situation Concerning Homophobia and Discrimination on Grounds of Sexual Orientation in Slovenia*. European Fundamental Rights Agency.

2011. "Use of the Europeanization Frame in Same Sex Partnership Issues across Europe." In *The Europeanization of Gender Equality Policies: A Discursive Sociological Approach*, eds. Emanuela Lombardo and Maxime Forest. Basingstoke, UK: Palgrave Macmillan, 168–91.

Kulpa, Robert, and Joanna Mizielińska. 2011. *De-Centring Western Sexualities: Central and Eastern European Perspectives*. Surrey, UK: Ashgate Publishing.

LaMar, Lisa, and Mary Kite. 1998. "Sex Differences in Attitudes toward Gay Men and Lesbians: A Multidimensional Perspective." *The Journal of Sex Research* 35(2): 189–96.

Landolt, Laura. 2004. "(Mis)constructing the Third World? Constructivist Analysis of Norm Diffusion." *Third World Quarterly* 25(3): 579–91.

Langlois, Anthony, and Cai Wilkinson. 2014. "Not Such an International Human Rights Norm? Local Resistance to LGBT Rights." *Journal of Human Rights* 13(3): 249–55.

Lang, Sabine. 2013. *NGOs, Civil Society, and the Public Sphere*. Cambridge University Press.

Lax, Jeffrey R., and Justin H. Phillips. 2009. "Gay Rights in the States: Public Opinion and Policy Responsiveness." *American Political Science Review* 103(3): 367–86.

Legro, Jeffrey W. 1997. "Which Norms Matter? Revisiting the 'Failure' of Internationalism." *International Organization* 51(1): 31–63.

Lieberman, Evan S. 2005. "Nested Analysis as a Mixed-Method Strategy for Comparative Research." *American Political Science Review* 99(3): 435–52.

Lind, Amy. 2014. "'Out' in International Relations: Why Queer Visibility Matters." *International Studies Review* 16(4): 601–4.

Linz, Juan J., and Alfred Stepan. 2011. *Problems of Democratic Transition and Consolidation: Southern Europe, South America, and Post-Communist Europe*. Baltimore: Johns Hopkins University Press.

Lipsky, Michael. 1968. "Protest as a Political Resource." *The American Political Science Review* 62(4): 1144–58.

Lloyd, Paulette, Beth Simmons, and Brandon Stewart. 2012. "The Global Diffusion of Law: Transnational Crime and the Case of Human Trafficking."

Paper presented at the University of California, Irvine, March 1, 2012. http://archives.cerium.ca/IMG/pdf/Lloyd_Simmons_Stewart_2012.pdf.

Lohmann, Susanne. 1993. "A Signaling Model of Informative and Manipulative Political Action." *American Political Science Review* 87(2): 319–33.

Mackey, Robert. 2014. "Latvian Minister Declares He's Gay, Exposing Fault Lines of New Culture War in Europe." *New York Times*. www.nytimes.com/2014/11/08/world/europe/after-latvian-minister-declares-hes-gay-new-front-opens-in-europes-cultural-war.html.

Makers.com. 2014. "Gloria Steinem: Feminist Activist," Youtube video, 4:12, posted on March 3, 2014, www.youtube.com/watch?v=8zl5qeFoaqs&feature= youtube_gdata_player.

Manalansan, Martin. 1995. "In the Shadows of Stonewall." *GLQ: A Journal of Lesbian and Gay Studies* 2(4): 425–38.

Maneo-Tolerancja. 2005. "Press Release; Grundrechte gelten auch für Lesben und Schwule!" www.maneo.de/infopool/flyer-und-infopakete.html?eID=dam_frontend_push&docID=288.

——— 2006. "Press Release; Europäische Solidarität gegen Homophobie in Polen." Berlin, Germany. www.maneo.de/infopool/flyer-und-infopakete.html?eID=dam_frontend_push&docID=288.

Maresca, Thomas. 2013. "Vietnam: Flawed on Human Rights, but a Leader in Gay Rights." *Atlantic*. www.theatlantic.com/international/archive/2013/04/vietnam-flawed-on-human-rights-but-a-leader-in-gay-rights/275413/.

Marks, Gary, and Doug McAdam. 1996. "Social Movements and the Changing Structure of Political Opportunity in the European Union." *West European Politics* 19(2): 249–78.

Marshall, Monty, Keith Jaggers, and Ted Robert Gurr. 2010. "POLITY IV PROJECT Dataset Users' Manual: Political Regime Characteristics and Transitions, 1800–2010." www.systemicpeace.org/inscr/p4manualv2012.pdf.

Martin, Lisa L., and Beth Simmons. 1998. "Theories and Empirical Studies of International Institutions." *International Organization* 52(4): 729–58.

Mastenbroek, Ellen. 2003. "Surviving the Deadline: The Transposition of EU Directives in the Netherlands." *European Union Politics* 4(4): 371–95.

Mazziotta, Agostino, Amélie Mummendey, and Stephen C. Wright. 2011. "Vicarious Intergroup Contact Effects Applying Social-Cognitive Theory to Intergroup Contact Research." *Group Processes & Intergroup Relations* 14(2): 255–74.

McAdam, Doug. 1988. *Freedom Summer*. Oxford University Press.

——— 1999. *Political Process and the Development of Black Insurgency, 1930–1970*. 2nd edn. University of Chicago Press.

——— 2013. "Cognitive Liberation." In *The Wiley-Blackwell Encyclopedia of Social and Political Movements*, eds. David A. Snow, Donatella della Porta, Bert Klandermans, and Doug McAdam. Oxford: Blackwell Publishing. http://onlinelibrary.wiley.com/doi/10.1002/9780470674871.wbespm030/abstract.

McAdam, Doug, and Yang Su. 2002. "The War at Home: Antiwar Protests and Congressional Voting 1965–1973." *American Sociological Review* 67(5): 696–721.

McAdam, Doug, Sidney Tarrow, and Charles Tilly. 2001. *Dynamics of Contention*. Cambridge University Press.

McCajor Hall, Timothy. 2009. "Stories from the Second World: Narratives of Sexual Identity in the Czech Republic across Three Generations of Men Who Have Sex with Men." In *The Story of Sexual Identity: Narrative Perspectives on the Gay and Lesbian Life Course*, eds. Phillip L. Hammack and Bertram J. Cohler. New York: Oxford University Press, 51–79.

McCarthy, John, and Mayer N. Zald. 1977. *The Dynamics of Social Movements.* Cambridge, MA: Winthrop Publishers.

McConahay, John B., and Joseph C. Hough. 1976. "Symbolic Racism." *Journal of Social Issues* 32(2): 23–45.

McDonald, James. 2015. "Ugandan Presidential Candidate Comes Out Against Homophobia." *Advocate.* www.advocate.com/world/2015/07/22/ugandan-presidential-candidate-comes-out-against-homophobia.

McGarry, Aidan. in press. "Parades, Pride and Prejudice: Roma and LGBTI Communities and Public Space in Post-Socialist Europe." *Communist and Post Communist Studies.*

Mepschen, Paul, Jan Willem Duyvendak, and Evelien H. Tonkens. 2010. "Sexual Politics, Orientalism and Multicultural Citizenship in the Netherlands." *Sociology* 44(5): 962–79.

Meyer, Christoph O. 2009. "International Terrorism as a Force of Homogenization? A Constructivist Approach to Understanding Cross-National Threat Perceptions and Responses." *Cambridge Review of International Affairs* 22(4): 647–66.

Meyer, David S. 2003. "How Social Movements Matter." *Contexts* 2(4): 30–5.

Meyer, John W., John Boli, George M. Thomas, and Francisco O. Ramirez. 1997. "World Society and the Nation-State." *American Journal of Sociology* 103(1): 144–81.

Michels, Mindy. 2012. "Albania: The Gay Movement You Never Imagined." *Huffington Post.* www.huffingtonpost.com/american-anthropological-association/albania-gay-rights_b_1497865.html.

Miller, Wentworth. 2013. "Re: St. Petersburg International Film Festival/'Guest of Honor' Invitation." www.glaad.org/blog/wentworth-miller-rejects-russian-film-festival-invitation-gay-man-i-must-decline.

Minkoff, Debra C. 1994. "From Service Provision to Institutional Advocacy: The Shifting Legitimacy of Organizational Forms." *Social Forces* 72(4): 943–69.

Mizielińska, Joanna. 2010. "Poland." In *The Greenwood Encyclopedia of LGBT Issues Worldwide*, ed. Chuck Stewart. Westport, CT: ABC-CLIO/Greenwood, 321–37.

Mole, Richard. 2011. "Nationality and Sexuality: Homophobic Discourse and the 'national Threat' in Contemporary Latvia." *Nations and Nationalism* 17(3): 540–60.

Montoya, Celeste. 2008. "The European Union, Capacity Building, and Transnational Networks: Combating Violence Against Women Through the Daphne Program." *International Organization* 62(2): 359–72.

——— 2013. *From Global to Grassroots: The European Union, Transnational Advocacy, and Combating Violence against Women.* Oxford University Press.

Morgan, Joe. 2014. "Russia's Biggest Gay Rights Protest Held since Anti-Gay Laws Were Enforced." *Gay Star News.* www.gaystarnews.com/article/russias-biggest-gay-rights-protest-anti-gay-laws-were-enforced020514.

Mos, Martijn. 2014. "Of Gay Rights and Christmas Ornaments: The Political History of Sexual Orientation Non-Discrimination in the Treaty of Amsterdam." *Journal of Common Market Studies* 52(3): 632–49.

Moscow Times. 2013. "87% of Russians Oppose Gay Parades." www .themoscowtimes.com/news/article/over-80-of-russians-oppose-same-sex-marriage-and-gay-parades/476773.html?.

Murai, Shusuke. 2015. "Tokyo's Shibuya and Setagaya Wards Issue First Same-Sex Partnership Papers." *Japan Times.* www.japantimes.co.jp/news/2015/11/05/national/social-issues/shibuya-set-issue-first-certificates-recognizing-sex-couples/#.VqZS_1KRLYd.

Nadelmann, Ethan A. 1990. "Global Prohibition Regimes: The Evolution of Norms in International Society." *International Organization* 44(4): 479–526.

Negro, Giacomo, Fabrizio Perretti, and Glenn R. Carroll. 2013. "Challenger Groups, Commercial Organizations, and Policy Enactment: Local Lesbian/Gay Rights Ordinances in the United States from 1972 to 2008." *American Journal of Sociology* 119(3): 790–832.

Newton, Huey. 1970. "A Letter from Huey Newton to the Revolutionary Brothers and Sisters about the Women's Liberation and Gay Liberation Movements." *The Black Panther*, August 21, 1970.

Nielsen, Nikolaj. 2014. "Malta Legalises Same-Sex Unions and Adoption." *EUobserver.com.* http://euobserver.com/social/123858.

NOP. 2011. "Historia NOP." www.nop.org.pl/historia-nop/.

Novak, Marja. 2015. "Slovenia Rejects Same-Sex Marriage Again." *Huffington Post.* www.huffingtonpost.com/entry/slovenia-gay-marriage_us_5678211fe4bo6fa6887de364.

Nussbaum, Martha Craven. 2010. *From Disgust to Humanity: Sexual Orientation and Constitutional Law.* New York: Oxford University Press US.

"ODWAGA." 2012. *ODWAGA.* www.odwaga.oaza.org.pl/homepage.html.

O'Dwyer, Conor. 2010. "From Conditionality to Persuasion? Europeanization and the Rights of Sexual Minorities in Post-Accession Poland." *Journal of European Integration* 32(3): 229.

2012. "Does the EU Help or Hinder Gay-Rights Movements in Post-Communist Europe? The Case of Poland." *East European Politics* 28(4): 332–52.

O'Dwyer, Conor, and Katrina Schwartz. 2010. "Minority Rights After EU Enlargement: A Comparison of Antigay Politics in Poland and Latvia." *Comparative European Politics* 8(2): 220–43.

Okeowo, Alexis. 2012. "Gay and Proud in Uganda." *New Yorker.* www .newyorker.com/online/blogs/newsdesk/2012/08/gay-and-proud-in-uganda.html#slide_ss_0=1.

Olzak, Susan. 2011. "Does Globalization Breed Ethnic Discontent?" *Journal of Conflict Resolution* 55(1): 3–32.

Owczarzak, Jill. 2009. "Defining Democracy and the Terms of Engagement with the Postsocialist State: Insights from HIV/AIDS." *East European Politics and Societies* 23(3): 421–45.

Pasek, Beata. 2003. "Polish Campaign Sparks Debate Over Gays." *Star Tribune, Associated Press (AP).* http://niechnaszobacza.queers.pl/strony/prasa/27.05.03_en_a.htm.

Paternotte, David. 2011. *Revendiquer le "mariage gay": Belgique, France, Espagne*. Brussels: Université de Bruxelles.

——— 2012. "Back into the Future: ILGA-Europe before 1996." *Destination Equality: Magazine of ILGA-Europe* 11(1): 5–8.

——— 2015. "Global Times, Global Debates? Same-Sex Marriage Worldwide." *Social Forces* (first view).

——— in press. "The NGOization of LGBT Activism: ILGA-Europe and the Treaty of Amsterdam." *Social Movement Studies* Online First(0): 1–15.

Paternotte, David, and Kelly Kollman. 2013. "Regulating Intimate Relationships in the European Polity: Same-sex Unions and Policy Convergence." *Social politics* 20(4): 510–33.

Pattillo, Mary E., David F. Weiman, and Bruce Western. 2004. *Imprisoning America: The Social Effects of Mass Incarceration*. New York: Russell Sage Foundation.

Petrova, Tsveta. 2012. "How Poland Promotes Democracy." *Journal of Democracy* 23(2): 133–47.

Pettigrew, Thomas F. 1998. "Intergroup Contact Theory." *Annual Review of Psychology* 49(1): 65–85.

Pettigrew, Thomas F., and Linda R. Tropp. 2006. "A Meta-Analytic Test of Intergroup Contact Theory." *Journal of Personality and Social Psychology* 90(5): 751–83.

Philpott, Daniel. 2007. "Explaining the Political Ambivalence of Religion." *The American Political Science Review* 101(3): 505–25.

Picq, Manuela Lavinas, and Markus Thiel, eds. 2015. *Sexualities in World Politics: How LGBTQ Claims Shape International Relations*. New York: Routledge.

Pinderi, Kristi. 2013. "Interview Transcript: 'Unbiased Voices of Reason in Albania Have No Outlet', Says US Ambassador." *Historia Ime*. http://historia-ime.com/en/english/135-%E2%80%9Cunbiased-voices-of-reason-in-albania-have-no-outlet%E2%80%9D,-says-us-ambassador.html.

Piven, Frances Fox, and Richard A Cloward. 1977. *Poor People's Movements: Why They Succeed, How They Fail*. 1st ed. New York: Pantheon Books.

Polletta, Francesca. 1999. "'Free Spaces' in Collective Action." *Theory and Society* 28(1): 1–38.

Polskie Radio. 2011. "Germans to Protest Nationalist Warsaw Independence Day Demo." *Polskie Radio dla Zagranicy*. www.thenews.pl/1/10/Artykul/57584,Germans-to-protest-nationalist-Warsaw-Independence-Day-demo.

Price, Richard. 2003. "Transnational Civil Society and Advocacy in World Politics." *World Politics* 55(4): 579–606.

Princen, Sebastiaan, and Bart Kerremans. 2008. "Opportunity Structures in the EU Multi-Level System." *West European Politics* 31(6): 1129–46.

Puar, Jasbir K. 2007. *Terrorist Assemblages: Homonationalism in Queer Times*. Durham: Duke University Press.

Public Broadcasting of Latvia. 2014. "Former Unity Board Member Provokes Storm with Twitter Rant." www.lsm.lv/en/article/politics/unity-councillor-quits-after-shocking-twitter-rant.a108522/.

Putnam, Robert D. 1988. "Diplomacy and Domestic Politics: The Logic of Two-Level Games." *International Organization* 42(3): 427–60.

Radaelli, Claudio M. 2004. "Europeanisation: Solution or Problem?" *European Integration online Papers (EIoP)* 8(16): 1–26.

Radeljić, Branislav. 2011. "Blessing the Collapse of Yugoslavia: The Vatican's Role in EC Policy-Making." *Serbian Studies Research* 2(1): 177–204.

Radio Poland. 2014. "Equality Parade Demands Civil Partnerships." www .thenews.pl/1/9/Artykul/173878,Equality-Parade-demands-civil-partnerships.

Rahman, Momin. 2014. "Sexual Diversity." In *Routledge International Handbook of Diversity Studies*, ed. Steven Vertovec. New York: Routledge, 75–82.

Ramet, Sabrina. 1982. "Catholicism and Politics in Socialist Yugoslavia." *Religion in Communist Lands* 10(3): 256–74.

    1998. *Nihil Obstat: Religion, Politics, and Social Change in East-Central Europe and Russia*. Durham: Duke University Press Books.

    2006. "Thy Will Be Done: The Catholic Church and Politics in Poland since 1989." In *Religion in an Expanding Europe*, eds. Peter J. Katzenstein and Timothy A. Byrnes. Cambridge University Press, 117–47.

Ratzinger, Joseph. 1986. "Letter to the Bishops of the Catholic Church on the Pastoral Care of Homosexual Persons." www.vatican.va/roman_ curia/congregations/cfaith/documents/rc_con_cfaith_doc_19861001_ homosexual-persons_en.html.

Raudenbush, Stephen W., and Anthony Bryk. 2002. *Hierarchical Linear Models: Applications and Data Analysis Methods*. Thousand Oaks, CA: SAGE.

Redakcja Fronda.pl. 2010. "Homoparady W Europie." www.fronda.pl/a/ homoparady-w-europie,7161.html.

Reynolds, Andrew. 2013. "Representation and Rights: The Impact of LGBT Legislators in Comparative Perspective." *American Political Science Review* 107(2): 259–74.

Riabov, Oleg, and Tatiana Riabova. 2014. "The Decline of Gayropa? – How Russia Intends to Save the World." *Eurozine*. www.eurozine.com/articles/ 2014-02-05-riabova-en.html.

Rimmerman, Craig A. 2014. *The Lesbian and Gay Movements: Assimilation or Liberation?* 2nd edn. Boulder, CO: Westview Press.

Ring, Trudy. 2014. "World Bank Delays Uganda Loan Due to Antigay Law." *Advocate*. www.advocate.com/world/2014/02/27/world-bank-delays- uganda-loan-due-antigay-law.

Risse-Kappen, Thomas, ed. 1995. *Bringing Transnational Relations Back In: Non-State Actors, Domestic Structures and International Institutions*. Cambridge: Cambridge University Press.

Risse, Thomas. 2000. "'Let's Argue!': Communicative Action in World Politics." *International Organization* 54(1): 1–39.

Risse, Thomas., ed. 2014. *European Public Spheres*. New York: Cambridge University Press.

Risse, Thomas, Stephen Ropp, and Kathryn Sikkink, eds. 2013. *The Persistent Power of Human Rights: From Commitment to Compliance*. New York: Cambridge: Cambridge University Press.

Roggeband, Conny. 2010. "Transnational Networks and Institutions." In *The Diffusion of Social Movements*, eds. Rebecca Givan, Kenneth M. Roberts, and Sarah A. Soule. Cambridge University Press, 19–33.

Rose, Deondra Eunique. 2012. "The Development of US Higher Education Policy and Its Impact on the Gender Dynamics of American Citizenship." PhD Dissertation. Cornell University.

Ross, Alex. 2015. "Berlin Story: How the Germans Invented Gay Rights–More than a Century Ago." *New Yorker*: 73–7.

Rousseau, David. 2006. *Identifying Threats and Threatening Identities: The Social Construction of Realism and Liberalism*. Palo Alto: Stanford University Press.

Rupp, Leila J. 2011. "The Persistence of Transnational Organizing: The Case of the Homophile Movement." *The American Historical Review* 116(4): 1014–39.

Rydström, Jens. 2008. "Legalizing Love in a Cold Climate: The History, Consequences and Recent Developments of Registered Partnership in Scandinavia." *Sexualities* 11(1–2): 193–226.

Sandro, Scabello. 2007. "Visite Dal Veterinario E Persecuzioni Essere Gay Al Tempo Dei Kaczyński." *Corriere della Sera*: 13.

Saner, Emine. 2013. "Gay Rights around the World: The Best and Worst Countries for Equality." *Guardian*. www.theguardian.com/world/2013/jul/30/gay-rights-world-best-worst-countries.

Sansalone, Dom. 2013. "Poll: Almost a Quarter of Russians Want 'Compulsory Treatment' for Gays and 5% Think Gay People Should Be 'Liquidated.'" *Pink News*. www.pinknews.co.uk/2013/03/12/poll-almost-a-quarter-of-russians-want-compulsory-treatment-for-gays-and-5-think-gay-people-should-be-liquidated/.

Scally, Derek. 2015. "German Politicians Demand Moves to Follow Irish Referendum." *Irish Times*. www.irishtimes.com/news/world/europe/german-politicians-demand-moves-to-follow-irish-referendum-1.2226873.

Schimmelfennig, Frank. 2007. "European Regional Organizations, Political Conditionality, and Democratic Transformation in Eastern Europe." *East European Politics and Societies* 21(1): 126–41.

Schmitt, Carl. 1996. *The Concept of the Political*. University of Chicago Press.

Schulenberg, Shawn. 2013. "LGBT Rights in Chile: On the Verge of a Gay-Rights Revolution?" Presented at the American Political Science Association Annual Meeting, Chicago, Ill, August 30, 2013.

Scott, James C. 1990. *Domination and the Arts of Resistance: Hidden Transcripts*. New Haven: Yale University Press.

Sears, David. 1988. "Symbolic Racism." In *Eliminating Racism: Profiles in Controversy*, eds. Phyllis Katz and Dalmas Taylor. New York: Plenum Press, 53–84.

Seckinelgin, Hakan. 2009. "Global Activism and Sexualities in the Time of HIV/AIDS." *Contemporary Politics* 15(1): 103–18.

Seidman, Steven. 2004. *Contested Knowledge: Social Theory Today*. 3rd edn. Malden, MA: Blackwell Publishing.

Seybert, Lucia. 2012. "The Trouble with 'Returning to Europe': New European Union Members' Reluctant Embrace of Nuclear Safety and Minority Rights." PhD Dissertation. Cornell University.

Shevtsova, Lilia. 2007. "Post-Communist Russia: A Historic Opportunity Missed." *International Affairs* 83(5): 891–912.

Sikkink, Kathryn. 2005. "Patterns of Dynamic Multilevel Governance and the Insider–outsider Coalitions." In *Transnational Protest and Global Activism*, eds. Donatella della Porta and Sidney Tarrow. New York: Rowman & Littlefield, 151–74.

Sil, Rudra, and Peter J. Katzenstein. 2010. *Beyond Paradigms: Analytic Eclecticism in the Study of World Politics*. Basingstoke, UK: Palgrave Macmillan.

Simmons, Beth A. 2009. *Mobilizing for Human Rights: International Law in Domestic Politics*. New York: Cambridge University Press.

Skrentny, John David. 2002. *The Minority Rights Revolution*. Cambridge, MA: Harvard University Press.

Slootmaeckers, Koen, and Heleen Touquet. in press. "The Co-evolution of EU's Eastern Enlargement and LGBT politics: An Ever Gayer Union?" In *The EU Enlargement and Gay Politics*, eds. Koen Slootmaeckers, Heleen Touquet, and Peter Vermeersch. Basingstoke, UK: Palgrave Macmillan.

Smith, Anna Marie. 1994. *New Right Discourse on Race and Sexuality: Britain, 1968–1990*. Cambridge University Press.

Smith, David. 2013. "Ugandan MPs Rush through Draconian Laws against Homosexuality." *Guardian*. www.theguardian.com/world/2013/dec/20/uganda-mps-laws-homosexuality.

Smith, Tom W. 2011. *Cross-National Differences in Attitudes towards Homosexuality*. The Williams Institute. http://escholarship.org/uc/item/81m7x7kb#page-5.

Snijders, Tom A. B., and Roel J. Bosker. 1999. *Multilevel Analysis*. London: Sage Publications.

Snow, David A., and Robert D. Benford. 1992. *Master Frames and Cycles of Protest*. New Haven: Yale University Press.

Soss, Joe, Richard Fording, and Sanford Schram. 2011. *Disciplining the Poor: Neoliberal Paternalism and the Persistent Power of Race*. University of Chicago Press.

Soule, Sarah A. 1997. "The Student Divestment Movement in the United States and Tactical Diffusion: The Shantytown Protest." *Social Forces* 75(3):855–82.

2004a. "Diffusion Processes within and across Movements." In *The Blackwell Companion to Social Movements*, eds. David A. Snow, Hanspeter Kriesi, and Sarah A. Soule. Oxford: Wiley-Blackwell, 294–311.

2004b. "Going to the Chapel? Same-Sex Marriage Bans in the United States, 1973–2000." *Social Problems* 51(4): 453–77.

Soule, Sarah A., and Jennifer Earl. 2001. "The Enactment of State-Level Hate Crime Law in the United States: Intrastate and Interstate Factors." *Sociological Perspectives* 44(3): 281–305.

Soule, Sarah A., and Brayden G. King. 2006. "The Stages of the Policy Process and the Equal Rights Amendment, 1972–1982." *American Journal of Sociology* 111(6): 1871–1909.

Soysal, Yasemin Nuhoglu. 1994. *Limits of Citizenship: Migrants and Postnational Membership in Europe*. University of Chicago Press.

Stathi, Sofia, and Richard J. Crisp. 2008. "Imagining Intergroup Contact Promotes Projection to Outgroups." *Journal of Experimental Social Psychology* 44(4): 943–57.

Stepan, Alfred. 2000. "Religion, Democracy, and the Twin Tolerations." *Journal of Democracy* 11(4): 37–57.

Stockdill, Brett C. 2003. *Activism against AIDS: At the Intersection of Sexuality, Race, Gender, and Class*. Boulder, CO: Lynne Rienner Pub.

Stoeckl, Kristina. 2014. *The Russian Orthodox Church and Human Rights*. London; New York: Routledge.

Strang, David. 1990. "From Dependency to Sovereignty: An Event History Analysis of Decolonization 1870–1987." *American Sociological Review* 55(6): 846.

Strang, David, and John W. Meyer. 1993. "Institutional Conditions for Diffusion." *Theory and Society* 22(4): 487–511.

Strehovec, Tadej. 2012. "Marriages and Cohabitations from Theological, Demographic and Social Perspective." *Pregledni znanstveni članek* 1(2): 195–203.

Strolovitch, Dara Z. 2007. *Affirmative Advocacy: Race, Class, and Gender in Interest Group Politics*. University of Chicago Press.

  2012. "Intersectionality in Time: Sexuality and the Shifting Boundaries of Intersectional Marginalization." *Politics & Gender* 8(3): 386–96.

Stychin, Carl Franklin. 1998. *A Nation by Rights: National Cultures, Sexual Identity Politics, and the Discourse of Rights*. Philadelphia: Temple University Press.

Swiebel, Joke. 2009. "Lesbian, Gay, Bisexual and Transgender Human Rights: The Search for an International Strategy." *Contemporary Politics* 15(1): 19–35.

Swimelar, Safia. in press. "The Struggle for Visibility and Equality: Bosnian LGBT Rights Developments." In *The EU Enlargement and Gay Politics*, eds. Koen Slootmaeckers, Heleen Touquet, and Peter Vermeersch. Basingstoke, UK: Palgrave MacMillan.

Symons, Jonathan, and Dennis Altman. 2015. "International Norm Polarization: Sexuality as a Subject of Human Rights Protection." *International Theory* 7(1): 61–95.

Takács, Judit, and Ivett Szalma. 2011. "Homophobia and Same-Sex Partnership Legislation in Europe." *Equality, Diversity and Inclusion: An International Journal* 30(5): 356–78.

Tarrow, Sidney. 2005a. "Rooted Cosmopolitans and Transnational Activism." http://government.arts.cornell.edu/assets/faculty/docs/tarrow/rooted_cosmopolitans.pdf.

  2005b. *The New Transnational Activism*. Cambridge University Press.

  2011. *Power in Movement: Social Movements and Contentious Politics*. Cambridge University Press.

Tarrow, Sidney, and Doug McAdam. 2005. "Scale Shift in Transnational Contention." In *Transnational Protest and Global Activism*, eds. Donatella della Porta and Sidney Tarrow. Lanham, MD: Rowman & Littlefield, 121–50.

Taylor, Adam. 2015. "A New Swedish Message to Russian Submarines: 'This Way If You Are Gay.'" *Washington Post*. www.washingtonpost.com/blogs/worldviews/wp/2015/05/12/swedens-new-message-to-russian-submarines-this-way-if-you-are-gay/.

Taylor, Verta. 1989. "Social Movement Continuity: The Women's Movement in Abeyance." *American Sociological Review* 54(5): 761–75.

Taylor, Verta, Leila J. Rupp, and Joshua Gamson. 2004. "Performing Protest: Drag Shows as Tactical Repertoire of the Gay and Lesbian Movement." In *Authority in Contention*, eds. Daniel Myers and Daniel Cress. Bingley, UK: Emerald Group Publishing Limited, 105–37. www.emeraldinsight.com/books.htm?chapterid=1758236&show=pdf.

Terkel, Amanda. 2015. "Marriage Equality In Germany 'Not A Goal' For Angela Merkel." *Huffington Post*. www.huffingtonpost.com/2015/05/27/angela-merkel-marriage-equality_n_7454090.html.

Thoreson, Ryan R. 2014. *Transnational LGBT Activism: Working for Sexual Rights Worldwide*. Minneapolis: University of Minnesota Press.

Tilly, Charles. 1978. *From Mobilization to Revolution*. Reading, MA: Addison-Wesley Pub. Co.

Tolbert, Pamela, and Lynne Zucker. 1983. "Institutional Sources of Change in the Formal Structure of Organizations: The Diffusion of Civil Service Reform, 1880–1935." *Administrative Science Quarterly* 28(1): 22–39.

Tolerantia Declaration. 2010. "Tolerantia Declaration." Maneo/Tolerantia Archive, Schwules Museum, Berlin, Germany.

Torstendahl, Rolf, ed. 1999. *State Policy and Gender System in the Two German States and Sweden 1945–1989*. Uppsala: Distribution, Dept. of History [Uppsala universitet].

Toshkov, Dimiter. 2008. "Embracing European Law: Compliance with EU Directives in Central and Eastern Europe." *European Union Politics* 9(3): 379–402.

Towns, Ann E. 2010. *Women and States: Norms and Hierarchies in International Society*. Cambridge University Press.

2012. "Norms and Social Hierarchies: Understanding International Policy Diffusion 'From Below.'" *International Organization* 66(2): 179–209.

Tremblay, Manon, David Paternotte, and Carol Johnson, eds. 2011. *The Lesbian and Gay Movement and the State*. Surrey, UK: Ashgate Publishing.

Trplan, Tomaz. 2005. "Slovenia." In *Racist Extremism in Central and Eastern Europe*, ed. Cas Mudde. New York: Routledge, 225–46.

Turner, Rhiannon N., Richard J. Crisp, and Emily Lambert. 2007. "Imagining Intergroup Contact Can Improve Intergroup Attitudes." *Group Processes & Intergroup Relations* 10(4): 427–41.

Vachudova, Milada Anna. 2005. *Europe Undivided: Democracy, Leverage, and Integration After Communism*. Oxford University Press.

van der Vleuten, Anna. 2014. "Transnational LGBTI Activism and the European Courts: Constructing the Idea of Europe." In *LGBT Activism and the Making of Europe: A Rainbow Europe?*, eds. Phillip M. Ayoub and David Paternotte. Basingstoke: Palgrave, 119–44.

Vogt, Andrea. 2015. "'We're next' Says Italy after Irish Gay Marriage Vote." *Telegraph*. www.telegraph.co.uk/news/worldnews/europe/italy/11627693/Were-next-says-Italy-after-Irish-gay-marriage-vote.html.

Voxerbrant, Diana. 2004. *Tolerancja! Who Would Have Thought Tolerance Could Be So Controversial*. Blackraw Productions. Documentary.

Waaldijk, Kees. 2000. "Civil Developments: Patterns of Reform in the Legal Position of Same-Sex Partners in Europe." *Canadian Journal of Family Law* 17(1): 62–88.

2009. "Legal Recognition of Homosexual Orientation in the Countries of the World." Presented at *The Global Arc of Justice Conference*, Los Angeles, CA, March 11, 2009.

Waaldijk, Kees, and M. T. Bonini-Baraldi. 2006. *Sexual Orientation Discrimination in the European Union: National Laws and the Employment Equality Directive*. T.M.C. The Hague: Asser Press. https://openaccess.leidenuniv.nl/handle/1887/16528.

Waever, Ole. 1993. "Societal Security: The Concept." In *Identity, Migration and the New Security Agenda in Europe*, eds. Ole Waever, Barry Buzan, Morten Kelstrup, and Pierre Lemaitre. New York: St. Martin's Press, 17–40.

Waites, Matthew. 2009. "Critique of 'Sexual Orientation' and 'Gender Identity' in Human Rights Discourse: Global Queer Politics beyond the Yogyakarta Principles." *Contemporary Politics* 15(1): 137–56.

Wald, Kenneth. 2013. "The State as a Religious Actor: New Thoughts on an Old Variable." Presented at the Religion, Identity, and Politics Conference, University of Michigan.

Warschauerpakt. 2007. "Warschauerpakt: Europa=Tolerancja." *Warschauerpakt: Europa=Tolerancja*. http://warschauerpakt2007.de/.

Way, Lucan and Levitsky, Steven. 2007. "Linkage, Leverage, and the Post-Communist Divide." *East European Politics and Societies* 21(1): 48–66.

Weber, Cynthia. 2015. "Why Is There No Queer International Theory?" *European Journal of International Relations* 21(1): 27–51.

Weeks, Jeffrey. 2000. *Making Sexual History*. Cambridge: Polity Press.

2007. *The World We Have Won: The Remaking of Erotic and Intimate Life*. London: Routledge.

2015. "Gay Liberation and Its Legacies." In *The Ashgate Research Companion to Lesbian and Gay Activism*, eds. David Paternotte and Manon Tremblay. Farnham: Ashgate Publishing, 45–58.

Weiss, Meredith L., and Michael J. Bosia. 2013. *Global Homophobia: States, Movements, and the Politics of Oppression*. Urbana-Champaign, IL: University of Illinois Press.

Wendt, Alexander. 1999. *Social Theory of International Politics*. New York: Cambridge University Press.

Whittier, Nancy. 2010. *Feminist Generations: The Persistence of the Radical Women's Movement*. Philadelphia: Temple University Press.

Wilkinson, Cai. 2014. "Putting 'Traditional Values' into Practice: The Rise and Contestation of Anti-Homopropaganda Laws in Russia." *Journal of Human Rights* 13(3): 363–79.

Wilson, Angelia R. 2013. *Why Europe Is Lesbian and Gay Friendly (and Why America Never Will Be)*. Albany, NY: SUNY Press.

Wright, Stephen C., Arthur Aron, Tracy McLaughlin-Volpe, and Stacy A. Ropp. 1997. "The Extended Contact Effect: Knowledge of Cross-Group Friendships and Prejudice." *Journal of Personality and Social Psychology* 73(1): 73–90.

Yeo, Andrew. 2011. *Activists, Alliances, and Anti-U.S. Base Protests.* New York: Cambridge University Press.

Zapryanova, Galina M., and Lena Surzhko-Harned. 2015. "The Effect of Supranational Identity on Cultural Values in Europe." *European Political Science Review* First View (1): 1–20.

Zaretsky, Robert. 2013. "Tocqueville and France's Gay Marriage Debate." *New York Times.* www.nytimes.com/2013/05/02/opinion/global/Tocqueville-and-Frances-Gay-Marriage-debate.html.

Zepeda-Millán, Chris. 2011. "Dignity's Revolt: Threat, Identity, and Immigrant Mass Mobilization." PhD Dissertation. Cornell University.

2016. "Weapons of the (Not So) Weak: Immigrant Mass Mobilization in the US South." *Critical Sociology* 42(2): 269–287.

Ziliak, Stephen Thomas, and Deirdre N. McCloskey. 2008. *The Cult of Statistical Significance: How the Standard Error Costs Us Jobs, Justice, and Lives.* Ann Arbor: University of Michigan Press.

Zito, Anthony R. 2009. "European Agencies as Agents of Governance and EU Learning." *Journal of European Public Policy* 16(8): 1224–43.

Zivi, Karen. 2012. *Making Rights Claims: A Practice of Democratic Citizenship.* New York: Oxford University Press.

Zürn, Michael, and Jeffrey T. Checkel. 2005. "Getting Socialized to Build Bridges: Constructivism and Rationalism, Europe and the Nation-State." *International Organization* 59(4): 1045–79.

Index

adoption, 62, 101, 123, 168t6.2, 178–80, 198, 218, 233tA.1

AIDS Quilt, 202

Altman, Dennis, 11, 25, 70, 215

Argentina, 4, 111, 118, 212–14

attitudes
  church authority, 137–53, 175t6.3
  homophobia, 4, 8, 38, 97, 162, 166, 189–97, 204, 215–20
  homosexuality, 8–10, 15–16, 20, 50–51, 62, 64–65, 77n21, 126, 127–57, 166–67 189, 211

Bączkowski and others v. Poland, 84–85, 158, 218n8

Beck, Volker, 74–75, 77, 81, 84, 122

Berlin, 1–3, 6, 16, 24, 28n4, 45–49, 53, 66–84, 120–22, 127, 135, 156, 159, 189, 199, 221, 226, 228, 237tA.3

Bernstein, Mary, 12n6, 23–24

Biedroń, Robert, 85–86, 171, 187, 193, 196

Bob, Clifford, 47, 192, 195–96

Bosnia-Herzegovina, 58, 173, 194

brokerage, 23, 33–36, 54, 61n7, 64t3.1, 71, 76–79, 90–91, 94, 118, 210, 233tA.1

Brysk, Alison, 4, 6, 213

Butler, Judith, 1–4, 204, 221–22

Catholicism, 5, 10, 13, 40, 51, 65, 76–78, 99–111, 117–24, 137, 142–52, 174–75, 182, 188–89, 199, 205, 226

Catholic Church, 42, 121, 137–38, 149, 159–65, 167–73, 177–81, 184, 194–97, 212, 217

channels of visibility, 16, 19, 20, 23, 30, 32–33, 36–38, 42–44, 165, 200, 207–10, 220, 223
  economic, 103, 106–9, 107t4.2, 124, 132, 134, 140, 146–49, 209, 234–39
  overall porousness of the state, 93, 97–98, 103, 106–16, 124–25, 142t5.1, 144, 148–52, 152t5.3, 234–39
  political, 10, 32–33, 38, 90, 93–94, 103, 107t4.2, 109, 146–47, 147t5.2, 234–39
  social, 38, 93–94, 97, 104–9, 126, 146–48, 147t5.2, 167t6.1, 209, 234–39

Checkel, Jeff, 13–14, 18, 33n10, 34n13, 49, 59, 77, 99n10, 136, 219

Clinton, Hillary, 5n2, 87

compliance, 14, 16–19, 23, 32, 36–39, 47, 57f3.1, 85, 90, 99, 121, 127, 200–1, 206–13

conditionality, 14, 91, 94, 96–98, 109, 115, 125, 132

cooperative transnationalism, 55, 84–85

Council of Europe (CoE), 8, 59, 85, 96, 208, 228

Croatia, 115, 173, 226

Currier, Ashley, 22, 46–47, 216

Czech Republic, 9–10, 13, 42, 101n17, 120, 144f5.2, 163, 197, 226

deliberation, 12, 23, 33–36, 42–45, 54,
    64t3.1, 79–80, 85, 96, 121, 134,
    154–55, 190–92, 198, 201, 205, 207,
    209–11, 217, 220–21
della Porta, Donatella, 26, 61
Denmark, 9–10, 87, 111–12, 117, 120,
    166n7, 213–15
diffusion, *see* international norms and
    diffusion
Dudgeon v. the United Kingdom,
    55–56
Duyvendak, Jan Willem, 13, 25, 101,
    118, 204

embassies, 2, 38, 66, 81, 92, 97, 103,
    166n7, 233–38
D'Emilio, John, 27, 103n22, 148
Equality Foundation, 70, 84
Estonia, 9–10, 13, 30–31, 42, 47, 113n29,
    123, 133n5, 144f5.2, 155, 164,
    226
European Court of Human Rights
    (ECtHR), 7–8, 55–58, 84, 158,
    165, 218n8
European Union (EU)
    Commission, 29, 55–63, 57f3.1,
        208n3, 230
    European Court of Justice, 7–9,
        56–58, 230
    Parliament, 8, 56–60, 65, 75, 80–81, 97,
        118, 188, 215, 227, 230
Europeanization, 37n16, 47, 54–66,
    69, 85, 89, 109, 112, 135–38, 160,
    206–207
Evangelista, Matthew, 41n21, 205

Fetner, Tina, 40, 105, 130, 130n2, 134,
    139, 176n13, 206
Finland, 9–10, 117, 214
Finnemore, Martha, 7–8, 13, 33, 96n9
frames
    defend the nation, 176–77, 181, 184,
        187–92
    European, 42, 60, 75–79, 179,
        194, 207
    wellbeing of children, 177–82, 190
France, 9–10, 28–29, 71n17, 77, 81, 111,
    117–20, 124, 169, 197n35, 197–98,
    214, 218
Frank, David, 17, 95n7, 101n16, 102, 104,
    110, 113, 210, 233tA.1

funding sources, 26, 29, 36, 59–61, 65,
    70n15, 72–74, 92–93, 119, 166,
    179–80, 182, 195n33, 202, 212, 232

geographic proximity, 66–67, 132–35,
    140–44, 147t5.2, 152t5.3, 237nA.3,
    239A.4
Germany, 9–10, 13–14, 19, 28–29, 45–55,
    61–83, 102n19, 111, 117–23, 135,
    164, 166n7, 185n24, 203, 226–28
Grodzka, Anna, 85–86, 196, 203–4

Hirschfeld, Magnus, 28, 45–46, 67
HIV/AIDS, 21, 30, 62, 113, 117, 202
homonationalism, 161n2, 221

Iceland, 199, 214
IGLYO, 166n7, 228, 229
ILGA, 29–30, 35, 37n16, 55n2, 59–61,
    65, 75, 85, 95–96, 100n12, 103, 111,
    119, 153–55, 157, 165–68, 211, 216,
    222n11, 226–29
Inglehart, Ronald, 13, 15, 99, 125, 138–39,
    237tA.3
Intergroup on LGBTI Rights, 57–60, 75
internalization, 11, 14–19, 23, 40–47,
    58f3.2, 127–51, 154–57, 160, 165,
    191f6.3, 200–1, 206–13, 220, 223
intersectionality, 48, 221–22
invisibility, 2–4, 25, 27, 31–32, 43–47, 191,
    198, 202–7
Ireland, 5, 9–10, 13, 42, 55, 71, 75,
    111–12, 121–123, 145, 164–65, 171,
    210, 214, 226
Irish "Yes" Campaign, 121–22, 210
Italy, 7n3, 9–10, 12n7, 56, 86, 102, 118,
    121, 123, 127, 141, 164–65, 171n11,
    195n33, 226, 228

Kampania Przeciw Homofobii (KPH), 65,
    69n12, 71n17, 83, 86, 166, 171, 185,
    189, 193, 195, 207
Katzenstein, Peter, 7, 18, 40–41, 91–94,
    137, 149, 170–72, 229
Kollman, Kelly, 5, 7, 67, 95n7,
    116–18, 206
Kuhar, Roman, 76, 135, 168t6.2,
    177–78, 188–89

Lambda Warsaw, 54, 72n17, 76
Lang, Sabine, 65, 211, 211n4, 221

Latvia, 9–10, 25–26, 37n16, 81, 92, 133n5,
144f5.2, 151, 154–56, 162n3, 164,
177, 195n33, 199, 226
Law and Justice Party, 80, 86, 97, 171,
181n19, 184, 187, 193, 197
learning, 23, 30–36, 34n13, 43–47, 54, 64,
79–80, 91, 94–97, 201, 205, 209–11,
220, 233tA.1
lesbian, gay, bisexual, transgender (LGBT),
see also trans
   activists, 15, 22–27, 47, 54–69, 76,
   84–85, 91–92, 124, 151, 162, 165,
   170–73, 178–97, 214–28
   legislation, 8–12, 19, 37f2.1, 40, 56,
   86–125, 130–31, 140, 151–57, 166,
   178–79, 194, 201, 209–17, 227–28
   norms, 11, 15–18, 23–24, 28, 41–44,
   90, 93n5, 128–31, 136–38, 149, 156,
   161–64, 172–77, 181, 190, 196–205,
   208, 212–23
   organizations/groups, 2, 7, 33–40, 44,
   52, 52–58, 64–75, 82–86, 90–123,
   141, 153–54, 165–68, 178–93,
   216–29, 234tA.1, 236tA.2
   rights, 6–17, 21–52, 204–6
Lithuania, 9–10, 32, 42, 81, 133n5,
144f5.2, 159, 164
LSVD, 75, 77, 118
Luxembourg, 9–10, 105n25, 108, 116,
120, 122, 166n7, 214

Malta, 5, 9–10, 13, 25, 49, 105n25, 108,
111–12, 114, 123, 133n5, 144f5.2, 226
Maneo, 71–74, 79, 82, 166n7
McAdam, Doug, 15, 25, 55n2, 60–61, 82,
113, 190n31, 226
Merkel, Angela, 79, 120–22
Meyer, John W., 12, 16–17, 38, 96n9, 99
Milk, Harvey, 21–22
Miller, Wentworth, 199
minority rights, 2, 17, 20, 29, 39n18, 85,
88, 95n7, 99, 121, 128, 166, 210, 230,
see also LGBT rights
Montoya, Celeste, 59n5, 92, 210, 221
Mothers of the Disappeared, 4
movement, *see also* LGBT activists;
   resistance; social movements
   civil rights, 82, 165, 219, 223
   countermovement, 39n18, 40, 87, 124,
   177, 186, 190n31, 193–94, 206
   homophile, 27–28, 87

immigrant rights, 4, 51, 202
LGBT, 7n3, 11, 23–31, 53–86, 92, 110,
112, 117–18, 124, 127, 157, 165, 171,
181, 184, 188, 190, 192, 197–206,
210, 210–13, 216, 223
queer, 1n1
women's, 24, 202–3
Mozaika movements, 26, 92

national identity, 11, 41–42, 70, 130–31,
137, 160–79, 184, 196, 202, 212, *see*
religious nationalism
nationalism, *see* religious nationalism
Netherlands, 7n3, 9–10, 13, 28–29, 29n6,
59, 102n19, 110, 117–18, 166n7,
214–15, 228
NGOization, 211n4
Nigeria, 215, 220
NOP, 184–85, 193, 195n33
norm brokers, 34–37, 43–48, 64, 79, 85,
90–93, 110f4.2, 119–20, 166–67, 191,
201, 205–7, 212–17, 222–23
norms, *see also* LGBT and norm, norm
   brokers
   diffusion, 6–7, 17–18, 37f2.1, 39, 87–93,
   127–32, 160, 205–6, 209, 213–23
   entrepreneur, 17n16, 19, 33, 39, 51,
   54–55, 64t3.1 69–75, 79–80, 99, 117,
   119, 219, 226
   international, 1n1, 6–17, 31, 34, 39–40,
   49, 64t3.1, 88, 91, 96n9, 104, 112,
   123, 126–37, 144, 151, 158–98,
   200–9, 212, 212–13
Norway, 75, 214–15

Obama, Barack, 120, 202, 215
O'Dwyer, Conor, 11, 37n16, 57n1, 59,
162n3, 190, 230–31
Oliari and other v. Italy, 56
Olympics
   Sochi, 199–200, 219–20
Open Society Foundations, 26, 92, 166n7
Orthodoxy, 99–100, 108t4.2, 109, 124,
124t5.1, 145, 147t5.2, 152t5.3, 169,
173, 238tA.3
Orthodox Church, 99, 137–38, 165, 217
parenting, *see* adoption

Palestinians, 222
Paternotte, David, 8, 13n8, 29–30, 48–49,
56, 59, 70, 95n7, 116–18, 211n4

perceived threat, *see* threat perception
persuasion, 33, 58
Philpott, Dan, 137n9, 162–64, 169
Poland, 3, 9–10, 13, 15, 19–20, 30–32,
    37n16, 42–45, 49–52, 53–55, 87–91,
    97–98, 102, 115, 124–26, 133n5,
    144f5.2, 157, 158–98, 205, 207,
    216–21, 226–28
police protection, 81–85
political opportunity structures, 44, 60–64
    horizontal, 60, 64, 69–70, 80, 82 85, 207
    vertical, 54–55, 60–62, 64, 69–70, 80,
        85, 207
Pope Benedict XVI, 170
Pope John Paul II, 149, 170–72, 180
post-materialism, 15, 131n2, 139, 142t5.1,
    145, 147t5.2, 152t5.3, 237tA.3
post-Soviet syndrome, 16, 163
Pride parades
    Budapest, 194
    Christopher Street Day, 1–3, 67, 73–74,
        76, 121–22, 221
    Europride, 3, 78f3.6, 80, 126, 158–59,
        182, 196, 227
    Ljubljana, 158–59, 178n14
    Lodz, 185–86
    Poznan, 66n11, 82, 172
    Warsaw equality marches, 3, 53–86, 180
public sphere, 3–5, 26–27, 62, 64t3.1, 65,
    79, 81, 85, 182, 183t6.4, 187, 192,
    198, 211
Putin, Vladimir, 2, 41, 218

radical flank theory, 190n31
religious nationalism, 11, 16, 162,
    197, 202
research method
    case selection, 49–51, 206, 225–45
    research design, 51–52, 225–45
resistance, 11, 14, 19–20, 27, 37, 39,
    42–47, 63n10, 99, 101, 131, 149,
    156–98, 201–2, 205–206, 209,
    211–13, 218–20, 223, 227, 229
    backlash, 14, 42–44, 113, 149,
        151–56, 190–91, 202, 205–6,
        211–12, 217–20
RFSL, 26, 166n7
Risse, Thomas, 34, 39n18, 41n21, 44–45,
    61, 79, 96
Romania, 7–10, 208
rooted cosmopolitans, 26, 35, 64t3.1,
    70–74, 207–8

Roth, Claudia, 53, 56, 74–81
Ruch Palikota, 81, 193
Russia, 2, 5, 41–42, 47–48, 77, 81, 85, 98,
    168t6.2, 168–69, 199, 211, 215–20,
    223, 228

same-sex unions
    marriage, 5, 8n5, 32, 69n2, 84,
        88n1, 101–2, 111, 115, 117,
        123, 131n2, 153, 156n13, 163,
        165, 168t6.2, 178–82, 197,
        210, 213–18
    registered partnership, 8n5, 9, 56,
        58, 60, 62n8, 73, 87–88, 90–92,
        98, 101–2, 105, 111, 113–23, 151,
        155n13, 168t6.2, 178–79, 180–81,
        196–97, 214, 233tA.1
Second World War (WWII), 21–22, 28,
    111, 169, 172
Seybert, Lucia, 6, 99n10
Sikkink, Kathryn, 7, 13, 15, 33–34, 44–45,
    61–62, 85, 94–96
Slovakia, 9–10, 25, 133n5, 144f5.2,
    155n13, 163–64, 170n10, 226
Slovenia, 9–10, 20, 42, 49–52, 113n29,
    117, 120, 123, 133n5, 144f5.2, 157,
    158–98, 226
social movement, *see also* movement
    mobilizing structures, 55, 64t3.1, 65,
        69n13, 71, 72, 207, 226
    repertoire of contention, 65, 94, 190
    scale shift, 61n7
    tactics, 54, 60–61, 79, 82, 159, 186, 192,
        207, 212, 227
social spaces, 45, 61–74, 84, 99–101,
    104–10, 107t4.2, 112, 206, 227,
    233tA.1, 236tA.2
socialization, 14, 18, 31–38, 54–55, 62, 70,
    75, 79–85, 90–91, 94–97, 109, 124,
    166, 209–10, 218–20
Solidarność Gejów 2, 73–74, 84
Soule, Sarah, 36–38, 91n3, 95n7, 99n10,
    104–5, 135–36
South Africa, 33n9, 214–17
Spain, 9–10, 13, 42, 102n19, 111, 118–21,
    145, 153, 163–64, 171, 195n33, 214,
    226, 228
Steinem, Gloria, 24
Stockdill, Brett, 25
Stonewall Rebellion, 2, 26–28, 101,
    188, 204
Strolovitch, Dara, 203–4, 222

Student Nonviolent Coordinating
  Committee, 82
Switzerland, 28

Tarrow, Sid, 26, 34n12, 36, 55, 60–61,
  69–71, 92–94, 176n13, 190n31,
  194, 226
Taylor, Verta, 1, 26
threat perception, 11, 40–47, 130–32,
  138–51, 151, 152t5.3, 156, 160–75,
  187, 196–97, 201, 206, 211–13,
  217–18, 217–22, 221, 223
trans, 1n1, 5, 12–13, 86, 101n18, 111–12,
  193, 196, 203–4, 227, *see also* LGBT
Turkey, 115, 226

Uganda, 214–23
Ukraine, 41, 44, 47, 96, 211
United Kingdom, 9–10, 29, 44, 55, 75,
  111, 124, 166n7, 185n24, 195n33,
  197, 214, 218
Uruguay, 120, 214

Verloo, Mieke, 222n11
Vietnam, 214
visibility, *see also* channels of visibility;
  invisibility
  coming out, 4–5, 21–31, 48, 70, 155,
    157, 199–203, 208, 217
  interpersonal, 23–26, 28n5, 45, 65, 73,
    139, 204, 208–9, 219n10
  norm, 11, 21–52, 90, 103, 116, 138,
    192, 200–2, 217
  public, 23–31, 45, 208–9, 217,
    219n10
  valence of, 23, 45–49

Warsaw, 3, 31, 53–54, 66–86, 97, 126,
  128, 158–59, 158–98, 180–86,
  195–96, 226–27
Wendt, Alex, 5
World League for Sexual Reform, 28
Wowereit, Klaus, 67, 74

Yugoslavia, 16, 163n4, 165–66, 172–74

Books in the Series (*continued from p. iii*)

Jack A. Goldstone, editor, *States, Parties, and Social Movements*

Jennifer Hadden, *Networks in Contention: The Divisive Politics of Climate Change*

Michael T. Heaney and Fabio Rojas , *Party in the Street: The Antiwar Movement and the Democratic Party after 9/11*

Tamara Kay, *NAFTA and the Politics of Labor Transnationalism*

Joseph Luders, *The Civil Rights Movement and the Logic of Social Change*

Doug McAdam and Hilary Boudet, *Putting Social Movements in Their Place: Explaining Opposition to Energy Projects in the United States, 2000–2005*

Doug McAdam, Sidney Tarrow, and Charles Tilly , *Dynamics of Contention*

Holly J. McCammon, *The U.S. Women's Jury Movements and Strategic Adaptation: A More Just Verdict*

Sharon Nepstad, *War Resistance and the Plowshares Movement*

Kevin J. O'Brien and Lianjiang Li, *Rightful Resistance in Rural China*

Silvia Pedraza, *Political Disaffection in Cuba's Revolution and Exodus*

Eduardo Silva, *Challenging Neoliberalism in Latin America*

Erica S. Simmons, *Meaningful Resistance: Market Reforms and the Roots of Social Protest in Latin America*

Sarah Soule, *Contention and Corporate Social Responsibility*

Yang Su, *Collective Killings in Rural China during the Cultural Revolution*

Sidney Tarrow, *The Language of Contention: Revolutions in Words, 1688–2012*

Sidney Tarrow, *The New Transnational Activism*

Ralph Thaxton Jr., *Catastrophe and Contention in Rural China: Mao's Great Leap Forward Famine and the Origins of Righteous Resistance in Da Fo Village*

Charles Tilly, *Contention and Democracy in Europe, 1650–2000*

Charles Tilly, *Contentious Performances*

Charles Tilly, *The Politics of Collective Violence*

Marisa von Bülow, *Building Transnational Networks: Civil Society and the Politics of Trade in the Americas*

Lesley J. Wood, *Direct Action, Deliberation, and Diffusion: Collective Action after the WTO Protests in Seattle*

Stuart A. Wright, *Patriots, Politics, and the Oklahoma City Bombing*

Deborah Yashar, *Contesting Citizenship in Latin America: The Rise of Indigenous Movements and the Postliberal Challenge*

Andrew Yeo, *Activists, Alliances, and Anti–U.S. Base Protests*